IF YOU THINK YOU'VE HEARD IT ALL, YOU PROBABLY HAVEN'T HEARD THIS . . .

A Labrador named Tubby has helped recycle an estimated 26,000 plastic bottles over the past six years by collecting them on his daily walks, crushing them, and passing them to his owner. This is the most bottles ever to be recycled by a dog.

The world's largest Santa hat measures a whopping 50 feet, 9 inches long, and 27 feet wide.

Kiran Harpal from the Netherlands holds the record for the most basketball bounces in one minute (384 bounces).

Published on August 1, 2008, in Japan, the audiobook *50 Lectures* by Takaaki Yoshimoto is the world's longest audiobook. It has a running time of 115 hours and 43 minutes.

A male goliath bird-eating spider (*Theraphosa blondi*) collected at Rio Cavro, Venezuela, in April 1965, had a record leg span of 11 inches—long enough to cover a dinner plate. It is still the largest spider on record.

Accreditation

Guinness World Records Limited has a very thorough accreditation system for records verification. However, while every effort is made to ensure accuracy, Guinness World Records Limited cannot be held responsible for any errors contained in this work. Feedback from our readers on any point of accuracy is always welcomed.

Abbreviations & Measurements

Guinness World Records Limited uses both metric and imperial measurements. The sole exceptions are for some scientific data where metric measurements only are universally accepted, and for some sports data. Where a specific date is given, the exchange rate is calculated according to the currency values that were in operation at the time. Where only a year date is given, the exchange rate is calculated from December of that year. "One billion" is taken to mean one thousand million. "GDR" (the German Democratic Republic) refers to the East German state, which was unified with West Germany in 1990. The abbreviation is used for sports records broken before 1990. The USSR (Union of Soviet Socialist Republics) split into a number of parts in 1991, the largest of these being Russia. The CIS (Commonwealth of Independent States) replaced it, and the abbreviation is used mainly for sporting records broken at the 1992 Olympic Games. Guinness World Records Limited does not claim to own any right, title, or interest in the trademarks of others reproduced in this book.

General Warning

Attempting to break records or set new records can be dangerous. Appropriate advice should be taken first, and all record attempts are undertaken at the participant's risk. In no circumstances will Guinness World Records Limited have any liability for death or injury suffered in any record attempt. Guinness World Records Limited has complete discretion over whether or not to include any particular records in the book. Being a Guinness World Record holder does not guarantee you a place in the book.

GUINNESS WRLD RECORDS 2011

BANTAM BOOKS
NEW YORK

Dedicated to Michael Jackson (1958–2009) & He Pingping (1988–2010)

2011 Bantam mass market edition

GUINNESS WORLD RECORDS™ 2011
Copyright © 2010 by Guinness World Records Limited.
Published under license.

GUINNESS WORLD RECORDS™ is a trademark of Guinness World Records Limited and is reproduced under license by Bantam Books, an imprint of The Random House Publishing Group, a division of Random House, Inc., New York.

Revised American editions copyright © 2011, 2010, 2009, 2008, 2007, 2006, 2005, 2004, 2003, 2002, 2001, 2000, 1999, 1998, 1997, 1996, 1995, 1994, 1993, 1992, 1991, 1990, 1989, 1988, 1987, 1986, 1985, 1984, 1983, 1982, 1981, 1980, 1979, 1978, 1977, 1976, 1975, 1974, 1973, 1972, 1971, 1970, 1969, 1968, 1966, 1965, 1964, 1963, 1962, 1960 by Guinness World Records Ltd.

For more information address: Guinness World Records Ltd.

BANTAM BOOKS and the rooster colophon are registered trademarks of Random House, Inc.

ISBN: 978-0-440-42310-2

Printed in the United States of America

www.bantamdell.com

9 8 7 6 5 4 3 2 1

Bantam mass market edition: May 2011

GUINNESS WORLD
RECORDS

EDITOR-IN-CHIEF
Craig Glenday

CONTENTS

```
★ BRAND-NEW RECORDS are indicated by a solid star, in both
the text and record headings

☆ BROKEN OR UPDATED RECORDS are indicated by an open
star, in both the text and record headings
```

RECORDS BY CITY (51°28'N 0°00'E): At the foot of many pages,
you'll find records associated with different cities. Starting in the UK, from
London's Greenwich meridian at 0°00'E, these cities are arranged in order
of their longitude (distance from the meridian), so as you read the book,
you can read your way around the world, eastward, city by city.

QUIZ!: What are these? they're simple quiz questions to test your family and friends. See p. 543 for all the answers.

INTRODUCTION

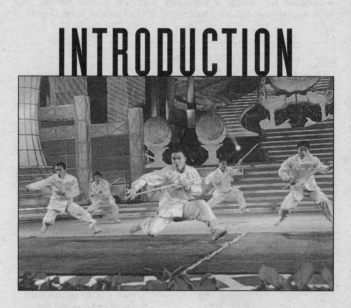

FIRE!

Farthest distance firewalking Trever McGhee (Canada) walked 597 ft. (181.9 m) over embers with temperatures in excess of 1,215.80°F (657.67°C) at Symons Valley Rodeo Grounds in Calgary, Alberta, Canada, on November 9, 2007.

★Longest run during a full-body burn The greatest distance run while performing a full-body burn is 259 ft. (78.9 m) and was achieved by

☆LONGEST FULL-BODY BURN (NO OXYGEN) On February 25, 2010, stuntman Ted A. Batchelor (U.S.A.) endured a full-body burn without oxygen for 2 min. 57 sec. on the set of *Lo Show dei Record* in Rome, Italy.

Previously, on September 19, 2009, Ted had led a group of 17 in the **largest simultaneous body burn**, when members of his team and the "Ohio Burns Unit" (U.S.A.) set themselves alight for 43 seconds in South Russell, Ohio, U.S.A.

professional stunt performer Keith Malcolm (UK) of The Stannage International Stunt Team at the Alton Show in Hampshire, UK, on July 5, 2009.

Longest-burning fire A burning coal seam lying beneath Mount Wingen in New South Wales, Australia, is thought to have started around 5,000 years ago when lightning struck the coal seam at the point where it reached the Earth's surface. The fire is still burning, around 100 ft. (30 m) underground, as it has slowly eaten away at the seam.

Largest fireworks display A fireworks display featuring 66,326 fireworks was achieved by Macedo's Pirotecnia Lda. in Funchal, Madeira, Portugal, on December 31, 2006. The display, which was part of the New Year celebrations on the island of Madeira, was launched from 40 different sites and was over in just eight minutes.

★ **LARGEST BURNING MAN FESTIVAL** The annual Burning Man festival staged in the Black Rock Desert in Nevada, U.S.A., attracted a record 49,599 visitors to the 2008 event. The week-long festival is named after the giant wooden effigy that is burned during the Saturday of Labor Day weekend. The event dates back to 1986.

Fire!   **xiii**

Worst fireworks disaster An estimated 800 people died as a result of an accident during a fireworks display staged beside the river Seine in Paris, France, on May 16, 1770, to mark the marriage of the future Louis XIV.

Most people burned at the stake The burning of "witches" at the stake reached its greatest intensity in Germany in the 16th and 17th centuries. At Quedlinburg, near Leipzig, 133 witches were burned in one day in 1589. Elsewhere, in the towns of Wurzburg and Bamberg, at least 1,500 witches were burned in less than a decade during the mid–17th century.

★ MOST PEOPLE SPINNING FIRE On August 15, 2009, in an event organized by The Arts Factory Lodge in New South Wales, Australia, 102 participants spun fire brands for a total of six and a half minutes. The high-temperature twirling was accompanied by a group of drummers, who kept track of time by beating on their instruments. A crowd of more than 300 people cheered on the fire spinners.

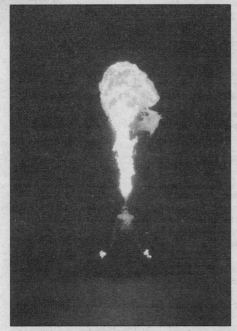

HIGHEST FLAME BLOWN BY A FIRE BREATHER Tim Black (Australia) blew a 23-ft. 7-in.-high (7.2-m) flame for *Zheng Da Zong Yi—Guinness World Records Special* in Beijing, China, on September 15, 2007.

☆ **LARGEST GATHERING OF FIRE BREATHERS** On October 15, 2008, 269 people got hot under the collar together in Eindhoven, the Netherlands, when they set the record for the largest gathering of fire breathers. The event was coordinated by the Dutch student association Intermate.

Fire!

★ **Tallest volcanic fire fountain** When the Izu-Oshima volcano, Japan, erupted in November 1986, it launched a fountain of fire into the air that was recorded as reaching 5,250 ft. (1,600 m) in height. A volcanic fire fountain is characterized by a violent, geyser-like eruption of incandescent lava, rather than an ash column.

☆ **Largest flaming image using candles** On December 10, 2009, 118 employees of the Sandoz (Pakistan) company created a flaming image with 35,478 candles at the Hotel Serena in Faisalabad, Pakistan. The image depicted the Sandoz logo and motto, and had an area of 9,800 ft.^{2} (910.45 m^2).

Worst tunnel fire On November 12, 2000, 155 skiers died in a tunnel fire on the Kaprun railway, which took passengers up the Kitzsteinhorn Glacier in the Austrian Alps. The fire occurred when a blocked heating ventilator caused leaking hydraulic oil to ignite.

☆ **Longest wall of fire** A wall of fire measuring 10,178 ft. 3 in. (3,102.3 m) long was created by the Marine Corps Community Services (U.S.A.) during the 2009 MCAS Yuma Air Show in Yuma, Arizona, U.S.A., on March 14, 2009.

Fastest jet-powered fire truck On July 11, 1998, in Ontario, Canada, the jet-powered *Hawaiian Eagle*, owned by Shannen Seydel of Navarre, Florida, U.S.A., attained a speed of 407 mph (655 km/h). The truck is a red 1940 Ford, powered by two Rolls-Royce Bristol Viper engines boasting 6,000 hp (4,470 kW) per engine and generating 12,000 lb. (5,443 kg) of thrust.

Largest bonfire A bonfire with a volume of 60,589 ft.^{3} (1,715.7 m^3) was built by ŠKD Mladi Boštanj and lit on April 30, 2007, in Boštanj, Slovenia, to celebrate Labour Day. Its 142-ft. 6.2-in. (43.44-m) height also qualifies the conflagration as the **tallest bonfire**.

EDITOR'S LETTER

Welcome to the explosive new edition of the world's biggest-selling copyright book. What a year it's been—we've literally gone from one extreme to another to bring you more pictures, more records, and more incredible achievements than ever. . . .

It's been a roller coaster of a year here at Guinness World Records (for actual *roller coaster* records, see p. 366). We've witnessed some incredible highs and experienced some poignant lows, but we've survived the ride for another year and the result is *Guinness World Records 2011*, the first edition of the new decade.

As ever, the **biggest-selling copyright book** is crammed with record-breaking facts and feats from across the United States and from all around the world. Once again, the U.S.A. tops the league table of both record claimants and record holders, with 736 successful attempts ratified out of 22,449 claims. We've tried to include as many of these new records as physically possible in these pages, so congratulations to everybody who succeeded in making it in, and commiserations to those who didn't quite make the grade. . . .

DONNA VANO A big thank-you goes out to action sports star Donna Vano (U.S.A.)—a long-time friend of GWR and a record holder in her own right—for keeping us on schedule at X Games 15 . . . and for the skateboard lessons! We survived the bruises and decided to stick to editing.

DONNA: Is the **oldest female competitor in the SuperPipe Pro Tour** as well as winner of the most gold medals in the U.S.A. Snowboarding Association in all five disciplines.

GREENWICH, LONDON, UK (51°28'N 0°0'): The **first surface circumnavigation via both the geographical Poles** was achieved by Sir Ranulph Fiennes and Charles Burton (both UK), who traveled south from Greenwich, London, UK, on September 2, 1979, and returned on August, 29, 1982, after a 56,000-km (35,000-mile) journey.

DEEGAN: Log on to www.guinnessworldrecords.com to see our exclusive interview with Brian Deegan and find out his best memory of competing in the X Games.

X GAMES 15 Guinness World Records was once again proud and honored to be present at the BMX and Skateboard Parks at the X Games X Fest this summer in Los Angeles, California. Moto X hero Brian Deegan (U.S.A., left) stopped by to say hello and pick up some of his GWR certificates, as did wheelchair athlete and X Games competitor Darwin Holmes (right), who demonstrated his skills using his adapted chair.

STAN THE MAN It's your friendly neighborhood Spider-Man creator Stan Lee accepting multiple GWR awards for his Marvel-ous comic books in June 2009.

MWAH, MWAH Congratulations to everyone at *Cosmopolitan* magazine and Maybelline New York for collecting a record 1,817 lipstick prints in 12 hours from venues across New York City for GWR Day 2009.

COMICS LEGENDS: Turn to p. 300 for all the best comics and graphic novels records. Check out the special header created for us by Lettering guru Todd Klein. Thanks, Todd!

ELF HELP GROUP Jenny McCarthy and Dean McDermott—stars of ABC Family's holiday movie *Santa Baby 2: Christmas Maybe*—joined in the festive fun on December 7, 2009, when they witnessed the **largest gathering of Santa's elves!** That heads you see in the background at left are indeed the 607 record-breaking elves hard at work!

To mark America's contribution to the world of record breaking, we've made this edition an American special. Look for the U.S.-themed areas throughout the book, such as *American Heroes* (p. 236), *American Wildlife* (p. 96), and *Route 66* (p. 263). Also, sports fans can enjoy an extended section of football, baseball, and basketball world records in the *Sports* chapter, which begins on p. 413.

So, what are our big stories of this year? First, Ashrita Furman of Queens, New York—the man with the record for having the most records—celebrated his 100th concurrent Guinness World Records achievement—the first person ever to do so. Find out more about Ashrita's truly awe-inspiring total (actually, it's now more like 114 at the time of going to press!) on p. 135.

What else? Well, as ever, Guinness World Records spent the year criss-crossing the country to attend some key events in the record-breaking calendar, including both the Summer and Winter X Games (see pp. 502–511), and the all-star *NBA Jam* session (p. 471). Our man on the road, Stuart Claxton, has worked tirelessly to bring record breaking to the public at these events, so look out for your name if you took part!

Beyond the United States, our international teams of *Adjudicators and Consultants* have been busier than ever dealing with claims from every country—making my job as editor even more difficult by unearthing ever more fascinating records. Find out what these two important teams do for Guinness World Records on pp. xxv–xxviii.

TALLEST MAN SAYS HELLO TO THE BIG APPLE As part of his whirlwind world tour, Turkey's Sultan Kösen—the world's tallest man—stopped off in the Bronx to shoot some hoops with a local team. Well, shoot's not the word—the 8-footer just stood by the hoop and dropped them in! *Find out more on pp. 104–105.*

SNUGGIES Here are fans of the LA Angels—a recordbreaking 42,690 of them—snuggling up warm in the **largest gathering of people wearing fleece blankets** at Angel Stadium in Anaheim, CA, on April 6, 2010.

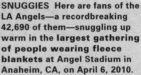

COMIC CON A highlight of the year was presenting Matt Groening with his many records for *The Simpsons* at the San Diego Comic Con (see p. 328 for more).

HULA HOOPS Thanks to everyone at *The Early Show* for hosting us on GWR Day 2009. Here's Paul "Dizzy Hips" Blair breaking the record for ☆ **most Hula Hoops spun simultaneously** with an amazing 136 hoops!

And now there's a new way to get *your* name into the records books—it's called *GWR Live!* and you can find out about this traveling hands-on record-breaking roadshow on pp. xxvi–xxxix.

Oh, and don't forget the other way to get your name listed here by setting or breaking a record on one of our global TV shows. For a round-up of global *GWR TV* output this year, see pp. xxx–xxxiii.

LE MANS, FRANCE (48°00'N 0°11'E): The **fastest lap in the Le Mans 24-hour race** is 3 min. 21.27 sec. (average speed 150.429 mph; 242.093 km/h) by Alain Ferté (France) in a Jaguar XJR-9LM on June 10, 1989.

SQUEEZE: Pictured below with Regis and Kelly are GWR's Stuart Claxton and record holder Leslie Tipton demonstrating the **fastest time to enter a zipped suitcase** (5.43 seconds).

REGIS & KELLY Many thanks once again to everyone at *LIVE! with Regis and Kelly*, who help us celebrate the launch of every new GWR book with a week long extravaganza of record breaking on their show. Hope to see you guys again next year!

DRAFT: A record eight high school seniors were chosen in the first round of the 2004 NBA Draft held in New York on June 24, 2004, including Dwight Howard (pictured below), who was #1 pick.

DWIGHT HOWARD The NBA All-Star Jam Session is where the top NBA players showcase their skills in front of an audience of thousands. This year, Dwight Howard from the Orlando Magic got in on the act—on center court during the Jam Session, he made a basket while *sitting down* from a record distance of 52 ft. 6 in. (16 m)! *View more NBA feats on p. 496.*

ROUEN, FRANCE (49°26'N 1°05'E): The **greatest distance walked by a woman in 24 hours** is 131.27 miles (211.25 km) by Annie van der Meer-Timmermann (Netherlands) at Rouen, France, on May 10–11, 1986.

BIG DOG GWR's Jamie Panas went to Tucson, Arizona, to measure record-breaking Giant George, a 43-in. (109-cm.) Great Dane, with his owner David Nasser.

With all these exciting new ways to source world records, it's been a job and a half trying to squeeze them all in. Still, it's allowed me to create some exciting new sections for this year's book:

• Did you miss the very first spread on *Fire!*? If so, turn back to pp. xii–xvi now for an explosive start to *GWR 2011*.

• We say goodbye to the *Space Shuttles* on p. 11, as NASA confirms the end of an era for reusable spacecraft.

• Find out how the **tallest man**'s world tour went in our picture feature on pp. 104–106 (and check out the latest news on the **shortest living mobile man** on p. 114).

• We've dedicated two chapters to animal records: *Living Planet* on p. 51, and *Animal Magic* on p. 267.

PET-ACULAR Natural Balance Pet Foods welcomed in 2010 by unveiling the ★ longest single-chassis parade float—113 ft. 8 in. (34.65 m)—during the Tournament of Roses Parade in Pasadena, CA, on New Year's Day.

RINGTONE RECORD Senegal-born R&B star Akon is awarded his GWR certificate by GWR's Danny Girton Jr., in recognition of being the **best-selling ringtone artist** of all time!

TRIVIA

The record-breaking parade float (above) was the first U.S. record approved by GWR judges in 2010.

PINGPING He might have been small in stature, but He Pingping (right) had a giant personality. The news of his passing made headlines around the world; the iconic Pingping was adored by millions, some of whom wrote to us to express their sadness.

Many of you also asked who would fill Pingping's small shoes as the new **shortest living mobile man**. The answer is Edward Niño Hernandez (above) of Colombia—*find his record on p. 114*.

HACHETTE JOB Our new American distributors proved they were the perfect people for the task by stacking up a record 1.4-m-tall (55-in) tower of *GWR* books in Chicago, Illinois, on November 13, 2009.

MAKEOVERS Here's GWR's Laura Plunkett with singer Adrienne Bailon presenting Sephora at Times Square in Manhattan their certificate for achieving a record 85 makeovers (by a team of five) in one hour.

IPSWICH, UK (52°03'N 1°09'E): The **most "hop the fence" yo-yo tricks in one minute** is 144, set by Arron Sparks (UK) during an event in Ipswich, Suffolk, UK, on July 27, 2008.

• Get the lowdown on your top *Cop & Crime Shows* (p. 311) and *Sci-Fi & Fantasy* TV (p. 316).
• Thanks to James Cameron's *Avatar* (see p. 291), the world's gone mad for *3D Cinema*, so don't miss our special feature on p. 336.
• Along the bottom of every page you'll find our *Records GPS* feature: go on a city-by-city tour of world records, starting at 0° on the map and traveling east around the world to various cities in order of longitude.
• And as usual, you'll find every major sporting record listed in our *Sports Reference* section, starting on p. 512.

DID YOU KNOW?

Michael Jackson was first referred to as the "King of Pop" during a visit to the Guinness World Records Museum on Hollywood boulevard in 1984!

IN MEMORIA

This year's edition is a particularly poignant one for us at Guinness World Records, as it is our tribute to two very special record holders we lost in the past year: Michael Jackson (p. 350) and He Pingping (p. xxiii).

Michael Jackson was always a big fan of the book, and always willing to give up his time for us, whether it was to open a new GWR Museum, or just to pop into the office to say hello. I was honored to be considered a friend of Michael's, and I'll always cherish the memories of his visit to the London office in 2006, and presenting him his award for *Thriller* at that year's World Music Awards alongside Beyoncé Knowles. Before his untimely passing, he was, I'm sure, the most famous living person on Earth.

A more recent addition to the GWR family was He Pingping, the world's **shortest living mobile man**. The cheeky, impish Pingping first lit up our lives in 2009 when he made the pages of our book, before going on to become an international superstar.

I was the lucky one who got to fly out to Inner Mongolia to measure the little man for the first time, and I knew from the moment I set eyes on him that he was going to be . . . well, a big hit!

As we traveled together, one thing became clear—his short stature was always going to have health implications. Yet he never let his size get in the way of having a good time, and he refused to be treated as an invalid. He wrung all he could out of the precious time he had, and made a major impact on the world, inspiring those with troubles of their own.

So, what better a message to take into the new decade than this: Life is there to be lived! Enjoy every frightening bank and turn of that roller coaster, and feel the thrill of the unknown highs and lows ahead of you. And if you break some records along the way, so much the better! Have a fantastic 2011.

Craig Glenday
Editor-in-Chief

ADJUDICATORS & CONSULTANTS

Meet the two teams that can turn your dreams into reality . . . the records adjudicators, with the power to say "yes" or "no" to your claim, and the consultants, who use their specialist knowledge to find world record facts and superlatives all year round.

ADJUDICATOR ON SITE Here's GWR Adjudicator Carlos Martínez (Spain) assessing a record claim for the **highest gas pipeline in Peru.** To find out how you can apply to have a judge on site, visit **www .guinnessworld records.com.**

Information flows into the *Guinness World Records* office in one of two main ways. The first is via our **Adjudicators**—these are the records managers who process the 65,000 claims we receive from the public each year.

This multilingual team divides itself among the various international GWR offices and visiting record attempts all around the world. As each record application comes in, it is assigned to one of the team, who will work

---

WE SPEAK: English, Spanish, Japanese, German, Dutch, Portuguese, French, Russian, Ukrainian, Hungarian, Romanian, Italian, Korean, Arabic, Chinese, and Welsh.

WE SEEK: GWR founding editor Norris McWhirter once described his job as "Finding the -ESTs from the -ISTs"—that is, finding superlatives from the experts.

---

on approving or rejecting the claim. These are the guys who also write the official rules—often in conjunction with a relevant governing body or acknowledged expert or consultant *(see below)*.

You might recognize some of these faces; they are often judges on GWR TV shows!

The Adjudicators

1. Louise Toms (UK)
2. Lucia Sinigagliesi (Italy)
3. Ralph Hannah (UK)
4. Louise Ireland (UK)
5. Aleksandr Vypirailenko (Ukraine)
6. Andrea Bánfi (Hungary)
7. Talal Omar (Yemen)
8. Marco Frigatti (Italy)
9. Jack Brockbank (UK)
10. Mariamarta Ruano-Graham (Guatemala)
11. Kristian Teufel (Germany)
12. Gareth Deaves (UK)
13. Amanda Mochan (U.S.A.)
14. Tarika Vara (UK)

TOULOUSE, FRANCE (43°36'N 1°26'E): The **highest-capacity jet airliner** is the double-deck Airbus 380, which first flew in Toulouse, France, on April 27, 2005. While it has a nominal seating capacity of 555, it has a potential maximum seating capacity of 853 depending on the interior fuselage fit.

YOUNG AND OLD Among those missing from the group photo on the previous page are Robert Young (left), pictured here with last year's oldest woman Gertrude Baines (U.S.A., 1894–2009) in Los Angeles, California, U.S.A., and our TV historian Dick Fiddy (right) of the British Film Institute.

Supporting the Adjudications team—and playing a crucial role as part of the Publishing team that actually designs and edits the book—are the **Consultants**. This is the international panel of experts who use their expert knowledge to proactively research records on behalf of Guinness World Records.

The spectrum of topics covered by the Consultants is what gives Guinness World Records its unique appeal—from the latest scientific breakthroughs, to all the most important sporting achievements, to the very latest gossip and showbiz news from the entertainment industry. In between, we have medical expertise from a range of specialists (including a gerontologist who researches old age and longevity, a trichologist—that's a "hair doctor"!—and an endocrinologist who advises us on giants and dwarves), as well as engineers, mountain climbers, retired Air Force officers, sailors, musicians, a couple of very on-the-ball sports experts—one of whom specializes in U.S. sports—and a TV historian from the British Film Institute.

Rounding off the list of experts are the countless (and often uncredited) academics, scientists, researchers, and inventors who help us ratify records across our wide range of topics.

Without all of these people—and feedback from you, the public—we wouldn't be able to produce such a compelling and diverse snapshot of our record-breaking year. So thanks to everyone who contributes to making the book—it's because of *you* that it continues to be the planet's **biggest-selling copyright book!**

....

VERSAILLES, FRANCE (48°48'N 2°08'E): The **largest garden** is that created by André Le Nôtre (France) at Versailles, France, in the late 17th century for King Louis XIV. It covers more than 15,000 acres (6,070 ha), of which the famous formal garden covers 247 acres (100 ha).

....

SHUKER: Also missing from the group shot is our zoology consultant (and cryptozoologist) Dr. Karl Shuker, who was on a field trip to Japan at the time.

SHOOT: Alas, the week in which we planned to photograph all our adjudicators and consultants was the week in which the Icelandic volcano Eyjafjallajökull erupted, so some of them couldn't make it.

The Consultants

1. Kenneth (and Tatiana, not in shot) Crutchlow: Ocean Rowing Society
2. Thomasina Gibson: showbiz, movies, entertainment
3. Christian Marais: world sports, gambling, games
4. Craig Glenday: Editor-in-Chief, Guinness World Records
5. David Hawksett: planets, science, technology, engineering
6. Stephen Wrigley: aircraft, military, crime, judiciary, society
7. Dr. Eleanor Clarke: anatomy, medicine, human body
8. Dave McAleer: music
9. Mike Flynn: journeys, adventuring.

GWR TV

The last 12 months have seen us filming breathtaking feats in 17 countries, putting together 120 hours of dynamic, primetime entertainment for shows seen in 85 countries, and featuring more than 250 record attempts.

ZOO: The latest Italian series was very "animal-friendly." It featured giant centipedes, tarantulas, king cobras, rattlesnakes, dogs, and a white ox!

WHO: GWR commissions photographers to attend filming at our TV shows to ensure we have the best and most up-to-date pictures of our record holders.

★ **OLDEST BODYBUILDER** On *Lo Show dei Record* in Italy on March 18, 2010, Ernestine Shepherd (U.S.A., b. June 16, 1936) set a record for the oldest competitive female bodybuilder. She was 73 years 9 months and 2 days old at that time, and still competes in international bodybuilding competitions.

BARCELONA, SPAIN (41°23'N 2°11'E): The **longest winning streak in UEFA Champions League matches** is 11 games by FC Barcelona in the 2002–03 season.

"Traveling to different shows around the world I get to meet truly talented people that inspire me and make my job fun!"

GWR's Marco Frigatti

POLAND Broadcast by Polsat, Poland's second-biggest television channel, *Guinness World Records* is a localized Polish edition of our popular Italian *Lo Show dei Record* featuring many of the same record-breaking guests as the Italian program. Now in its second series, our Polish show is presented by the former TV sports news anchor Maciej Dowbor. He is pictured here, in a return to his sporting roots, talking to Federica Pellegrini (Italy), women's 200 m freestyle (long course and short course) and 400 m (long course) freestyle world record holder.

JAPAN In Japan we have a series called *Guinness World Records Special* featuring the feats of a fair few talented individuals, such as competitive eater extraordinaire Takeru Kobayashi (Japan, above, left), who munched six hotdogs in 3 minutes in Kashiwanohakoen Stadium just outside Tokyo on August 25, 2009 (*see p. 246 for details*).

GREECE The second series of *Guinness World Records* in Greece saw an audience share of over 25% of the country's viewing public! The show, broadcast by MEGA, the country's largest broadcaster, stars Kostas Fragolias, Lorentzo Cariere, and Giorgos Lianos, pictured here celebrating with new record holder Daniele Seccarecci (Italy), the heaviest competitive bodybuilder (male) at 297 lb. 9.9 oz. (135 kg).

AUSTRALIA Produced by Eyeworks and airing on the Seven Network, Australia's *Guinness World Records* takes record breaking to the masses, with location shoots where attempts are performed live before an astounded public. Studio feats included Mon Tanner's record for fire eating—most torches extinguished in one minute, with 88. But like so many before him he lost his record just a few months later. . . .

CHINA This was our fifth year working with CCTV, China's state broadcaster, and record breaking has never been so popular—*Zheng Da Zong Yi–Guinness World Records Special* has a regular audience of more than 50 million! The show mixes highly competitive record-breaking spectaculars with popular acts and demonstrations of skill, such as an exhilarating performance by the Shaolin warrior monks, pictured above.

NEW ZEALAND Hosted by Marc Ellis, former All Black player and a Guinness World Record holder, TV2's *NZ Smashes Guinness World Records* saw a slight twist to our format—Eyeworks, the production company behind the show, handpicked record attempts that had been featured in other TV shows, and lined up ambitious Kiwis to try to claim the records as their own! The success of this format in New Zealand—it frequently got an audience twice as large as that of *The Simpsons* (see p. 328) when shown—led to a similar production in Australia, whereby these famously competitive nations could go head-to-head to see who could break the most Guinness World Records. The picture above shows two of 121 New Zealanders attempting the record for the **largest human mattress dominoes**.

ITALY Euro Produzione, our long-standing production partners in Europe, hit gold with *Lo Show dei Record* in Italy, with 143 fresh record attempts and a new hostess in the shapely form of former model Paola Perego. Paola's personal touch was key to getting all the people who are "unici al mondo" (unique in the world) to reveal the stories behind their attempts and achievements. Among the many successful record breakers were White Rope Skippers (all UK, pictured above) setting the record for the **most consecutive double Dutch style skips by a team**, with 362.

FRANCE *Le Monde des Records* is now in its 11th year in France and is as popular as ever. We broadcast more programs by volume in this country than any other territory, and have also featured on more TV channels here than anywhere else. Pictured is Bruno Wattier's attempt at the **most stripper trousers worn and removed in one minute.** He set this record with five on September 29, 2009, but lost it on March 18, 2010 when it was beaten on the set of *Lo Show dei Record* in Rome, Italy!

EXTRA! For more record-breaking tv, turn to pp. 304–311.

★**HEAVIEST SHOES WALKED IN** Physical fitness fan Zhang Zhenghui (China) appeared on the set of *Lo Show dei Record* in Rome, Italy, on March 18, 2010, where he managed to walk 32 ft. 9 in. (10 m) while wearing cast-iron shoes weighing a hefty 270 lb. 11.6 oz. (122.8 kg).

BEHIND THE SCENES AT GWR TV
There were 11 cameras on set at all times during the making of *Lo Show dei Record* in Rome, Italy, which began filming on February 25 and wrapped on April 29, 2010. It had a production team of 118 behind it (who ate 330.6 lb./150 kg of food between them while working), and it took 40 days to construct the set, which measured 131 ft. 2 in. x 131 ft. 2 in. (40 m x 40 m).

INTERVIEW MEET MR MOLLOY . . .

Rob Molloy (pictured right with champion gurner Tommy Mattinson) is Director of Television at Guinness World Records.

He took time out from his busy schedule to tell us what it's like on the set of a Guinness World Records show. . . .

Well, each show is different. Many of them reflect the cultures of the country they are based in, and that's always interesting to see. Sometimes filming can be stressful, but it's always entertaining.

What are your favorite records that have featured on GWR TV programs?

My personal favorite is the man who ran through 15 sheets of tempered glass on our New Zealand show. Or the record for the longest duration for three contortionists in a box. That was pretty crazy; they were filmed in countries all over Europe doing that!

And what exciting new projects can we expect in the next year?

As well as our studio-based shows we are planning on taking audiences behind the scenes and on the road with our adjudicators, allowing them to see world records as they happen!

....

AMIENS, FRANCE (49°53'N 2°17'E): Isabelle Dinoire (France) underwent the **first partial face transplant** at Amiens University Hospital, Amiens, France, on November 27, 2005. Ms Dinoire was left with severe facial disfigurement after her pet dog ripped off her nose, lips, and chin trying to wake her after she accidentally overdosed on pills in May 2005.

....

GUINNESS WORLD RECORDS LIVE!

Guinness World Records Live! is all about taking record breaking on the road. We've invited people from all around the globe to come to our Challenge Fairs—the only places in the world where you can walk in a humble mortal and walk out a genuine GWR record holder!

DID YOU KNOW?

GWR Live! has witnessed over 250 records being broken in eight countries. The most culturally diverse Challenge Fair was at Global Village in Dubai, UAE, which was attended by 34 different nationalities.

CROWD PLEASERS: Redcoats Micheala Lormier and Dave Clark hosted Guinness World Records Live! at the Butlins Resort in Bognor Regis, UK.

PARIS, FRANCE (48°52'N 2°20'E): The first cinema in operation was the Cinématographe Lumière at the Salon Indien, Paris, France, which opened on December 28, 1895. At the opening, an audience of 35—who had paid 1 franc each—watched L'*Arrivée d'un train en gare* (France, 1895) by the Lumière brothers.

DALLAS, USA ★ MOST POINTS SCORED AS KOBE BRYANT PLAYING THE 2K SPORTS NBA 2K10 VIDEO GAME Chico Kora (U.S.A., above) scored 29 points playing as Kobe Bryant on *NBA 2K10* at the NBA Jam in Dallas, Texas, U.S.A., on February 13, 2010.

X GAMES LA, CA & ASPEN, CO, U.S.A. GWR Live! got involved once again in the Summer and Winter X Games. Various BMX records were attempted (above and left), and Phil Smage (U.S.A., above) successfully set the record for the ☆**highest ollie on a snowskate**, at 28.5 in. (72.4 cm).

BOGNOR REGIS, UK ★ FASTEST TIME TO DRESS A BARBIE DOLL This challenge proved endlessly fascinating for younger guests (left) at Butlins. The record to dress a Barbie doll in three items of clothing, shoes, and an accessory is jointly held by Andrea Benjamin (UK) and Debbie Watson (UK), with a time of 36.99 sec., on 15 April 2010.

BED HEADS A team of six (all UK) made up a bunk bed in 1 min. 11 sec. at a GWR LIVE! event at Butlins, Minehead, UK, on March 7, 2010.

TURKEY ☆ CAN STACKING The GWR Live! Challenge Fair for Multi Corporation in Turkey started at Europe's largest shopping mall, the Forum Istanbul, and then toured Forum malls in cities across Turkey. Pictured is Deniz Özeskici (Turkey), who built a 20-can pyramid in just 6.49 sec. on April 4, 2010.

OSAKA, JAPAN ★MOST BALLS CAUGHT, NO HANDS The Guinness World Records Live! Challenge in the Park in Tokyo Midtown saw massive crowds trying their hand at rolling, spinning, throwing, sorting, folding, recycling, and leap-frogging as they attempted to win a place in history. Pictured is 61-year-old Tsuyoshi Kitazawa from Akasaka, Tokyo, who set the record for the ★most tennis balls caught with no hands in one minute, with 15.

DUBAI LOUDEST SHOUT . . . At Global Village in Dubai, UAE, members of the public broke 61 records over 110 days throughout early 2010. One of the most popular challenges was the loudest shout (pictured left), but no one was able to equal Annalisa Wray (UK), who achieved a shout of 121.7 dBA way back on April 16, 1994. It's still the record to beat. . . .

DUNKIRK, FRANCE (51°02'N 2°22'E): The **greatest evacuation in military history** was carried out by 1,200 Allied naval and civil craft from Dunkerque (Dunkirk), France, between May 26 and June 4, 1940. A total of 338,226 British and French troops were rescued.

HOW TO BE A RECORD BREAKER

So, you fancy yourself as a record breaker? Want to get your name in print? Here's our idiot's guide to turning your ideas into action. Applying is free and easy, so you've got no excuses. . . .

NEW CATEGORY

This is what we call a record claim that we've never seen before (as opposed to an "existing category"). But you have to convince us that your idea is a good one before we open a new category!

STEP 1 Think of a record! Or better, flick through a copy of the GWR book and find a record you think you can break. Looking through the book will also give you an idea of the kinds of records we like.

STEP 2 Visit **www.guinnessworld records.com** and click on "APPLY NOW"—then tell us about your record idea. Give us as much notice as you can (about three months is ideal!).

ALGIERS, ALGERIA (36°42'N 3°13'E): The world's **largest bowl of couscous** weighed 13,315 lb. (6.04 tonnes) and was made by Semoulerie Industrielle de la Mitidja and displayed at the International Fair of Algiers, Algeria, on June 3, 2004.

EXTRA! If animation gets you animated, take a trip to toon world on p. 325.

STEP 3 The next bit's easy—you just have to wait while our Records Management Team (RMT) plow through their (enormous) inbox and get to your claim. This is why we need the time—also, we might need expert help assessing your idea.

STEP 4 If your record category already exists, we'll email you the guidelines that the last claimant followed. If it's a new category—and we like it—we'll create new guidelines and email them to you asap.

If you get a "no" from Marco's Records Management Team, don't despair—rethink your idea and then reapply. We reject about 85% of claims because they're too dangerous or too stupid . . . or just not impressive enough!

STEP 5 Congratulations, we like your idea and you've got the guidelines. Read and follow them carefully—if you ignore them, you're unlikely to succeed.

FAST TRACK: If you're in a rush, why not try our three-day fast track service? You pay a fee for a dedicated records manager to process your claim asap.

SNAP!: If you *really* want to see your record in the book, be sure to submit the best possible photos—we love records with exciting, dynamic photography!

STEP 6 Now you practice, practice, practice. This is Luke, by the way, and he wants to try the **longest time juggling three objects blindfolded.**

STEP 7 When you're ready, attempt your record as per the guidelines. Be sure to have at least two independent witnesses, and film the entire event. Invite the press, too!

STEP 8 Next, mail us your evidence, your video footage, your signed witness statements, and whatever else we've requested in the guidelines. Then there's more waiting to do. . . .

STEP 9 Back at GWR Towers, we'll watch your video, assess your witness statements, and consult with any necessary governing body or expert. Have you followed the guidelines? Have you beaten the record?

STEP 10 Congratulations—if you're a record breaker, we'll send you your official GWR certificate. You're now a member of an elite group, a special family of high achievers, a crack squad of record holders!

STEP 11 There's one last stage: if you're *really* lucky, your record will be selected for the annual GWR book. Not every record makes it—only the best of the best! Good luck, everyone!

GHENT, BELGIUM (51°03'N 3°44'E): Jos de Troyer (Belgium) created the **largest hanging basket** measuring 34 ft. 5 in. (10.5 m) in diameter and weighing 99,208 lb. (45 tonnes) in Ghent, Belgium. It went on display in April 2000 above the Emile Braunplein Square.

How to Be a Record Breaker

GWR DAY

Guinness World Records Day is our annual global celebration of record breaking, when hundreds of thousands of people around the world get together to set or break records. Here is just a small selection of feats attempted on or around GWR day 2009!

GWR DAY 2009

RECORD	NAME	COUNTRY OF ORIGIN
Most push-ups with claps (73)	Stephen Buttler	UK
Tallest matchstick model (21 ft. 5 in.; 6 million matches)	Toufic Daher	Lebanon
Largest sports lesson (884)	multiple	Ireland
Fastest hot water bottle burst (18.81 seconds)	Shaun Jones	UK
Fastest time to peel and eat three lemons (28.5 seconds)	Jim Lyngvild	Denmark
Largest cup of hot chocolate (4 gallons; 4.5 liters)	Serendipity 3	U.S.A.
Largest paintbrush mosaic (32 ft. 9 in. x 8 ft. 6 in.; 10 x 2.6 m)	Saimir Strati	Albania
Highest wall climb on darts (16 ft. 4 in.; 5 m)	Maiko Kiesewetter	Germany

NORTHERN IRELAND ★ STORYBOOK CHARACTERS The largest gathering of people dressed as storybook characters is 300, achieved by Carr's Glen Primary School in Belfast, Northern Ireland, UK.

THE HAGUE, THE NETHERLANDS (52°04'N 4°18'E): The **largest clog dance** involved 475 participants at an event organized by Introdans Education and Dance and Child International at the Spuiplein in The Hague, the Netherlands, on July 8, 2006.

UK ★ FARTHEST DISTANCE TO PULL A BUS WITH THE HAIR Manjit Singh (UK), the "Iron Man of Leicester," pulled an 8.8-ton (8-tonne) double-decker bus 69 ft. 6 in. (21.2 m) using just his hair as part of the GWR celebrations in London. He tried the same stunt in 2007 using his ears but failed to move the bus the required distance.

ITALY ★ FASTEST TIME TO EAT PASTA Ernesto Cesario (Italy) ate his way into the record books on GWR Day 2009 by eating a 5.2-oz. (150-g) bowl of pasta in 1 min. 30 sec. in Milan.

GERMANY ★ FARTHEST JOURNEY BY WATERSLIDE To commemorate GWR Day in Germany, a team of 10 (all Germany) broke the 24-hour water-slide distance record, covering a fantastic 843.33 miles (1,357.22 km) at the Galaxy Erding indoor waterpark, the largest of its kind in Europe.

USA ★ LARGEST CHEERLEADING DANCE

GWR Day is now so popular in America, it takes up the entire week! One of our favorite events from last year involved 297 participants from the University Cheerleaders Association (U.S.A.) performing the largest cheerleading dance at the University of Memphis in Tennessee. Each participant danced for a muscle-pounding 5 min. 43 sec.!

FINLAND ★ FASTEST 40 M BY HUMAN WHEELBARROW

The truly international team of Adrian Rodriguez (Mexico, standing) and Sergiy Vetrogonov (Ukraine) achieved the fastest 40 m (131 ft.) by a human wheelbarrow, taking just 17 seconds, in Helsinki, Finland. The dynamic duo averaged a speed of 0.951 ft./s. (0.29 m/s.).

NETHERLANDS ☆ MOST BASKETBALL BOUNCES (1 MIN.)

Congratulations to Kiran Harpal (Netherlands), who broke the one-minute basketball-bounce record at the Hiernasst Youth Center in Wijchen with 384 consecutive bounces in the allotted time!

....

BRUSSELS, BELGIUM (50°50'N 4°21'E): The largest deliberately buried hoard of coins ever found was the so-called Brussels hoard of 1908, comprising approximately 150,000 coins.

....

TURKEY ☆ MOST CONCRETE BLOCKS BROKEN (30 SEC.) Martial arts expert Ali Bahçetepe (Turkey) broke 655 blocks using just his hands in 30 seconds in Datça Cumhuriyet Meydani, Turkey, on November 11, 2009.

UK ☆ MOST PEOPLE HUGGING (1 MIN.) To kick off GWR Day in the UK, a total of 112 morning commuters hugged one another at St. Pancras station in London for one minute.

NORWAY ☆ LARGEST GINGERBREAD MAN Getting in on the action was IKEA Furuset in Oslo, Norway, where this ginormous gingerbread man weighing 1,435 lb. 3 oz. (651 kg) was baked and decorated.

ITALY ☆ LONGEST PLATFORM-TO-PLATFORM BICYCLE JUMP Bicycle daredevil Vittorio Brumotti (Italy) successfully cleared a jump of 13 ft. 2 in. (4.02 m) between the top of two trucks in Fiera Milano, Milan, Italy.

EXTRA! For more shows of strength, flex your muscles and turn to pp. 141–146.

NEW ZEALAND ☆FARTHEST MALTESER BLOW Over in NZ, we could rely on multiple record holder Alistair Galpin to lead the charge. First off was the **farthest distance to blow a Malteser** (a chocolate-covered honeycomb malt ball) using a straw—37 ft. (11.29 m).
• Later the same day, Alistair achieved the ★**farthest distance to spit a champagne cork** at 16 ft. 3 in. (5 m).
• He then rounded the day off with the ★**farthest distance to blow a coin**—an epic 14 ft. 4 in. (37.6 cm).

SPACE

CONTENTS

A SENSE OF SCALE

Largest spiral galaxy Discovered in 1986, from photographs taken by the Anglo-Australian astronomer David Malin, and later named after him, Malin 1 is a spiral galaxy some 1.1 billion light-years away. In terms of its diameter, it is the largest known spiral galaxy in the Universe, measuring around 650,000 light-years across—several times the size of our Milky Way, which has a diameter of around 100,000 light-years. Malin 1 contains some 50 billion suns' worth of free-floating hydrogen.

Largest globular cluster Omega Centauri, in the southern constellation of Centaurus, is the most massive of the roughly 140 globular clusters surrounding our galaxy. Consisting of several million stars with a combined mass equivalent to 5 million suns, it is visible to the naked eye as a hazy star. However big this might seem, it would still take around a thousand Omega Centauris to equal just one spiral galaxy such as the galaxy in which we live, the Milky Way.

LARGEST PLANET IN THE SOLAR SYSTEM Jupiter, with an equatorial diameter of 89,405 miles (143,884 km) and a polar diameter of 83,082 miles (133,708 km), is the largest of the eight major planets, with a mass 317 times that of the Earth. However, despite its large size, Jupiter has a very short period of rotation, resulting in a Jovian day of only 9 hr. 55 min. 29.69 sec.—the ★ shortest planetary day in the Solar System.

NÎMES, FRANCE (43°50'N 4°21'E): The **largest surviving ancient Roman aqueduct** is the Pont du Gard near Nîmes in southern France, which stands 155 ft. (47 m) tall and is 902 ft. (275 m) long at its highest level. It was built in the late 1st century BC or the early 1st century AD and carried water across the river Gard.

LARGEST NEBULA VISIBLE TO THE NAKED EYE The Tarantula Nebula in the constellation of Doradus, in the southern sky, is large and bright enough to be visible to the naked eye, despite being at a distance of 170,000 light-years (10.7 billion AU). The huge cloud of glowing gas has a diameter of around 1,000 light-years (63 million AU) and is the only nebula outside our galaxy which is visible to the naked eye.

Largest star Due to the physical difficulties in directly measuring the size of a distant star, not all astronomers agree on the largest star, but the most likely candidate is VY Canis Majoris, a red supergiant some 5,000 light-years away. Estimates of its size give it a diameter of between 1.55 and 1.86 billion miles (2.5–3 billion km). If placed at the center of the Solar System, its outer surface would reach beyond the orbit of Jupiter.

Largest star with a planet In January 2003 astronomers announced their discovery of a planet orbiting the orange giant star HD 47536. This star is expanding at the end of its life and currently measures around 20.5 million miles (33 million km, or 23 times the size of the Sun) across. The planet is some 186 million miles (300 million km) from its star but will eventually be consumed in a few tens of millions of years as the star continues to expand into a red giant.

DELFT, THE NETHERLANDS (52°01'N 4°22'E): The **largest flying paper aircraft**, with a wingspan of 45 ft. 10 in. (13.97 m), was constructed by a team of students from the Faculty of Aerospace Engineering at Delft University of Technology, the Netherlands, and flown on May 16, 1995.

EXTRA! For large-scale manmade objects, turn to Big Stuff on p. 378.

LARGEST STRUCTURE IN THE UNIVERSE A team of astronomers led by Richard Gott III and Mario Juric (both U.S.A.) of Princeton University, Princeton, New Jersey, U.S.A., have discovered a huge wall of galaxies some 1.37 billion light-years long. They used data from the Sloan Digital Sky Survey, which is mapping the locations of one million galaxies in the universe. Their discovery was announced in October 2003.

☆**Largest extrasolar planet** Discovered in 2006, TrES-4 is an extrasolar planet some 1,400 light-years away, orbiting its parent star GSC 02620–006648 once every 3.5 days. It was discovered using the transit method, where the planet eclipses its star during its short orbit as seen from Earth. With a diameter of around 150,000 miles (240,000 km), it is some 1.7 times the size of Jupiter.

LARGEST GALAXY The central galaxy of the Abell 2029 galaxy cluster, located 1,070 million light-years away from the Earth in the constellation Virgo, has a major diameter of 5,600,000 light-years—80 times the diameter of our own Milky Way galaxy—and a light output equivalent to 2,000,000,000,000 (two trillion) Suns. Scientists suspect Abell 2029 attained its massive size by pulling in nearby galaxies.

ANTWERP, BELGIUM (51°13'N 4°24'E): The **largest ever gem theft** occurred at the Antwerp Diamond Center, Belgium, when 123 of the 160 vaults were emptied in a weekend raid on February 15–16, 2003, resulting in an estimated loss of $100 million.

LARGEST SPACE TELESCOPE NASA's Hubble Space Telescope (HST, left), named after the eminent American astronomer Edwin P. Hubble, celebrated its 20th anniversary in April 2010. The telescope, which weighs 24,250 lb. (11 tonnes) and is 43 ft. (13.1 m) in overall length, with a 94.8-in. (240-cm) reflector, was launched into space by the U.S. space shuttle *Discovery* on April 24, 1990. It has been serviced five times while in orbit and is currently due to remain in use until at least 2014. During its operational lifespan, the HST has captured spectacular images of many deep-space objects.

> "Space is big. You just won't believe how vastly, hugely, mind-bogglingly big it is. I mean, you may think it's a long way down the road to the chemist's, but that's just peanuts to space."
>
> **Douglas Adams, *The Hitchhiker's Guide to the Galaxy***

Largest dwarf planet The icy world Eris was discovered in January 2005. It has a highly elliptical orbit, with its distance from the Sun ranging from between 3.4 and 9.07 billion miles (5.6 and 14.6 billion km), and a diameter of around 1,490 miles (2,400 km). Before the reclassification of

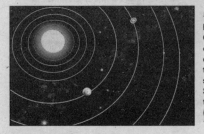

★**LARGEST KNOWN PLANETARY SYSTEM** Of the 429 planets orbiting other stars discovered to date, none are yet known to exist within a planetary system as large as our own Solar System, which is thought to be 100,000 AU (9.3 billion miles; 15 billion km) across.

DORDRECHT, THE NETHERLANDS (51°48'N 4°39'E):
The **largest flotilla of tugboats** was composed of 148 vessels and was achieved by Vereniging de Binnenvaart in Dordrecht, the Netherlands, on June 16, 2007.

Pluto as a dwarf planet, Eris was regarded by many as the tenth planet of the Solar System. Eris has a small moon, Dysnomia, around 217 miles (350 km) across.

Largest Kuiper Belt Object The Kuiper Belt is the cloud of frozen gases and debris at the edges of our Solar System around 55 AU (5 billion miles; 8.1 billion km) from the Sun. The Kuiper Belt object 50000 Quaoar measures around 800 miles (1,300 km) across and was discovered by Chad Trujillo and Mike Brown (both U.S.A.) at Caltech, Pasadena, California, U.S.A., on June 4, 2002. The object, originally dubbed 2002 LM60, is named after a creation god of the Tongva tribe—the original inhabitants of the Los Angeles area. It orbits the Sun at a distance of around 4 billion miles (6 billion km) and has an orbital period of 288 years.

Largest asteroid in the asteroid belt Among all the objects in the asteroid belt between Mars and Jupiter, Ceres is the largest, with an average diameter of 584.7 miles (941 km). Discovered by Giuseppe Piazzi in Palermo, Sicily, on January 1, 1801, Ceres is large enough to have an almost spherical shape. It is classified as the **smallest dwarf planet** and is due to be visited by NASA's *Dawn* probe in 2015.

★ **Largest asteroid visited by spacecraft** First discovered in 1885, 253 Mathilde, like Ceres, is found in the Asteroid Belt. It measures 41 x 29 x 28 miles (66 x 48 x 46 km) and became the third and largest asteroid to be encountered by a spacecraft in June 1997, when NASA's *NEAR Shoemaker* spacecraft passed it.

SATURN

Least round planet A combination of its low density (less than water) and rapid rotation (10.6 hours) gives Saturn the most oblate shape among the planets. Its equatorial diameter is 74,897.5 miles (120,536 km) while its polar diameter is just 67,560 miles (108,728 km).

★ **Longest-lasting lightning storm** A lightning storm in Saturn's upper atmosphere raged for more than eight months in 2009. Monitored by the *Cassini* spacecraft, the storm, with a diameter of several thousand miles, caused lightning flashes in Saturn's atmosphere around 10,000 times the intensity of their terrestrial counterparts.

···
HAARLEM, THE NETHERLANDS (52°23'N 4°39'E): The **longest water polo marathon** lasted 24 hours and was played by Rapido 82 Haarlem at the De Planeet pool, Haarlem, the Netherlands, between April 30 and May 1, 1999.
···

☆ **LARGEST PLANETARY RING** The Phoebe ring, discovered by NASA's Spitzer Infrared Telescope and announced on October 6, 2009, is a sparse disk of dust that extends to the orbit of the moon Phoebe, some 8,050,335 miles (12,955,759 km) from Saturn itself. It is believed to be formed by dust kicked off the surface of Phoebe by micrometeorite impacts.

★ **Largest eruptive ice plumes** Active cryovolcanism on Enceladus, Saturn's sixth-largest moon, had been predicted by scientists ever since the encounters by the two *Voyager* spacecraft in the early 1980s had revealed the geologically young surface of this icy moon. In 2005, observations from the *Cassini* spacecraft showed immense plumes of water ice above the moon's south pole. They are formed by the eruption of pressurized water reservoirs beneath the ice, forced to the surface by volcanic activity. They are at least as tall as the moon's 313-mile (505-km) diameter.

★ **Closest moon to Saturn** Discovered in July 2009 using observations from the *Cassini* spacecraft, S/2009 S 1 is a tiny moon just 985 ft. (300 m) across that orbits Saturn at a distance of just 35,251 miles (56,732 km), less than the radius of the planet. It orbits within the outer B Ring and was discovered using the shadow it cast across the rings themselves.

Colombo Gap Maxwell Gap   Huygens Gap Encke Gap Keeler Gap

D RING   C RING   B RING   A RING   F RING

GREATEST RING SYSTEM The intricate system of rings around Saturn have a combined mass of around 9×10^{19} lb. (4×10^{19} kg)—equivalent to the mass of an icy moon around 250 miles (400 km) across, or 1,800 times less massive than our moon. Gaps in the ring (such as the Colombo Gap) are caused by the gravitational influence of Saturn's moons. Rings G and E are more distant and not shown above.

EXTRA! Turn to page 11 for everything you need to know about the space shuttle.

☆ **SMALLEST ROUND WORLD** Mimas, the 20th largest moon in the Solar System, is just 246.4 miles (396.6 km) across. It is the smallest known body in the Solar System whose shape has been rounded due to its own gravity. The largest crater on Mimas is Herschel, which is 80 miles (130 km) across. It has 3-mile-high (5-km) walls, and a 4-mile-high (6-km) central peak.

LEAST DENSE PLANET Saturn is composed mostly of hydrogen and helium, the two lightest elements in the universe. It has an average density of only 0.71 times that of water. As Saturn is actually less dense than water, it would float—if there were an area of water in the Solar System large enough to accommodate it!

....

LYON, FRANCE (45°46'N 4°50'E): An international team of eight surgeons carried out the **earliest hand transplant operation** when they stitched the hand of a dead man to the wrist of 48-year-old Clint Hallam (New Zealand) in 1998, after he had suffered a chainsaw accident nine years previously.

....

★ **LARGEST METHANE SEA** Kraken Mare, on Titan, is a body of liquid methane 727 miles (1,170 km) across and with an area similar to that of the Caspian Sea on Earth (1,400,000 miles^2; 3,626,000 km^2). In July 2009, *Cassini* imaged the glint of reflected sunlight off Kraken Mare.

★**Outermost discrete ring** The most outwardly discrete ring, as opposed to a diffuse dust disk, is the contorted F Ring, with an orbital radius of 87,600 miles (141,000 km). It lies some 2,500 miles (4,000 km) beyond the edge of the main ring system and is probably the most dynamically active ring in the Solar System. Just a few hundred miles wide, the F Ring is thin and held in place by two shepherd moons, Pandora and Prometheus, whose gravitational interactions with the ring particles produce twisted knots within the ring that can change appearance in just a few hours.

Tallest ridge in the Solar System Observations of Saturn's moon Iapetus by the NASA/ESA spacecraft *Cassini-Huygens* on December 31, 2004, revealed a ridge at least 800 miles (1,300 km) long, reaching an altitude of around 12 miles (20 km) above the surface. Iapetus is just 890 miles (1,400 km) across.

Largest chaotically rotating object Saturn's moon Hyperion measures 254 x 161 x 136 miles (410 x 260 x 220 km) and is the largest highly irregularly shaped body in the Solar System. It is one of only two bodies in the Solar System discovered to have completely chaotic rotation, tumbling in its orbit around Saturn. The other is asteroid 4179 Toutatis, measuring 2.7 x 1.5 x 1.1 miles (4.5 x 2.4 x 1.9 km).

Closest moons to each other Janus and Epimetheus share the same average orbit some 56,500 miles (91,000 km) above Saturn. As their orbital paths are only 31 miles (50 km) apart, one of the moons is always catching the other up. Every four years they come within 6,200 miles (10,000 km) of each other and swap orbits, before drifting apart again.

Satellite with the thickest atmosphere Saturn's large moon Titan has the thickest atmosphere of any moon in the Solar System, exerting a surface pressure of 1.44 bar. It consists mainly of nitrogen gas and is the most similar atmosphere to our own in the Solar System.

SPACE SHUTTLES

THE SPACE SHUTTLE—or, more accurately, the Shuttle Transportation System (STS)—made its first test flights in 1981, and orbital missions began the following year. It is the world's first—and to date only—spacecraft to make multiple orbital flights and landings.

Now, 30 years later, NASA has announced the retirement of the space shuttle program. With its end in sight, we take a look at the shuttle's record-breaking history and its major achievements.

☆ **Most reused spacecraft** NASA's space shuttle *Discovery* was last launched on April 5, 2010, beginning its 38th spaceflight, STS-131. *Discovery*, the third orbiter in the shuttle fleet, first flew in August 1984.

Longest shuttle flight The lengthiest shuttle flight was by *Columbia* and its crew of five astronauts during the STS-80 mission. Launched on November 19, 1996, it had 17 days 15 hr. 53 min. 26 sec. of mission elapsed time.

LARGEST SOLID ROCKET BOOSTER The two boosters that assist the launch of the U.S. space shuttle use solid rather than liquid fuel. They are the largest solid rocket boosters (SRBs) ever flown. Each booster is 149 ft. (45.4 m) long and 12 ft. (3.6 m) wide. Each contains more than 1,000,000 lb. (450,000 kg) of propellant and provides a thrust of 3.3 million lb. (1.49 million kg), or about 83% of liftoff power. Unlike the shuttle's external fuel tank, the SRBs are reusable.

FIRST!: Space Shuttle *Columbia* was the first spacecraft to land on wheels. Before this, spacecraft used parachutes to reach Earth.

LAST!: At the time of going to press, the last shuttle mission planned by NASA was STS-133, a discovery flight due to launch on September 16, 2010.

★ FIRST SPACECRAFT WITH A GLASS COCKPIT Glass cockpits are characterized by electronic instrument displays, replacing older consoles that relied on mechanical gauges to display flight information. All three of NASA's operational shuttles have glass cockpits, the first to receive one being *Atlantis*, which flew with the new interface in 2000 during STS-101.

LARGEST OBJECTS TRANSPORTED BY AIR Although not the heaviest, the largest single objects to be transported by air are the 122-ft. 2-in. (37.23-m) space shuttles, which are "piggybacked" on top of modified Boeing 747 jets from alternative airstrips back to Cape Canaveral in Florida, U.S.A. *Discovery, Atlantis,* and *Endeavour* each weigh around 110 tons (100 tonnes) when transported.

....

AMSTERDAM, THE NETHERLANDS (52°22'N 4°53'E): The **largest painting** is a depiction of the sea that measures 92,419 ft.^{2} (8,586 m^2), the size of nearly four American football fields. It was completed by ID Culture at The Arena, Amsterdam, the Netherlands, to mark the venue's opening on August 14, 1996.

....

★ **FIRST SHUTTLE DOCKING**
On June 29, 1995, *Atlantis* docked with the Russian *Mir* space station, beginning the Shuttle-*Mir* Program. This was the 100th spaceflight by the U.S.A. *Atlantis* brought cosmonauts Anatoly Solovyev and Nikolai Budarin to *Mir*, and returned Vladimir Dezhurov, Gennady Strekalov (both Russia), and Norm Thagard (U.S.A.) to Earth. This was the first time a shuttle crew had changed in orbit.

Largest shuttle crew The shuttle mission with the largest crew to date was STS-61-A, which launched on October 30, 1985, carrying eight astronauts on board *Challenger*. This flight carried the West German *Spacelab* D-1 laboratory. The flight lasted 7 days 44 min. 51 sec.

Largest door Each of the four doors in the NASA Vehicle Assembly Building near Cape Canaveral, Florida, U.S.A., is 460 ft. (140 m) high, as tall as a 35-story building. Their massive size was originally to allow fully assembled Saturn V rockets to pass through them.

★ **Most people on a spacewalk** The first flight of *Endeavour* on May 7, 1992, was to repair the failing *Intelsat VI* satellite. Retrieving the satellite proved problematic until Pierre Thuot, Richard Hieb, and Thomas Akers (all U.S.A.) performed a spacewalk and were able to capture *Intelsat VI* by hand. In the meantime, mission commander Daniel Brandenstein (U.S.A.) maneuvered *Endeavour* to within a few feet of the stricken satellite. This is the only occasion in history that three people have walked in space at the same time.

★ **First manned maiden spaceflight** The first ever shuttle launch was a test flight by astronauts John Young and Robert Crippen (both U.S.A.) on

QUIZ!: What was the name given to NASA's first space shuttle? See p. 543 for the answer.

SPACE TOILET

The toilet on the space shuttle uses foot straps and thigh bars to hold the user in place. Solids are stored on board until landing, and waste liquids are vented into space.

★FIRST INFLIGHT REPAIR On July 26, 2005, the shuttle *Discovery* launched on the STS-114 mission. During a spacewalk, Stephen Robinson (U.S.A.) was able to pull out manually two protruding "gap fillers" between the thermal tiles on *Discovery*'s underbelly. This photograph was taken by Robinson, using a digital camera. It shows the thermal tiles on the underside of the shuttle, reflected in the visor of his helmet.

April 12, 1981. This was the first time a new spacecraft system had ever flown in space without a prior unmanned spaceflight.

★**Heaviest glider** The heaviest shuttle landing was *Columbia* during the STS-83 mission, which touched down on April 8, 1997, with a mass of 213,060 lb. (96,642 kg). To return to Earth, the shuttle fires its orbital maneuvering engines to slow down and decrease its altitude, and uses friction to reduce speed in the upper atmosphere. From then on, the landing sequence is unpowered, with the shuttle acting as a glider, performing a series of high-altitude turns to dissipate speed, and eventually approaching the runway and touching down with the rear wheels first.

★**Heaviest component** At liftoff, the space shuttle consists of the orbiter itself, the external fuel tank that feeds its main engines, and two solid rocket boosters attached to the tank that provide additional thrust. The heaviest component at liftoff is the tank, weighing 1,680,000 lb. (760,000 kg).

Heaviest payload launched The *Chandra X-ray Observatory* was launched by *Columbia* on July 23, 1999. With a mass of 50,161 lb. (22,753 kg), this was the heaviest satellite that has ever been launched by the space shuttle.

DID YOU KNOW?

The ★**first orbital space shuttle mission**—STS-1—was the 54.5-hour maiden flight of *Columbia,* commanded by NASA astronaut John Young.

UTRECHT, THE NETHERLANDS (52°05'N 5°08'E): The most people spinning plates simultaneously was 1,026 at the official opening of the Sportcampus in Utrecht, the Netherlands, on September 25, 2007.

THE SUN

★**First flyby of the Sun's poles** The joint NASA/ESA *Ulysses* space-craft was launched from the space shuttle *Discovery* in 1990. It headed out to Jupiter, where it used a gravitational slingshot to send it into a polar orbit around the Sun, from where it has directly observed both solar poles. The spacecraft ceased operations on June 30, 2009.

SOL

The scientific term for the Sun. It is found in Latin, among other languages, as is the word for the Moon: "Luna."

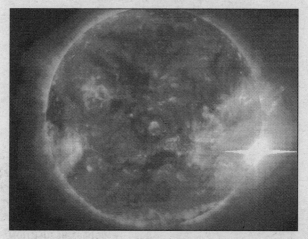

LARGEST SOLAR FLARE On November 4, 2003, a solar flare—seen at the lower right-hand side of this photograph—erupted from the surface of the Sun. It was rated as an X28 event by the Space Environment Center of the National Oceanic and Atmospheric Administration (NOAA), in Boulder, Colorado, U.S.A.

....

MARSEILLE, FRANCE (43°18'N 5°22'E): The **last use of the guillotine** was on September 10, 1977, at Baumettes Prison, Marseille, France, for the torturer and murderer Hamida Djandoubi, who was age 28 at the time.

....

EXTRA! Take a trip to Saturn by turning back to pp. 7–11.

★ **HIGHEST-RESOLUTION SOLAR TELESCOPE** The Swedish 3-ft. 2-in. (1-m) Solar Telescope on La Palma in the Canary Islands uses a mirror in the path of the sunlight that minutely changes shape a thousand times per second to counter the effects of atmospheric turbulence. It can see details on the surface of the Sun (inset) as small as 43 miles (70 km) across.

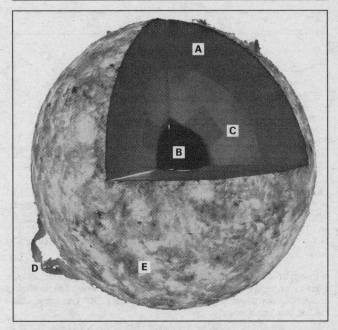

HOTTEST PLACE IN THE SOLAR SYSTEM The very center of the Sun is the hottest place in the Solar System. The latest estimates of the temperature put it at 28,080,000°F (15,600,000°C). The pressure in the core is also immense, around 250 billion times the pressure at sea level on Earth. These conditions allow nuclear fusion to take place, which is what makes the Sun shine.

A. CONVECTIVE ZONE Energy from the core moves through this zone by convection, similar to the turbulent movement in boiling water.

B. CORE The Sun's core is approximately 28,080,000°F (15,600,000°C). Around 661 million tons of hydrogen are fused into around 657 million tons of helium every second by nuclear fusion.

C. RADIATIVE ZONE Radiation produced in the core can "bounce around" among the matter in the radiative zone for millions of years.

D. PROMINENCE Vast eruptions of plasma from the photosphere can extend into space for hundreds of thousands of miles.

E. PHOTOSPHERE The visible surface of the Sun is where we see phenomena such as sunspots. Its average temperature is around 9,932°F (5,500°C). Sunspots are cooler, at around 5,432°F (3,000°C).

Largest sunspot group On April 8, 1947, the largest sunspot group ever identified was found in the Sun's southern hemisphere. At its greatest length, it measured 187,000 miles (300,000 km), with a maximum width of 90,000 miles (145,000 km). It was roughly 36 times greater than the surface area of the Earth and was even visible to the naked eye, close to sunset.

★**Longest-lasting sunspot group** Between June and December 1943, a group of sunspots was observed to last for 200 days. The smallest sunspots, known as pores, and less than 1,553 miles (2,500 km) across, can last less than one hour.

★**Longest and shortest solar cycles** The solar cycle is a periodic change in the number of sunspots on the surface of the Sun and relates directly to solar magnetic activity. It was first discovered in 1843 and, by examining older observations of sunspots, astronomers now have data on sunspot activity going back to the early 17th century. The cycle lasts an average of 11 years, with the longest so far ending in 1798 having lasted 13.7 years, and the shortest ending in 1775 having lasted just nine years.

BERGEN, NORWAY (60°22'N 5°24'E): The **longest road tunnel** is between Aurland and Lærdal on the main road between Bergen and Oslo, Norway, and measures 15.2 miles (24.5 km) in length. It was opened to the public in 2001.

★Biggest object in the Solar System The Sun has a mass 332,900 times greater than that of Earth, and a diameter of 865,000 miles (1,392,000 km). It accounts for 99.86% of the mass of the whole Solar System.

Closest approach to the Sun by a spacecraft The unmanned spacecraft *Helios 2* approached within 27 million miles (43.5 million km) of the Sun, carrying both U.S. and West German instrumentation, on April 16, 1976.

Due for launch in 2015, NASA's *Solar Probe+* will attempt to study the Sun from as close as 3.9 million miles (6.2 million km), from within the Sun's outer atmosphere or corona. Traveling at a speed of 125 miles/sec. (200 km/sec.), the spacecraft will have to survive temperatures of up to 2,600°F (1,420°C).

★ Strongest geomagnetic storm On September 1, 1859, at 11:18 a.m., British astronomer Richard Carrington observed two blinding explosions occurring on the surface of the Sun. The following dawn, all over the world the skies were ablaze with auroras caused by the charged particles from the eruptions interacting with Earth's magnetosphere, having taken just 18 hours to cross the space between the Sun and the Earth (the journey normally takes three or four days).

The study of ice cores suggest that events of this magnitude occur roughly every 500 years. The magnetic disruptions caused by the "Carrington Event" affected telegraph systems all over Europe and North America.

Most destructive geomagnetic storm The "Great Geomagnetic Storm" of March 13, 1989, was the most destructive geomagnetic storm ever recorded. The record-breaking event was classified G5 (the most severe rating) on the space weather scale. The result of an abnormally strong solar wind, it caused large-scale disruption to the power grid in Canada and the U.S.A., and even changed the orbit of a satellite. The power outages—caused by failures at the Hydro-Québec systems in Canada—saw 6 million people losing electricity for nine hours.

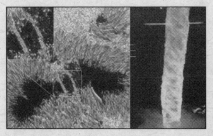

★LARGEST TORNADOES IN THE SOLAR SYSTEM In April 1998, scientists announced the discovery of rotating tornado-like storms in the atmosphere of the Sun, using observations made by the *SOHO* satellite. Occurring mainly near the poles of the Sun, these phenomena are around the size of Earth, and the ionized gas within them moves at around 300,000 mph (500,000 km/h).

★Nearest star The pioneering work of Father Angelo Secchi (Italy, 1818–78) in spectroscopy led to his classification scheme for stars, and to his conclusion that our own Sun was a star and not a phenomenon unique to the Solar System. At just 93,000,000 miles (149,000,000 km) from Earth, the Sun is astronomically close. The next nearest star, Proxima Centauri, is 4.2 light years away, or 24,000,000,000,000 miles (40,000,000,000,000 km).

EARTH

CONTENTS

PEAKS & TROUGHS

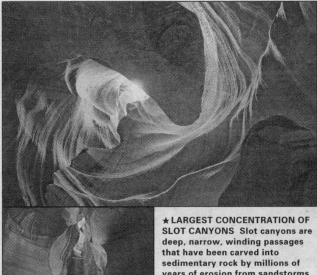

★LARGEST CONCENTRATION OF SLOT CANYONS Slot canyons are deep, narrow, winding passages that have been carved into sedimentary rock by millions of years of erosion from sandstorms, rain, and fast-flowing waters. They are characterized by narrow openings and deep sides, often with cavernous interiors and beautifully colored striations. According to SummitPost, the climbing and outdoor activity group, the Colorado Plateau in southwestern North America has a greater number of slots than anywhere on Earth, perhaps as many as 10,000.

☆ **DEEPEST MINE** TauTona, which means "great lion" in the Setswana language, is a gold mine situated near Carletonville, South Africa, owned by AngloGold Ashanti. Originally built by the Anglo American Corporation, the 1.24-mile (2-km) original main shaft was sunk in 1957. The mine began operation in 1962 and, by 2008, had reached a depth of 2.4 miles (3.9 km). At this depth, the temperature of the rock faces can reach 140°F (60°C). The mine now has around 497 miles (800 km) of tunnels and employs 5,600 miners.

AIX-EN-PROVENCE, FRANCE (43°22'N 5°27'E): The **largest known dinosaur eggs** are those of *Hypselosaurus priscus* ("high ridge lizard"), a 40-ft.-long (12-m) titanosaurid that lived about 80 million years ago. Examples found in the Durance valley near Aix-en-Provence, France, in October 1961 would have had, uncrushed, a length of 12 in. (30 cm).

EXTRA! Explore fascinating fish & sealife by turning to p. 71.

HIGHS

Tallest mountain Mauna Kea on the island of Hawaii, U.S.A., is the world's tallest mountain. Measured from its submarine base in the Hawaiian Trough to its peak, the mountain has a height of 33,480 ft. (10,205 m), of which 13,796 ft. (4,205 m) is above sea level.

Tallest unclimbed mountain At 24,835 ft. (7,570 m), Gangkar Punsum in Bhutan is ranked as the world's 40th highest peak, and the highest mountain yet to be climbed. Unsuccessful attempts were made to summit the peak in the 1980s, then in 1994, a partial ban of mountaineering in the country was declared. Since 2003, all climbing in Bhutan has been outlawed—for religious reasons—so it could remain unclimbed for many years to come.

Tallest mountain face The Rupal face of Nanga Parbat, in the western Himalayas, Pakistan, is a single rise of some 15,000 ft. (4,600 m) from the valley floor to the summit. The mountain itself, with a summit of 26,656 ft. (8,125 m), is the world's ninth highest mountain.

★Highest polar ice cap Dome Argus is a vast ice plateau near the center of eastern Antarctica. Its highest point is 13,428 ft. (4,093 m) above sea level. It is the highest ice feature on Antarctica and it overlies the 745-mile-long (1,200-km) Gamburtsev Mountain Range.

★Highest historically active volcano Llullaillaco, on the Argentina–Chile border, is a stratovolcano on a plateau within the Atacama Desert. Its last eruption was in 1877 and, at 22,109 ft. (6,739 m) high, it is the highest recorded active volcano.

Fastest-rising mountain Nanga Parbet in Pakistan is growing taller at a rate of 0.27 in. (7 mm) per year. Part of the Himalayan Plateau, it formed when India began colliding with the Eurasian continental plate between 30 and 50 million years ago.

GRENOBLE, FRANCE (45°12'N 5°42'E): The late Michel Lotito (France) of Grenoble, France, known as Monsieur Mangetout, ate metal and glass from the age of nine—without doubt the **strangest diet** on record. Gastroenterologists who had X-rayed his stomach described his ability to consume 2 lb. (900 g) of metal per day as unique.

UP!: Mount Thor has an average angle of 105°, which makes it very popular with climbers. It was first scaled in 1953 (see below).

☆ **GREATEST VERTICAL DROP Mount Thor** on Baffin Island, Nunavut, Canada, is a granite peak whose west face consists of a vertical drop of 4,101 ft. (1,250 m). It is technically an overhang, with the average angle of repose of the cliff being at 105°—15° beyond the vertical. The mountain was first climbed in 1953 by a team from the Arctic Institute of North America (AINA).

Largest subglacial mountain range The Gamburtsev Mountains in eastern Antarctica extend for approximately 745 miles (1,200 km) across the continent. They reach up to 8,850 ft. (2,700 m) high and are permanently buried under more than 1,968 ft. (600 m) of ice. Discovered by a Soviet team in 1958, the mountains are believed to be around 500 million years old.

DOWN!: Mount Thor is made of granite and is part of the Baffin Mountains. These, in turn, form part of the Arctic Cordillera Mountain Range.

TOULON, FRANCE (43°10'N 5°55'E): The 9,548-ton (8,662-tonne), 333-ft. 8-in.-long (101.7-m) *Richelieu*, the **heaviest wooden ship** ever, was launched in Toulon, France, on December 3, 1873.

LONGEST UNDERWATER CAVE SYSTEM Sistema Ox Bel Ha (meaning "Three Paths of Water" in the Mayan language), in the state of Quintana Roo, Mexico, is a complex series of underwater passages accessible by exposed lakes called cenotes. As of May 2009, some 111.870 miles (180.038 km) of underwater passages had been explored and mapped by cave divers.

GENEVA, SWITZERLAND (46°12'N 6°09'E): The **most expensive cell phone** was designed by GoldVish of Geneva, Switzerland, and was sold for €1,000,000 ($1,287,200) at the Millionaire Fair in Cannes, France, on September 2, 2006.

★HIGHEST ACTIVE CARBONATITE VOLCANO Oldoinyo Llengai, Tanzania, is a rare type of volcano that erupts natrocarbonatite lava. At 9,718 ft. (2,962 m) high, it is the only active volcano of this type on Earth. It erupts a bizarre runny lava that appears like molten chocolate at 930–1,110°F (500–600°C) and turns white upon cooling.

Longest submarine mountain range The Mid-Ocean Ridge extends some 40,000 miles (65,000 km) from the Arctic Ocean to the Atlantic Ocean, around Africa, Asia, and Australia, and under the Pacific Ocean to the west coast of North America. It has a maximum height of 13,800 ft. (4,200 m) above the base ocean depth.

LOWS

Deepest cave In September 2007, cavers from the Ukrainian Speleological Association reached a record depth of 7,188 ft. 3 in. (2,191 m) in the Krubera Cave (also known as the Voronya Cave) in the Arabika Massif, Georgia. More than 8,202 ft. (2.5 km) of new cave passages were explored during this 29-day underground expedition.

Deepest penetration into the Earth's crust A geological exploratory borehole near Zapolyarny on the Kola peninsula of Arctic Russia, which began on May 24, 1970, had reached a depth of 40,236 ft. (12,261 m) by 1983, when funding stopped. The temperature of the rocks at the bottom of the hole is about 410°F (210°C).

Largest sea cave The Sea Lion Caves, close to Florence on the coast of Oregon, U.S.A., have a chamber 310 ft. (95 m) long, 165 ft. (50 m) wide, and around 50 ft. (15 m) high in a wave-cut passage measuring 1,315 ft. (400 m) long.

Deepest valley The Yarlung Zangbo valley in Tibet has an average depth of 16,400 ft. (5,000 m), but in 1994 explorers discovered that its deepest point was 17,657 ft. (5,382 m). This deepest point is more than three times deeper than the Grand Canyon, which is the **largest land gorge** with a depth of 1 mile (1.6 km) and a width ranging from 0.25 to 8 miles (0.5 to 29 km).

The peaks on either side of the Yarlung Zangbo valley are Namche Barwa (25,436 ft; 7,753 m) and Jala Peri (23,891 ft; 7,282 m). They are just 13 miles

(21 km) apart, with the Yarlung Zangbo River flowing between them at an elevation of 8,000 ft. (2,440 m).

Largest cave opening The entrance to Cathedral Caverns in Grant, Alabama, U.S.A., is the world's largest cave opening. At 126 ft. (38.4 m) wide and 25 ft. (7.6 m) high, Cathedral Caverns was originally known as the Bat Cave until it was developed into a tourist attraction in 1955.

Deepest lava cave Kazumura Cave in Hawaii, U.S.A., is both the deepest and also the longest lava cave—an open tube down the inside of a lava flow. It is 36.9 miles (59.3 km) long and descends 3,605 ft. (1,099 m) down the eastern flank of Kilauea volcano.

RIVERS & LAKES

Highest level of alkalinity in a lake system The Magadi-Natron basin in the Great Rift Valley of Kenya-Tanzania contains saline (salt) bodies of water with temperatures as high as 120°F (50°C) and alkalinity that reaches levels as high as pH 10–12—strong enough to burn the skin. The corrosiveness of these lakes—notably Natron, Magadi, and Nakuru—is caused by high concentrations of minerals from hot springs, along with a high evaporation rate. Lake Natron's characteristic deep-red color is the result of pigments produced by algae that live in the hypersaline environment.

★ **Largest rapids by flow rate** Inga Falls, on the Congo river in the Democratic Republic of Congo, drops in height by 315 ft. (96 m) over a length of around 9 miles (15 km). The average flow rate has been measured at around 1,500,000 ft³/sec. (42,400 m³/sec.), enough to fill London's Albert Hall in around two seconds. Inga Falls has a maximum flow rate of around 2,500,000 ft³/sec. (70,800 m³/sec.).

★ **Largest inland delta** The Okavango Delta in Botswana is formed by the Okavango river as it enters an endorheic basin in the Kalahari Desert. (The term "endorheic" means it has no outlets other than evaporation for its water.) Millions of years ago it emptied into an inland sea until tectonic activity interrupted the river and formed the delta. The size of the delta varies seasonally from around 6,100 miles² (16,000 km²) to around 3,400 miles² (9,000 km²).

....

OBERHAUSEN, GERMANY (51°28'N 6°51'E): The **most pirouettes on a motorcycle in 30 seconds** is 21, performed by Horst Hoffmann (Germany) during the Centro Festival in Oberhausen, Germany, on September 9, 2006.

....

SALTIEST LAKE Don Juan Pond in Wright Valley, Antarctica, has such a high salt content that it remains a liquid even at temperatures as low as −63.4°F (−53°C). At its saltiest, the lake's percentage of salt by weight is 40.2%, compared with 23.1% in the Dead Sea and an average of 3.38% in the world's oceans as a whole.

★**LARGEST EPHEMERAL LAKE** Like Lake Turkana (see p. 31), Lake Eyre—which is located at the lowest point in Australia—is an example of an endorheic system. It usually contains little or no water but occasionally floods due to heavy monsoon rains. In 1974, the greatest flooding of this salt flat basin created a temporary inland sea with an area of around 3,600 miles² (9,500 km²).

★ **DEEPEST HYPERSALINE LAKE** The Dead Sea on the Israel–Jordan border is the deepest hypersaline (very salty) lake in the world, with a maximum depth of 1,240 ft. (378 m). The Dead Sea has an average salinity of more than 8.5 times that of seawater. Dead Sea mud is believed by many people to have healing properties when rubbed on the skin.

★ **Largest tidal bore** Tidal bores are formed when the front of the incoming tide forms a wave or series of waves that travels up a river against its direction of flow. This phenomenon occurs in several dozen locations around the world, but by far the largest and most spectacular happens in the Qiantang River, China, where it can form a massive wave of water up to 30 ft. (9 m) high, traveling upstream at up to 25 mph (40 km/h). The bore is so dangerous that it is thought only a handful of people have been able to surf it.

★ **Largest desert lake** Lake Turkana in the Great Rift Valley, Kenya, has a surface area of 2,472 miles^2 (6,405 km^2) and an average depth of 99 ft. (30.2 m). It is the fourth-largest salt lake in the world and is fed by the Omo, Turkwel, and Kerio Rivers. There is no outflow from Lake Turkana, and the only method of water loss is by evaporation.

COLOGNE, GERMANY (50°57'N 6°58'E): The **longest journey by automobile using alternative fuel** is 23,697 miles (38,137 km), by a team of four (all Germany) in a Volkswagen Caddy EcoFuel using natural gas. The journey started in Cologne, Germany, on October 15, 2006, and finished in Leipzig, Germany, on April 13, 2007.

☆ LARGEST WATERFALL (VERTICAL AREA) Victoria Falls, on the Zambezi River between Zimbabwe and Zambia, is neither the tallest nor the widest in the world, but it is the largest by vertical area. Being 5,604 ft. (1,708 m) wide and 354 ft. (108 m) high, it creates a sheet of falling water with an area of around 1,984,000 ft.² (184,400 m²).

Largest tropical lake With a surface area of around 26,563 miles² (68,800 km²), Lake Victoria is the biggest lake in the world that lies within the tropics. Containing some 659 miles³ (2,750 km³) of water, it is ranked as the seventh-largest freshwater lake in the world. It is the main source of the Nile river, the world's **longest river**.

Greatest river flow The Amazon river in South America has the greatest flow of any river, discharging an average of 7,100,000 ft.³/sec. (200,000 m³/sec.) into the Atlantic Ocean, which increases to more than 12,000,000 ft.³/sec. (340,000 m³/sec.) in full flood. The lower 900 miles (1,450 km) averages 55 ft. (17 m) in depth, but the river has a maximum depth of 407 ft. (124 m).

The Amazon is fed by more than 1,000 tributaries and its flow is 60 times greater than that of the Nile. The river accounts for about 20% of the freshwater that drains into the world's oceans.

★ **LARGEST CRATER LAKE** Lake Toba, on the Indonesian island of Sumatra, is the site of a supervolcanic eruption around 75,000 years ago that was probably the largest anywhere on Earth during the last 25 million years. The crater formed by the eruption is now filled with water that makes Lake Toba, which is around 60 miles (100 km) by 18 miles (30 km) in extent, and 1,656 ft. (505 m) deep at its deepest point.

OCEANS & SEAS

★**First proven rogue wave** Rogue waves are waves with abnormal height compared to others, and were long believed to be legendary. On January 1, 1995, the first confirmed measurement of this phenomenon occurred as a wave with a height of 84 ft. (25.6 m) struck the Draupner platform in the North Sea.

★**Largest dead zone** Regions of coastal waters where seawater is depleted of oxygen are called "dead zones." More than 400 have been mapped around the world, but the Baltic Sea, with an area of around 145,000 miles^2 (377,000 km^2), is the largest. The bottom of the Baltic lacks oxygen year-round.

Widest continental shelf The Siberian continental shelf extends 750 miles (1,210 km) off the coast of Siberia, Russia, into the Arctic Ocean. Huge concentrations of methane exist beneath this shelf. In 2008, scientists found evidence that global warming is starting to allow this trapped methane to enter the atmosphere.

SMALLEST COASTLINES

	STATE/NATION	DISTANCE (IMPERIAL)	DISTANCE (METRIC)
1	Monaco (above left)	3.5 miles	5.6 km
2	Nauru (above right)	12 miles	19 km
3	Bosnia	13 miles	20 km
4	Jordan	16 miles	25 km
5	Slovenia	19 miles	30 km

★**Youngest ocean** Of the major oceans of the world, the Southern Ocean (also known as the Antarctic Ocean and the South Polar Ocean) is the youngest. It formed when Antarctica split away from Australia and South America around 30 million years ago, also forming the Drake Passage in the process.

★**Newest forming ocean** In 2005, a rift some 35 miles (56 km) long opened up in the Afar Depression (also known as the Danakil Depression, the lowest point in Africa) in Ethiopia. In November 2009, scientists an-

CANNES, FRANCE (43°33'N 7°00'E): The **largest movie festival** is the Festival International du Film de Cannes, held in the south of France in May each year. The event attracts between 40,000 and 50,000 movie industry workers annually.

KRAKA-: Pictured is island-volcano Krakatoa erupting in May 2009. An eruption on August 27, 1883 was the loudest noise ever recorded . . .

★ LARGEST VOLCANIC ZONE The Pacific Ring of Fire is a huge horseshoe-shaped arc of concentrated earthquake and volcanic activity around 24,800 miles (40,000 km) long, located in the Pacific Ocean. It comprises some 452 volcanoes and more than 75% of the world's active and dormant volcanoes.

nounced that results of their analysis showed that this rift is the beginning of the formation of a new ocean. The tectonic processes occurring under Afar are the same as those on the ocean floor at the ridges where new crust is formed and existing crust is pushed apart.

It is expected that, around a million years from now, seawater from the Red Sea will pour into the Afar Depression as it stretches and thins, and the resulting body of sea will gradually grow, possibly to become as large as the Atlantic or Pacific Oceans.

Largest submarine tar flow In 2003, a team of scientists led by Texas A&M University, U.S.A., discovered the world's first asphalt-erupting volcano 9,842 ft. (3,000 m) deep on the seafloor of the Gulf of Mexico. Using

-TOA!: . . . the explosion was heard from more than 3,100 miles (5,000 km) away. That's 8% of the Earth's surface!

☆ **DEEPEST OBSERVED VOLCANIC ERUPTION** On December 18, 2009, U.S. scientists announced the discovery of a volcanic eruption around 3,900 ft. (1,200 m) deep in the Pacific Ocean. The footage, captured in May 2009 by a robotic submersible, shows molten lava erupting from the West Mata volcano, which is 125 miles (200 km) southwest of the Samoas and is one of the most active submarine volcanoes in the world.

a remotely operated camera, the team found tar flows from the volcano, named Chapopote, covering at least 0.4 miles² (1 km²). Their results were published in the journal *Science* in May 2004.

★ **Shallowest ocean** The Arctic Ocean is the shallowest (and smallest) of the five main oceans. At 5,426,000 miles² (14,056,000 km²) it is roughly the size of Russia and covers 2.8% of the Earth's surface but has an average depth of 3,450 ft. (1,050 m).

★ **Highest ocean temperature** In August 2008, an international team of scientists announced they had recorded water at a temperature of 867°F

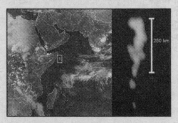

★ **LARGEST AREA OF GLOWING SEA** In 1995, scientists at the US Naval Research Laboratory discovered an area of luminous sea in the Indian Ocean off the coast of Somalia using satellite images. The patch of water (pictured) was more than 155 miles (250 km) long, with an area of around 5,400 miles² (14,000 km²). Bioluminescent bacteria are thought to have been responsible for the water's appearance.

BERNE, SWITZERLAND (46°57'N 7°28'E): The **largest solar-slate roof** is on a former grain storage facility in Berne, Switzerland. The building is fitted with a solar-slate roof measuring 22,066 ft.² (2,050 m²) and made of 16,650 photovoltaic cell-embedded slates known as "Sunslates."

★ **OLDEST SEAWATER** The seawater at the bottom of the 12,400-ft.-deep (3,800-m) Canada Basin has remained unstirred for several thousand years. The Basin, which is north of Canada and Alaska, U.S.A., is connected to the Pacific Ocean only by the 230-ft.-deep (70-m) Bering Strait and is protected from the power of the Atlantic Ocean by tall submarine ridges.

(464°C) spewing from a hydrothermal vent on the ocean floor, 9,842 ft. (3,000 m) deep at the Mid-Atlantic Ridge. Above 764°F (407°C) at this depth, water becomes "supercritical" and lighter than normal water. The water at the "black smoker" was measured using sensors on a remote-controlled robot.

★ **Fastest seafloor spreading center** The East Pacific Rise is a tectonic plate boundary that runs from Antarctica to the west coast of the U.S.A. At this boundary, a new crust is being created and the continental plates are moving apart. A portion of the East Pacific Rise—the Pacific-Nazca boundary—is pushing continental plates apart at a rate of around 93 miles/million years (150 km/million years).

★ **Warmest ocean** The Indian Ocean has the warmest surface temperature of all the world's oceans, as most of it is found in the tropics. Its minimum surface temperature is around 72°F (22°C) but can be as high as 82°F (28°C) toward the east; temperatures in the south can be considerably lower. At 28,400,000 miles^2 (73,556,000 km^2) the Indian Ocean is the third-largest of the Earth's oceanic divisions, covering approximately 20% of the Earth's surface.

ISLANDS & REEFS

Largest island Greenland, the largest island, is about 840,000 miles^2 (2,175,600 km^2) in size—just over three times larger than the U.S. state of Texas.

At around 39,768 miles^2 (103,000 km^2), the **largest volcanic island** is Iceland, formed from eruptions from the Mid-Atlantic Ridge, on which it sits. Iceland is essentially seafloor exposed above the ocean.

LONGEST REEF The Great Barrier Reef off Queensland, northeastern Australia, is 1,260 miles (2,027 km) in length. This mammoth feature is not actually a single structure, but consists of thousands of separate reefs. The reef is the **largest marine structure built by living creatures**, because it consists of countless billions of dead and living stony corals (order Madreporaria and Scleractinia).

★ **LARGEST ISLAND IN A LAKE ON AN ISLAND IN A LAKE ON AN ISLAND** The island of Luzon in the Philippines is home to Lake Taal, and within the lake lies the Taal volcano; the central volcanic crater of Taal is now a lake, named Crater Lake, and Vulcan Point is an island, approximately 130 ft. (40 m) across, situated within Crater Lake.

★ **Largest river island** Majuli, in the Brahmaputra River in northeast India, covers around 340 miles^2 (880 km^2)—twice the size of Barbados. Many years ago, the island was a long, thin strip of land called Majoli ("land between two parallel rivers") until earthquakes and floods in the 17th and 18th centuries changed the rivers' flow.

★ **Longest barrier island** Barrier islands are narrow, run parallel to mainland coasts, and are formed by the action of waves and currents. Padre Island in the Gulf of Mexico, off the Texas coast, formed just a few thousand years ago and is around 130 miles (210 km) long.

★ **Archipelago with the most islands** The Archipelago Sea lies within Finnish waters in the Baltic Sea and contains around 40,000 islands. The whole archipelago—or chain or group of islands—is slowly rising, as the land is still "rebounding" since the weight of ice from the last Ice Age was removed.

··

TURIN, ITALY (45°03'N 7°40'E): On December 11, 1993, Alberto Bolaffi (Italy) became the proud owner of the **most expensive telegram sold at auction** after paying $68,500 at Sotheby's, New York City, U.S.A. His purchase was the congratulatory telegram sent by Soviet premier Nikita Khrushchev on April 12, 1961, to the **first man in space**, Yuri Gagarin.

··

EXTRA! For a review of the world's worst natural disasters, go to pp. 46–50.

★ **YOUNGEST ISLAND** The island of Surtsey, off the south coast of Iceland, formed on November 14, 1963, when the new land being created by an undersea volcano finally breached the surface of the ocean. The volcanic activity, which had begun 426 ft. (130 m) below the surface, lasted until June 5, 1967. By this time, Surtsey had grown to around 1 mile^2 (2.7 km^2). Since then, the island has been gradually shrinking because of erosion.

★ **Largest atoll** An atoll is a marine structure that comprises a body of water (lagoon) enclosed by a ring (or partial ring) of coral. The Great Chagos Bank in the Indian Ocean is an atoll covering 4,881 miles^2 (12,642 km^2)—yet the seven named islands that form its rim have an area of just 1.7 miles^2 (4.5 km^2).

★ **Most islands within an atoll** Huvadhu Atoll in the Indian Ocean comprises around 255 islands and covers an area of 1,120 miles^2 (2,900 km^2).

★ **Largest submerged bank** The reef Saya de Malha Bank in the Indian Ocean covers 15,756 miles^2 (40,808 km^2). It rises to within 22 ft. (7 m) of the surface and would be the world's largest atoll—three times the size of the Great Chagos Bank—if it were above sea level.

REEFS

USS *Oriskany*, the **largest artificial reef**, is affectionately known as the "Great Carrier Reef." Why? See page 41.

ALESSANDRIA, ITALY (44°55'N 8°37'E): The **largest chocolate bar** weighed 7,892 lb. 8 oz. (3,580 kg) and was made by Elah Dufour-Novi in Alessandria, Piemonte, Italy, on October 11, 2007.

★ **Oldest coral reef** The Chazy Reef Formation is a fossilized coral reef that extends from the U.S. state of Tennessee to Newfoundland in Canada. Its most significant outcrop occurs at Isle La Motte in Vermont, U.S.A. It originally formed *c.* 450 million years ago in what was then the Iapetus Ocean. It is the oldest known example of structures built by coral.

★ **Largest fringing reef** Fringing reefs occur right off the shoreline of a landmass—unlike a barrier reef, which occurs farther out into the ocean and often forms a lagoon. Ningaloo Reef, on the shore of Western Australia, extends for around 180 miles (300 km) in length and is just 330 ft. (100 m) from the shore at its closest point.

Largest artificial reef The U.S. Navy's attack aircraft carrier USS *Oriskany* (aka the "Mighty O," laid 1944) was decommissioned in 1976 after a long service, and was scheduled for scrapping until the decision was made to sink it as an artificial reef in the Gulf of Mexico, 24 miles (38 km) off Pensacola, Florida, U.S.A. It was sunk on May 17, 2006, using 500 lb. (226 kg) of C4 explosives, and took 37 minutes to reach the seabed.

It is around 150 ft. (45 m) tall and 888 ft. (270 m) long, and attracts an abundance of marine life rarely seen in the northern Gulf of Mexico.

WEATHER & CLIMATE

★ **Highest storm phenomena** Elves are ethereal reddish phenomena that occur above thunderstorms. They were discovered in 1992 using a low-level camera on board the space shuttle. Lasting less than a millisecond, they appear as disk-shaped luminous regions up to 300 miles (480 km) across and occur at altitudes of around 60 miles (97 km).

Greatest snowfall (depth) The deepest snowfall recorded to date measured 37 ft. 7 in. (11.46 m) at Tamarac, California, U.S.A., in March 1911. The **greatest snowfall in 12 months** fell between 1971 and 1972, when a total of 1,224 in. (31,102 mm) was recorded at Paradise, Mount Rainier, Washington, U.S.A.

Most trees destroyed by storms A record 270 million trees were felled or split by storms that hit France on December 26–27, 1999.

Fastest wind speed On April 10, 1996, a wind speed of 253 mph (408 km/h) was recorded at Barrow Island, Australia, during Tropical Cyclone Olivia. This is the fastest wind speed ever recorded on Earth not associated with a tornado.

Hottest place on Earth For a fraction of a second, the air around a lightning strike is heated to around 54,000°F (30,000°C), or roughly five times hotter than the visible surface of the Sun.

★ **MOST RECENTLY CLASSIFIED CLOUD FORMATION** The last cloud type to be recognized as distinct was cirrus intortus in 1951. In 2009, a new type, undulatus asperatus, was proposed by experts as a new type of cloud formation. Its characteristic appearance (pictured) resembles ocean waves, although it is rare. Undulatus asperatus clouds tend to dissipate without forming storms.

MAINZ, GERMANY (50°01'N 8°14'E): It is widely accepted that the **oldest mechanically printed book** was the Gutenberg Bible, printed in Mainz, Germany, *c.* 1455, by Johann Henne zum Gensfleisch zur Laden (*c.* 1398–1468), who was known as *zu Gutenberg*.

MOST VIOLENT PLACE IN A TROPICAL CYCLONE Just beyond the calm eye of a hurricane or typhoon is the eye wall. This is a complete circle of storm clouds, often in a towering vertical structure, whirling around the eye. It is here that the highest winds and strongest rainfall occur. In cyclones with very high wind speeds of above 110 mph (177 km/h), a second eye wall will often form around the first.

Worst damage toll from an ice storm The most damaging ice storm on record occurred in the first week of January 1998 in eastern Canada and adjoining parts of the U.S.A. The storm, which began on January 6, shut down airports and railway stations, blocked highways, and cut off power to 3 million people—almost 40% of the population of Québec. Over five days, freezing rain coated power lines with 4 in. (10 cm) of ice, more weight than they could carry, and tens of thousands of poles were toppled. The bill was estimated at a massive CAN $1 billion ($650 million U.S.).

....

MANNHEIM, GERMANY (49°29'N 8°29'E): The **oldest modern symphony orchestra**—basically, four sections consisting of woodwind, brass, percussion, and bowed string instruments—was founded at the court of Duke Karl Theodor at Mannheim, Germany, in 1743.

....

POW!: Positive lightning strikes are known as "bolts from the blue," as they often break forth out of clear or only slightly cloudy skies.

ZAP!: As well as thunder storms, lightning can be caused by volcano eruptions and forest fires, which can create enough dust in the atmosphere to generate a static charge.

★ MOST POWERFUL LIGHTNING No one knows exactly how lightning is created, but ice in clouds may be a factor, perhaps helping to divide electrical current into positive and negative charges. Less than 5 percent of all lightning strikes involve positive lightning—in which the net transfer of charge from the cloud to the ground is positive. Positive lightning outlasts normal (negative) lightning strikes and causes a stronger electrical field, giving rise to strikes of up to a billion volts and an electrical current that may reach 300,000 amperes.

★ **GREATEST CLOUD COVER DUE TO HUMAN ACTIVITY** Contrails are condensation trails in the atmosphere left by aircraft. Depending upon local atmospheric conditions, they can last between seconds and hours. In the busiest air corridors, the combined effect of aircraft contrails can increase the cloud cover by up to 20 percent.

★ **First cloud seeding experiment on a tropical cyclone** On October 13, 1947, the U.S. military dumped 80 lb. (36 kg) of dry ice into an Atlantic hurricane. "Pronounced modification of the cloud deck seeded" was recorded by the crew before the hurricane changed direction and hit the coast of Georgia. The damage caused by the cyclone was blamed on the experiment, and the program, Project Cirrus, was canceled.

★ **Strongest hurricane** The category-5 Hurricane Wilma, which occurred during October 2005 and caused damage to the Yucatán Peninsula, Mexico, was the strongest hurricane since records began in 1851. A hurricane hunter plane measured a barometric pressure in the eye of just 882 millibars—the lowest ever recorded for a hurricane. Wind speeds in Wilma's eye wall reached 165 mph (270 km/h).

★ **Largest blue jet** Blue jets are electrical phenomena that project upward in a cone from the tops of cumulonimbus clouds during thunderstorms. They were discovered in 1989. On September 14, 2001, scientists in Puerto Rico recorded a blue jet that reached around 49 miles (80 km) above a storm, and lasted less than a second.

EXTRA! What happens when the natural world turns violent? To find out, see page 46.

★ First identical snow crystals One often-heard statement about snow is that no two snowflakes are ever alike. However, in 1988, Nancy Knight (U.S.A.), a scientist at the National Center for Atmosphere Research in Boulder, Colorado, U.S.A., found two identical examples while using a microscope to study snow crystals from a storm in Wisconsin, U.S.A.

Clouds with the greatest vertical range Cumulonimbus clouds have been observed to reach a vertical height of almost 65,600 ft. (20,000 m— or nearly three times the height of Mount Everest) in the tropics.

Most cows killed by lightning A single bolt of lightning killed 68 Jersey cows that were sheltering under a tree at Warwick Marks' farm near Dorrigo, NSW, Australia, on October 31, 2005. So, don't shelter under trees in a storm!

NATURAL DISASTERS

★ Highest death toll from a blizzard A weeklong blizzard from February 3 to 9, 1972, dumped more than 10 ft. (3 m) of snow across parts of rural Iran, ending a four-year drought. Approximately 4,000 people are estimated to have died as a result of the blizzard.

HIGHEST DEATH TOLL FROM A TSUNAMI On December 26, 2004, an earthquake with a magnitude of 9 occurred under the Indian Ocean, off the coast of Indonesia. The resulting tsunami wave inundated the coastlines of nine different countries around the Indian Ocean. The total death toll will never be known, but as of January 20, 2005, at least 226,000 people are known to have perished.

ZURICH, SWITZERLAND (47°22'N 8°33'E): Scientists at the IBM Research Division's Zurich laboratory, in Switzerland, built the world's **smallest abacus** in November 1996. Using individual molecules as beads, the device had a diameter of less than one nanometer (one-millionth of a millimeter).

★ **HIGHEST MUDSLIDE DEATH TOLL** In December 1999, a torrential storm dumped 35 in. (911 mm) of rain on Vargas state, Venezuela, in just a few days. The resulting mudslides from the mountainous areas close to the coast caused massive loss of life and infrastructure damage. Estimates of the death toll range from 10,000 to as high as 30,000, though—as with all natural disasters—exact figures are practically impossible to determine.

HEIDELBERG, GERMANY (49°24'N 8°42'E): The **largest wooden wine cask** is the Heidelberg Tun, which lies in the cellar of the Friedrichsbau in Heidelberg Castle, Heidelberg, Germany. Installed in 1751, it is 23 ft. (7 m) tall and 28 ft. (8.5 m) across, with a capacity of 48,773 gallons (221,726 liters).

EXTRA! Turn back to pp. 15–20 to read about the awesome power of the Sun.

★**FASTEST VOLCANIC HAZARD** Pyroclastic flows are the most dangerous of volcanic hazards. They are a mixture of gas and rock that travel down and away from a volcano at temperatures of up to 1,830°F (1,000°C) and speeds of up to 450 mph (720 km/h). In 1902, a pyroclastic flow at Mount Pelée on Martinique overwhelmed the city of Saint-Pierre, killing 30,000 people.

DID YOU KNOW?

A pyroclastic flow is like a fast-moving liquid, with rocks and debris suspended in it by hot, expanding gases and its forward momentum. It flows like a snow avalanche.

TRIVIA

More people have been killed by pyroclastic flow than by any other type of volcanic hazard.

★**Highest death toll from a wildfire** On October 8, 1871, forest fires burned through northeast Wisconsin and upper Michigan, U.S.A., killing an estimated 1,200 to 2,500 people. More than 1,500 miles^2 (3,800 km^2) of forest and farmland was destroyed. The event is known as the "Peshtigo tragedy," after a village that lost half its population in the fire.

★**Closest point to human extinction** The eruption of the Toba supervolcano around 75,000 years ago threw some 191 miles^3 (800 km^3) of ash into the atmosphere, creating Earth's largest volcanic crater. The resulting tsunamis and volcanic winter are thought to have reduced the human population to 10,000.

☆ **MOST DAMAGE CAUSED BY A CYCLONE** Hurricane Katrina, which devastated the coast of Louisiana, U.S.A., and surrounding states on August 29, 2005, caused damage estimated to be as high as $156 billion. At least 1,836 people lost their lives in the hurricane and subsequent floods. Katrina was the first category-5 hurricane of the 2005 season, the sixth strongest Atlantic hurricane ever recorded, and represents the ☆ **costliest natural disaster**.

★ **HIGHEST DEATH TOLL FROM A HEAT WAVE** The hottest August on record for the northern hemisphere was in 2003. At least 35,000 fatalities are thought to have resulted from the extreme heat, with some estimates as high as 52,000. France suffered worst, with 14,802 deaths, mainly among the elderly; the temperature reached 104°F (40°C) on seven consecutive days there.

Costliest year for natural disasters According to reinsurers Swiss Re, the Asian tsunami, an unusually active hurricane season, and disasters such as floods pushed the total economic loss for 2005 to $225 billion.

★ **Highest death toll from a fire whirl** Under the right circumstances, tornado-like phenomena can occur within fires. The deadliest example on record happened as a result of the Great Kanto Earthquake of September 1,

1923, which devastated the Kanto region of Honshu, Japan. Around 38,000 people were incinerated by a fire whirl while packed into the Former Army Clothing Depot in Tokyo.

Worst avalanche disaster—most people trapped At least 265 people died and more than 45,000 were trapped on January 20, 1951, during the "Winter of Terror," when a series of 649 reported avalanches, caused by a combination of hurricane-force winds and wet snow overlaying powder snow, thundered through the Swiss, Austrian, and Italian Alps.

Most extensive flood damage Flooding from the Hwai and Yangtze Rivers in China in August 1950 destroyed 890,000 homes and left 490 people dead and 10 million homeless. Around 5 million acres (2 million ha) of land was left under water, rendering 3.5 million acres (1.4 million ha) unfit for the planting season.

Most powerful earthquake The Valdivia earthquake or Great Chilean Earthquake of May 22, 1960, had a magnitude of 9.5 on the moment magnitude scale. (Like the Richter scale, this records the energy released in an earthquake.) It is estimated to have killed between 2,231 and 5,700 people and left 2 million homeless.

LIVING PLANET

CONTENTS

AYE!: Aye-ayes are thought to use echolocation to seek out prey—like bats. They are the only primates to do so.

AYE!: These nocturnal lemurs have squirrel-like front incisor teeth that continue to grow and never wear down.

LARGEST NOCTURNAL PRIMATE The aye-aye (*Daubentonia madagascariensis*) of Madagascar has a body length of 16 in. (40 cm), a tail length of 20 in. (50.5 cm), and weighs approximately 6 lb. (2.76 kg). These solitary animals spend up to 80% of the night foraging for food in the tree canopies and most of the daytime sleeping in tree nests.

Aye-ayes are also known for their skeletal, dexterous middle finger, which is used to tap tree bark to listen for evidence of edible insect larvae inside. They then make a hole in the tree trunk and use the middle finger to hook out the larvae—the primate equivalent of the woodpecker!

QUIZ!: No tall tales—how long is the aye-aye's tail? See p. 543 for the answer.

DINOSAURS

★**Largest ammonite** An incomplete fossil shell of the ammonite *Parapuzosia seppenradensis* discovered in Germany in 1895 measured 6 ft. 3 in. (1.95 m) across, but the complete shell is thought to have been around 8 ft. 4 in. (2.55 m). Ammonites were related to squids and octopuses but lived inside coiled shells, and this particular species was alive during the late Cretaceous Period (99.6 million to 65.5 million years ago).

Largest dinosaur footprint In 1932, the gigantic footprints of a large bipedal hadrosaurid ("duckbill") measuring 53.5 in. (136 cm) in length and 32 in. (81 cm) wide were discovered in Salt Lake City, Utah, U.S.A.

Largest and most complete Tyrannosaurus rex skeleton The largest, most complete, and best-preserved *Tyrannosaurus rex* skeleton ever found is "Sue," measuring 13 ft. (4 m) tall and 41 ft. (12.5 m) long and approximately 90% complete. It was found in South Dakota, U.S.A., on August 12, 1990 by explorer Sue Hendrickson (U.S.A.), after whom the skeleton has been named.

BIG: Another titanosaurid, *Antarctosaurus giganteus* (Giant Antarctic lizard), found in Argentina and India, is estimated to have weighed between 40 and 80 tonnes (44 and 88 tons).

HEAVIEST DINOSAUR In 1994, dinosaur researcher Gregory Paul used the fossil remains of a titanosaurid from Argentina called *Argentinosaurus* (left) to calculate that it had originally weighed up to 110 tons (100 tonnes), making it the heaviest dinosaur to have walked the Earth. Paul based his calculations on the creature's vertebrae.

....

BREMEN, GERMANY (53°04'N 8°47'E): Visible to the eye, *Thiomargarita namibiensis* is the **largest bacterium**. Heide Schulz, from Bremen's Max Planck Institute for Marine Microbiology, found samples up to 0.029 in. (0.75 mm) wide off the Namibian coast.

....

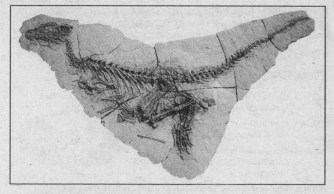

★ LARGEST *SINOSAUROPTERYX* FOSSIL A complete *Sinosauropteryx* fossil measuring 12 ft. 5 in. (3.8 m) long is housed at the Shandong Tianyu Natural History Museum in Shandong Province, China. The *Sinosauropteryx* is the first dinosaur found that displayed evidence of having had feathers.

☆ **Largest prehistoric carnivorous bird** *Brontornis burmeisteri*, which lived in Patagonia, South America, during the Miocene Epoch, is recognized as the largest carnivorous bird ever. Standing approximately 9 ft. 3 in. (2.8 m) tall, this huge flightless bird weighed 770–880 lb. (350–400 kg), more than twice the weight of today's largest bird, the ostrich (*Struthio camelus*).

Longest dinosaur genus name *Micropachycephalosaurus*, meaning "small thick-headed lizard," is the longest generic name for a dinosaur, with an impressive 23 letters and nine syllables. Named in 1978 by Chinese paleontologists, this very small dinosaur, only 6–12 in. (50–100 cm) long, is a thick-skulled plant-eater that lived in China around 83–73 million years ago, in the Cretaceous Period.

★ **Largest mosasaur** Mosasaurs were prehistoric sea lizards, related to modern-day varanids or monitor lizards. The largest mosasaur known to science is *Hainosaurus*, which had a total length of up to 49 ft. 2.5 in. (15 m).

STUTTGART, GERMANY (48°48'N 9°10'E): The **most tap dancers in a single routine** was 6,951, who gathered at the City Square, Stuttgart, Germany, on May 24, 1998. The routine, choreographed by Ray Lynch (U.S.A.), lasted 2 min. 15 sec. and was performed to the tune "Klicke-di-Klack," which Ray had composed.

| ERA | **MESOZOIC** (251–65 MYA) *from the Greek for "middle life"* |

| PERIOD | **TRIASSIC** (251–206 MYA) |

245 MYA Globe is dominated by the "supercontinent" Pangea, the **largest ever continent**

230 MYA First dinosaurs—in the form of small, bipedal predators—emerge

225 MYA The shrewlike *Adelobasileus cromptoni* is the **first known mammal**

225 MYA Pterosaurs take to the skies; giant reptiles such as the ichthyosaur *Cymbospondylus* dominate seas

210 MYA **Longest dinosaur**, *Amphicoelias*, estimated at around 197 ft. (60 m)

| PERIOD | **JURASSIC** (206–144 MYA) |

200 MYA Extinction event, but dinosaurs flourish and dominate life

180 MYA Archosaurs (dinosaurs, pterosaurs, crocodilians) dominant on land; marine reptiles continue to rule the waves

160 MYA Global warming leads to humid climates and lush jungles; large trees (conifers) and cycads common

155 MYA *Allosaurus* among the largest land predators of the Jurassic Period

150 MYA Emergence of *Archaeopteryx* marks the start of the evolution of the **first birds** from therapod dinosaurs

| PERIOD | **CRETACEOUS** (144–65 MYA) |

130 MYA Earth is now the land of the giants, with the appearance of *Giganotosaurus* and *Argentinosaurus*, the **largest-ever land animals**

115 MYA Mammals remain small in size but increasingly large in number; their size, shape, and diversity is restricted by the dominance of the dinosaurs

100 MYA Dinosaurs, the most dominant land vertebrates since the Jurassic Period, are at their most diverse

90 MYA Flowering plants diversify thanks to the emergence of pollinating insects

65 MYA Mass extinction event at the end of the Cretaceous Period removes 40% of animal families, including dinosaurs; the Age of the Reptile is over

CENOZOIC (65–0 MYA) *from the Greek for "new life"*

PALEOGENE (65–23 MYA)

64 MYA Continents continue to drift toward their present position; supercontinent Laurasia not yet divided

60 MYA Following mass extinction, only animals smaller than a crocodile remain alive; birds are the largest creatures and biggest predators

55 MYA Explosion in (often giant) mammalian life as environment niches filled; elephants, rodents, primates, and whales appear

36 MYA Antarctica begins to freeze over, cooling the oceans' climate; 25% of life on Earth perishes

30 MYA New mammal species (ancestors of modern horses, pigs, and camels) emerge, many dinosaur-sized, such as the **largest-ever land mammal**, *Indricotherium*

NEOGENE (23–5 MYA)

23 MYA First true carnivores appear; grassland becomes a dominant part of the landscape, covering one-fifth of the planet

20 MYA Herbivores evolve new teeth and digestive systems to deal with the abundance of grass; they also herd and migrate with the seasons

15 MYA Golden era for *Deinotherium*—the second-largest land mammal ever—a proboscidian related to the modern-day elephant

10 MYA The ★ **largest ever predatory shark** is *Carcharodon megalodon*, around 53 ft. (16 m) long, with a mouth perhaps 6 ft. (2 m) wide

4 MYA Our ancestors are prey to the saber-toothed *Dinofelis*, a successful carnivore mammal of the felid (cat) family

QUARTENARY (5–0 MYA)

2.5 MYA The tool-using *Homo habilis*, the ★ **first recognizable human**, evolves from a hominid such as *Australopithecus aferensis*

2 MYA The elephantine woolly mammoth *Mammuthus* appears; its shaggy coat and thick skin are perfect for surviving harsh winters during the last Ice Age

190,000 YA *Homo sapiens*—yes, that's us—evolve in eastern Africa; within 40,000 years, we have spread across Asia, Europe, and the Far East

*Source: International Commission on Stratigraphy; *informal, not ratified by the ICS*

SMALL: The ☆ **smallest species of dinosaur** is the feathered Microraptor *zhaoianus*. It has a total length of 15.3 in. (39 cm), of which 9.4 in. (24 cm) is accounted for by its tail.

LARGEST LAND-BASED CARNIVORES The therapods (beast-footed) are the group of dinosaurs that many scientists believe evolved into birds. They included the fearsome *Tyrannosaurus rex*, *Allosaurus*, and the even bigger *Giganotosaurus* (left), which lived 93–89 million years ago and could grow to an estimated 43 ft. (13 m) long with a weight of 13,230 lb. (6 tonnes).

LONG: The ★ **longest dinosaur tail** was that of the North American sauropod D*iplodocus*. it measured up to 42 ft. 7 in. (13 m) long.

★**Longest dinosaur horns** The longest horns of any dinosaur were the paired horns borne above the eyes by the North American ceratopsian dinosaur *Triceratops*. Each horn measured up to 39 in. (1 m) long and may have been used in courtship jousting bouts.

....

BREGENZ, AUSTRIA (47°30'N 9°45'E): The **longest table soccer marathon** lasted 51 hr. 52 min. and was set by Alexander Gruber, Roman Schelling, Enrico Lechtaler, and Christian Nägele (all Austria) in Bregenz, Austria, between June 27 and 29, 2008.

....

EXTRA! Can't get enough of old-timers? Check out golden oldies on pp. 124–128.

LARGEST CROCODILE EVER *Sarcosuchus imperator* was a prehistoric species of crocodile that lived approximately 110 million years ago. Recent fossilized remains found in the Sahara Desert, Africa, suggest that this creature took 50–60 years to grow to its full length of around 37–40 ft. (11–12 m) and its maximum weight of approximately 17,636 lb. (8 tonnes).

★ **SMALLEST-BRAINED DINOSAUR** The *Stegosaurus* ("plated lizard")—which, about 150 million years ago, roamed the lands that comprise the present-day U.S. states of Colorado, Oklahoma, Utah, and Wyoming—measured up to 30 ft. (9 m) in length but had a walnut-sized brain weighing only 2.5 oz. (70 g). This represented 0.002% of its computed body weight of 7,275 lb. (3,300 kg)—compared to 0.06% for an elephant, or 1.88% for a human.

HAMBURG, GERMANY (53°35'N 9°59'E): The **largest fashion catalog** had 212 pages and measured 3 ft. 11 in. x 4 ft. 11 in. (1.2 m x 1.5 m) when unveiled in Hamburg, Germany, on August 30, 2003. It was a replica of the Bon Prix S2 catalog *Voila!*

BEASTS

★**Largest bear** The giant short-faced bear (*Arctodus simus*) was the largest bear of all time. This prehistoric species, also known as the bulldog bear, had an estimated weight of 1,322–1,763 lb. (600–800 kg). Males were bigger than females, and when on all fours would have stood around 5 ft. 3 in. (1.6 m) at the shoulder.

Smallest hominid Discovered by Indonesian and Australian scientists in a cave on the island of Flores, Indonesia, in 2003, *Homo floresiensis* stood just 3 ft. 3 in. (1 m) tall. A species of great ape, *Homo floresiensis* lived on Flores as recently as 13,000 years ago.

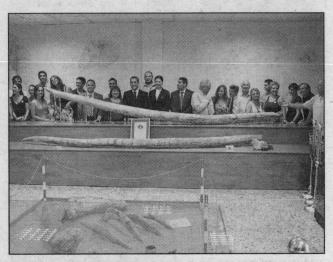

★**LONGEST MASTODON TUSK** A mastodon tusk measuring 16 ft. 6 in. (5.02 m) was excavated between July 17 and 28, 2007, at a dig in Milia, Grevena, Greece, supervised by Evangelia Tsoukala, Dick Mol, and a paleontological team from the Aristotle University of Thessaloniki and the School of Geology.

OSLO, NORWAY (59°57'N 10°45'E): The **largest band** ever assembled was one of 20,100 bandsmen from Norges Musikkorps Forbund bands, who came together at the Ullevaal Stadium, Oslo, Norway, on June 28, 1964.

LARGEST ELEPHANT EVER The Steppe mammoth *Mamuthus trogontherii* roamed over what is now central Europe a million years ago. A fragmentary skeleton of this species found in Mosbach, Germany, indicates a shoulder height of 14 ft. 9 in. (4.5 m)—this compares to the largest African elephant recorded, which had a shoulder height of 12 ft. (3.6 m) and weighed more than 9 tons (8.1 tonnes).

★ **Most complete fossil primate** On May 19, 2009, an international team of scientists unveiled the fossilized remains of a primate dating back 47 million years—the most complete fossil of an early primate found to date. The 3-ft.-long (1-m) female specimen, closely resembling a modern-day lemur and named *Darwinius masillae*, had been found in Germany in 1993. The lengthy delay between discovery and announcement was the consequence of many years spent authenticating and preparing the specimen for sale. Time will tell how significant this fossil find proves to be.

EXTRA! All these beasts are long extinct. For much more on modern mammals, look lively and turn to pp. 88–91.

LARGEST PREHISTORIC MAMMAL *Indricotherium*, of the family Hyrachyidae, was a long-necked, hornless rhinocerotid that lived in western Asia and Europe about 35 million years ago. It measured 17 ft. 9 in. (5.41 m) to the top of the shoulder hump and was 37 ft. (11.27 m) long.

★**Largest thunder beast** Also known as *brontotheres* or *titanotheres*, thunder beasts were huge prehistoric odd-toed ungulates (mammals that, like horses, walk on their toenails) that resembled rhinoceroses. The largest thunder beast was *Brontotherium*, which lived in North America around 55.8–33.9 million years ago. Characterized by a very large Y-shaped, hornlike structure of bone on its nose, this mighty herbivorous mammal stood around 8 ft. 2 in. (2.5 m) high at the shoulder, and may have weighed up to 2,200 lb. (1,000 kg). When native American Indians first found the huge fossilized bones of this mammal, they mistook them for those of a legendary beast called the thunder horse that jumped down from the sky to Earth and made loud noises during thunderstorms. Based on this folklore, scientists named the animal *Brontotherium* ("thunder beast").

★**Largest egg-laying mammal** Hackett's long-beaked echidna (*Zaglossus hacketti*), known from fossil remains in Western Australia, weighed up to 220 lb. (100 kg) and was the size of a sheep. A massive relative of modern echidna, or spiny anteaters, it lived around 2.6 million to 12,000 years ago.

★ **LARGEST SLOTH**
Megatherium,
a giant ground sloth, lived in what is now South America during the Pliocene and Pleistocene epochs for around 5.3 million years. It stood 16 ft. 8 in. (5.1 m) high on its hind legs, and had an estimated average weight of 4.9 tons (4.5 tonnes).

★ **LARGEST SABER-TOOTHED CAT**
Smilodon populator
lived in what is now South America from around 1 million years ago to around 10,000 years ago and stood 5 ft. 5 in. (1.56 m) at the shoulder. Each of its two serrated saber-like canine teeth were up to 12 in. (30 cm) long.

AUGSBURG, GERMANY (48°22'N 10°54'E): The **oldest complete stained glass** in the world can be found in a window of the Cathedral of Augsburg, Germany. The window, which dates from the second half of the 11th century, represents the Prophets.

INSECTS & ARACHNIDS

★**Longest animal name** The longest scientific binomial (two-part) name given to any animal is *Parastratiosphecomyia stratiosphecomyioides* (containing 42 letters), aka the soldier fly, which is a species of stratiomyid fly with a metallic-green thorax and abdomen.

★**Largest animal family** The largest taxonomic family of animals is the weevil or snout beetle family, Curculionidae, which contains more than 60,000 species currently known to science.

★**Longest ant memory** Worker ants of two different species—*Formica selysi* and *Manica rubida*—that had been reared together for three months and then separated could still recognize one another after 18 months—the most tenacious ant memory demonstrated.

Deadliest ant The bulldog ant (*Myrmecia pyriformis*), found in coastal regions of Australia, uses its sting and jaws simultaneously. It has caused at least three human fatalities since 1936.

Largest beetle The largest beetle in terms of weight, and indeed the **heaviest insect**, is Africa's goliath beetle (*Goliathus goliathus*), which can obtain larval weights (that is, its weight during its juvenile stage) up to 3.5 oz. (100 g).

★**HARDIEST BEETLE** The world's most indestructible beetle is a small species known as ***Niptus hololeucus***. Researcher Malcolm Burr revealed that 1,547 specimens were discovered alive and thriving inside a bottle of casein (a chemical present in milk) that had been stoppered for 12 years. Burr also discovered another collection found living for 15 years inside a can of leaves from the powerful poison plant *Datura stramontium*.

"Dear GWR, my giant millipede is 15¼ inches—is this a world record?"
Jim Klinger, Jungle Jim's Bugs of the World. Erm, yes!

TRENTO, ITALY (46°04'N 11°08'E): The ☆ **longest-running international speed-skating competition** is the Alberto Nicolodi Trophy, organized by Sportivi Ghiaccio Trento, Trento, Italy, which had its 49th anniversary on February 20–21, 2010.

100s: Despite their names, centipedes (meaning "100 feet") don't have 100 legs, and millipedes ("1,000 feet") don't have 1,000 legs!

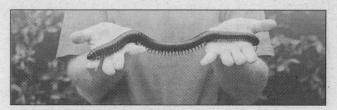

LARGEST MILLIPEDE A fully grown African giant black millipede (*Archispirostreptus gigas*) owned by Jim Klinger of Coppell, Texas, U.S.A., measures 15.2 in. (38.7 cm) in length, 2.6 in. (6.7 cm) in circumference, and has 256 legs.

LARGEST SCORPION A specimen of *Heterometrus swannerdami* found during World War II in Krishnarajapuram, India, measured 11.5 in. (29.2 cm) in overall length, from its stinger to its "pincer."

"Pedipalps" (pincers) are used to catch prey and dig burrows, as well as playing a role in mating and defense.

1,000s: The record for the **animal with most legs** goes to a specimen of *Illacme plenipes*—a millipede from California, U.S.A., which had 750 legs.

STRANGEST DEFENSE MECHANISM The bombardier beetle (genus *Brachinus*) stores two harmless chemicals in a special chamber in its abdomen. When it feels threatened, the liquids are released into a second chamber and mix with an enzyme, resulting in a violent chemical reaction and the release of considerable heat (up to 212°F, or 100°C) from the anus.

★Largest crane fly The world's largest species of crane fly or daddy longlegs is *Holorusia brobdignagius*. This species of crane fly can grow up to 9 in. (23 cm) long, but is exceedingly slender and fragile.

★Largest orb-weaver spider In 2000, an enormous female specimen of orb-weaver spider was discovered by Slovenian biologist Dr. Matjaz Kuntner in a collection of specimens owned by the Plant Protection Institute in Pretoria, South Africa. Not only did it prove to belong to a hitherto unknown species—which Dr. Kuntner later named *Nephila komaci*—but it was also found to constitute the world's largest orb-weaver spider species. Further specimens have since been obtained, some from Madagascar, revealing that females have a leg span of up to 4.7 in. (12 cm), and can spin webs up to 3 ft. 3.3 in. (1 m) wide.

STRONGEST SPIDERWEBS The extremely tough webs spun by spiders of the genus *Nephila* can catch small birds and frogs (pictured), and are even capable of slowing down the passage of mammals up to the size of humans.
  Spiders of the tropical African species *N. senegalensis* have a special garbage line in their web, in which the sucked-out remains of small birds have been found.

PADUA, ITALY (45°25'N 11°52'E): The world's **oldest botanical garden** to remain on its original site is the Orto Botanico in Padua, Italy, which was created in 1545. The original design of a circular central plot (symbolizing the world), surrounded by a ring of water, is still in place.

EXTRA! Check out some creepy crustaceans below and amazing mammals on pp. 88–91.

★ **LONGEST SNOUT ON A BEETLE** South Africa's long-snouted cycad weevil (*Antliarhinus zamiae*) has the longest snout of any beetle. The 0.79-in.-long (2-cm) snout is used for drilling holes in cycad seeds, inside which the 3-cm-long (1.18-in.) weevil can then lay its eggs.

Largest spider A male goliath bird-eating spider (*Theraphosa blondi*) collected at Rio Cavro, Venezuela, in April 1965 had a record leg span of 11 in. (28 cm)—long enough to cover a dinner plate.

CRUSTACEANS & MOLLUSKS

★ **Largest copepod** Copepods are small marine crustaceans, typically 0.04–0.07 in. (1–2 mm) in length, that constitute the biggest biomass in the oceans. The largest species of copepod is *Pennella balaeonpterae*, which lives exclusively as a parasite upon the backs of fin whales (*Balaenoptera physalus*). It can attain a maximum length of 12.5 in. (32 cm).

★ **SHARPEST NIGHT VISION** *Gigantocypris* is a marine crustacean (pictured) that lives at depths of more than 3,300 ft. (1,000 m), where there is virtually no sunlight. Luckily, this genus of ostracod has the best night vision of any animal, boasting eyes with an f-number (a measure of light sensitivity) of 0.25 (humans measure around f-2.55). Each eye possesses a pair of high-powered parabolic reflectors that direct the very dim available light onto the retina at their center.

GOTHENBURG, SWEDEN (57°43'N 11°59'E): George Olesen (Denmark) pulled a 11,350-ton (10,300-tonne) passenger ferry a distance of 16 ft. 8.8 in. (5.1 m) at Gothenburg Ferry Terminal, Gothenburg, Sweden, in June 2000. This represents the **heaviest boat pulled**.

Crustaceans & Mollusks   **67**

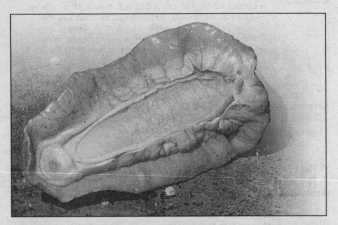

★**LARGEST CHITON** Chitons (from the Greek for "tunic") are primitive marine mollusks. The largest is the gumboot or giant Pacific chiton (*Cryptochiton stelleri*), found off the Pacific coasts of North America and Japan, which grows up to 1 ft. (33 cm) long and 0.43 in. (13 cm) wide. Its red, leathery mantle (or "girdle") wraps around its body (like a tunic, hence its name), covering a series of armored plates that run down the chiton's back.

★**Most recently described class of crustaceans** In 1979, while diving in Lucayan Cavern beneath the island of Grand Bahama, biologist Dr. Jill Yager (U.S.A.) encountered tiny wormlike crustaceans that proved to be a new species, dubbed *Speleonectes lucayensis*. So different was *S. lucayensis* from all crustaceans that, in 1981, an entirely new taxonomic class—Remipedia—was created in order to accommodate it. Several additional, related species have since been discovered, all of which are blind and characterized by their oarlike limbs, hence these crustaceans are termed remipedes ("oar-footed").

★ **LARGEST BARNACLE**
Barnacles are marine crustaceans that "encrust" themselves to surfaces. The largest is the giant acorn barnacle, *Balanus nubilis*, standing up to 5 in. (12.7 cm) high.

★ **Most maternal crab** The Jamaican bromeliad crab (*Metopaulias depressus*), which actually lives on land in mountainous forests, is the world's most maternal crab. The female lays her eggs in puddles of rainwater that collect in the large leaves of bromeliad plants, and three months after the eggs hatch she feeds her offspring with small insects and also chases away would-be predators such as lizards and large spiders.

QUIZ!: To which group do the following creatures belong, mollusk or crustacean?
A. crab B. octopus C. slug
See p. 543 for the answer.

VENICE, ITALY (45°27'N 12°21'E): Venice is the **most waterlogged city** on Earth. By the end of the 20th century, the city flooded up to 40 times a year; in the next 50 years it is estimated that the water level there will rise by a further 8 in. (20.3 cm).

GASTROPOD

From the Greek for "stomach foot," on the misunderstanding that slugs glide around on their bellies.

LARGEST CLAM The largest of all existing bivalve shells is that of the marine giant clam (*Tridacna gigas*), found on the Indo-Pacific coral reefs. One specimen measuring 3 ft. 9.25 in. (1.15 m) in length and weighing 734 lb. (333 kg) was collected off Ishigaki Island, Okinawa, Japan, in 1956; it probably weighed a little more than 750 lb. (340 kg) when it was alive.

★**Largest mollusk** An adult male colossal squid (*Mesonychoteuthis hamiltoni*) weighing around 990 lb. (450 kg) and measuring 33 ft. (10 m) long was caught by fishermen in the Ross Sea of Antarctica. It was taken to New Zealand, and the catch was announced on February 22, 2007. Colossal squid are usually shorter than giant squid, but much heavier.

Most venomous mollusk The two closely related species of blue-ringed octopus, *Hapalochlaena maculosa* and *H. lunulata*, are found around the coasts of Australia and parts of Southeast Asia. They carry a neurotoxic venom so potent that their relatively painless bite can kill in a matter of minutes. It

★**LARGEST SLUG** The world's largest species of terrestrial slug is the ash-black slug, *Limax cinereoniger*. Found in ancient woodlands throughout all but the most northerly regions of Europe, this gastropod mollusk can grow to a length of up to 12 in. (30 cm), and eats fungi.

CHOMP!: Some slugs possess tens of thousands of tiny, razor-sharp teeth that are continually being replaced.

LARGEST LAND CRUSTACEAN The coconut or rubber crab (*Birgus latro*), which lives on tropical islands and atolls in the Indo-Pacific, is the largest land-living crustacean. Weights of up to 9 lb. (4.1 kg) and leg spans of up to 39 in. (1 m) have been recorded. The largest crustacean is the Japanese spider crab (*Macrocheira kaempferi*), with a claw span of up to 12 ft. 1.6 in. (3.7 m).

has been estimated that each individual carries sufficient venom to cause the paralysis (or even death) of 10 adult people. Fortunately, blue-ringed octopuses are not considered aggressive and normally bite only when they are taken out of the water and provoked. These mollusks have a radial spread of just 4–8 in. (100–200 mm).

Largest eye-to-body ratio The vampire squid (*Vampyroteuthis infernalis*) has the largest eye-to-body ratio of any animal. Its body can reach 11 in. (28 cm) in length, while its eyes may have a diameter of 0.9 in. (2.5 cm).

Oldest mollusk In 2006, a quahog clam (*Arctica islandica*) that had been living on the seabed off the north coast of Iceland was dredged by a team from Bangor University's School of Ocean Sciences, Wales, UK. On October 28, 2007, researchers revealed that it was between 405 and 410 years old. The clam was nicknamed "Ming," after the Chinese dynasty in power when it was born!

FISH & SEALIFE

★**Largest barracuda** A barracuda specimen weighing 85 lb. 1 oz. (38.6 kg) was caught on April 11, 2002, off Christmas Island, Kiribati, in the Pacific Ocean.

LEIPZIG, GERMANY (51°18'N 12°22'E): The largest bicycle bell ensemble was organized by Professor Jörg Kärger and consisted of 503 participants playing German folk songs and hymns at the University of Leipzig, Germany, on November 23, 2003.

QUIZ!: Of all the fish in the sea, which is the largest? see p. 543 for the answer.

★ **LARGEST SEA LILY** Despite looking like flowers, sea lilies are not plants. The largest sea lilies inhabit the Pacific Ocean and belong to the genus *Metacrinus*. They have a maximum stalk height of 2 ft. (61 cm), with a 5.98-in. (15.2-cm) arm length.

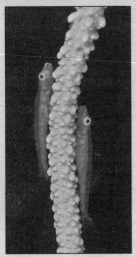

★ **LARGEST FAMILY OF MARINE FISH** Family Gobiidae, the goby family, contains more than 2,000 species (including the whip coral goby *Bryaninops yongei*, left). Gobies range in length from less than 0.2 in. to 12 in. (1–30 cm), their most distinctive feature being their disk-shaped sucker derived from their fused pelvic fins.

Largest fish egg The crew of a shrimp trawler in the Gulf of Mexico found a whale shark egg (*Rhincodon typus*) measuring 12 x 5.5 x 3.5 in. (30.5 x 14 x 8.9 cm) on June 29, 1953.

★ **Smallest sea urchin** The *Echinocyamus scaber* species of sea urchin, which is native to the seas off New South Wales, Australia, has a test (shell) diameter of just 0.22 in. (5.5 mm).

★ **Largest family of fish** Family Cyprinidae, the carp family of freshwater fish, contains more than 2,400 species, housed in approximately 220 genera. Among its most familiar members are the carps (including goldfish), tench, barbs, and minnows.

URCHIN

An old-fashioned word for the spiny hedgehogs that sea urchins resemble!

★ **HOTTEST FISH EYES** Swordfish (*Xiphias gladius*) have special organs that heat up their eyes to as much as 82°F (28°C), improving their efficiency in cold water and enabling them to swiftly spot prey.

Longest fish fin All three species of thresher shark (family Alopiidae) have huge scythe-shaped caudal (tail) fins that are roughly as long as their entire bodies. The largest of the three species is the common thresher shark (*Alopias vulpinus*), which is found worldwide in temperate and tropical seas. Common threshers may grow to a length of 19 ft. 8 in. (6 m), of which almost 9 ft. 10 in. (3 m) consists of its greatly elongated upper tail fin; the fish's body itself is sleek and slender.

VATICAN CITY (41°54'N 12°27'E): The **oldest army** is the Pontifical Swiss Guard in the Vatican City, which comprises 80 to 90 individuals. The unit's foundation dates back to January 21, 1506; its earliest origins, however, predate 1400.

★ **LARGEST BRAIN CORAL COLONY** As large as a truck, a brain coral approximately 9 ft. 10 in. (3 m) high and 16 ft. 4 in. (5 m) across can be found on a dive site called Kelleston Drain, south of the island of Little Tobago, Trinidad and Tobago. Like all colonial corals, brain corals are not a single organism but composed of millions of individual coral polyps living together.

Fastest fish In short-distance speed trials carried out at the Long Key Fishing Camp, Florida, U.S.A., a cosmopolitan sailfish (*Istiophorus platypterus*) took out 300 ft. (91 m) of line in 3 seconds, equivalent to a velocity of 68 mph (109 km/h). By comparison, cheetahs run at 62 mph (100 km/h). Sailfish achieve their incredible bursts of speed thanks to their highly oxygenated red muscles.

Most venomous jellyfish The box jellyfish (*Chironex fleckeri*, aka Flecker's sea wasp), found off the north coast of Australia, typically con-

★ **LONGEST PREGNANCY** The common frilled shark (*Chlamydoselachus anguineus*), a primitive species native to all oceans, has a longer gestation period (pregnancy) than any other animal: an average of 3.5 years.

DOWN: The **deepest-living fish** is the *Abyssobrotula galatheae* species of cusk eel, which lives at a depth of 27,460 ft. (8,370 m).

★ **HEAVIEST STARFISH** On September 14, 1969, a specimen of *Thromidia catalai*, a hefty five-armed species of starfish native to the western Pacific, was caught off Ilot Amédée, New Caledonia. The starfish, which weighed an estimated 13 lb. 3 oz. (6 kg), was later deposited at New Caledonia's Nouméa Aquarium.

tains enough venom to kill 60 humans and is responsible for one death per year, on average.

Longest fish migration A bluefin tuna (*Thunnus thynnus*) was tagged off Baja California, Mexico, in 1958 and was caught again 300 miles (483 km) south of Tokyo, Japan, in April 1963, by which time it had traveled a straight-line distance of at least 5,800 miles (9,335 km). Its weight also increased from 35 lb. (16 kg) to 267 lb. (121 kg) between catches.

★ **Heaviest fish** A scientifically recorded specimen of whale shark (*Rhincodon typus*) captured off Baba Island, near Karachi, Pakistan, on November 11, 1949 measured 41 ft. 6 in. (12.65 m) long, making it the **largest fish**, but it also weighed an estimated 33,000–46,200 lb. (15–21 tonnes), giving it the record for heaviest fish, too. Sharks and rays are cartilaginous fish—their skeletons are composed of cartilage instead of the hard bone of many other fish species. The **heaviest bony fish** is the ocean sunfish (*Mola mola*), which has been recorded as weighing 4,400 lb. (2 tonnes) and measuring 10 ft. (3 m) from fin tip to fin tip.

Largest jellyfish Most jellyfish have a body diameter, or bell, ranging from 0.8 in. to 15.8 in. (2–40 cm), but some species grow considerably larger. The largest recorded specimen was an Arctic giant jellyfish (*Cyanea capillata arctica*) that washed up in Massachusetts Bay, U.S.A., in 1870; it had a bell diameter of 7 ft. 6 in. (2.28 m) and tentacles stretching 120 ft. (36.5 m).

Longest survival out of water for a fish Six species of lungfish live in freshwater swamps that dry out for months or even years at a time. Two of the four species found in Africa (*Protopterus annectens, P. aethiopicus, P. dolloi*, and *P. amphibius*) are considered to be real survival experts. As their swamp water recedes, they burrow deep into the ground and secrete mucus to form a moisture-saving cocoon around their bodies. They then build a porous mud plug at the entrance of the burrow—and wait. Abandoning gill breathing in favor of their air-breathing lungs, they can live for up to four years in this dormant position.

AMPHIBIANS

Largest frog A specimen of the African goliath frog (*Conraua goliath*), captured in April 1899 on the Sanaga River, Cameroon, had a snout-to-vent length of 14.5 in. (36.83 cm) and an overall length of 34.5 in. (87.63 cm) with its legs extended, about the size of a house rabbit.

The world's **smallest frog**, and the **smallest known amphibian**, is *Eleutherodactylus limbatus* of Cuba, which is 0.33–0.47 in. (8.5–12 mm) long from snout to vent.

☆**Rarest amphibians** The Red List of Threatened Species lists two toads as "Extinct in the Wild":

•The Wyoming toad (*Bufo baxteri*) exists only within the Mortenson Lake National Wildlife Refuge in Wyoming, U.S.A.; believed extinct in 1980, it was rediscovered in 1987, but no known mating in the wild has occurred since 1991.

•The hundreds of remaining Kihansi spray toads (*Nectophrynoides aspergi- nis*), a dwarf toad native to Tanzania, live at the Bronx Zoo, New York City, U.S.A.

★**Least fecund amphibian** Fecundity is the capacity for producing offspring. The world's least fecund frog is the Cuban frog (*Sminthillus limbatus*), a tiny species of poison-arrow frog whose female lays only a single egg.

In stark contrast, a single female of the world's **most fecund amphibian**, the cane toad (*Bufo marinus*), will lay as many as 30,000–35,000 eggs per spawning.

★MOST TRANSPARENT AMPHIBIAN
Some so-called glass frogs (of the family Centrolenidae), native to the rainforests of Central and South America, have partially transparent abdominal skin that resembles frosted glass. Their heart, liver, and gut can be readily seen through it when viewed from underneath. The remainder of their skin is usually lime green.

ROME, ITALY (41°54'N 12°30'E): On February 15, 2003, the **largest anti-war rally** occurred in Rome, Italy, where a crowd of 3 million people gathered to protest the U.S.A.'s threat to invade Iraq.

LARGEST AMPHIBIAN The giant salamanders (family Cryptobranchidae) are the greatest of the amphibians. The record-holder is the Chinese giant salamander (*Andrias davidianus*, pictured), which lives in mountain streams in northeastern, central, and southern China. One record-breaking specimen collected in Hunan Province measured 5 ft. 11 in. (1.8 m) in length and weighed 143 lb. (65 kg).

Most poisonous . . .

Frog: The golden poison frog (*Phyllobates terribilis*) of South and Central America may measure only 1.6–2 in. (4–5 cm) long, but it secretes enough toxin to provide a lethal dose to 10 adult humans or 20,000 lab mice.

Newt: One drop of blood from the California newt (*Taricha torosa*), which contains the toxic and powerful nerve poison tetrodotoxin, could kill several thousand mice.

QUIZ!: Which classic arcade video game features an amphibian attempting to cross a busy road and a fast-flowing river? See p. 543 for the answer.

Largest newt The Spanish ribbed newt (*Pleurodeles waltl*), found in central and southern Iberia and Morocco, is 6–12 in. (15–30 cm) long.

The world's **smallest newt** or **salamander** is the Mexican lungless salamander (*Bolitoglossa mexicana*), which attains a maximum length of approximately 1 in. (2.54 cm).

★ **LARGEST GENUS OF FROG**
The *Pristimantis* genus of frog comprises more than 400 species, with new ones being discovered each year. These small frogs are native to southern Central and northern South America, and are notable for laying their eggs on land. These hatch directly as froglets, thus bypassing the tadpole stage.

★ **LARGEST AMPHIUMA**
Amphiumas are three highly distinctive species of aquatic North American salamander with elongated, superficially eel-like bodies, minute legs, and no tongue. The largest of these very unusual amphibians is the three-toed amphiuma (*Amphiuma tridactylum*), pictured. It can grow to 3 ft. 3 in. (1 m) long, possesses gill slits but lacks eyelids, and lives in marshes and lakes within the southeastern U.S.A.

EXTRA! Discover more about humanity's relationship with animals in our animal magic chapter, from p. 267.

★ LARGEST CAECILIAN
Extant (living) amphibians can be divided into Anura (frogs and toads), Caudata (newts and salamanders), and Gymnophiona (caecilians). This last order are limbless tropical amphibians that generally resemble earthworms, and have eyes hidden beneath a layer of skin. The world's largest is Thompson's caecilian (*Caecilia thompsoni*), a Colombian species that can attain a length of 4 ft. 11 in. (1.51 m). It is native to moist tropical and subtropical lowland forests as well as plantations and even rural gardens.

★ HIGHEST FROG CROAK
The concave-eared torrent frog (*Odorrana tormota*) of eastern China emits a croak of 128 kHz—well beyond the range of human hearing, which cannot detect sound frequencies above 20 kHz.

COPENHAGEN, DENMARK (55°40'N 12°34'E): Bakken, located in Klampenborg, north of Copenhagen, Denmark, opened in 1583 and is the **oldest operating amusement park** in the world. The park claims to have more than 150 attractions, including a wooden roller coaster built in 1932.

REPTILES

★**Largest gecko** Delcourt's giant gecko (*Hoplodactylus delcourti*) is known from only a single mounted and stuffed specimen measuring 2 ft. (61 cm) long. It had been on display at the Marseille Natural History Museum in France for more than a century before, in 1979, it was recognized by curator Alain Delcourt as representing a species unknown to science. This gecko was formally named and described in 1986.

Fastest lizard In a series of experiments conducted by Professor Raymond Huey from the University of Washington, U.S.A., and colleagues at the University of California at Berkeley, U.S.A., the highest burst speed recorded for any reptile on land was 21.7 mph (34.9 km/h), achieved by *Ctenosaura*, a spiny-tailed iguana from Central America.

★**Longest reptilian incubation period** Of all the egg-laying reptiles the tuataras (see *Instant Expert*, p. 83) have to keep their eggs warm the

★MOST ACUTE NOCTURNAL COLOR VISION Unlike most other animals with nocturnal vision, the helmeted gecko (*Tarentola chazaliae*) can perceive colors at night. This is thought to be due to the higher density of color-sensitive large cone cells in the lizard's retinas.

★FASTEST CROCODILE ON LAND The freshwater crocodile (*Crocodylus johnstoni*) can attain speeds reaching 10.56 mph (17 km/h) when in full gallop—a mode of terrestrial locomotion that only a few species of crocodile can accomplish. Native to Australia, this crocodile rarely grows larger than 8–10 ft. (2.5–3 m).

UDINE, ITALY (46°03'N 13°14'E): The most participants in a cycling event is 48,615 for the 18.2-mile-long (29.3-km) Udine Pedala 2000, organized by Rolo Banca 1473, at Udine, Italy, on June 11, 2000.

★LARGEST VENOMOUS LIZARD Measuring up to 10 ft. 3 in. (3.13 m) and weighing around 154 lb. 5 oz. (70 kg), the Komodo dragon (*Varanus komodoensis*) is the largest lizard. In 2009, researchers at Melbourne University, Australia, discovered that the reptile also possesses a pair of venom glands in its lower jaw that secrete a venom containing several different toxic proteins.

longest before they are ready to hatch. Scientists have recorded tuataras incubating eggs for as long as 13 to 15 months before their offspring emerge from their shells.

★Largest crocodile eggs The false gharial (*Tomiostoma schlegelii*), a crocodilian with long, narrow jaws and a slender snout native to southeast Asia, lays eggs that typically measure 3.94 x 2.76 in. (10 x 7 cm). Despite its name, recent studies have shown that the false gharial is more closely related to other gharials than to crocodiles and alligators.

Largest tortoise The giant tortoises (*Chelonoidis nigra*) of the Galápagos Islands are the largest tortoise species. A specimen named Goliath, who resided at the Life Fellowship Bird Sanctuary in Seffner, Florida, U.S.A., from 1960 until his death in November 2002, was 4 ft. 5.5 in. (1.35 m) long, 3 ft. 3.6 in. (1.02 m) wide, and 2 ft. 3 in. (68.5 cm) tall, and weighed 920 lb. (417 kg).

★LARGEST TUATARA
There are only two species of tuatara, both of which are found exclusively in the islands off the main coast of New Zealand. Of the two, the greatly endangered Brothers Island tuatara (*Sphenodon guntheri*) is the largest. It can grow up to 2 ft. 6 in. (76 cm) long and have a maximum weight of 3 lb. 1 oz. (1.4 kg).

★Country with most venomous snake species Australia not only has more species of venomous snake than any other country on Earth, but also includes among those snakes no less than nine of the world's top 10 most venomous snake species. These include such (in)famous serpents as the inland taipan (*Oxyuranus microlepidotus*)—perhaps the world's most venomous snake—the eastern brown snake (*Pseudonaja textilis*) at the number-two spot, the coastal taipan (*Oxyuranus scutellatus*) third, and the tiger snake (*Notechis scutatus*) fourth.

Oldest snake The greatest reliable age recorded for a snake in captivity is 40 years 3 months 14 days for a male common boa (*Boa constrictor*) named Popeye, who died at Philadelphia Zoo, Pennsylvania, U.S.A., on April 15, 1977.

Largest crocodilian The estuarine, or saltwater, crocodile (*Crocodylus porosus*) is found throughout the tropical regions of Asia and the Pacific. The Bhitarkanika Wildlife Sanctuary in Orissa State, India, houses four measuring more than 19 ft. 8 in. (6 m) in length, the largest being more than

....

PALERMO, ITALY (38°07'N 13°22'E): The **largest Mafia trial** took place in Palermo, Sicily, Italy, on February 10, 1986. A total of 426 people were found guilty and 19 were sentenced to detention in perpetuity.

....

EXTRA! For more cold-blooded creatures, plod along to pp. 53–59 to explore the land of the dinosaurs.

★SMALLEST CHELONIAN Of all the chelonians—turtles, tortoises, and terrapins—the smallest is the speckled cape tortoise or speckled padloper (*Homopus signatus*). It has a shell length of 2.3–3.7 in. (6–9.6 cm)—so small that the tortoise can hide in tiny gaps between rocks.

23 ft. (7 m) long. There are several unauthenticated reports of specimens up to 33 ft. (10 m) in length. Adult males average 14–16 ft. (4.2–4.8 m) in length and weigh about 900–1,150 lb. (408–520 kg).

Smallest Crocodilian The dwarf caiman (*Paleosuchus palpebrosus*) of northern South America is the smallest crocodilian in the world today. Females rarely exceed a length of 4 ft. (1.2 m), and males seldom grow to more than 4 ft. 11 in. (1.5 m).

Rarest lizard Until it was rediscovered in 1990, the Jamaican iguana (*Cyclura collei*) was thought to be extinct. With no more than 100 adult specimens located since 1990, the species is considered critically endangered, and it is clinging to survival in southern Jamaica's remote Hellshire Hills—the only sizable area of dry forest remaining on the island.

Longest venomous snake The venom of a single bite from the king cobra (*Ophiophagus hannah*), found in southeast Asia and India, is enough to kill an elephant, or 20 people. What's more, it can grow to 12–15 ft. (3.65–4.5 m) in length and can stand tall enough to look an adult human in the eye.

INSTANT EXPERT

• Tuataras might look like lizards, but they are actually the only living representatives of an otherwise extinct group of reptiles named the sphenodontids, a group that thrived at the time of the dinosaurs.

• Not all reptiles live on dry land. The marine iguana (*Amblyrhynchus cristatus*) and various species of sea snake live in salt water.

• The common Basilisk (*Basiliscus basiliscus*) is known as the "Jesus lizard" for its ability to run on water!

Rarest crocodilian There were fewer than 200 Chinese alligators (*Alligator sinensis*) living in the wild in 2002. Found in the lower parts of the Yangtze River in wetlands, the species can grow to 6 ft. 6 in. (2 m) and weigh 88 lb. (40 kg). Their numbers have dwindled over time due to habitat destruction and killing by local farmers.

BIRDS

Fastest birds

•In level flight: The mean estimated speed recorded for a satellite-tagged gray-headed albatross (*Thalassarche chrysostoma*) is 78.9 mph (127 km/h) sustained for more than eight hours.

•In a dive: A peregrine falcon (*Falco peregrinus*) was recorded at a velocity of 168 mph (270 km/h) at a 30° angle of stoop, rising to a maximum of 217 mph (350 km/h) at 45°.

•On land: The **fastest (flightless) bird on land** is the ostrich (*Struthio camelus*), which can reach 45 mph (72 km/h) when running.

•In water: The fastest bird swimmer is the gentoo penguin (*Pygoscelis papua*), which has a burst of speed of about 17 mph (27 km/h).

Strongest bird of prey The female harpy eagle (*Harpia harpyja*) regularly kills and carries away animals equal or superior to its 20 lb. (9 kg) weight.

Smallest birds Male bee hummingbirds (*Mellisuga helenae*) of Cuba and the Isle of Youth measure 2.24 in. (57 mm) in total length, half of which is taken up by the bill and tail, and weigh just 0.056 oz. (1.6 g). Females of the species are slightly larger.

Hummingbirds also have the **fastest wing beat**. The ruby-throated hummingbird (*Archilochus colubris*) can produce a wing-beat rate of 200 beats per second.

RATITE

"Flightless." The name is from the Latin for "raft": just as a raft has no keel, these birds have no lengthwise ridge in their breastbone.

BERLIN, GERMANY (52°31'N 13°25'E): The **largest single rock concert**, in terms of participants and organization, was Roger Waters's production of Pink Floyd's *The Wall*, staged on July 21, 1990, in Potsdamer Platz, straddling East and West Berlin, Germany, when 600 people performed on stage.

LAZY!: Kori bustards—the **heaviest flying birds**—are rarely seen in the air: they are so heavy, they prefer to walk everywhere!

HEAVIEST BIRDS
The **heaviest bird of prey** is the Andean condor (*Vultur gryphus*, pictured), males of which average 20–27 lb. (9–12 kg) and have a wingspan of 10 ft. (3 m). The **heaviest flying bird** is the kori bustard (*Ardeotis kori*) of south and east Africa; males can reach 40 lb. (18.2 kg). The **heaviest (and largest) of all birds** is the ratite male ostrich (*Struthio camelus camelus*). It can grow 9 ft. (2.75 m) tall and may weigh 345 lb. (156.5 kg).

Keenest smell for a bird Few birds have a developed sense of smell, but the black-footed albatross *(Diomedea nigripes)* can smell bacon fat poured into the ocean from at least 18 miles (30 km) away.

Smallest nest The nest of the vervain hummingbird (*Mellisuga minima*) is about half the size of a walnut shell, while the deeper but narrower one of the bee hummingbird (*M. helenae*) is thimble-sized.

Largest communal nest The sociable weaver (*Philetairus socius*) of southwestern Africa builds a nest that can be up to 26 ft. (8 m) long and 6 ft. 6 in. (2 m) high. Resembling a giant haystack that hangs from a tree or telegraph pole, it contains up to 300 individual nests. Not surprisingly, these enormous communal nests can get so heavy that the tree on which they are built sometimes collapses.

BONES!: Andean natives collect the bones of the Andean condor—the **heaviest bird of prey**—believing that they have healing powers.

★ **LOWEST NESTING ALTITUDE** The little green bee-eater (*Merops orientalis*) nests at 1,312 ft. (400 m) below sea level in the Dead Sea area of the Middle East. This is the lowest nesting altitude recorded for any species of bird.

★ **Highest nests** The highest tree nest constructed by any bird is that of the marbled murrelet (*Brachyramphus marmoratus*), a small North Pacific member of the auk family of seabirds. Its nests have been discovered as high as 147 ft. (45 m), usually on moss-covered branches of old conifer trees.

This may explain why the first formally identified nest from this species was not recorded by science until as recently as 1961, in Asia; the first North American example was not found until 1974.

★ **LONGEST BIRD TONGUE** Relative to body size, the longest tongue of any bird is that of the wryneck (*Jynx torquilla*), a European relative of woodpeckers. Its tongue is two-thirds of its 6.4-in. (16.5-cm) body length. On a human scale, this would mean you could lick your knees without bending over!

JINX!: Because a wryneck can twist its head and neck through nearly 180°, some people believed that witches used the bird to make curses. The word "jinx" derives from their latin genus name: *jynx*!

EXTRA! see how well we humans do when we take to the skies by visiting pp. 196–200.

★ **HIGHEST YOLK CONTENT** The bird eggs with the highest yolk content to egg volume are those of New Zealand's kiwis (order Apterygiformes). Some 60% of a kiwi egg's volume is taken up by yolk (compared with 31% of a hen's egg), and it contains so much nutrients that the kiwi chick does not have to eat for several days after hatching.

★ **HUNGRIEST BIRDS** The world's hungriest birds are the hummingbirds (family Trochilidae), which have such high metabolic rates that they need to consume at least half of their total body weight in food every day in order to survive. Their food consists mostly of tiny insects and nectar.

★ **SMALLEST EGGS** Surprisingly, bearing in mind that it lays the **largest eggs** of any bird, the bird that lays the smallest eggs relative to body weight is the ostrich (*Struthio camelus*). This is because the egg's weight is only 1.4–1.5% of the ostrich's total weight. A comparable percentage has also been recorded for the emperor penguin (*Aptenodytes forsteri*).

PRAGUE, CZECH REPUBLIC (50°05'N 14°25'E): The **largest ancient castle** in the world is Hradcany Castle or Prague Castle in Prague, Czech Republic, built in the 9th century with a surface area of 18 acres (7.28 ha).

★**Most birdsongs recorded** The red-eyed vireo (*Vireo olivaceus*), a small New World species of songbird, has been recorded singing 22,197 songs in a 10-hour period, an average of more than 2,000 songs per hour!

★**Shortest migration** In stark contrast to the thousands of miles flown by certain migrating birds, North America's blue grouse (*Dendragapus obscurus*) descends a mere 984 ft. (300 m) from its winter home in the mountainous pine forests to deciduous woodlands in order to feed upon the early crop of seeds and fresh leaves.

MAMMALS

★**Largest mammal family** Family Muridae, a group containing many rodents, is the largest of all mammal families. The group contains more than 600 species, including the true mice and rats, as well as the gerbils and jirds. Rodents were already widely distributed globally, but have since been introduced by man to many islands that were previously rodent-free.

Tallest mammal Native to the dry savannah and open woodland areas of sub-Saharan Africa, a typical adult male giraffe (*Giraffa camelopardalis*) measures between 15 ft. and 18 ft. (4.6–5.5 m) tall. The tallest recorded giraffe was a 19-ft. (5.8-m) Masai bull (*G. c. tippelskirchi*) named George, received by Chester Zoo, UK, on January 8, 1959.

Slowest mammal Despite its undeserved reputation, the three-toed sloth (*Bradypus tridactylus*) of tropical South America is not really a lazy creature—it is just very slow. On the ground its average speed is 6–8 ft. (1.8–2.4 m) per minute (0.07–0.1 mph; 0.1–0.16 km/h), but in the trees it can accelerate to 15 ft. (4.6 m) per minute (0.17 mph; 0.27 km/h)!

★**STRONGEST MAMMAL BITE** In tests, the Tasmanian devil (*Sarcophilus harrisii*) produced a bite force quotient (the scientific measure of the power of an animal's bite relative to its size) of 181. By comparison, the tiger's bite force quotient is 127 and the lion's a mere 112.

MARIBOR, SLOVENIA (46°33'N 15°39'E): Maribor, Slovenia, is home to the **oldest vine**. A scientific measurement of the vine in 1972 established that it was then at least 350 years old and may have been up to 400 years in age.

★ **HUNGRIEST BEAR** The giant panda (*Ailuropoda melanoleuca*) can digest only 21% of all the bamboo that it consumes. Consequently, it must eat up to 38% of its own weight in bamboo shoots each day.

★ **Smallest Hyrax** Africa's hyraxes are small mammals that superficially resemble rodents but are most closely related to the African elephant (*Loxodonta africana*)—the **largest land mammal** at 8,800–15,400 lb. (4–7 tonnes). Despite links to the biggest of land beasts, the yellow-spotted rock hyrax (*Heterohyrax brucei*) is no bigger than 18.5 in. (47 cm) in total length—adult specimens can be as short as 12.7 in. (32.5 cm)—and weighs a mere 5.29 lb. (2.4 kg), at most.

By comparison, the **smallest land-dwelling mammal** is Savi's pygmy shrew (*Suncus etruscus*), an insect-eating mammal that inhabits the Mediterranean and southern Asia regions. The shrew is about the size of a human thumb, with an average body length of 1.4–2 in. (36–53 mm), a tail length of 0.9–1 in. (24–29 mm), and weighs just 0.05–0.09 oz. (1.5–2.6 g).

★ **Lightest egg-laying mammal** Of the five species of monotreme (see *Did You Know?* on p. 91), the platypus (*Ornithorhynchus anatinus*) of mainland Australia and Tasmania is the lightest. Male platypuses typically weigh 2.2–5.2 lb. (1.0–2.4 kg) while females weigh just 1.5–3.5 lb. (0.7–1.6 kg).

★ **FASTEST-PANTING WILD DOG** The big-eared fennec fox (*Fennecus zerda*) has a novel way of cooling down in its Saharan home. When the temperature reaches 100°F (38°C), it loses heat by panting at a rapid rate of 690 breaths per minute!

EXTRA! For more on mammals, don't forget to check out life down on the farm on pp. 282–288.

BIG!: The **largest mammal** is the blue whale (*Balaenoptera musculus*), with an average length of 80 ft. (24 m)!

★ **LONGEST WHALE TOOTH** The ivory tusk of the male narwhal (*Monodon monoceros*) grows to an average length of roughly 6 ft. 6 in. (2 m) but can exceed 9 ft. 10 in. (3 m) and weigh up to 22 lb. (10 kg). In past centuries, the single (or, very rarely, paired) spiraled tusks were sometimes thought to be unicorn horns when found washed up on the beach.

★**Largest mammal genome** An animal's genome is the map of all of its genetic information and is found in the nucleus of every cell in its body. The red vizcacha rat (*Tympanoctomys barrerae*) has a genome containing 16.8 picograms (1 picogram = 1 trillionth of a gram) of DNA. Most other mammals have a genome containing only 6–8 picograms. The red vizcacha also has the ★ **most chromosomes of any mammal** with a total of 102 chromosomes, split into 51 pairs. By comparison, humans have only 46 chromosomes, divided into 23 pairs.

★**BONIEST MAMMAL TAIL** The long-tailed pangolin (*Manis tetradactylus*) has up to 47 vertebrae in its tail—more than any other mammal. All eight species of pangolin, or scaly anteater, have impressive spines and claws that are composed of keratin, the same substance as human fingernails.

SMALL!: The **smallest mammal** is the bumblebee bat (*craseonycteris thonglongyai*), with a head–body length of only 1.14–1.29 in. (29–33 mm).

FASTEST

When measured over a short distance, the cheetah (*Acinonyx jubatus*) can maintain a steady maximum speed of approximately 62 mph (100 km/h) on level ground, making it the **fastest land mammal over short distances**.

A prime example of a speedy cheetah is Sarah, an eight-year-old that ran 328 ft. (100 m) in 6.13 seconds at the Cincinnati Zoo, Ohio, U.S.A., on September 10, 2009, giving her the record for the ★ **fastest 100 m by a land mammal**, trouncing Usain Bolt's (Jamaica) 100 m time of 9.59 seconds (see p. 91).

However, Sarah's speed has no staying power compared with that of a pronghorn (*Antilocapra americana*). Native to western North America, pronghorns have been recorded traveling continuously at 35 mph (56 km/h) for as far as 4 miles (6 km), giving them the title of the **fastest land mammal over long distances**.

Finally, the **fastest marine mammal** is the bull killer whale (*Orcinus orca*). On October 12, 1958, one specimen was recorded traveling at 34.5 mph (55.5 km/h) in the northeastern Pacific.

★ **LONGEST-LIVED RODENT** The naked mole rat (*Heterocephalus glaber*) is a bizarre-looking mammal that spends its life in underground burrow systems beneath East Africa's drier tropical grasslands. An extremely social creature, mole rats reside in colonies and can live for up to 28 years.

VIENNA, AUSTRIA (48°12'N 16°22'E): The **longest human beatbox marathon** is 24 hours and was achieved by Michael Krappel (Austria) during the event Vienna Recordia, in Vienna, Austria, on September 30, 2007.

PLANT LIFE

★**Rarest flax plant** Flax is a fibrous plant that has long been used to make fabric. The rarest species of flax plant is the Floreana flax (*Linum cratericola*), native to the Galápagos Islands. Only discovered by science in the 1960s, then feared extinct from 1981 until rediscovered in 1997, this small subshrub is presently limited to three small groups on Floreana Island. Here it is threatened with extinction by feral goats, invasive plants, and periods of dry weather.

Smallest plant kingdom Of the six biogeographical plant zones—Boreal, Neotropical, Paleotropical, South African, Australian, and Antarctic—the South African is the smallest.

Most selective carnivorous plant *Nepenthes albomarginata* is a carnivorous plant that grows in Malaysia and Indonesia and feeds only on *Hospitalitermes bicolor* termites. The termites

SMELLIEST PLANT Native to the Sumatran rainforests, the "corpse flower," or titan arum, *Amorphophallus titanum*, is believed to be the smelliest plant on Earth. When it blooms, it releases a foul odor similar to that of rotting flesh to attract flies to aid in its pollination. The stench can be smelled up to half a mile (0.8 km) away.

> "[The corpse flower] smells like a dead person. . . . I happen to be a nurse and that is exactly what it smells like."
> **A visitor to Huntington Botanical Gardens, San Marino, California, U.S.A., tells it like it is.**

BRNO, CZECH REPUBLIC (49°12'N 16°37'E): The farthest distance covered on a penny-farthing bicycle in 24 hours is 522.504 km (324.668 miles) by Josef Zimovčák (Czech Republic) in Brno, Czech Republic, on 20–21 June 1996.

are attracted to edible hairs, called trichomes, on the plant, but sometimes slip down the plant's "throat" and are digested by liquids at the bottom of the flower.

Highest concentration of endangered plant species South Africa's Cape Flats hosts 15 species per square kilometer that are threatened by extinction.

★Rarest willow Deciduous willows are a common tree throughout the northern hemisphere. However, one species, the Tarragonès willow (*Salix tarraconensis*) is considered critically endangered and is known only from a few dispersed populations of 10–40 specimens located between Castellón and Tarragona in Spain.

★MOST CHROMOSOMES IN A PLANT All living organisms contain chromosomes—the part of a cell that contains all the genetic information that determines what characteristics the organism will possess. While humans have 46 chromosomes in 23 pairs, many other organisms have far more. The adder's tongue fern (*Ophioglossum reticulatum*) is reported to have 1,440 chromosomes arranged into 720 pairs, making it the record holder for both the greatest number of chromosomes in a plant and the **★most chromosomes in an organism.**

DID YOU KNOW?

Lycopodium powder, the dried spores of club moss, is highly flammable and has been used in stagecraft for centuries to produce short-lived fireballs.

TRIVIA

In 1978, Bulgarian Georgi Markov was assassinated in London, UK, by a ricin-coated umbrella tip that was jabbed into his leg.

★ **Oldest yew** The world's oldest yew tree is a specimen of common yew (*Taxus baccata*) that grows in the churchyard of St. Digain's parish church, in Llangernyw, North Wales, UK. It is estimated to be 4,000 years old.

Highest concentration of heathers The fynbos (Afrikaans for "fine bush") plant ecosystem, exclusive to South Africa's Cape floristic region, contains more than 600 species of heather (genus *Erica*). Only 26 species of heather occur in the rest of the world.

★ **Rarest onion** The rarest member of the onion genus *Allium* is *Allium rouyi*, a Spanish species with fewer than 300 known specimens fragmented among five subpopulations confined within a very small area of Bética Province in Andalusia, Spain.

Most toxic plant Based on the amount it takes to kill a human, the most toxic common plant in the world is the castor bean (*Ricinus communis*). The toxin—ricin—causes the clumping and breakdown of red blood cells and internal bleeding. It is 6,000 times more toxic than cyanide and 12,000 times more toxic than rattlesnake venom.

★ **Rarest club moss** Club mosses are a primitive form of plant endemic to wet forests and cliffside shrublands. The wawae'iole (*Huperzia nutans*) is the rarest variety and grows only on Koolau Mountain on Oahu in Hawaii, U.S.A.

★ **TALLEST HARDWOOD TREE** A specimen of Australian swamp gum tree (*Eucalyptus regnans*) known as "Centurion" stands 331.36 ft. (101 m) tall and has a diameter of 13.12 ft. (4 m). It is located just 49 miles (80 km) from Tasmania's capital, Hobart.

POZNAŃ, POLAND (52°25'N 16°55'E): The **largest beer tankard** can hold more than 7,000 liters (1,539 gal), is made of bronze, and was manufactured to celebrate the new Stary Browar cultural and commercial center in Poznań, Poland, on March 11, 2007.

Fastest entrapment by a plant Carnivorous plants trap their prey in movements considered to be among the fastest in the entire plant kingdom. On land, the clamshell-like leaves of the Venus flytrap (*Dionaea muscipula*) shut in one-tenth of a second (100 milliseconds) from the moment they are stimulated. Underwater, the hinged trapdoor of the bladderwort (*Utricularia vulgaris*) captures its victim in 1/15,000th of a second.

☆ **Largest seed collection** The Millennium Seed Bank Project, housed at the Wellcome Trust Millennium Building, Wakehurst Place, West Sussex, UK, had 24,200 species collected as of March 20, 2010.

Smallest orchid The platystele (*Platystele jungermannioides*) found in the lower cloud forest of Mexico, Guatemala, Costa Rica, and Panama at an elevation of 656–3,280 ft. (200–1,000 m) grows around 0.25 in. (6.3 mm) high and 0.78 in. (20 mm) wide. This smallest of orchid species blooms in the spring with just two or three tiny flowers that are a mere 0.09 in. (2.5 mm) wide. With roughly 25,000 species, the orchid family is also the second-largest flowering plant family behind the Compositae family of daisies, the ☆ **largest family of flowering plants**, with more than 26,000 species.

★ **OLDEST CYPRESS** A cypress tree (*Cupressus sempervirens*) known as Sarv-e-Abarkooh, or Zoroastrian Sarv, is a tourist attraction in Abarkooh, Yazd, Iran. It is estimated to be more than 4,000 years old and is a national monument.

Most visited garden (paying visitors) The Royal Botanic Gardens, Kew, Surrey, UK, has an average of 1 million paying visitors per year. The 326-acre (132-ha) site has 40 historically important buildings and collections of more than 40,000 species of plants. Kew Gardens became a United Nations World Heritage site on July 3, 2003.

AMERICAN WILDLIFE

Largest structure built by a land animal Found throughout the U.S.A. and Canada, the North American beaver (*Castor canadensis*) uses mud, wood, and stones to dam up streams, ensuring a plentiful supply of fish, and then builds a lodge within its dam for winter refuge. The largest lodge ever recorded was 40 ft. (12.1 m) across and 16 ft. (4.8 m) high.

Smelliest animal The striped skunk (*Mephitis mephitis*), a member of the mustelid family found throughout the U.S.A., ejects a truly foul-smelling liquid from its anal glands if threatened. This defensive secretion contains seven major volatile and stench-filled components. Two of these substances, both sulfur-containing thiols, are responsible for the secretion's strongly repellent odor, and are known respectively as (E)-2-butene-1-thiol and 3-methyl-1-butanethiol. They are so potent that they can be detected by humans at a concentration of 10 parts per billion—a low dilution that is equivalent to a teaspoonful in an Olympic-sized swimming pool of water!

Most restricted amphibian distribution The Peaks of Otter salamander (*Plethodon hubrichti*) is confined to an 11.8-mile-long (19-km) expanse in the Blue Mountains of Virginia, U.S.A.—the most limited range for any species of amphibian.

FASTEST-RUNNING FLYING BIRD Native to the southwestern U.S.A., the North American roadrunner (*Geococcyx californianus*) has been clocked at 26 mph (42 km/h) when pursued by an automobile.

BRATISLAVA, SLOVAKIA (48°10'N 17°07'E): Motorcycle enthusiasts Peter Schmidl and Anna Turceková had a wedding procession of 597 motorcycles when they tied the knot in Bratislava, Slovakia, on May 6, 2000, the **largest motorcycle wedding procession**.

LARGEST MAMMAL COLONY A black-tailed prairie dog (*Cynomys ludovicianus*) colony found in 1901 contained 400 million individuals and covered an estimated 23,705 miles² (61,400 km²).

FASTEST EATER According to research published in February 2005 by Dr. Kenneth Catania at Vanderbilt University, Tennessee, U.S.A., the star-nosed mole (*Condylura cristata*) handles its food for an average of 230 milliseconds before eating it. The fastest recorded handling time in the study was 120 milliseconds.

LONGEST TERRESTRIAL MIGRATION Grant's caribou (*Rangifer tarandus granti*), aka the porcupine caribou, lives in western Alaska and the Yukon Territory of Canada and travels up to 2,982 miles (4,800 km) during its regular migration to more sheltered wintering grounds.

COUGAR

A term thought to come ultimately from "susuarana" ("false deer") from the Tupi people of Brazil.

MAMMAL WITH THE MOST NAMES With a range that extends from the Yukon in Canada to the southern Andes of South America and includes the entire continental U.S.A., the puma (*Puma concolor*) has more than 40 common names in English, including "cougar," "mountain lion," "catamount," and "Florida panther."

EXTRA! For more Great American records, go get your kicks on Route 66 (pp. 263–266).

LARGEST DEER When it comes to deer, the biggest beast is the Alaskan moose (***Alces alces gigas***). A bull standing 7 ft. 8 in. (2.34 m) and weighing an estimated 1,800 lb. (816 kg) was shot in the Yukon Territory, Canada, in September 1897.

Smallest bee A bee that nests in the sandy soil of southwestern U.S.A., *Perdita minima* is just under 0.07 in. (2 mm) long and weighs just 0.333 mg.

Animal most likely to procreate quadruplets Native to the southeastern states from Arizona to Florida, U.S.A., the nine-banded armadillo (*Dasypus novemcinctus*) is a close relative of the anteater and is the only mammal known to bear identical quadruplets regularly. All four, all of the same sex, develop from the same egg and share one placenta in the womb.

TARANTO, ITALY (40°28'N 17°14'E): The **largest focaccia bread** weighed 6,172 lb. (2,800 kg) and was made by Catucci Pietro and Latte Antonio (both Italy) in the Piazza Mercato, Mottola, Taranto, Italy, on August 6, 2005.

★**Largest piece of natural spider silk** On September 25, 2009, an 11 x 4 ft. (3.3 x 1.2 m) piece of cloth made from natural spider silk was put on display at the American Museum of Natural History in New York, U.S.A. A team of 70 people spent four years collecting golden orb spiders from telephone poles in Madagascar (although their natural range includes the southeastern U.S.A., from North Carolina to Texas). A second team of 12 removed up to 80 ft. (24 m) of silk filament from each spider. To create 1 oz. (28 g) of silk, 14,000 spiders must be "milked"—the equivalent of 50,000 spiders for 2.2 lb. (1 kg) of silk.

Most dangerous American lizard The Gila monster (*Heloderma suspectum*) is a large lizard that can measure up to 2 ft. (60 cm) and inhabits Mexico and the southwestern U.S.A. from California to Arizona. Its main claim to fame are the venom glands in its jaw that carry enough venom to kill two adult humans. The venom is not injected, but seeps into the wound the reptile causes when it bites and chews its victims with its sharp fragile teeth. In a study of 34 people bitten by these animals, there were eight recorded fatalities. Fortunately, the lizard, like the similarly venomous Mexican beaded lizard (*Heloderma horridum*) and the Komodo dragon (*Varanus komodoensis*, see p. 81) attacks only when provoked.

Largest flea The largest known flea species is *Hystrichopsylla schefferi*, which was described from a single specimen taken from the nest of a mountain beaver (*Aplodontia rufa*) at Puyallup, Washington, U.S.A., in 1913. Females measure up to 0.3 in. (8 mm) long—roughly the diameter of a pencil.

HUMAN BEINGS

CONTENTS

"People often just want to look at me or touch me. Some even want to kiss me."

Elaine Davidson, most pierced woman

MOST PIERCED PEOPLE Since having her first piercing in January 1997, Elaine Davidson (UK) has had 4,225 pieces of metal attached to, and inside, her body. Elaine is the world's **most pierced person**. Her male equivalent is John Lynch (UK, aka Prince Albert), who had, at the last count, 241 piercings, including 151 in his head and neck.

LABRET

A piercing or adornment of the lip, and in particular the lower lip. Ornaments range from simple studs to enormous clay plates.

TALLEST MAN

SULTAN AND THE METS
Of all the places Sultan Kösen (Turkey) visited, nowhere made as big an impression on him as New York City. It was the size of the buildings that impressed him the most—he had never seen so many skyscrapers before!

DID YOU KNOW?

Sultan has grown so tall because of a tumor on his pituitary gland. The tumor has now been removed, and he has finally stopped growing.

TRIVIA

The pituitary gland controls the release of growth hormone: too much and you're a giant; too little, you're a dwarf.

STOCKHOLM, SWEDEN (59°21'N 18°04'E): The world's **first banknotes** (or *banco-sedlar*) were issued in Stockholm, Sweden, in July 1661 by the Bank of Palmstruch. The oldest surviving note is one of five dalers dated December 6, 1662.

TALL TOUR 2009 Sultan once lived a quiet life on a farm in the Mardín region of Turkey. Now he's an international jet-setter! Here he is making a big impression in London, UK (left), Madrid, Spain (above left), and Milan, Italy (above right). He also traveled to Reykjavik, Iceland, where he enjoyed a spa bath, and Vienna, Austria, where he became a media star!

CAPE TOWN, SOUTH AFRICA (33°55'S 18°25'E): The **first heart transplant operation** was performed on Louis Washkansky (South Africa) at the Groote Schuur Hospital, Cape Town, South Africa, on December 3, 1967, by a team of 30 headed by Prof. Christiaan Neethling Barnard (South Africa).

HIGH HOPES

So what are the newly famous gentle giant's dreams for the future? "I want what everyone else wants," says Sultan. "A wife, a family, a nice home. I'd also like the chance to find some decent clothes that fit! I've already had a suit made for me, and at least one dream has come true: I now own a pair of jeans made specially for me!"

TALLEST LIVING MAN At 8 ft. 1 in. (246.5 cm), Sultan is the world's ☆ **tallest living man** and ☆ **tallest living human being.** Indeed, he is the tallest person to exceed 8 ft. (243.8 cm) in 20 years, and only the 11th person in history to be officially ratified as over 8 ft. by Guinness World Records.

Sultan was first measured by GWR's Editor-in-Chief, Craig Glenday, in Ankara, Turkey, on February 11, 2009. "To avoid any controversy, I had to measure him myself," said Craig. "It's the only way to be totally sure of a claimant's height. There is too much at stake to leave it to anyone other than a GWR representative."

One of the most difficult aspects of being so tall, says Sultan, is finding clothes and shoes to fit. His 1-ft.-2-in.-long (36.5-cm) feet—the ☆ **largest feet on a living person**—require extra-large shoes (above, compared with a U.S. size-9.5 sneaker), which are expensive to make.

Sultan also holds the record for the ☆ **largest hands on a living person,** measuring 10.83 in. (27.5 cm) from the wrist to the tip of the middle finger.

EXTRA! For more tall tales and short stories, turn to p. 111.

BODY PARTS

☆ **Most teeth in the mouth** The record for the most teeth in the mouth belongs to Kanchan Rajawat (India) and Luca Meriano (Italy), both of whom had 35 adult teeth as of October 17, 2008.

★ **Smallest tooth extracted** A primary tooth extracted from Colton Laub (U.S.A.) on October 30, 2002, by Dr. Scott Harden at Fountain View Family Dentistry, Acworth, Georgia, U.S.A., measured 0.1 in. (3 mm).

Longest milk tooth Ahmed Afrah Ismail (Maldives) had a milk tooth measuring 0.9 in. (2.3 cm). The tooth was measured in Male, Republic of Maldives, on December 28, 2000.

Largest gape J. J. Bittner (U.S.A.) is able to open his mouth to a gap of 3.4 in. (8.4 cm). His gape was measured from the incisal edge of his maxillary central incisors to the incisal edge of his mandibular central incisors—that is, between the tips of the front teeth in his upper and lower jaws.

☆ **LONGEST TOOTH REMOVED** Loo Hui Jing (Singapore) had a tooth measuring 1.26 in. (3.2 cm) extracted by Dr. Ng Lay Choo at the Eli Dental Surgery, Singapore, on April 6, 2009.

★ **WIDEST TONGUE** Here's a record that will take some lickin'! The tongue of Jay Sloot (Australia) was measured to be 3.1 in. (7.9 cm) at its widest point on the set of *Lo Show dei Record* in Rome, Italy, on March 18, 2010.

Longest tongue Jay might have the edge in width, but when it comes to length, Stephen Taylor (UK) is the tongue champ. Stephen's tongue was 3.86 in. (9.8 cm) from its tip to the middle of his closed top lip when it was measured at the Westwood Medical Centre, Coventry, UK, on February 11, 2009.

....

BELGRADE, SERBIA (44°49'N 20°27'E): Chess masters Goran Arsovic and Ivan Nikolic (both Yugoslavia, now Serbia) played a game with 269 moves on February 17, 1989—the **most moves in a chess game**. The drawn game was played in Belgrade, Yugoslavia (now Serbia), and took 20 hr. 15 min.

....

LONGEST TOENAILS Since 1982, Louise Hollis (U.S.A.) has been growing her toenails to exceedingly great lengths. When measured at their longest in 1991, the combined length of all 10 toenails was 87 in. (221 cm).

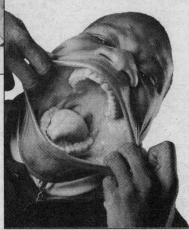

★ MOST ELASTIC MOUTH The lips (oral labia) and cheeks (buccal cavity) of Francisco Domingo Joaquim "Chiquinho" (Angola), at full stretch, measured 6.69 in. (17 cm) wide on March 18, 2010. Incredibly, he does not have the widest gape (see p. 107). Chiquinho suffers from a connective tissues disorder.

EXTRA! For more medical records, go to pp. 128–132.

Largest hands Robert Wadlow (U.S.A.), the **tallest man ever** (see pp. 104–106 to discover the heights he reached), had hands that measured 12.75 in. (32.3 cm) from the wrist to the tip of his middle finger. He wore a size 25 ring.

Longest fingernails on a single hand The aggregate measurement of the five nails on the left hand of Shridhar Chillal (India, b. August 18, 1937) was 23 ft. 1.5 in. (705 cm) on February 4, 2004. His thumb measured 62.2 in. (158 cm), his index finger 51.5 in. (131 cm), his middle finger 54.3 in. (138 cm), his ring finger 55.1 in. (140 cm), and his little finger 54.3 in. (138 cm). Chillal last cut his fingernails in 1952.

Longest fingernails ever (female) Lee Redmond (U.S.A.) started to grow her fingernails in 1979 and, over the years, she carefully manicured them to reach a total length of 28 ft. 4.5 in. (8.65 m), as measured on the set of *Lo Show dei Record* in Madrid, Spain, on February 23, 2008. Sadly, Lee lost her nails in a motor vehicle accident in early 2009, but since that time no one has beaten her all-time record.

★ **LONGEST FINGERNAILS** We were saddened in December 2009 to learn of the passing of Melvin Boothe (U.S.A.). Melvin first contacted us about his fantastic fingernails in 2006, and when last measured on May 30, 2009, at his home in Troy, Michigan, U.S.A., they had a combined length of 32 ft. 3.8 in. (9.85 m).

MISKOLC, HUNGARY (48°07'N 20°50'E): The **highest score in an international handball match** was recorded when the USSR beat Afghanistan 86–2 in the "Friendly Army Tournament" at Miskolc, Hungary, in August 1981.

Fewest toes The two-toed ("ostrich-foot") syndrome exhibited by some members of the Wadomo tribe of the Zambezi Valley in Zimbabwe, and the Kalanga tribe of the eastern Kalahari Desert in Botswana, is hereditary via a single mutated gene.

Narrowest waist Cathie Jung (U.S.A.) is 5 ft. 8 in. (1.73 m) tall, but her waist is much smaller than you might expect—just 21 in. (53.34 cm). And that figure narrows to just 15 in. (38.1 cm) when she is wearing a corset, which pulls in the lower ribs. Cathie developed her tiny waist as part of her enthusiasm for Victorian clothing. Look at pictures of ladies in the Victorian era, when corsets were normal attire, and see how narrow their waists and rib cages were!

Longest legs (female) Svetlana Pankratova's (Russia) legs measured 51.9 in. (132 cm) long in Torremolinos, Spain, on July 8, 2003. Her unique gift presents certain challenges—she has to have some clothes specially made, she ducks through doorways, and she needs lots of legroom when traveling in automobiles and planes.

LONGEST NOSE ON A LIVING PERSON The nose of Mehmet Ozyurek (Turkey) was measured at 3.46 in. (8.8 cm) long from bridge to tip on the set of *Lo Show dei Record* in Rome, Italy, on March 18, 2010.

CHOO!: It is claimed that Thomas Wedders, who lived in England in the 1770s, had a record-breaking nose that was 7.5 in. (19 cm) long.

Largest feet ever Robert Wadlow (U.S.A.) wore U.S. size 37 AA shoes (UK 36; approx. European 75), equivalent to 18.5 in. (47 cm) long. To say thanks to the International Shoe Company (U.S.A.), who provided his $100 shoes for free, Wadlow visited an estimated 800 U.S. cities on a goodwill promotional tour.

SIZE

Shortest man

Ever: The shortest mature human of whom there is independent evidence was Gul Mohammed (India, 1957–97). On July 19, 1990, he was examined at Ram Manohar Hospital, New Delhi, India, and found to have grown to a height of 22.5 in. (57 cm).

Living: Lin Yih-Chih (Taiwan), who is wheelchair-bound, owing to the condition osteogenesis imperfecta, measures 27 in. (67.5 cm).

Living (mobile): See p. 114.

Shortest woman

Ever: Pauline Musters (Netherlands, 1876–95) measured 12 in. (30 cm) at birth and 21.5 in. (55 cm) tall at the age of nine. When she died of pneumonia with meningitis in New York City, U.S.A., on March 1, 1895, at the age of 19, she had reached a height of 2 ft. (61 cm).

Living: Madge Bester (South Africa) measures 2 ft. 1.5 in. (65 cm) tall. A sufferer of the skeletal disorder type III osteogenesis imperfecta, she has extremely brittle bones and is confined to a wheelchair in a home in Bloemfontein, South Africa. Her mother, Winnie (d. 2001), also a sufferer, measured 2 ft. 3.5 in. (70 cm).

Living (mobile): This category remains unfilled as of May 10, 2010.

DID YOU KNOW?

At a modest 5 ft. 4 in. (163 cm), the current French president Nicolas Sarkozy is the shortest man ever to lead his country.

TRIVIA

At his peak, Tonga's King Taufa'ahau Tupou IV was the world's heaviest ruler, at 462 lb. (209.5 kg).

KOSICE, SLOVAKIA (48°42'N 21°15'E): The **largest litter of brown bears** (*Ursus arctos*) born in captivity is five. Miso, Tapik, Dazzle, Bubu, and Cindy (three males, two females) were born on January 6, 2002, in Zoo Kosice, Kosice-Kavecany, Slovakia.

☆ **HEAVIEST LIVING MAN** At his last weigh-in (December 2009), Mexico's Manuel Uribe registered 918 lb. (416.5 kg; 65.5 st)—a reversal of fortune for the dieting 43-year-old, who had been experiencing regular weight loss since peaking at 1,235 lb. (560 kg; 88 st) in 2006. Despite being bed-bound, Uribe married his second wife, Claudia Solis, (above, left) in 2008.

BED!: Manuel married Claudia from his bed, which had been adorned with white and gold silk and fresh sunflowers; it was transported to the altar on the back of a truck.

WED!: Manuel's doctors and nutritionists were among the guests at the low-calorie wedding to ensure that their patient didn't tuck into the five-tiered cake.

★ **SHORTEST LIVING MOTHER** Stacey Herald (U.S.A.), who stands 2 ft. 4.5 in. (72.39 cm) tall, gave birth to her first child, Kateri, in Dry Ridge, Kentucky, U.S.A., on October 21, 2006. Her second baby girl, Makaya, was born on January 1, 2008. Stacey is pictured here with her husband, Will, and their two girls. Her third child, a boy named Malachi, was born in November 2009.

Lightest person

Lucia Xarate (Mexico, 1863–89) of San Carlos, Mexico, an emaciated
ateleiotic dwarf of 26.8 in. (67 cm), weighed 2.8 lb. (1.1 kg) at birth and
only 4 lb. 11 oz. (2.13 kg) at the age of 17. She fattened up to 13 lb. (5.9 kg)
by her 20th birthday.

Most variable stature

Adam Rainer (Austria, 1899–1950) measured just 3 ft. 10.5 in. (1.18 m) at
the age of 21 but then started growing at a rapid rate. By 1931, he had nearly
doubled to 7 ft. 1.75 in. (2.18 m), but became so weak that he was bedridden

for the rest of his life. At the
time of his death, he measured
7 ft. 8 in. (2.34 m)—twice his
height at 21. He remains the
only person in history to have
been both a dwarf and a giant.

☆**HEAVIEST LIVING WOMAN
TO GIVE BIRTH** Donna
Simpson of New Jersey,
U.S.A., weighed 532 lb.
(241 kg; 38 st) when she
delivered daughter Jacqueline
in February 2007. It took a
team of up to 30 medics to
help perform the high-risk
cesarean birth. "I want this
record made public to remind
women of size that they too
may be able to bear a child,"
said Donna.

THESSALONIKI, GREECE (40°38'N 22°57'E): Made by the
Alpani Brothers factory in Thessaloniki, Greece, in 2008, the ★ **longest
leather belt** measured 206 ft. 36 in. (62.91 m).

★ **SHORTEST TEENAGERS** Jyoti Amge (India, b. December 16, 1993) measured 2 ft. (61.95 cm) on September 6, 2009, in Tokyo, Japan. The shortest male teenager is Khagendra Thapa Magar (Nepal, b. October 14, 1992), who measured 2 ft. 1.8 in. (65.58 cm) on February 25, 2010, when measured by doctors.

☆ **SHORTEST MAN** Following the death of He Pingping (China) in 2010, the title of shortest mobile man passed to Edward Niño Hernandez (Colombia, b. May 10, 1986), who measures 2 ft. 3.46 in. (70.21 cm) tall.

Edward's reign as holder of this famous category may be one of the briefest in GWR history, however. It is expected that Khagendra Thapa Magar (*see Shortest teenagers, above*) will assume the title of the world's shortest man in October 2010, upon turning 18.

EXTRA! The human body is a remarkable thing. For proof, consult medical records, pp. 128–132.

Tallest man
Ever: When Robert Pershing Wadlow (U.S.A., 1918–40) was last measured—on June 27, 1940—he was 8 ft. 11.1 in. (2.72 m) tall, the tallest height ever authenticated in medical history.
Living: *See pp. 104–106.*

Tallest woman
Ever: Zeng Jinlian (China, 1964–82) of the Bright Moon Commune, Hunan Province, China, measured 8 ft. 1.75 in. (2.48 m) on her deathbed.
Living: ☆ Yao Defen (China) recorded an average height of 7 ft. 7 in. (233.3 cm) when last documented. Evidence suggests that Defen may still be growing, as a portion of tumor remains on her pituitary gland, the organ that regulates the production of growth hormone. She is too ill to be remeasured at present.

Heaviest twins Billy Leon (1946–79) and Benny Loyd (1946–2001) McCrary, alias McGuire (both U.S.A.), were of average size until the age of six. By November 1978, however, Billy and Benny weighed 743 lb. (53 st 1 lb; 337 kg) and 723 lb. (51 st 9 lb.; 328 kg) respectively, and each had waists measuring 84 in. (2.13 m).

SKIN DEEP

Largest organ An organ is defined loosely as any part of an animal or plant that is adapted for a particular function—for example, respiration, digestion, or excretion. When it comes to the human body, the skin is the largest organ. It provides a protective covering for the body, insulates us from the cold, regulates our temperature, and protects us from infection.

☆ **Most body piercings in one session** Josh Brown and Yuri Dubon (both U.S.A.) carried out 1,200 piercings in one session lasting 2 hr. 53 min. at the Sign of the Times, Norco, California, U.S.A., on August 16, 2009.

Most tattooed senior citizens The **most tattooed female senior citizen** is 73-year-old grandmother Isobel Varley (UK). Isobel had her first tattoo—a small bird on her right shoulderblade—on August 14, 1986, after a visit to a tattoo convention in Hammersmith, London, UK. As of April 2010, she had 93% body coverage.

....

ATHENS, GREECE (37°58'N 23°43'E): The **greatest number of medals awarded at one Olympic Games** is 931 (comprising 303 golds, 301 silvers, and 327 bronzes), which were awarded at the 2004 Games held in Athens, Greece.

....

The ★ **most tattooed male senior citizen** is Tom Leppard (UK)—see opposite.

★ **Most people tattooed simultaneously** A total of 178 people were tattooed at the same time at the 5th annual London Tattoo Convention 2009, held at the Tobacco Dock in London, UK, on September 24, 2009.

☆ **MOST TATTOOED WOMAN** Julia Gnuse (U.S.A., left) has had approximately 95% of her body decorated with tattoos; her first tattoo was in 1991. She shares her ink-redible record with Krystyne Kolorful (Canada), who has taken 10 years to achieve 95% coverage.

★ **FARTHEST DISTANCE TO PULL A VEHICLE USING MEAT HOOKS** Hannibal Helmurto (Germany) pulled an 8,818-lb. (4-tonne) van a total of 351 ft. (107 m) using two meat hooks inserted through the skin in the small of his back in Edinburgh, UK, on August 13, 2007.

EXTRA! If you're a sucker for sideshow arts, don't hang around—turn to p. 155.

★ **MOST TATTOOED SENIOR CITIZEN** Former **most tattooed man** Tom Leppard (aka Tom Woodbridge, UK), has 99.9% of his body covered in a saffron-yellow and black leopard-print tattoo. The 73-year-old ex-soldier lived for 20 years in the wilds of the island of Skye in the Scottish Hebrides before finally changing his spots and moving into an assisted living facility in the Skye village of Broadford in 2008.

★ **MOST NEEDLES IN THE HEAD** Wei Shengchu (China) had 2,009 needles inserted into his head on the set of **Lo Show dei Record** in Milan, Italy, on April 11, 2009.

☆ **Longest tattoo session** Andy Kynes (UK) underwent a grueling 48-hr. 11-min. tattoo session under the needle of Lady Kaz Wilson (UK) at the Diamond Tattoo Studio in Wigan, Lancashire, UK, on November 18–21, 2009. The event was organized to raise money for UK charity Children in Need.

★ **Most tattoos by a single artist (24 hours)** Hollis Cantrell (U.S.A.) created 801 tattoos in 24 hours at Artistic Tattoo in Phoenix, Arizona, U.S.A., on November 16, 2008.

Stretchiest skin Garry Turner (UK) is able to stretch the skin of his stomach to a length of 6.25 in. (15.8 cm), thanks to a rare medical condition called Ehlers-Danlos Syndrome, a disorder of the connective tissues affecting the skin, ligaments, and internal organs. With this condition, the collagen that strengthens the skin and determines its elasticity becomes defective, resulting in, among other things, a loosening of the skin, and "hypermobility" of the joints. In more serious cases, it can cause the rupturing of blood vessels.

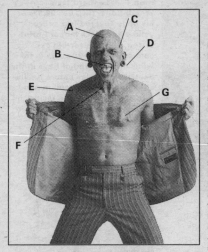

MOST TATTOOED PERSON Lucky Diamond Rich (Australia, b. NZ) has spent over 1,000 hours having an entire "body-suit" of tattoos (plus a layer of solid black) applied—coverage in excess of 200%.

A. COLORED INK Inked in red across his face and scalp is the Tibetan mantra "Om Mani Padme Hum," usually translated as "Praise to the Jewel in the Lotus."

B. METAL TEETH Gone are Lucky's original teeth, and in their place are silver fangs.

C. SCALP Lucky has gouged out three strips of skin from his scalp, revealing the skull beneath!

D. STRETCHED EARLOBES Lucky's ears are not just pierced, they're stretched and fitted with a spacer or "flesh tunnel."

E. BLACK INK An all-over "bodysuit" of black ink.

F. WHITE INK Lucky has started inking white tattoos on top of the black.

G. CHEST IMPLANTS Through his pectoral muscles, Lucky has placed two titanium rods; these will eventually be removed, creating a hollow through which he can attach weights and hooks.

> **OUCH!:** Lucky is tattooed on the eyelids, the delicate skin between the toes, and down into the ears. He even has his gums tattooed!

RIGA, LATVIA (56°56'N 24°06'E): The **most Mentos and soda fountains** created in the same place is 1,911 and was achieved by the people of Latvia and students of TURIBA in Riga, Latvia, on June 19, 2008.

First plastic surgery Walter Ernest O'Neil Yeo (UK, 1890–1960) was the first person in the world to have plastic surgery. In 1917, skin grafts were transferred from his shoulder to his face in order to replace his upper and lower eyelids. The gunnery warrant officer had lost them while manning the guns aboard HMS *Warspite* in 1916, in the Battle of Jutland, during World War I. The pioneering surgery was performed by Sir Harold Gillies (UK), regarded as the father of plastic surgery.

Most common skin infection *Tinea pedis*, usually called "athlete's foot," is the most common skin infection in humans. The fungus afflicts up to 70% of the worldwide population, and almost everyone will get it at least once in our lifetime. The infection manifests when the skin between the toes becomes soft and peels away, and it may even crack, ooze, and bleed.

ATHLETE'S FOOT

AKA *Tinea pedis*—a contagious fungal infection of the skin that afflicts most men between the ages of 20 and 40.

HAIR

★**Largest ball of human hair** Over the past 50 years, Henry Coffer (U.S.A.) has been collecting human hair and amassing a giant hairball that, as of December 8, 2008, weighs 167 lb. (75.7 kg) and measures 14 ft. (4.26 m) in circumference. Coffer, a 77-year-old barber from Charleston, Missouri, began saving hair at the request of a customer. Over the years he has been collecting, he has found many uses for his hair clippings, including patching potholes, gardening, and fertilizing soil.

Largest human hairball "Trichobezoar" is the medical name for a hairball, which occurs as a result of Rapunzel Syndrome or "trichophagia"—the eating of one's own hair (from the Greek for "hair eating"). The largest trichobezoar surgically removed from a human was a hairball weighing 10 lb. (4.5 kg) found in the stomach of an unnamed 18-year-old woman treated at Rush University Medical Center in Chicago, Illinois, U.S.A., in November 2007.

....

TALLINN, ESTONIA (59°26'N 24°44'E): Intan Pragi (Estonia) spun a roulette wheel more than 1,650 times over 48 hours during the **longest croupier marathon** at the Olympic Casino in Tallinn, Estonia, on February 18–20, 2005.

....

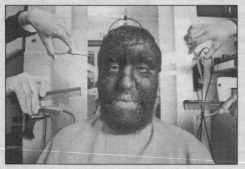

HAIRIEST FAMILY Pictured is "Chuy" Jesus Fajardo Aceves, one of a family of 19—covering five generations—from Mexico that suffers from hypertrichosis, aka "werewolf syndrome." The women are covered with a light to medium coat of hair, while the men of the family have thick hair on every inch of their body, apart from their hands and feet.

☆ **LONGEST BEARD** On March 4, 2010, Sarwan Singh's (Canada) beard was measured at 7 ft. 9 in. (2.37 m) on the set of *Lo Show dei Record* in Rome, Italy, the longest beard on a living person. The iconic Sikh—head Giani (priest) at Guru Nanak Sikh Temple in Surrey, Canada—said, "It's not a talent, like playing music. . . . It's a gift from God."

EXTRA! The human body is more amazing than you can imagine. Find out more on pp. 107–111.

★ **Most hairstyles applied (8 hours)** Rachel Brown (U.S.A.) of Salon Mimosa in Lake Park, Florida, U.S.A., styled the hair of 32 customers in eight hours on February 16, 2009. Each client had to have his/her hair washed and rinsed, and then cut, completely dried, and styled before Rachel moved on to the next client.

☆ **Most haircuts by a team (24 hours)** Ten hairdressers from Supercuts in Houston, Texas, U.S.A., cut 349 heads of hair on October 10, 2009.

Most expensive haircut An Italian customer of the Stuart Phillips Salon in Covent Garden, London, UK, paid £8,000 ($16,420) on October 29, 2007, for a luxury haircut.

★ **Most hair dyed (24 hours)** Ten hairdressers and their assistants from Schwarzkopf & Sergio & Margarida Hair Salon in Lisbon, Portugal, dyed 380 heads of hair in 24 hours on October 21, 2009.

LONGEST BEARD (FEMALE) Melinda Maxie—the stage name of Vivian Elaine Wheeler (U.S.A.)—has a beard that, when last measured in 2000, had a maximum length of 11 in. (27.9 cm). "A sideshow wouldn't be a sideshow without the bearded lady," said Melinda, who has been in and out of circuses since the age of 8.

DID YOU KNOW?

The Sikh faith opposes the cutting of facial hair, so Sarwan Singh has never shaved in his life. "My beard is my favorite body part."

TRIVIA

In 2001, Ismael Rivas Falcon (Spain) pulled a train weighing 6,069 lb. (2,753.1 kg) with his beard.

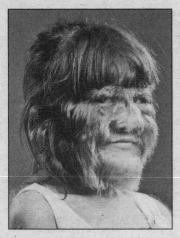

★ **HAIRIEST TEENAGE GIRL** The most hirsute female teen—according to the Ferriman-Gallwey method—is Supatra "Nat" Sasuphan (Thailand). She was assessed on the set of *Lo Show dei Record* in Rome, Italy, on March 4, 2010. The Ferriman-Gallwey score is a method of quantifying hirsutism (hairiness) in women.

LONGEST HAIR The world's longest documented hair belongs to Xie Qiuping (China), at 18 ft. 5.54 in. (5.627 m) when measured on May 8, 2004. She has been growing her hair since 1973, from the age of 13. "It's no trouble at all. I'm used to it," she said. "But you need patience and you need to hold yourself straight when you have hair like this."

QUIZ!: Which of these measures the most: the longest beard, the longest mustache, or the highest hairstyle? See p. 543 for the answer.

☆**Highest hairstyle** A hairdo measuring 8 ft. 8 in. (2.66 m) high was created by several hairdressers in an event organized by KLIPP unser Frisör in Wels, Austria, on June 21, 2009.

☆**Tallest wig** An enormous wig of human hair was made by Emilio Minnicelli (Italy) and modeled in the main square of the Bologna Piazza Maggiore in Italy on May 15, 2004. It measured 46 ft. 11 in. (14.3 m) tall and weighed 57 lb. (26 kg).

☆**Tallest mohican** The tallest mohawk measures 31.5 in. (80 cm) and belongs to Stefan Srocka (Germany). The length was verified at Hairgallery Daniela Schorn in Marktrodach, Germany, on June 2, 2009.

☆**Longest female dread-locks** The dreadlocks of Asha Mandela (U.S.A.) reached a record 19 ft. 6.5 in. (5.96 m) when professionally unknotted and measured on CBS's *The Early Show* in New York City, U.S.A., on November 11, 2009, for GWR Day.

☆**Longest extensions** A hair extension piece of 53 ft. 10 in. (16.25 m) in length was applied by Kay Meinecke (Germany) to the hair of a model at a shopping mall in Hamburg, Germany, on November 10, 2007.

☆**Longest mustache** Ram Singh Chauhan (India) has a mustache that measured 14 ft. (4.29 m) on the set of *Lo Show dei Record* in Rome, Italy, on March 4, 2010.

LONGEST HAIRS
☆**Arm:** 5.75 in. (14.61 cm), Justin Shaw (U.S.A.), October 7, 2009.
Chest: 9 in. (22.8 cm), Richard Condo (U.S.A.), April 29, 2007.
Ear: 7.12 in. (18.1 cm), Anthony Victor (India), September 17, 2007.
Eyebrow: 7.01 in. (17.8 cm), Toshie Kawakami (Japan), July 22, 2008.
Eyelash: 2.75 in. (6.99 cm), Stuart Muller (U.S.A.), December 7, 2007.
Leg: 6.5 in. (16.51 cm), Wesley Pemberton (U.S.A.), February 9, 2008.
Nipple: 5.07 in. (12.9 cm), Douglas Williams (U.S.A.), May 26, 2007.

....

HELSINKI, FINLAND (60°10'N 24°56'E): As of June 19, 2008, Seppo Mäkinen (Finland) had amassed 30,105 different badges from more than 50 countries, the **largest collection of badges**. He began his record-breaking collection in 1994.

....

GOLDEN OLDIES

Oldest living . . .

☆ **Person** (and ☆ **woman**): Eugénie Blanchard, who lives on the French-owned island of St. Barthélemy in the Caribbean, was born on February 16, 1896, and became the world's oldest human at the age of 114 years old 75 days; *see table right for the top 10 oldest living people as of May 11, 2010.*

☆ **Man:** Walter Breuning (U.S.A.). *See p. 126.*

☆ **Twin:** The oldest living single twin is 110-year-old Ruth Peter Anderson (U.S.A., b. July 24, 1899). Her fraternal twin, Abel, died in 1900 at the age of one year. *To our knowledge, no pair of twins has ever reached supercentenarian status (over 110).*

Twins: As we go to press, Guinness World Records is attempting to identify the holders of the record for the **oldest identical twins**. Widespread media coverage has been devoted to the claim of Cao Daqiao and Cao Xiaoqiao (China, b. October 3, 1905), said to be 104 years old, though GWR is still to secure documentary evidence confirming this age. The twins live in Weifang in east China's Shandong Province.

Conjoined twins: Ronnie and Donnie Galyon (U.S.A., b. October 25, 1951) are the oldest living conjoined twins. For 36 years, they traveled in circuses, but retired in 1991. They share a passport but can cast two votes.

Married couple (aggregate age): Karl Dølven (Norway, b. August 31, 1897) married Gudrun Haug (Norway, b. October 14, 1900) on June 4, 1927. They were married until Gudrun's death on April 24, 2004, when she was 103 years 193 days and Karl was 106 years 237 days—an aggregate age of 210 years 65 days.

The ☆ **longest marriage** is currently 86 years for Herbert and Zelmyra Fisher. For more on this record-breaking couple, see p. 208.

DID YOU KNOW?

On February 20, 2010, there were 76 people confirmed and authenticated as being over the age of 110. Of these, only three were men!

TRIVIA

The chance of you living to 128 years old is about 1 in 2,560,000,000,000 (that's 1 in 2.56 trillion)!

BUCHAREST, ROMANIA (44°26'N 26°06'E): The Palace of the Parliament in Bucharest, Romania, is the **heaviest building**, constructed from 1.5 billion lb. (700,000 tonnes) of steel and bronze with 35 million ft.^{3} (1 million m^3) of marble, 7.7 million lb. (3,500 tonnes) of crystal glass, and 31.7 million ft.^{3} (900,000 m^3) of wood.

	NAME	AGE	DATE OF BIRTH
1	*Eugénie Blanchard (St. Barts/France)*	114	Feb 16, 1896
2	*Eunice Sanborn (U.S.A.)*	113	Jul 20, 1896
3	*Besse Cooper (U.S.A.)*	113	Aug 26, 1896
4	*Walter Breuning (U.S.A.) **m***	113	Sep 21, 1896
5	*Chiyono Hasegawa (Japan)*	113	Nov 20, 1896
6	*Venere Pizzinato-Papo (Italy)*	113	Nov 23, 1896
7	*Shige Hirooka (Japan)*	113	Jan 16, 1897
8	*Mississippi Winn (U.S.A.)*	113	Mar 31, 1897
9	*Dina Manfredini (U.S.A.)*	113	Apr 4, 1897
10	*Mineno Yamamoto (Japan)*	113	Apr 8, 1897

Source: Gerontology Research Group, extracted May 11, 2010   *m* = male

★LONGEST WORKING ICE-CREAM SELLER Charlie D'Angelo
(b. September 26, 1919) of Clifton, New Jersey, U.S.A., has been
working as an ice-cream man nonstop for 30 years, delivering
confections from his Iggy's Igloo ice-cream truck since 1979. He has
worked in the ice-cream trade intermittently since the age of 12!

★OLDEST SIBLINGS With a
combined age of 325 years
289 days, the Thornton sisters
of Shreveport, Louisiana,
U.S.A., are the oldest ever
siblings. All three passed away
within a few weeks of each
other: Rosie Thornton Warren
(left) on December 18, 2009;
Carrie Thornton Miller (right)
on January 5, 2010; and Maggie
Lee Thornton Renfro (pictured
middle) on January 22, 2010.

YOGA: Grandmother Bette has taught yoga for 40 years. Here she is pictured in the (demanding) peacock position!

★ **OLDEST FEMALE YOGA TEACHER** At 83 years old, Australia's Bette Calman is the oldest woman to teach the Indian mental and physical discipline of yoga.

☆ **OLDEST LIVING MAN** On the death of Henry Allingham (UK, 1896–2009), the title of oldest living man passed to 113-year-old Walter Breuning (b. September 21, 1896, left) of Great Falls, Montana, U.S.A. At his last birthday, he became only the 12th man in history verified to reach 113 or older.

DAME: The **oldest person**—and **oldest woman**—whose age has been authenticated was Jeanne Calment (France), who died at age 122 years.

EXTRA! Not old enough for you? Shuffle on over to Dinosaurs on pp. 53–59.

★ **OLDEST SALSA DANCER** In December 2009, salsa dancer Sarah Paddy Jones (UK, born July 1, 1935) and her partner, Nicko, took first prize on the Spanish TV talent show *Tu Si Que Vales*.

GAMES: The World Masters Games are the ★ **largest participatory multi-sport event** on the planet. The 2002 games attracted a record 24,886 athletes.

★ **OLDEST FEMALE TRACK AND FIELD RECORD HOLDER** On October 11, 2009, 100-year-old Ruth Frith (Australia) threw a record 13-ft. 4-in. (4.07-m) shot put in the over-100s category at the World Masters Games in Sydney, Australia. The Games are open to athletes of all abilities.

EDIRNE, TURKEY (41°40'N 26°34'E): The world's **oldest continuously sanctioned sporting competition** is the Kırkpınar Oil Wrestling Festival, which has been held since 1460. The event is currently staged on the Sarayiçi Peninsula near Edirne, Turkey.

☆**Oldest man ever** New evidence has come to light that casts doubt on the long-standing longevity record held by Shigechiyo Izumi (Japan). The birth certificate submitted as evidence might actually belong to his older brother, who died at a young age; if the family used Izumi as a "necronym"—that is, gave him his dead brother's name, as the new research suggests—this means his final age was 105 years old, not 120.

The title of oldest man ever, then, passes to Thomas Peter Thorvald Kristian Ferdinand "Christian" Mortensen (Denmark/U.S.A., August 16, 1882–April 25, 1998), who died at the age of 115 years 252 days—the only Nordic person to live beyond the age of 113.

★**Oldest Michelin three-star chef** Jiro Ono (Japan, b. October 27, 1925), owner of the Sukiyabashi Jiro sushi restaurant in Tokyo, Japan, was first acknowledged as a three-star chef in the *Michelin Guide Tokyo 2008* when he was 82.

MEDICAL RECORDS

★**Most eye tests carried out in an hour** Volunteers from Specsavers International BV conducted a total of 648 eye tests in 92 locations throughout the Netherlands on May 15, 2009.

Largest tummy tuck operation performed on a woman Plastic surgeons at the Hospital de Cruces in Barakaldo, Spain, removed an "apron" of fat weighing 132 lb. (60 kg) from a morbidly obese woman in March 2006. During the nine-hour operation, surgeons needed small cranes to help support the fat and skin removed from her stomach. The weight removed is similar to that of an average 17-year-old girl, and had an energy content of 462,000 calories.

> *"We chose him because he is tenacious, motivated, and persistent."*
> **Arm transplant surgeon Dr Jean-Michel Dubernard on his patient,**
> **Denis Chatelier (see page 129)**

IZMIR, TURKEY (38°25'N 27°08'E): The world's **oldest datable bridge** still in use is the slab-stone single-arch bridge over the River Meles in Izmir (formerly Smyrna), Turkey, which dates from *c.* 850 B.C. Remnants of Mycenaean bridges dated *c.* 1600 B.C. exist in the neighborhood of Mycenae, Greece, over the River Havos.

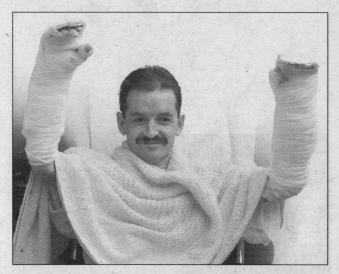

★FIRST DOUBLE ARM TRANSPLANT In January 2000, an international team of 18 surgeons and 32 support staff led by Professor Jean-Michel Dubernard (France) made history by performing the first double arm transplant. The recipient—Denis Chatelier, a 33-year-old French explosives worker (pictured) who had lost his arms in an accident four years previously—received the forearms of an 18-year-old cadaveric donor.

The procedure took 17 hours to complete and was performed at the Edouard-Herriot Hospital in Lyon, France. Dubernard had previously performed the **first arm transplant** back in 1998.

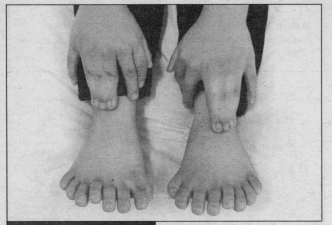

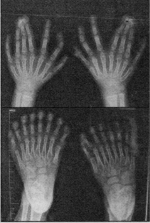

☆ **MOST FINGERS AND TOES** On March 19, 2010, an anonymous six-year-old boy was admitted to a hospital in Shenyang, Liaoning Province, China, with 31 fingers and toes (15 fingers and 16 toes). Three fingers on each hand are fused; however, x-rays show each finger had full skeletal development.

★ **Longest-living Hydrocephalic** The medical condition hydrocephalus is marked by excess cerebrospinal fluid in the skull, which puts pressure on the brain, often harming it. The most common treatment is a "shunt," a technique developed in 1952 that uses tubing inserted into the skull to carry the excess fluid safely to another part of the body. In 1985, the death rate for sufferers was 52%, making the case of Theresa Alvina Schaan (Canada, b. March 17, 1941) all the more striking. As of August 7, 2009, she's been living with the condition for 68 years 143 days.

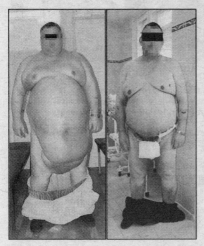

☆ **LARGEST TUMMY TUCK** According to Russian news website www.life.ru, in early 2010 a 49-year-old man known only as Petr F (pictured at left, before and after) underwent a three-hour operation to remove 264 lb. (120 kg) of fat and skin in Voronezh, Russia. Prior to the operation, Petr weighed 529 lb. (240 kg), but his inability to walk for prolonged periods drove him to seek medical help.

★ **Longest-surviving multi-organ transplant patient** Mark Dolby (UK) received a heart-lung-liver transplant on August 21, 1987, and a kidney transplant in December 2005, all at Harefield Hospital, London, UK. As of April 22, 2009, he had survived 21 years 244 days as a multi-organ transplantee.

Least blood transfused in a transplant operation In June 1996, a team from St. James University Hospital, Leeds, UK, performed a liver transplant on 47-year-old housewife Linda Pearson (U.S.A.) without any blood being transfused. Such an operation usually requires 4–6 pints (2.3–3.4 liters) of blood, but as a Jehovah's Witness Mrs. Pearson chose to refuse the transfusion on religious grounds.

VARNA, BULGARIA (43°13'N 27°55'E): The **largest legal document** is an insurance policy measuring 29 ft. 4 in. x 19 ft. 8 in. (9 x 6 m), issued by ING Asigurari de Viata (Romania) and signed in Varna, Bulgaria, on March 15, 2008.

EXTRA! For the lowdown on some bizarrely big body parts, go to p. 107.

JAN 2004   FEB 2004   AUG 2004   JAN 2007   OCT 2007

HIGHEST PERCENTAGE OF BURNS TO THE BODY
- Tony Yarijanian (U.S.A., above) underwent 25 surgeries after suffering burns to 90% of his body in an explosion at his wife's beauty spa on February 15, 2004.
- David Chapman (UK) also survived 90% burns after an accident with a gasoline canister on July 2, 1996.

Most hand amputations on the same arm Clint Hallam (New Zealand) has had his right hand amputated a total of three times. He first lost his hand in 1984 after an accident with a circular saw. Surgeons managed to reattach the severed limb, but an infection developed and it was removed in 1988. In September 1998, doctors gave him a hand transplant, but Clint later requested that it be amputated.

Youngest multi-organ transplant patient Sarah Marshall (Canada, b. February 14, 1997) became the youngest patient to receive a multi-organ transplant when, on August 7, 1997, she was given a liver, a bowel, a stomach, and a pancreas at the Children's Hospital in London, Western Ontario, Canada.

SUPER STUNTS

CONTENTS

STUNTS

☆ **MOST GUINNESS WORLD RECORDS HELD** Since 1979, Ashrita Furman of Queens, New York City, U.S.A., has set or broken 259 official Guinness World Records, and at the time of going to press currently holds 100 records. Why is Ashrita—born Keith, but given the Sanskrit name Ashrita, meaning "protected by God," by his meditation teacher Sri Chinmoy—so passionate about record breaking? "I'm trying to show others that our human capacity is unlimited if we can truly believe in ourselves."

(SOME OF) ASHRITA'S ACHIEVEMENTS

1. Fastest 100-m egg-and-spoon race (19.90 seconds)
2. Fastest mile balancing a baseball bat on the finger (7 min. 5 sec.)
3. Fastest 1-mile sack race (16 min. 41 sec.)
4. Longest balance board duration (1 hr. 49 min. 5 sec.)
5. Longest duration on an exercise ball (3 hr. 38 min. 30 sec.)
6. Fastest 1-mile fireman's carry (15 min. 11.87 sec.)
7. Fastest 10-km hula hooping (1 hr. 25 min. 9 sec.)
8. Fastest mile on a pogo stick while juggling balls (23 min. 28 sec.)
9. Fastest 1-mile piggyback race (13 min. 1 sec.)
10. Longest table-tennis-bat-and-ball duration (3 hr. 7 sec.)
11. Fastest mile on spring-loaded stilts (7 min. 13 sec.)
12. Fastest mile on a space hopper (15 min. 3 sec.)
13. Greatest distance traveled with a cue stick balanced on the chin (5,472 ft.; 1,668 m)
14. Most star jumps in 1 minute (61)

WHEELED WONDERS

Most automobiles driven on two wheels simultaneously On November 26, 2000, a team of Renault drivers drove 16 automobiles on two wheels simultaneously, in a continuous line, at Evreux, France, for the TV show *L'Émission des Records*.

★**Longest vehicle drift** Driving a 2010 Ford Mustang GT, Vaughn Gittin Jr. (U.S.A.) pulled off a drift of 6,280 ft. (1,914.15 m) at the Speedway in Las Vegas, U.S.A., on December 18, 2008.

★**Longest UTV ramp jump** Junior Quisquis (U.S.A.) performed a jump of 47 ft. 8 in. (14.53 m) in a utility terrain vehicle (UTV) in Pauma Valley, California, U.S.A., on October 31, 2009.

Fastest speed dragged behind a motorcycle Gary Rothwell of Liverpool, UK, was dragged behind a motorcycle at 156.3 mph (251.54 km/h) on 0.07-in. (2-mm) titanium-soled boots at Bruntingthorpe Proving Ground, Leicester, UK, on April 18, 1999.

Most motorcyclists in a globe of death On November 2, 1999, a team of five motorcyclists rode their vehicles around a person placed at the center of a 14-ft.-3-in.-diameter (4.33-m) steel sphere. The daredevil feat

★**HIGHEST AIR ON A MOTORCYCLE (QUARTER PIPE)** Ronnie Renner (U.S.A.) achieved a 35-ft. 4-in. (10.77-m) air—launching himself into the air off a quarter pipe— on a motorcycle (see left) during the Red Bull High Rise in Grant Park at Butler Field in Chicago, Illinois, U.S.A., on July 25, 2009.

took place at The Riviera Hotel, Versailles Theater, Las Vegas, Nevada, U.S.A., by a team led by Bela Tabak and featuring Gary Lurent, Humberto Fonseca Pinto, Kurtis Kunz, and Humberto H. Fonseca Pinto Jr. (all U.S.A.). Bela's wife, Robin, was the person in the middle!

Wall of death—endurance Martin Blume (Germany) performed on a "wall of death" for 7 hr. 13 sec. in Berlin, Germany, on April 16, 1983. He rode a Yamaha XS 400 for 12,000 laps on a wall with a diameter of 33 ft. (10 m), averaging 30 mph (48 km/h) over 181 miles 880 yd (292 km).

★LONGEST CABLE WALK The longest walk on a cable-car cable is 3,624 ft. (995 m)—the length of 14 jumbo jets—by Freddy Nock (Switzerland) at Zugspitze, near Garmisch-Partenkirchen, Germany, on August 30, 2009. The cable thickness was 1.96 in. (50 mm), and the height difference was 1,141 ft. (348 m) at the lowest point to 8,202 ft. (2,500 m) above sea level at the highest!

JOHANNESBURG, SOUTH AFRICA (26°12'S 28°02'E): Vic Toweel (South Africa) knocked down Danny O'Sullivan (UK) 14 times in 10 rounds in their world bantamweight fight at Johannesburg, South Africa, on December 2, 1950, before the latter retired. You can hardly blame O'Sullivan for retiring—he'd just suffered the **most knockdowns in a boxing match**.

☆**Most donuts in one minute** Emilio Zamora (Spain) achieved 24 donut (360°) spins on a motorbike in Cheste, Valencia, Spain, on November 6, 2009. This event took place during the 2009 World Grand Prix motorcycle championships.

☆**Most gyrator spins on a bmx bike (one minute)** Jason Plourde (Canada) performed 39 gyrator (360°) spins in a minute on the set of *Zheng Da Zong Yi—Guinness World Records Special* in Beijing, China, on November 22, 2009.

☆**LONGEST DISTANCE COVERED BY AN AUTOMOBILE DRIVEN ON TWO SIDE WHEELS** Michele Pilia (Italy) drove his automobile for 230.57 miles (371.06 km) using only two side wheels at Sant'Elia Stadium in Cagliari, Italy, on February 26, 2009.

TIP THE BALANCE

Michele uses a ramp to get the automobile up onto its side. He then uses his body weight to maintain the automobile's balance.

ISTANBUL, TURKEY (41°0'N 28°58'E): Ilker Yilmaz (Turkey) squirted milk from his eye a distance of 9 ft. 2 in. (279.5 cm) at the Armada Hotel, Istanbul, Turkey, on September 1, 2004, the **farthest distance to squirt milk from the eye.**

☆**MOST BARS JUMPED ON THE BACK WHEEL OF A TRIAL BIKE** Benito Ros Charral (Spain) successfully jumped 48 gapping bars on the back wheel of a trial bike on the set of *Lo Show Dei Record* in Milan, Italy, on April 19, 2009.

MISCELLANY

★**Fastest time to escape from three pairs of handcuffs underwater** Matthew "Matt the Knife" Cassiere (U.S.A.) escaped from three pairs of handcuffs while underwater in 44 seconds on the set of *Zheng Da Zong Yi—Guinness World Records Special* in Beijing, China, on December 17, 2006. (For more escapology, see pp. 155–156.)

★ **Most repeated backward flips on spring-loaded stilts** Yuan Shi-wei (China) made 25 consecutive backward flips on spring-loaded stilts in Dengfeng city, Henan Province, China, on September 17, 2008.

Highest altitude reached using helium-filled toy balloons Mike Howard (UK) and Steve Davis (U.S.A.) ascended to a height of 18,300 ft. (5,580 m) by means of 1,400 helium-filled latex toy balloons near Albuquerque, New Mexico, U.S.A., on August 4, 2001.

Greatest distance flown in a wing suit Adrian Nicholas (UK) flew 10 miles (16 km) in a wing suit over Yolo County, California, U.S.A., on March 12, 1999. Exiting the airplane at 33,850 ft. (10,317 m), he reached speeds of up to 150 mph (241 km/h) and "flew" for 4 min. 55 sec.

☆ **Oldest wing walker** Thomas Lackey (UK) made a wing walk across the English Channel at age 89 years 33 days on July 25, 2009.

ST. PETERSBURG, RUSSIA (59°56'N 30°20'E): The city of St. Petersburg, Russia, has the **most extensive streetcar system**, with approximately 2,400 cars running on its routes and more than 430 miles (690 km) of track.

☆ **HEAVIEST AIRCRAFT PULLED BY AN INDIVIDUAL** Revd. Kevin Fast (Canada) pulled a CC-177 Globemaster III, weighing 416,299 lb. (188.83 tonnes), a distance of 28 ft. 10 in. (8.8 m) on September 17, 2009.

★ **Highest bungee jump restrained with the hands** On September 28, 2008, Patrick Schurf (Austria) performed a bungee jump measuring 203 ft. 4 in. (61.99 m). He was secured only to strongman Frank Müllner (Austria), who held the bungee cord by hand!

☆ **Fastest time to run through ten locked doors** Vennessa Mayer, aka Lady Fairy Floss (Australia), successfully ran through 10 locked doors in a time of 17.32 seconds on January 10, 2010. The record attempt took place on the set of *Australia Smashes Guinness World Records* in Sydney, New South Wales, Australia.

....

CAIRO, EGYPT (30°03'N 31°13'E): A raised obelisk at Heliopolis, near Cairo, Egypt, has remained in place since it was erected *c.*1750 B.C. by Senusret I to mark 30 years of his rule. It is the **oldest obelisk to remain in situ**.

....

STRENGTH & BALANCE

STRENGTH

★**Fastest ice climber** Pavel Gulyaev (Russia) climbed a 49-ft.-high (15-m) vertical ice wall in a record time of 8.748 seconds at the Ice Climbing World Cup held in Bustemi, Romania, on February 8, 2009.

☆**Heaviest vehicle pulled by the hair** He Jianma (China) pulled a bus weighing 18,254 lb. (8,280 kg), attached to his hair, for a distance of 98 ft. (30 m) in You County, Hunan Province, China, on May 25, 2009.

★**Longest time to restrain a vehicle on an incline** Using a chain attached to a handle, Ervin Katona (Serbia) restrained an automobile weighing 2,160 lb. (980 kg) while resting on a 45° incline for 1 min. 2 sec. in Milan, Italy, on April 25, 2009.

★**Most telephone directories torn behind the back in three minutes (male)** Alexander Muromskiy (Russia) tore a total of six telephone directories (each 1,048 pages thick) behind his back in three minutes at the Moscow Center of Martial Arts in Moscow, Russia, on October 17, 2009.

★**Most one-finger push-ups in 30 seconds** Fu Bing Li (China) managed 25 one-finger push-ups in 30 seconds in Beijing, China, on November 23, 2009.

★ **GREATEST WEIGHT SUPPORTED WHILE SKIPPING A ROPE The** heaviest weight supported while simultaneously skipping a rope 10 times is 394 lb. 10 oz. (179 kg), by James Brewster Thompson (U.S.A.) in Milan, Italy, on April 18, 2009.

EXTRA! For some truly breathtaking stunts, backflip to page 136.

★ **LONGEST DURATION BALANCING ON FOUR FINGERS** On November 9, 2008, Wang Weibao (China) managed to balance his entire body weight on just four fingers for a painful 19.23 seconds. He achieved his fantastic finger feat in Beijing, China.

☆ **Farthest throw of a person** Jonathan Macfarlane threw Andrew Rainford (both New Zealand) 15 ft. 11 in. (4.87 m) in Auckland, New Zealand, on July 25, 2009.

★ **Heaviest road vehicle pulled by teeth** Georges Christen (Luxembourg) pulled a bus weighing 19,982 lb. (9,064 kg) using just his teeth in Beijing, China, on November 18, 2009.

☆ **Fastest car push over one mile** On June 12, 2009, Mario Mlinaric (Croatia) pushed a 4,144-lb. 11-oz. (1,880-kg) automobile 1 mile (1.6 km) in a time of 15 min. 21 sec. in Zagreb, Croatia.

☆ **Heaviest weight lifted by the ear** Using only one ear, Zafar Gill (Pakistan) lifted a weight of 160 lb. 15 oz. (73 kg) in Lahore, Pakistan, on January 3, 2009. Zafar lifted gym weights, which hung from a clamp that was attached to his right ear.

BALANCE

★ **Longest time to balance a tire on the teeth** Frank Simon (U.S.A.) held a 110-lb. (50-kg) tire on his teeth for 31 seconds in Beijing, China, on June 21, 2009.

★ **Longest time to balance a lawn mower on the chin** On October 31, 2009, Preacher Muaddib (UK) balanced a 16-lb. 4-oz. (7.4-kg) lawn mower on his chin for 1 min. 11 sec. at the Spa Theatre, Whitby, UK.

....

LUXOR, EGYPT (25°41'N 32°39'E): The **earliest known example of an alphabet**—i.e., a writing system in which a number of symbols are used to represent single sounds rather than concepts—dates back to around 1,900 B.C. and was found in Wadi el Hol near Luxor, Egypt.

....

★ **FASTEST 20 M CARRYING 300 KG ON THE SHOULDERS** Agris Kazelniks (Latvia) covered a distance of 65 ft. 7 in. (20 m) carrying 661 lb. 5 oz. (300 kg) on his shoulders in a time of 11.4 seconds on the set of *Lo Show dei Record* in Milan, Italy, on April 18, 2009.

★ **Most knee bends on a Swiss ball in one hour** Balancing for one hour on an exercise ball, Stephen Buttler (UK) managed 1,716 knee bends at Hope House, Shropshire, UK, on November 12, 2009.

★ **Farthest distance traveled with a soccer ball balanced on the head** Yee Ming Low (Malaysia) covered 6.915 miles (11.129 km) with a soccer ball balanced on his head in Selangor, Malaysia, on August 21, 2009.

★ **Heaviest weight balanced on feet** On November 20, 2009, Li Chunying (China) balanced 573 lb. (260 kg) on his feet in Beijing, China.

☆ **Longest hold of the "human scale"** Scott Fidgett and Cole Armitage (both UK) maintained the punishing "human scale" acrobalance position for an incredible 50.13 sec., on the set of *Lo Show dei Record* in Rome, Italy, on April 1, 2010.

★ **MOST PEOPLE TO BE LIFTED AND THROWN IN TWO MINUTES (FEMALE)** Aneta Florczyk (Poland) picked up and threw 12 people in two minutes in Madrid, Spain, on December 19, 2008.

MARINELLI

The Marinelli bend is named after contortionist and theatrical agent H. B. Marinelli (1864–1924).

★**LONGEST TIME TO HOLD THE MARINELLI BEND POSITION** The longest duration to maintain a Marinelli bend—a back bend in which the weight of the body is supported only by the teeth—is 50 seconds, set by Iona Oyungerel Luvsandorj (Mongolia) in Milan, Italy, on April 18, 2009.

ARGH!: "It's not painful—if it was I wouldn't be here now. But there are very few people that can do it." —Iona

UNIQUE!: Iona claims to be the only person in the UK who can perform the Marinelli bend.

☆ **GREATEST WEIGHT LIFTED WITH THE TONGUE** Thomas Blackthorne (UK) attached a weight of 27 lb. 8.96 oz. (12.5 kg) to a hook that pierced his tongue on the set of *El Show Olimpico* in Mexico City, Mexico, on August 1, 2008.

★ **Most dance spins by a couple (one minute)** Lisa Anscomb-Smith and Giles Eadle (both UK) performed 125 dance spins in a minute at the Great British Salsa Experience in Manchester, UK, on November 22, 2008.

☆ **Most revolutions with head and feet on ground (one minute)** Zhang Disheng (China) executed 52 body revolutions with head and feet on the ground on the set of *Lo Show dei Record* in Rome, Italy, on February 25, 2010.

☆ **Most horizontal bar backward spins (one minute)** Wang Jue (China) achieved 164 spins on the set of *Lo Show dei Record* in Rome, Italy, on February 25, 2010.

★ **Longest human scale** Scott Fidgett and Cole Armitage (both UK) held the acrobalance position for 48.17 seconds in London, UK, on April 21, 2009.

TEL AVIV, ISRAEL (32°04'N 34°47'E): The **longest period of active service reported for a guide dog** is 14 years 8 months (August 1972–March 1987), by a Labrador retriever bitch named Cindi-Cleo, owned by Aron Barr of Tel Aviv, Israel.

PARTY TRICKS

☆**Most cartwheels in a minute** Marcio Barbosa (Brazil) managed 55 cartwheels in one minute at the Arpoador beach in Rio de Janeiro, Brazil, on February 6, 2009.

★**Longest burp** The lengthiest burp lasted 1 min. 13 sec., and was achieved by Michele Forgione (Italy) at the 13th annual Hard Rock Beer festival "Ruttosound" competition held in Reggiolo, Italy, on June 16, 2009.

★**Most balloons blown up in an hour (individual)** The greatest number of balloons blown up in an hour by an individual is 320 by Felipe Nascimento (Brazil) at Animasom Store, Leblon Shopping, Rio de Janeiro, Brazil, on February 4, 2009.

☆**Fastest hot water bottle burst** The fastest time to blow up a standard hot water bottle until it bursts is 18.81 seconds, a record set by Shaun Jones (UK) in London, UK, on November 3, 2009.

ERUCTATION

The expulsion of air from the stomach through the mouth, better known as "burping."

☆ **LOUDEST BURP (MALE)** Paul Hunn (UK) unleashed a burp of 109.9 dB at Butlins, Bognor Regis, UK, on August 23, 2009. The ☆ **loudest burp by a female** is 107.0 dB, by Elisa Cagnoni (Italy) at the 13th annual Hard Rock Beer festival "Ruttosound" competition in Reggiolo, Italy, on June 16, 2009.

WINDY: Paul practices his strange talent by drinking copious amounts of fizzy drinks and allowing the gas to build up in his stomach!

☆ **MOST STRAWS IN THE MOUTH** Mega-mouthed Simon Elmore (Germany) held 400 straws in his mouth for a regulation 10 seconds in Sollhuben, Bavaria, Germany, on August 6, 2009.

★ **MOST BALLOONS INFLATED BY THE NOSE IN THREE MINUTES** Andrew Dahl (U.S.A.) inflated 23 balloons using only his nose in three minutes on the set of *Lo Show dei Record* in Rome, Italy, on March 18, 2010.

BLOW OUT: Andrew can inflate two balloons—one by each nostril—at the same time.

DID YOU KNOW?

Andrew also holds the record for the most balloons inflated by the nose in one hour: 308 in New York, U.S.A., on September 16, 2008.

TRIVIA

Andrew found he could blow up balloons with his nose when he was seven years old and bored on a long automobile journey.

"It all started at school, it just went from there. I never grew up."
Loudest burper Paul Hunn talks about his emerging talent

QUIZ!: Anssi Vanhala solved a rubik's cube in 36.77 seconds using which body part? See p. 543 for the answer.

☆**MOST KICKS TO THE HEAD IN ONE MINUTE** Nick Gatelein (U.S.A., left) matched Cody Warden's (U.S.A.) record of 77 kicks to the head while visiting X Games 15 in Los Angeles, California, U.S.A., on August 2, 2009.

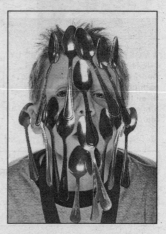

☆**MOST SPOONS BALANCED ON THE FACE** The greatest number of spoons balanced on the face is 17, achieved by Aaron Caissie (Canada) on the set of *Lo Show dei Record* in Milan, Italy, on April 18, 2009.

☆**Most Maltesers thrown and caught with the mouth (one minute)** Bipin Larkin (U.S.A.) threw 59 Maltesers (chocolate malt balls) across a distance of 15 ft. (4.5 m) into the mouth of catcher Ashrita Furman (U.S.A.) in a minute in New York City, U.S.A., on August 22, 2009.

☆**Most rope jumps (one minute)** Beci Dale (UK) performed 332 rope jumps in one minute at Pinewood Studios, UK, on April 4, 2009.

....

HAIFA, ISRAEL (32°49'N 34°59'E): The **shortest operating subway (metro) system** is the Carmelit in Haifa, Israel. Opened in 1959, the Carmelit is just 1 mile 626 ft. (1,800 m) long. The only subway in the country, it starts at Paris Square and finishes at Carmel Central, and has a total of six stations.

....

☆ **MOST TENNIS BALLS HELD IN THE HAND** The greatest number of tennis balls held in one hand is 21, achieved by Rohit Timilsina (Nepal) for 14.32 seconds in Kathmandu, Nepal, on June 14, 2008.

★ **Most CDs flipped and caught (one minute)** Mohammad Rohail Riaz (Pakistan) successfully flipped and caught 58 CDs in one minute in Dubai, UAE, on February 21, 2009.

★ **Most grapes caught in the mouth (three minutes)** Ashrita Furman (U.S.A.) successfully caught a total of 182 grapes in his mouth from a distance of 15 ft. (4.5 m) at the Grand National Park, Arizona, U.S.A., on July 10, 2009.

☆ **Most rubber bands stretched over the face** On September 20, 2009, at the Sylvia Park shopping mall in Auckland, New Zealand, Shay Horay (New Zealand) managed to stretch 71 regular elastic bands over his face on the set of *NZ Smashes Guinness World Records*.

★ **Fastest time to duct-tape oneself to a wall** Ashrita Furman (U.S.A.)—aka Mr. Versatility—stuck himself to a wall with duct tape in 6 min. 32.87 sec. in New York City, U.S.A., on September 19, 2009.

★ **Most bras worn and removed in one minute** Model Rosie Jones (UK) was able to put on and fully remove a bra seven times in a minute at the offices of *The Sun* newspaper in London, UK, on November 9, 2009.

☆ **Fastest time to solve a Rubik's Cube**
• Hai Yan Zhuang (China) solved a Rubik's cube while blindfolded in just 30.90 seconds in Xi'an, China, on April 4, 2010.
• On November 7, 2009, at Kose in Estonia, Anssi Vanhala (Finland) solved a cube using his feet in 36.72 seconds.

EXTRA! For some super-talented circus acts, turn to pp. 158–163.

JERUSALEM, ISRAEL (31°47'N 35°13'E): The world's **largest mezuzah parchment** measured 37 in. (94 cm) long and 30 in. (76 cm) wide and its container measured 43.3 in. (110 cm) long on May 19, 2004. It was scribed by Avraham-Hersh Borshevsky of Jerusalem, Israel.

URBAN ARTS

★**Most backflips against a wall in one minute** Miguel Marquez (Spain) made 29 backflips against a wall in a minute on the set of *Zheng Da Zong Yi—Guinness World Records Special* in Beijing, China, on June 19, 2009.

★**Most double Dutch skips in one minute** The greatest number of double Dutch skipping jumps carried out in 60 seconds is 202. It was set by Nobuyoshi Ando (Japan) at DoubleDutch Harbor Festival 09GW, Urban Dock Lalaport Toyosu, Tokyo, Japan, on May 3, 2009.

★ The **most consecutive double Dutch–style skips by a team** is 194, by the Blue and White Rope Skippers (all UK) on the set of *Guinness World Records Smashed* at Pinewood Studios, UK, on April 17, 2009.

The **most people skipping simultaneously on two ropes** is 38, at the studios of *El Show de los Récords* in Madrid, Spain, on December 5, 2001. They completed three full rotations of the ropes.

Longest climb by a human fly On May 25, 1981, Daniel Goodwin (U.S.A.) ascended 1,454 ft. (443.2 m) up the outside of the Sears Tower in Chicago, U.S.A., using only suction cups and metal clips.

☆**LONGEST TIME TO CONTROL A SOCCER BALL** Dan Magness (UK) controlled a soccer ball for 24 hours during an event run by Sony PlayStation in Covent Garden, London, UK, on April 30–May 1, 2009. Dan also holds the record for the ★**longest time to control a soccer ball on the back**—3 min. 40 sec.—set on April 19, 2009.

KURSK, RUSSIA (51°48'N 36°11'E): The **largest tank battle** ever is generally acknowledged to be the Battle of Kursk, Russia, during World War II. On July 12, 1943, in the Prokhorovka region near Kursk, a total of 1,500 German and Russian tanks amassed for close-range fighting.

EXTRA! For world-beating wheel skills and daredevil feats, jump to p. 158.

★ FARTHEST BACKFLIP OFF A WALL
Chase Armitage (UK) achieved a backflip of 9 ft. 11 in. (3.04 m) off a wall on the set of *Guinness World Records Smashed* at Pinewood Studios, UK, on March 25, 2009. Chase is also able to clear an automobile driven in front of the wall, just as he is running up it.

★ MOST POGO BACKFLIPS The greatest number of consecutive backflips performed on a pogo stick is eight by Fred Grzybowski (U.S.A.) in Ohio, U.S.A., in August 2009. Fred has been an avid pogoer since his school days.

JUMP? Did you know it is permitted to base jump from the Perrine Memorial Bridge (see p. 153)? But jump from a bridge elsewhere in the U.S.A. and you could be in trouble with the law!

★ MOST BREAKDANCE ELBOW SPINS
Mark Dossenbach (Switzerland) performed 16 continuous spins on one elbow at Zug, Switzerland, on August 19, 2005. He's put the work in, though: Mark started practicing acrobatics at the age of eight, and he's had more than 20 years to perfect the art of elbow spinning!

★ MOST HEADSPINS (ONE MINUTE)
B-Girl Roxy (aka Roxanna Milliner, UK) performed a dizzying 71 headspins during a warm-up session at the UK B-Boy Championships World Finals held at the O2 Academy Brixton in London, UK, on October 11, 2009.

HOP!: Jordy (France)—**the youngest rapper**—topped the French chart with "Dur dur d'être bébé," aged four and a half, in September 1993.

GRAFFITI

★ **Largest spray-painted picture** An 8,183.58-ft.^{2} (760.28-m^2) picture, titled *There Is Life on the Streets*, was spray-painted for Coca-Cola Ýcecek by 580 students from nine Turkish universities. It was completed at Hezarfen Airport, Istanbul, Turkey, on August 16, 2004.

Longest graffiti scroll On December 16, 2008, the children's charity "To hamogelo tou pediou" made a 2,299-ft.-7-in-long (700.92-m) graffiti scroll in Kerkyra, Greece.

BASE JUMPING

Highest exit point Dr. Glenn Singleman and Heather Swan (both Australia) made a BASE jump from a ledge 21,666 ft. (6,604 m) up Mount Meru in Garwhal Himalaya, India, on May 23, 2006. The husband-and-wife team wore wingsuits for their jumps.

☆ **Largest group jump** A total of 30 skydivers from more than seven different countries performed a base jump from the Ostankino television and radio tower in Moscow, Russia, on July 3, 2004.

Most jumps in 24 hours Special Ops Officer Dan Schilling (U.S.A.) jumped off the 486-ft.-high (148-m) Perrine Memorial Bridge over Snake River in Twin Falls, Idaho, U.S.A., 201 times on July 7–8, 2006. He averaged one jump every 6 min. 20 sec.!

Oldest base jumper James Talbot Guyer (U.S.A.) parachuted off the Perrine Memorial Bridge on the north side of Twin Falls in Idaho, U.S.A., on August 2, 2002, at the age of 74 years 47 days.

DAMASCUS, SYRIA (33°30'N 36°17'E): As of May 15, 2008, the **largest restaurant** in the world is the 6,014-seater Bawabet Dimashq Restaurant (Damascus Gate Restaurant) owned by Mr. Shaker Al Samman in Damascus, Syria.

☆**MOST BUILDINGS CLIMBED
SOLO** As of 2010, Alain
"Spiderman" Robert (France) had
scaled more than 100 towers,
monuments, and skyscrapers
without ropes, suction devices,
or safety equipment. Alain uses
pipes, window frames, cables,
and the gaps between brickwork to scale structures often more than
1,300 ft. (400 m) tall.

One of Alain's most notable endeavors was reaching the top of the
Petronas Towers (pictured) in Kuala Lumpur, Malaysia, on September 1,
2009, after two failed attempts. In the picture above right, he is seen
standing triumphantly atop the building's antenna.

BREAKING

★**Most flares in one minute** Victor Ortiz (Spain) performed 37 flares
in a minute in the Spanish capital, Madrid, on January 9, 2009.

★**Most one-hand jumps** Victor Mengarelli (Sweden) achieved 93 one-
hand jumps at ICA Maxi in Haninge, Sweden, on November 2, 2007.

★**Longest hand wave** Nana Mizuki fan club S C NANA NET (Japan)
organized a breakdance hand wave involving 7,014 participants at the Tokyo
Big Site, Japan, on November 21, 2009.

★**Longest marathon** Arulanantham Suresh Joachim, Troy Feldman,
Jesse Catabog, Donald F. Geraghty, Lance Johnson, Eva Nikitova, Damian
Dobrowolski, Dan Rossignoli, Darren Bryan, Karl Alba, and Joseph Hersco
(all Canada) breakdanced continuously for 24 hours at the Vaughan Mills
shopping mall in Vaughan, Ontario, Canada, on March 23–24, 2007.

★**Most windmills in 30 seconds** LeeRoy Bailey (UK) carried out 46
"mills" in 30 seconds on the set of *Guinness World Records Smashed* at
Pinewood Studios, UK, on March 31, 2009.

SIDESHOW ARTS

☆**Fastest straitjacket escape** Jackson Rayne (U.S.A.) exited a Posey straitjacket in 7.26 seconds at the Hilton Convention Center, Las Vegas, U.S.A., on November 17, 2009.

★**Fastest chains escape** Matt "The Knife" Cassiere (U.S.A.) escaped from a set of chains in 49.67 seconds on the set of *Zheng Da Zong Yi* in Beijing, China, on November 13, 2008.

DID YOU KNOW?

By night, Dr. Adamovich performs as "impalement artist" The Great Throwdini. By day, he runs a wedding business, and has married thousands of people as a certified minister!

MOST KNIVES THROWN AROUND A HUMAN TARGET IN ONE MINUTE
Dr. David R. Adamovich (U.S.A., aka The Great Throwdini) hurled 102 throwing knives, each 14 in. (36 cm) long, around his partner in one minute in Freeport, New York, U.S.A., on December 26, 2007. (See "Top 100," below.) Throwdini also holds the record for the **fastest time to throw 10 knives around a human target**: 4.29 seconds.

TOP 100: Visitors to GWR's website have voted this record by the Great Throwdini as one of the top 100 GWR records of all time!

☆**Fastest handcuff escape** Escapologist Zdenek Bradac (Czech Republic) escaped from a set of handcuffs in 1.66 seconds in Hamburg, Germany, on June 6, 2009.

On September 9, 2009, he escaped from a pair of handcuffs while underwater in a time of 10.66 seconds, in Jablonec nad Nisou, Czech Republic, the ☆**fastest escape from handcuffs underwater**.

☆**GREATEST WEIGHT LIFTED WITH THE NIPPLES** On September 26, 2009, blacksmith, welder, and sculptor Sage Werbock (U.S.A., aka The Great Nippulini) lifted a total weight of 70 lb. 8 oz. (31.9 kg) from piercings in his nipples. The weight comprised a 55-lb. (24.9-kg) anvil, a 15-lb. (6.8-kg) anvil, and chains weighing 8 oz. (0.2 kg).

PETS!: The Great Nippulini owns two dogs, three cats, seven reptiles, a blue-faced Amazon parrot, and a Madagascar hissing cockroach.

★**MOST BEVERAGE CANS BROKEN WITH A WHIP IN THREE MINUTES** Adam Winrich (U.S.A.) split 23 beverage cans with a whip in three minutes on the set of *Lo Show dei Record* in Milan, Italy, on April 11, 2009. Winrich also set a record on June 20, 2009, when he achieved 257 cracks in a minute with a bullwhip at The Stone's Throw Bar in Eau Claire, Wisconsin, U.S.A.—the ☆**most whip cracks in one minute**.

MOSCOW, RUSSIA (55°45'N 37°36'E): At 751 ft. 3 in. (229 m) above street level, the world's **highest clock** sits atop the Federation Tower "West" in Moscow, Russia. The clock was first activated on April 24, 2008.

★ **YOUNGEST SWORD SWALLOWER** According to the Sword Swallowers Association International (SSAI), the youngest recorded sword swallower is Erik Kloeker (U.S.A., b. October 27, 1989), who swallowed a solid-steel sword, up to the hilt, at the age of 16 years 267 days on July 21, 2006.

☆**Fastest time to pass through a tennis racket three times** Ashrita Furman (U.S.A.) passed his body through a tennis racket three times in 8.1 seconds at the Panorama Café in New York City, U.S.A., on October 4, 2009.

Most layered bed of nails Lee Graber, Todd Graber, Chris Smith, and Doreen Graber (all U.S.A.) formed a four-person bed of nails (6-in. [15.25-cm] nails set 2 in. [5 cm] apart) at Tallmadge, Ohio, U.S.A., on October 8, 2000.

Lee Graber of Tallmadge, Ohio, U.S.A., was sandwiched between two beds of nails, with a weight of 1,658 lb. (752.5 kg) placed on top for 10 seconds on June 24, 2000—the **heaviest weight endured on an "Iron Maiden" bed of nails**. The nails were spaced 2 in. (5 cm) apart.

☆**Heaviest concrete block break on a bed of nails** Neal Hardy (Australia) had 16 concrete blocks weighing 1,173 lb. 8 oz. (532.3 kg) in total placed on his chest while he was lying on a bed of nails. The blocks were then broken with a sledgehammer at Vikings Auditorium, Erindale, Canberra, Australia, on February 16, 2008.

Most people swallowing the same object A group of four sword swallowers—Thomas Blackthorne (UK), Chayne Hultgren (Australia), Captain Frodo (Norway), and Gordo Gamsby (Australia)—swallowed the four steel legs of the same bar stool. This gut-wrenching record was set in front of a live audience during a show at the Edinburgh Fringe Festival in Scotland, UK, on August 21, 2007.

★**Most swords swallowed at once** A group of 19 sword swallowers (from Italy, Sweden, and the U.S.A.) swallowed a total of 50 swords among them, simultaneously, in Wilkes-Barre, Pennsylvania, U.S.A., on August 30, 2002.

....

MECCA, SAUDI ARABIA (21°25'N 39°49'E): The annual pilgrimage (Hajj) to Mecca, Saudi Arabia, regularly attracts the **most Muslim pilgrims**: an average of 2 million people a year, from 140 countries.

....

LONGEST SWORD SWALLOWED Natasha Veruschka (U.S.A.) swallowed a sword 29.5 in. (74 cm) in length on February 28, 2009. Natasha also holds the record for the most swords swallowed simultaneously by a female, at 13 blades.

Greatest weight lifted by the beard In the world of beard weightlifting, no one surpasses the achievements of Lithuania's Antanas Kontrimas. On September 16, 2007, he tied a 139-lb. (63.2-kg) girl to his beard and lifted her 3.93 in. (10 cm) off the ground on the set of *Zheng Da Zong Yi—Guinness World Records Special* in Beijing, China.

CIRCUS SKILLS

Juggling The ★**longest duration juggling four objects** was 2 hr. 23 min. and was achieved by David Slick (U.S.A.) in North Richland Hills, Texas, U.S.A., on March 1, 2009.

David also holds the record for the ☆**longest duration juggling three objects**—12 hr. 5 min.—set at North Richland Hills Public Library, Texas, U.S.A., on July 22, 2009.

And just to make things even more challenging . . . the ☆**longest duration juggling three balls while suspended upside down** by gravity boots is 5 min. 20 sec. and was set by Ashrita Furman (U.S.A.) in the hallway of the Sri Chinmoy Centre in Jamaica, New York City, U.S.A., on November 21, 2009.

EXTRA! For sensational strongman feats and breathtaking balancing, see p. 141–145.

☆**Most juggling catches (one minute)** On July 12, 2009, Zdenek Bradac (Czech Republic) beat his own record for the most juggling catches in a minute, with 339, at the Prinzenraub Festival in Altenburg, Germany.

☆**Most hula hoops spun simultaneously** Paul "Dizzy Hips" Blair (U.S.A.) spun 136 hula hoops simultaneously on CBS's *The Early Show* in New York City, U.S.A., on November 12, 2009, to celebrate Guinness World Records Day.

☆**Tallest stilts** The tallest stilts ever mastered measured 53 ft. 10 in. (16.41 m) from ground to ankle. Saimaiti Yiming (China) walked 10 steps on them, without touching his safety lines, in Shanshan county, Xinjiang, China, on November 15, 2006.

★**Fastest tightrope walk over 100 m** Aisikaier Wubulikasimu (China) covered 100 m on a tightrope in 44.63 seconds at Taimu Mountain Scenic Spot, Fuding City, Fujian Province, China, on October 27, 2009.

The attempt was an outdoor event for *Zheng Da Zong Yi—Guinness World Records Special 2009*.

★**HIGHEST STATIC TRAPEZE ACT** Amanda Vicharelli (U.S.A., left), John "Chuck" Berry (New Zealand), and Johannes "Jojo" Rose (Germany) performed a static trapeze act at a height of 2,171 ft. (662 m) in Xiaozhai Tiankeng Cave, China, on October 2, 2008.

SARATOV, RUSSIA (51°32'N 46°01'E): Eugene Andreev (USSR) holds the official World Air Sports Federation (FAI) record for the **longest freefall parachute jump**, after falling for 80,380 ft. (24,500 m) from an altitude of 83,523 ft. (25,458 m) near the city of Saratov, Russia (then USSR), on November 1, 1962.

☆ **THREE CONTORTIONISTS IN A BOX—DURATION** On September 20, 2009, Skye Broberg, Nele Siezen, and Jola Siezen (all New Zealand) climbed into a box with a 26 x 27 x 22-in. (66.04 x 68.58 x 55.88-cm) interior and remained there for 6 min. 13.52 sec. on the set of *NZ Smashes Guinness World Records* at the Sylvia Park mall, Auckland, New Zealand.

CIRCUS STYLE The ★ **most open umbrellas balanced is eight**, by Liu Lina (China, left) for *Zheng Da Zong Yi—Guinness World Records Special* in Beijing, China, on June 21, 2009. Qiu Jiangning (China, right) made the ★ **highest jump through a hoop**—10 ft. 2 in. (3.12 m)—on the show four days earlier.

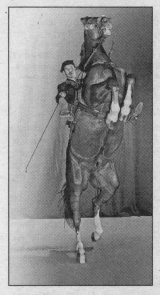

★LONGEST DISTANCE BY A HORSE ON HIND LEGS The greatest distance covered by a horse walking on only two legs is 95 ft. 5 in. (30 m) and was achieved by a horse named Doc, ridden by Gregory Ancelotti (Italy), on the set of *Lo Show dei Record*, in Milan, Italy, on April 25, 2009.

★Most 360° spins on a tightrope (two minutes) On September 20, 2007, Maimaitiaili Abula (China) performed 41 full-circle spins on a tightrope on the set of *Zheng Da Zong Yi—Guinness World Records Special* in Beijing, China.

★Most rotations hung from the neck of another person (30 seconds) Liu Xiaogao and Liu Jiangshan (both China), from the Shenyang Jinying Youth Acrobatic Troupe, performed 82 rotations suspended from each other's neck by a belt in 30 seconds on the set of *Zheng Da Zong Yi—Guinness World Records Special* in Beijing, China, on November 21, 2009.

☆Most bullwhip cracks (one minute) Adam Winrich (U.S.A.) carried out 257 bullwhip cracks in a minute at The Stone's Throw Bar in Eau Claire, Wisconsin, U.S.A., on June 20, 2009.

Most consecutive somersaults horseback riding In 1856, James Robinson (U.S.A.) performed 23 consecutive somersaults on horseback at Spalding Rogers Circus, Pittsburgh, Pennsylvania, U.S.A.

☆ **HIGHEST SHALLOW DIVE** On October 9, 2009, Darren Taylor (U.S.A.) performed a shallow dive from a height of 35 ft. 9 in. (10.9 m) at the Gwinnett Arena, Atlanta, Georgia, U.S.A. In doing so, he broke his own record by 1 in. (2.5 cm).

Farthest jump riding a lion Edgard and Askold Zapashny (both Russia), of the Russian State Circus Company, performed a 7-ft. 6-in. (2.3-m) jump astride a lion named Michael on July 28, 2006.

Heaviest elephant lifted In 1975, while performing with Gerry Cottle's Circus (UK), Khalil Oghaby (Iran) lifted an elephant off the ground using a harness and platform above the animal. At 4,400 lb. (2 tonnes), this is the heaviest elephant ever lifted by a human.

Longest-running circus Ringling Bros. and Barnum & Bailey Circus (U.S.A.) is the world's longest running, with Barnum & Bailey's "Greatest Show on Earth" established in 1870 and later merging with the Ringling Brothers in 1919. At its height, the circus carried 150 clowns and traveled in three trains with a staff of 1,500 to 2,500 people.

"Pain lasts for a minute. The glory lasts for a lifetime."
Shallow dive supremo Darren Taylor, aka Professor Splash

KUWAIT CITY, KUWAIT (29°22'N 47°58'E): The **largest kite flown** had a lifting area of 10,225.7 ft.² (950 m²). Laid flat, it had a total area of 10,968.4 ft.² (1,019 m²) and was 83 ft. 7 in. (25.475 m) long and 131 ft. 3 in. (40 m) wide. The kite was made by Abdulrahman Al Farsi and Faris Al Farsi (both Kuwait) and flown at the Kuwait Hala Festival in Flag Square, Kuwait City, Kuwait, on February 15, 2005.

Largest circus audience A crowd of 52,385 people gathered to see the Ringling Bros. and Barnum & Bailey Circus at the Superdome, New Orleans, Louisiana, U.S.A., on September 14, 1975.

MASS PARTICIPATION

★ **Largest backward race** The record for the largest backward race was achieved by 539 people at an event organized by Mater Salvatoris Institute in Kapellen, Belgium, on March 13, 2009.

☆ **Largest bikini parade** A bikini parade involving 287 women set a world record at an event held by Kellogg's Special K in Johannesburg, South Africa, on November 7, 2009.

☆ **Most people crammed in a Smart Car** A total of 16 members of the Candy Lane Dancers troupe (all New Zealand) squeezed into a standard Smart Car at the Sylvia Park shopping mall in Auckland, New Zealand, on August 23, 2009.

☆ **Largest family reunion** A reunion involving 2,585 people was achieved by the Lilly family at Flat Top, West Virginia, U.S.A., on August 9, 2009.

☆ **LARGEST "THRILLER" DANCE** The largest Michael Jackson "Thriller" dance was performed by 13,597 participants at an event organized by the Instituto de la Juventud del Gobierno del Distrito Federal at the Monumento a la Revolución, Mexico City, Mexico, on August 29, 2009.

TEHRAN, IRAN (35°41'N 51°25'E): Official Iranian estimates gave the size of the crowds lining the 20-mile (32-km) route to Tehran's Behesht-e Zahra cemetery on June 11, 1989, for the funeral of Ayatollah Ruhollah Khomeini, as 10,200,000 people. That figure represented one-sixth of Iran's population, the **largest percentage of a population to attend a funeral**.

☆**Largest human beatbox ensemble** Michael Krappel (Austria) assembled a beatbox ensemble with 327 participants in Vienna, Austria, on September 27, 2009.

★**Most people gold panning** The greatest number of people gold panning at the same time was 100, at an event held by Primaria Rosia Montana in Rosia Montana, Romania, on August 30, 2009.

★**Most people chanting** At an event held in Gärdet Park, Stockholm, Sweden, 2,558 people chanted together on August 15, 2009.

☆**Largest Bollywood dance** A Bollywood dance featuring 1,082 students and teachers of the Anglo Chinese School was performed in Singapore on April 29, 2009.

☆**LARGEST MARTIAL ARTS DISPLAY** A martial arts display featuring 33,996 participants practicing tai chi took place at an event organized by Beijing Municipal Bureau of Sports in Beijing, China, on August 8, 2009.

DID YOU KNOW?

Tai chi chuan, to give its full name, is a Chinese martial art. The name means "supreme ultimate fist," and it dates back to around 1580.

TRIVIA

Ken Dickenson and Kevin Bartolo performed a tai chi marathon lasting for 25 hr. 5 min. in Australia on March 17–18, 2006.

☆**LARGEST DANCE CLASS** The biggest dance class was achieved by an unprecedented 7,770 participants at an event organized by DanceSport Team Cebu International Inc. at the Cebu City Sports Center in Cebu City, the Philippines, on June 27, 2009. The participants were trained more than three weeks prior to the event to ensure the success of the attempt.

★**Most people dressed as bees** A total of 1,901 participants dressed up as bees on July 15, 2009, in Staffordshire, UK.

★**Most people holding their breath underwater** On October 11, 2009, a total of 280 people held their breath underwater in Torri del Benaco, Verona, Italy. The record was achieved by "La Scuola del Mare 2" (Italy).

☆**Largest Christmas-cracker pulling** A group of 1,478 people engaged in a mass Christmas-cracker pull in Tochigi, Japan, on October 18, 2009.

ABU DHABI, UAE (24°28'N 54°22'E): The **most expensive vehicle license plate**—made up of the single digit "1"—was sold to Saeed Abdul Ghaffar Khouri (UAE) for Dh52.2 million ($14.2 million) at a special license-plate auction organized by Emirates Auction Company and held at Emirates Palace, Abu Dhabi, UAE, on February 16, 2008.

☆**LARGEST GATHERING OF SMURFS** The most people dressed as Smurfs was 2,510 and was achieved by Jokers' Masquerade with the help of Swansea University at Swansea Oceana in Swansea, UK, on June 8, 2009. Everyone's faces, arms, and legs had to be painted blue to qualify.

★**Largest charity walk** A charity walk by 1,903 participants took place at an event organized in Rathcoole Park, Rathcoole, County Dublin, Ireland, on September 5, 2009.

☆**Largest group hug** A group of 9,758 people encircled the citadel of Alba Iulia in Transylvania, Romania, in a communal hug on May 29, 2009.

☆**Largest coffee party (single venue)** A coffee party comprising an incredible 8,162 participants was held by Krüger GmbH & Co. KG (Germany) at the Jugendpark in Cologne, Germany, on August 30, 2009.

★**Most people exercising to a video game** On May 22, 2009, 605 people performed an exercise routine to a video game at the Electronic Arts Burnaby Campus Sports Field in Burnaby, British Columbia, Canada.

★**Most people knitting** On August 7, 2009, at the "Sock Summit" in Portland, Oregon, U.S.A., 937 people took part in a mass knitting event.

☆**Largest annual gathering of women** Attukal Pongala in Kerala, India, is a celebration of womenhood in which offerings (*pongala*) are made to Attukal Amma, the mother goddess. The 2010 event attracted more than 3 million women.

☆**MOST KITES FLOWN SIMULTANEOUSLY** For an initiative organized by United Nations Relief and Works Agency (UNRWA), children at Al-Waha beach, Gaza Strip, on July 30, 2009, flew 3,710 kites, the greatest number in the air together at one time.

★**LARGEST PARADE OF MINIS** The London & Surrey Mini Owners Club organized a parade of Minis consisting of 1,450 vehicles as part of the London to Brighton Mini Run, in Crystal Palace, London, UK, on May 17, 2009.

★**Largest picnic (multiple venue)** A total of 12,934 picnickers assembled across 79 venues in a record attempt organized in the UK for National Family Week on May 25, 2009.

☆**Most people in a multi-legged race** The greatest number of participants in a multi-legged race was achieved by 261 people at an event held at the Nogata North Elementary School in Nogata, Japan, on November 21, 2008.

DUBAI, UAE (25°16'N 55°18'E): The **largest prize for a single horse race** is for the Dubai World Cup, held in Dubai, UAE, which carries a total purse of $6 million. Of this, $3.6 million goes to the winner of the race.

★ LARGEST SCUBA-DIVING LESSON
A "class" of 2,465 people took part in a scuba lesson in the water of Malalayang Beach in Manado, Indonesia, on August 16, 2009.

MOST . . .

★ Models in a fashion show The Muaa Summer 2010 show in Buenos Aires, Argentina, saw 260 models take to the runway on October 8, 2009.

★ Backing dancers to a singer A total of 251 members of an audience were trained to perform a choreographed routine for singer Alesha Dixon (UK) in London, UK, on April 2, 2009.

★ Automobiles washed in eight hours (multiple venues) During the Soaps It Up! National Car Wash Fundraiser event coordinated by Victory Management Group (U.S.A.) on June 20, 2009, 4,105 people gathered across the U.S.A. to wash automobiles and raise money for cystic fibrosis research.

★ Golf balls hit simultaneously A record 1,873 balls were hit simultaneously at the Real Federacion Español de Golf course in Madrid, Spain, on September 27, 2009.

★ MOST PARTICIPANTS IN A BADMINTON RALLY A total of 96 participants played in a badminton rally on May 23, 2009. The record was set by Aviva (Singapore), in Raffles City Mall, Singapore.

☆ **LONGEST CONGA ON ICE** An impressive 252 participants performed a conga on ice at the Alexandra Palace Ice Rink in London, UK, to celebrate Guinness World Records Day on November 11, 2009.

★ **Champagne bottles sabered simultaneously** At an event organized by International Sabrageurs Anonymous in Portarlington, Co. Laois, Ireland, on July 18, 2009, 152 participants simultaneously sabered bottles of champagne.

☆ **Sky lanterns flown simultaneously** An amazing 10,318 sky lanterns were launched at an event organized by Freedom Faithnet Global (Indonesia) in Ancol Carnaval Beach, Jakarta, Indonesia, on December 5, 2009.

☆ **LARGEST SOCCER TOURNAMENT** Copa Telmex 2009 was contested by 187,765 players, in 11,280 teams, and held in Mexico between May 1 and November 29, 2009. It was staged with the aim of providing a brighter future for Mexican youth.

MUSCAT, OMAN (23°37'N 58°35'E): Made from Swarovski crystal, the world's **largest chandelier** hangs in the Sultan Qaboos Grand Mosque in Muscat, Oman. It is 46 ft. (14.1 m) tall and 26 ft. (8 m) in diameter, with 1,114 bulbs.

EXTRA! For more eccentric behavior, turn to pp. 255–258 for some record-breaking collectors!

☆ **LARGEST GATHERING OF SUPERHEROES** A record 1,091 people gathered at Twickenham Stadium, London, UK, while dressed as superheroes at an event organized by the Rugby Football Union and facilitated by event360 at the Emirates Airline London Sevens on May 23, 2010. Various hulks, bananamen, and Ninja Turtles attended, but Elvises and Santas were disqualified!

☆ **Karaoke participants** The largest karaoke session took place at Bristol Motor Speedway in Bristol, Tennessee, U.S.A., on August 22, 2009, when 160,000 people sang "Friends in Low Places," by Garth Brooks (U.S.A.), before the NASCAR Sharpie 500 race.

LARGEST . . .

☆ **Halloween gathering** A group of 508 people in scary costumes assembled in Bloomington, Indiana, U.S.A., on Halloween 2009.

On September 24, 2009, the ★ **largest gathering of skeletons** featured 197 people, in London, UK.

★ **Gathering of people dressed as storybook characters** On November 12, 2009, 300 people dressed up as storybook characters for Guinness World Records Day. The record was set by Carr's Glen Primary School, in Belfast, Northern Ireland, UK.

★ **Sports lesson** A record 882 students at Ballyclare High School in Northern Ireland took part in a sports lesson on November 12, 2009. Also top of the class were 5,401 participants who enjoyed the ★ **largest physics lesson** in Denver, Colorado, U.S.A., on May 7, 2009.

HUMAN
ENDEAVORS

Prima ego velivolis ambivi cursibus Orbem,
Magellane novo te duce ducta freto.
Ambivi merito? circum VICTORIA

CONTENTS

GRAND TOURS

★ **YOUNGEST FEMALE TO ROW THE INDIAN OCEAN** Sarah Outen (UK, b. May 26, 1985) single-handedly crossed the Indian Ocean, east to west, between April 1 and August 3, 2009, in her boat *Serendipity* (which she affectionately termed *Dippers*). At the start of her trip, Sarah was aged 23 years 310 days. Her journey began in Australia and ended 4,180 nautical miles (4,810 miles; 7,740 km) later in Mauritius. During the epic trip, she lost 44 lb. (20 kg) in weight—despite scoffing a stomach-bulging 500 chocolate bars—and also broke two oars.

INDIAN OCEAN The Indian Ocean is the planet's third-largest ocean, accounting for around 20% of the planet's surface water. It is the second-deepest ocean—after the Pacific—with an average depth of 12,260 ft. (3,736 m).

The route from Australia to Mauritius stretches for 3,100 nautical miles (see green line, left), but Sarah clocked up 4,180 nautical miles (see red line), thanks to "feisty currents, teasing winds, and general unpredictable weather."

> *"If you're strong up top and have prepared well, then you have the best chance—stubborn and strong, and with a bit of luck, you'll weather the worst of the storms. It's all about attitude, endurance, and keeping happy."*
>
> **Sarah Outen, ocean rower**

EXTRA!: If you love record-breaking tales of the high seas, turn to p. 200.

☆**GREATEST DISTANCE ON A HAND-CRANKED CYCLE IN 24 HOURS**
Thomas Lange (Germany) covered 403.80 miles (649.85 km) on a hand-cranked cycle in 24 hours during the Bike Sebring 12/24 Hours, in Sebring, Florida, U.S.A., on February 14–15, 2009.

LONGEST JOURNEY BY . . .

★**Motorized bicycle** Eddie Sedgemore (UK) cycled 1,912.1 miles (3,077 km) on a motorized bicycle in 28 days from May 9 to June 5, 2009.

☆**A pilgrim** The greatest distance claimed for a "round the world" pilgrimage is 38,102 miles (61,319 km) by Arthur Blessitt (U.S.A.) since December 25, 1969. He has crossed 315 "nations, island groups, and territories" carrying a 12-ft.-tall (3.7-m) wooden cross and preaching from the Bible throughout.

☆**Powered paraglider** Benjamin Jordan (Canada) traveled 4,975.93 miles (8,008 km) by powered paraglider flying west to east across Canada from Tofino (British Columbia) to Bay St. Lawrence (Nova Scotia) from May 15, 2009, to August 24, 2009. He landed and took off from Canadian schools along the way, where he gave presentations to the children to encourage them to challenge their fears and realize their own dreams.

Punt Aided by four other crew members, John Pearse (UK) traveled by punt from Oxford, UK, to Leeds, UK, and back to Oxford from June 19 to August 10, 1965, a total of 721 miles (1,160 km).

KARACHI, PAKISTAN (24°51'N 67°00'E): Nargis Bhimji of Karachi, Pakistan, celebrated her birthday for 35 hr. 25 min. by crossing time zones, flying from Karachi to Singapore and then to San Francisco, U.S.A., on June 27, 1998—thereby giving her the record for the **longest birthday**.

☆**LONGEST JOURNEY SWIMMING**
Martin Strel (Slovenia) covered a distance of 3,273.38 miles (5,268 km) when he swam the entire length of the Amazon River, in Peru and Brazil, from February 1 to April 8, 2007.

Walking backward Aged 36, Plennie L. Wingo (U.S.A.) completed an 8,000-mile (12,875-km) backward walk from Santa Monica, California, U.S.A., to Istanbul, Turkey, in 517 days between April 15, 1931, and October 24, 1932. Wingo averaged 15.47 miles (24.89 km) each day of his trip.

Wheelchair Rick Hansen (Canada) wheeled his wheelchair 24,901 miles (40,075 km) through four continents and 34 countries, starting from Vancouver, BC, Canada, on March 21, 1985, and returning there on May 22, 1987.

FASTEST . . .

Paris–London journey On September 24, 1983, David Boyce of Stewart Wrightson (Aviation) Ltd traveled the 214 miles (344 km) from central Paris, France, to central London, UK (BBC TV Centre), in 38 min. 58 sec. He traveled by motorcycle and helicopter to Le Bourget, France; then via Hawker Hunter jet (piloted by the late Michael Carlton) to Biggin Hill, UK; and last by helicopter to the TV Centre parking lot.

MUMBAI, INDIA (18°57'N 72°49'E): The **longest dosa** (rice flour pancake) measured 30 ft. (9.14 m) and was prepared by chefs at the Sankalp Restaurant in Andheri, Mumbai, India, on February 12, 2006.

EXTRA!: More of a homebody than a globe-trotting grand tourist? Then switch to p. 304 to find out what's on TV.

☆**FASTEST TIME TO CYCLE THE LENGTH OF THE PAN-AMERICAN HIGHWAY** Scott Napier (UK) cycled the Pan-American Highway from Prudhoe Bay, Alaska, U.S.A., to Ushuaia, Argentina, in 125 days from June 22 to October 25, 2009. Napier cycled a total of 14,099.11 miles (22,690.36 km) on his trip.

Unpowered crossing of the Bering Strait

The fastest crossing of the Bering Strait—the sea channel that separates Asia from North America—on foot and skis was completed by Dmitry Shparo and his son Matvey (both Russia), achieved when they reached Chariot, Alaska, U.S.A., on March 20, 1998. They had begun their journey in Mys Dezhneva, East Cape, Russia, on March 1, and traveled a total distance of approximately 180 miles (290 km).

★**Time to visit all sovereign countries** Kashi Samaddar (India) visited all 194 United Nations member countries in 6 years, 10 months, and 7 days, between July 18, 2002, and May 24, 2009.

Relay cycle around Australia Starting and finishing in Brisbane, Queensland, a team of eight cyclists took 18 days 8 hr. 39 min. to cycle 8,894 miles (14,314 km) around Australia between October 22 and November 9, 2001, taking in 19 coastal cities along the way.

DID YOU KNOW?

Giampietro Marion (Italy) cycled the South American portion of the Pan-American Highway, from Chigorodo, Colombia, to Ushuaia, Argentina, in 59 days in 2000.

TRIVIA

The Pan-American highway is broken by a small impassable section called the Darién Gap.

OMSK, RUSSIA (54°59'N 73°22'E): The **smallest book ever printed** measures 0.035 x 0.035 in. (0.9 x 0.9 mm) and is an edition of *Chameleon* by the Russian author Anton Chekhov. The book was made and published by Anatoliy Konenko of Omsk, Russia, in 1996.

CLASSIC JOURNEYS

On every continent there is a classic journey to be found; it may be from one extreme point to another, or it may be between two points that have a historical or even romantic association. Whatever the journey may be, you can be sure that someone is going to attempt to complete that journey, either using an outlandish mode of transport or in the quickest time possible, and, more often than not, both! These are a few of our favorite fastest journeys.

JOURNEY	FROM	TO	DISTANCE	HOW	WHO	TIME	WHEN
Cairo to Cape	Cairo, Egypt	Cape Town, South Africa	approximately 6,835 miles (11,000 km)	Bicycle	Chris Evans, David Genders, Michael Kennedy (all UK); Paul Reynaert (Belgium); Jeremy Wex, Steve Topham, Scotty Robinson, Andrew Griffin (all Canada); and Sascha Hartl (Austria)	119 days 1 hr. 32 min.	January 18 to May 17, 2003
John O'Groats to Land's End	John O'Groats, Scotland, UK	Land's End, England, UK	874 miles (1,407 km)	Foot	Andrew Rivett (UK)	9 days 2 hr. 26 min.	May 4–13, 2002
Land's End to John O'Groats	Land's End, England, UK	John O'Groats, Scotland, UK	874 miles (1,407 km)	Unicycle	Robert Ambrose (UK)	12 days 1 hr. 59 min.	August 13–25, 2000
Pan-American Highway	Ushuaia, Argentina	Prudhoe Bay, Alaska	19,019 miles (30,431 km)	Foot	George Meegan (UK)	2,426 days	January 26, 1977, to September 18, 2009
Trans-Australia	Perth, Western Australia	Sydney, New South Wales	approximately 2,485 miles (4,000 km)	Bicycle	Richard Vollebregt (Australia)	8 days 10 hr. 57 min.	October 13–21, 2006
Trans-U.S.A.	Jacksonville, Florida	San Diego, California	2,595 miles (4,175 km)	Inline skates	Russell "Rusty" Moncrief (U.S.A.)	69 days 8 hr. 45 min.	January 5 to March 15, 2002
Trans-U.S.A.	Newport, Oregon	Washington, D.C.	3,261 miles (5,248 km)	Unicycle	Akira Matsushima (Japan)	43 days	July 10 to August 22, 1992
Trans-U.S.A.	San Francisco, California	New York City	3,100 miles (4,989 km)	Foot	Frank Giannino, Jr. (U.S.A.)	46 days 8 hr. 36 min.	September 1 to October 17, 1980

PUSH!: In 2001, 30 South African school pupils pushed an unpowered soapbox cart 1,280 miles (2,061 km) between Komatipoort and Cape Town, South Africa, in 19 days.

★ **LONGEST JOURNEY ON A POCKETBIKE (MINIMOTO)** Ryan Galbraith and Chris Stinson (both U.S.A.) traveled a record 445.26 miles (716.58 km) on pocketbikes (minimotos) from August 5 to August 8, 2009. Galbraith and Stinson began their journey in Colorado, U.S.A., and ended in South Dakota, U.S.A.

☆ **LONGEST JOURNEY BY SKATEBOARD** Starting in Leysin, Switzerland, on June 24, 2007, and finishing in Shanghai, China, on September 28, 2008, Rob Thomson (New Zealand) traveled a staggering 7,555 miles (12,159 km) on his skateboard in 463 days.

CRAWL!: Arulanantham Suresh Joachim (Canada) crawled for a record 35.18 miles (56.62 km) around a circuit in Sydney, New South Wales, Australia, on May 18–19, 2001.

NEW DELHI, INDIA (28°37'N 77°12'E): The **highest road in the world** is in Khardungla pass at an altitude of 18,640 ft. (5,682 m). It is one of the three passes of the Leh–Manali road in Kashmir, completed in 1976 by the Border Roads Organization, New Delhi, India. Motor vehicles have been able to use it since 1988.

AROUND THE WORLD

FIRST . . .

Circumnavigation by aircraft without refueling Richard G. "Dick" Rutan and Jeana Yeager (both U.S.A.) traveled the globe westward from Edwards Air Force Base, California, U.S.A., in nine days from December 14 to 23, 1986, without refueling. The key to their success was their aircraft, *Voyager*—created by Dick's brother Burt, the man behind *SpaceShipOne*, the vehicle used in the **first privately funded manned spaceflight**.

Circumnavigation by balloon solo Steve Fossett (U.S.A.) circled the globe in *Bud Light Spirit of Freedom*, a 140-ft.-tall (42.6-m) mixed-gas balloon, from June 19 to July 2, 2002. He took off from Northam, Western Australia, and landed at Eromanga, Queensland, Australia, after covering 20,627 miles (33,195 km) over 14 days 19 hr. 50 min.—the **longest duration flown by a balloon solo**.

FIRST UNPOWERED EQUATORIAL CIRCUMNAVIGATION Mike Horn (South Africa) circumnavigated the globe along the Equator by bicycle, dugout canoe, sailing trimaran, and on foot in 513 days between June 2, 1999, and October 27, 2000. His journey started and finished near Libreville in the west African state of Gabon, and proceeded in six legs that included crossing the Amazon and central Africa.

EXTRA!: All these record holders have skipped over oceans—make sure you don't by setting sail for pp. 33–37.

☆ **YOUNGEST PERSON TO SAIL AROUND THE WORLD SOLO AND UNSUPPORTED** Michael Perham (UK, b. March 16, 1992) sailed nonstop around the world in *TotallyMoney.com*, starting and finishing at the Ushant/Lizard line, in 284 days from November 15, 2008 to August 27, 2009, arriving aged 16 years 7 months 30 days. It is a record that is unlikely to be beaten as GWR no longer accepts claims for this category by anyone under 16 years of age.

FIRST CIRCUMNAVIGATION BY AMPHIBIOUS VEHICLE Ben Carlin (Australia) and his American wife Elinore left Montreal, Canada, in *Half-Safe*, a modified amphibious jeep, on July 24, 1950, intent on going around the world. It was an eventful trip—Elinore left her husband in India and filed for divorce—but eventually Ben arrived back in Montreal on May 8, 1958, after traveling 39,000 miles (62,765 km) over land and 9,600 miles (15,450 km) by water.

HYDERABAD, INDIA (17°22'N 78°28'E): The **largest film studio** is Ramoji Film City, Hyderabad, India, which opened in 1996 and measures 1,666 acres (674 ha). Comprising 47 sound stages, it has permanent sets ranging from railroad stations to temples.

FIRST CIRCUMNAVIGATION BY AIRCRAFT Two U.S. Army Douglas DWC seaplanes, the *Chicago*, piloted by Lt. Lowell H. Smith (left), and the *New Orleans*, flown by Leslie P. Arnold, flew around the world in 57 "hops" between April 6 and September 28, 1924, beginning and ending at Seattle, Washington, U.S.A.

Person to sail around the world (solo and nonstop)

Robin Knox-Johnston (UK) set sail from Falmouth, Cornwall, UK, in his yacht *Suhaili* on June 14, 1968, as one of nine participants in the *Sunday Times* Golden Globe Race. By the time he returned to Falmouth on April 22, 1969, he was the only remaining competitor and claimed both the record and the £5,000 ($8,070) prize money.

Woman to sail nonstop around the world in both directions On February 16, 2009, former PE teacher Dee Caffari (UK) finished the Vendée Globe round-the-world yacht race in sixth place. This achievement means that Dee is the first woman to sail both ways around the world, alone and unaided. What's more, she is only the fourth person ever to do so. This remarkable feat is now added to her previous achievement of becoming the **first woman to circumnavigate westward solo and nonstop** in May 2006.

FIRST CIRCUMNAVIGATION While Ferdinand Magellan is often credited with the first round-the-world voyage, he died on the way and never completed the journey. He led a fleet of five ships that left Spain on September 20, 1519. Of these, only the *Vittoria* returned, on September 8, 1522, under the command of navigator Juan Sebastián de Elcano and with just 17 of the original crew.

Prima ego velivolis ambire cursibus Orbem,
Magellane novo te duce ducta freto.

···

LUCKNOW, INDIA (26°51'N 80°55'E): First established in 1959, the City Montessori School in Lucknow, India, had an enrollment of 32,114 pupils on February 5, 2008, for the 2007–08 academic year, making it the **largest school by number of pupils**.

···

FASTEST TIME AROUND THE WORLD BY A SAILING CREW Bruno Peyron (France) captained a crew of 14 around the world in 50 days 16 hr. 20 min. 4 sec. aboard the maxi catamaran *Orange II* from January 24 to March 16, 2005. The journey started and finished in Ushant, France.

FASTEST . . .

Circumnavigation by passenger aircraft The fastest flight under the Fédération Aéronautique Internationale (FAI) rules, which permit flights that exceed the length of the Tropic of Cancer or Capricorn (22,858.8 miles; 36,787.6 km), was one of 31 hr. 27 min. 49 sec., set by an Air France Concorde, flight AF1995 (Capts Michel Dupont and Claude Hetru, both France). The Concorde flew from JFK airport in New York, U.S.A., eastbound via Toulouse, Dubai, Bangkok, Guam, Honolulu, and Acapulco on August 15–16, 1995, with a crew of 18 plus an additional 80 passengers.

Also according to the FAI rules, the **fastest time to fly around the world on scheduled flights** is 44 hr. 6 min. by David J. Springbett (UK). His route took him over a course of 23,068 miles (37,124 km), from Los Angeles, California, U.S.A., eastbound via London, Bahrain, Singapore, Bangkok, Manila, Tokyo, and Honolulu on January 8–10, 1980.

Circumnavigation by helicopter John Williams and Ron Bower (both U.S.A.) flew west around the world (against the prevailing winds) in a Bell 430 helicopter in 17 days 6 hr. 14 min. 25 sec. from August 17 to September 3, 1996, starting and finishing in Fair Oaks, London, UK.

Circumnavigation by car The record for the first and fastest man and woman to have circumnavigated the Earth by car, covering six continents, under the rules applicable in 1989 and 1991 embracing more than an Equator's length of driving (24,901 road miles; 40,075 km), is held by Saloo Choudhury and his wife, Neena Choudhury (both India). The journey took 69 days 19 hr. 5 min. from September 9 to November 17, 1989. The couple drove a 1989 Hindustan "Contessa Classic," starting and finishing in Delhi, India.

ENDURANCE

FARTHEST . . .

☆**Distance to surf on a river bore** On June 8, 2009, Sergio Laus (Brazil) surfed the Pororoca bore on the Araguari River, Amapa, Brazil, for 36 minutes, covering 7.33 miles (11.8 km).

Treadmill runs The ★**farthest distance run on a treadmill in 48 hours (team)** is 539.86 miles (868.64 km), by the 12-strong Porsche Human Performance (UK) team at the Festival of Speed, Goodwood, UK, on July 3–5, 2009.

Lee Chamberlain (UK) traveled 468.04 miles (753.24 km) on a treadmill at the Camberley Shopping Centre, Surrey, UK, from July 18 to 25, 2009, the ☆**farthest distance run on a treadmill in a week**.

★**Paddleboard journey (team)** Stéphanie Geyer-Barneix, Alexandra Lux, and Flora Manciet (all France) completed a paddleboard journey extending 3,001 miles (4,830 km; 2,607 nautical miles), from the island of Cap Breton (Canada) to Capbreton (France) on August 28, 2009. The journey took 54 days to complete, and the three women paddled from a kneeling or lying position, using only their hands to propel them through the water.

☆**Distance by motorcycle in 24 hours** Omar Hilal Al-Mamari (Oman) rode 1,321.65 miles (2,127 km) on a motorcycle on a road between Marmool and Thamrait in Oman on August 18–19, 2009.

MEDAN, NORTH SUMATRA, INDONESIA (3°35'N 98°40'E): A young pointer puppy named Judy was captured by the Japanese in 1942 and interned at a makeshift POW camp at Medan, Indonesia, along with the captured crew of HMS *Grasshopper*, of which she was the mascot. The upside of this is that she achieved a Guinness World Record—as history's **only puppy POW**.

EXTRA!: For aerial daredevilry, take off for p. 196, and for tales of bravery and endurance on the world's oceans, wave hello to p. 200.

★FASTEST MILE IN A BOMB DISPOSAL SUIT Lt. Jonathan Kehoe (U.S.A.) ran a mile wearing a bomb disposal suit in a time of 10 min. 16 sec. at Camp ECHO in Diwaniyah provence, Iraq, on February 2, 2009. Jonathan is a lieutenant in the U.S. Navy Explosive Ordnance Disposal (USN EOD). He wore a 75-lb. (34-kg) EOD 9 bomb suit.

★LONGEST TIME TO HOLD THE BREATH VOLUNTARILY (FEMALE) Karoline Mariechen Meyer (Brazil) held her breath underwater for an astonishing 18 min. 32.59 sec. at the Racer Academy swimming pool, Florianopolis, Brazil, on July 10, 2009. A professional freediver, Karoline trained for four months to try to break the record. Prior to the attempt, she inhaled oxygen for 24 minutes.

☆ **MOST CONSECUTIVE POGO-STICK JUMPS (MALE)** The greatest number of consecutive jumps achieved on a pogo stick is 186,152, by James Roumeliotis (U.S.A.) in Massachusetts, U.S.A., on September 22–23, 2007.

☆ **Distance run in one hour (female)** Dire Tune (Ethiopia) ran 60,751 ft. (18,517 m) in one hour at the IAAF World Athletics Grand Prix meeting in Ostrava, Czech Republic, on June 12, 2008.

★ **Open-water swim relay** A team of 200 participants swam a total of 425.48 miles (684.75 km) in an open-water relay at Lake Camlough, Camlough, Northern Ireland, UK, between September 9 and 19, 2009.

Distance walked over hot plates Rolf Iven (Germany) walked 75 ft. 1 in. (22.90 m) over hot plates on the set of *Lo Show dei Record*, in Milan, Italy, on April 18, 2009.

∙∙

BANGKOK, THAILAND (13°45'N 100°29'E): In its most scholarly transliteration, Krungthep Mahanakhon, the official name for Bangkok, the capital of Thailand, has 168 letters and is the **longest placename**. The official short version (without capital letters, which are not used in Thai) is krungthephphramahanakhon bowonratanakosin mahintharayuthaya mahadilokphiphobnovpharad radchataniburirom udomsantisug (111 letters).

∙∙

IRON: If conventional triathlons aren't testing enough, try an Ironman: a 2.4-mile (3.86-km) swim and a 112-mile (180.25-km) cycle, followed by a marathon!

☆**LONGEST STATIC CYCLING MARATHON** Switzerland's Mehrzad Shirvani rode a static cycle for a record eight days (192 hours) at the Kortrijk Xpo, Kortrijk, Belgium, from January 17 to 25, 2009. Shirvani beat the previous record by more than six hours.

LONGEST . . .

☆**Reading-aloud marathon (team)** Elizabeth Sánchez Vegas, Ana María Leonardi, María Cristina Alarcón, Lilly Blanco, Devorah Sasha, and Isabel Viera, from International Solidarity for Human Rights, read the Universal Declaration of Human Rights aloud at the InterAmerican Campus of the Miami Dade College in Miami, Florida, U.S.A., for 240 hr. 15 min. 27 sec. from November 3 to 13, 2009.

☆**Dance marathon (individual)** Dr. Vattikotta Yadagiriacharya (India) danced for 108 hours continuously at the Ravindra Bharathi Auditorium, Hyderabad, India, from November 25 to 29, 2008.

Tennis marathons The ☆**longest doubles tennis match** lasted 50 hr. 00 min. 8 sec. and was played between Vince Johnson, Bill Geideman, Brad Ansley, and Allen Finley (all U.S.A.) at the YMCA of Catawba Valley, Hickory, North Carolina, U.S.A., from November 7 to 9, 2008.

The ☆**longest singles tennis match** lasted 36 hours and was achieved by Dennis Schrader and Bart Hendriks (both Netherlands), in Zandvoort, the Netherlands, on September 10–11, 2009.

★**Stand-up comedy show (individual)** Comedian Tommy Tiernan (Ireland) performed a stand-up set lasting 36 hr. 15 min. at Nuns Island Theatre, Galway, Ireland. The event began at 3 p.m. on Friday, April 10, 2009, and ended two days later, at 3:15 a.m.

MAN: The **fastest time to complete an Ironman race** is 7 hr. 50 min. 27 sec., by Luc van Lierde (Belgium) at Roth, Germany, on July 13, 1997.

★ GREATEST DISTANCE RUN BY A RELAY TEAM The longest distance run by a relay team is 1,923 miles (3,096 km) and was achieved by the Gillette Phenomenal Tour over 14 days, from September 21, 2009, to October 5, 2009.

★ **Time to hold a live scorpion in the mouth** Kanchana Ketkaew (Thailand) held a living scorpion in her mouth for 2 min. 23 sec. on the set of *Lo Show dei Record* in Milan, Italy, on April 11, 2009. Her husband placed the scorpion in her mouth.

☆ **Full-body ice contact** Chen Kecai (China) spent 1 hr. 48 min. 21 sec. in direct contact with ice in the frozen Jingbo Lake, Mudanjiang City, China, on March 14, 2010.

☆ **Handshake**
• On September 21, 2009, Jack Tsonis and Lindsay Morrison (Australia) shook hands for 12 hr. 34 min. 56 sec. in Sydney, Australia.
• George Posner and John-Clark Levin (both U.S.A.) then shook for 15 hours in California, U.S.A., on October 4, 2009.
• And on November 21, 2009, Matthew Rosen and Joe Ackerman (both UK) shook for 15 hr. 30 min. 45 sec. in London, UK.

LAND SPEED RECORD

In late 2011 (or early 2012), a new attempt will be made at the land speed record. The team behind the attempt is led by the UK's Richard Noble and Andy Green, who set the current record of nearly 763 mph (1,228 km/h) in 1997. This time, the aim is to break the 1,000 mph (1,609 km/h) barrier. . . .

Land speed record The official land speed record (measured over one mile) is 763.035 mph (1,227.985 km/h; Mach 1.020), set by Andy Green (UK) on October 15, 1997, in the Black Rock Desert, Nevada, U.S.A., in *Thrust SSC* (SuperSonic Car).

Thrust SSC was the brainchild of former land speed record holder Richard Noble (UK).

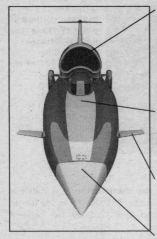

INTAKE DUCT A single, central intake duct delivers airflow to the engine. The procedure is: 1. air enters; 2. air is compressed and pressurized; 3. fuel is added, then ignited; 4. expanded air is forced through the turbines; 5. gases are expelled through a nozzle out of the back of the engine.

COCKPIT The driver is secured in a rigid carbon-fiber safety cell based on the design of a fighter plane's cockpit. Its designer, Andy Green (who will drive the *Bloodhound*), calls it the "world's fastest office"!

WINGLETS Dynamic (computer-controlled) winglets above the wheels help to maintain a constant wheel load—i.e., they keep the car on the ground!

BODYWORK The carbon-fiber and aluminum shell can withstand an air pressure of more than 2,457 lb./ft.^{2} (12 tonnes/m^2). Changes to the bodywork are constantly fed to the onboard computer.

★**First car to break the sound barrier** When Andy Green set the land speed record in 1997 in the Black Rock Desert, it was the first time that anyone on land had gone faster than the speed of sound—about 768 mph (1,236 km/h) in dry air at 68°F (20°C). The resultant sonic boom shook a school and caused sprinkler covers to fall off in the nearby town of Gerlach. Pilot Green achieved the record 50 years and a day after the sound barrier was broken in the air by pilot Chuck Yeager (U.S.A.).

Fastest speed on a conventional motorcycle John Noonan (U.S.A.) reached a speed of 252.662 mph (406.62 km/h) on a modified 1,350 cc Suzuki Hayabusa at Bonneville Salt Flats, Utah, U.S.A., on September 7, 2005.

Fastest rocket car The highest speed ever attained in a rocket-powered car is 631.367 mph (1,016.084 km/h) over the first measured kilometer by *The Blue Flame*, on the Bonneville Salt Flats, Utah, U.S.A., driven by Gary Gabelich (U.S.A.) on October 23, 1970. Momentarily, Gabelich exceeded 650 mph (1,046 km/h). The car was powered by a liquid natural gas/hydrogen peroxide rocket engine.

....

KUALA LUMPUR, MALAYSIA (3°08'N 101°41'E): The 426-ft. 5-inch tall (130-m) tower at Kuala Lumpur International Airport (KLIA) in Malaysia is the **tallest air traffic control tower** in the world. The tower, designed by a local architect, is shaped like a giant Olympic torch.

....

PARACHUTE After the attempt, the throttle is closed and airbrakes are deployed to begin *Bloodhound*'s deceleration. When the car slows to about 600 mph (950 km/h), a parachute is deployed, decreasing acceleration to 3 g. The car should stop within 4.5 miles (7 km).

FIN Directional stability is provided by a relatively small fin—too big and the car can be affected by crosswinds; too small and it will be unstable.

EJ200 ENGINE Approximately half of the thrust is provided by a 2,204-lb. (1,000-kg) Rolls-Royce EJ200 engine—a military turbofan normally found in the engine bay of a Eurofighter Typhoon. And located beneath the engine is the . . .

HYBRID SOLID-FUEL ROCKET At 350 mph (563 km/h), the 882-lb. (400-kg) hybrid solid-fuel rocket kicks in; together, the jet and rocket have a power of 47,500 lb. (212 kN)—equivalent to 180 Formula One cars.

REAR WHEELS The 35.8-in. (90-cm) solid-aluminum wheels turn 12,000 times a minute. They are protected by front- and rear-pointing covers that not only reduce drag but also protect the wheels from debris.

Fastest wheel-driven vehicle The fastest speed reached by a vehicle powered through its wheels—i.e., where the power of the engine is directed to the vehicle's wheels, as opposed to jet power—is 458.444 mph (737.794 km/h) by the turbine-powered *Vesco Turbinator*, driven by Don Vesco (U.S.A.) at Bonneville Salt Flats, Utah, U.S.A., on October 18, 2001.

Fastest car crash survived In September 1960, during trials to set a new land speed record at Bonneville, multiple world record holder Donald Campbell (UK) crashed his car *Bluebird* while traveling at a speed of 360 mph (579 km/h). The vehicle rolled over and Campbell fractured his skull; against all the odds, the daredevil driver survived.

QUIZ!: How long after the sound barrier was first broken did Andy Green set the current land speed record? See p. 543 for the answer.

GEE!: As he accelerates, Driver Andy Green will experience a G-force of 2.5 G, which will push him back into his seat and force the blood into his head.

SUPER-SONIC CAR Shown here is a CGI of the 14,148-lb. (6,422-kg), 50-ft.-long (12.8-m) *Bloodhound*, the SuperSonic Car (SSC) that Richard Noble (right) hopes will jet driver Andy Green (left) to more than 1,000 mph (1,609 km/h)—faster than the current low-altitude air speed record. The target being set for *Bloodhound* is a 31% improvement on the team's previous record-breaking *Thrust SSC* time!

WHIZZ!: As he slows down, Andy will feel a force of 3 G in the opposite direction, draining the blood from his head to his feet. It is hoped that he won't lose consciousness!

TRACK!: The *Bloodhound* team have chosen to attempt the record on a dried-up lake bed known as the Hakskeen Pan in the Northern Cape of South Africa.

Longest skid mark The skid mark made by the jet-powered *Spirit of America*, driven by Norman Craig Breedlove (U.S.A.), after the car went out of control at Bonneville in Utah, U.S.A., on October 15, 1964, was nearly 6 miles (10 km) long.

LAND SPEED MILESTONES

MPH	KM/H	YEAR	CAR	DRIVER	LOCATION
39.24	63.15	1898	*Jeantaud*	Gaston de Chasseloup-Laubat (France)	Achères, France
(100)					
103.56	166.66	1904	*Gobron Brillié*	Louis Rigolly (France)	Ostend, Belgium
(200)					
203.7	327.82	1927	*Sunbeam*	Henry Segrave (U.S.A.)	Daytona, Florida, U.S.A.
(300)					
301.12	484.60	1935	*Bluebird*	Donald Campbell (UK)	Bonneville, Utah, U.S.A.
(400)					
407.45	655.72	1963	*Spirit of America*	Craig Breedlove (U.S.A.)	Bonneville
(500)					
526.28	846.96	1964	*Spirit of America*	Craig Breedlove (U.S.A.)	Bonneville
(600)					
600.60	966.57	1965	*Spirit of America*	Craig Breedlove (U.S.A.)	Bonneville
(700)					
763.03	1,227.98	1997	*Thrust SSC*	Andy Green (UK)	Black Rock Desert, U.S.A.
(1000)					
1,000+	*1,609+*	*2011?*	Bloodhound *SSC*	*Andy Green (UK)*	*Hakskeen, SA*

The selected entries show the progression of the land speed record as each 100-mph milestone is reached.

SINGAPORE (1°22'N 103°48'E): The **largest walk** was The New Paper Big Walk 2000, in which 77,500 pedestrians set off from the National Stadium in Singapore on May 21, 2000, in order to promote healthy living and raise money for charity.

HIGH ACHIEVERS

☆ **Most conquests of Mount Everest** Apa Sherpa (Nepal) reached the summit of Mount Everest, on the Nepal-Tibet border, for the 19th time on May 21, 2009, the most times anyone has ever successfully climbed the world's highest mountain.

Apa began climbing in the late 1980s because he, like many other Sherpa people, found that being a guide was a good way to make money to support a family.

☆ **Oldest man to climb Mount Kilimanjaro** Reginald W. Alexander (UK, b. October 1, 1930) reached the summit of Mount Kilimanjaro, Tanzania, on August 3, 2009, aged 78 years 306 days.

> *"It will be a case of mind over matter. We want to show people that if we can do it, anyone can."*
>
> **Amputee John Sandford Hart (UK), preparing to climb Kilimanjaro on crutches**

★ **HIGHEST ALTITUDE SCUBA DIVING** Scuba dives have been made on several occasions at an altitude of 19,357 ft. (5,900 m), in a lagoon in the crater of Licancabur, a volcano on the border between Chile and Bolivia. One diver to investigate the lagoon was Henri Garcia of the Chilean Expedición America team; he spent 1 hr. 8 min. at depths of 16–23 ft. (5–7 m) on January 16, 1995.

CHENGDU, CHINA (30°39'N 104°04'E): The **largest panda cub born in captivity** weighed 7.6 oz. (218 g) when he was born at the Wolong Giant Panda Research Center, Chengdu, Sichuan Province, China, on August 7, 2006. The cub is the first offspring of Zhang Ka, who was in labor for 34 hours, itself the **longest recorded labor for captive pandas**.

MALE: According to the Senior Citizen Mount Everest Expedition, Min Bahadur Sherchan (Nepal) reached the top of Everest on May 25, 2008, at the record age of 76 years 340 days.

☆ **HIGHEST ALTITUDE CYCLING** Gil Bretschneider and Peer Schepanski (both Germany) rode their mountain bikes at an altitude of 23,658 ft. (7,211 m) on the slopes of the Muztagata peak in Xinjiang Province, China, on July 10, 2009.

The challenge started on June 23, 2009, when the pair were at an altitude of 17,552 ft. (5,350 m), and it took them 17 days to reach their goal.

★ **FIRST MARRIED COUPLE TO REACH THE SUMMIT OF MOUNT EVEREST** Phil and Susan Ershler (U.S.A.) were the first married couple to successfully climb Mount Everest, reaching the summit on Thursday, May 16, 2002—the same day that a record 54 people reached the top.

FEMALE: Tamae Watanabe (Japan) reached the summit of Mount Everest at the age of 63 years 177 days on May 16, 2002, becoming the oldest woman ever to do so.

★FASTEST ASCENT OF MOUNT KILIMANJARO ON CRUTCHES John Sandford Hart (UK, left center) completed an ascent of Mount Kilimanjaro on crutches in 4 days 20 hr. 30 min. Sandford Hart, who had his right leg amputated as the result of a boating accident, completed the challenge on October 24–29, 2009.

☆**Highest altitude reached by motorcycle** A team of six from the North Calcutta Disha Motorcycle Club (all India) rode their Hero Honda motorcycles to an altitude of 20,488 ft. (6,245 m) on the Changchemno Range near Marsemikla, India, on August 29, 2008.

Highest marathon The Everest Marathon, first run on November 27, 1987, begins at Gorak Shep (17,100 ft.; 5,212 m) and ends at Namche Bazar, (11,300 ft.; 3,444 m). The fastest time for a man to complete this race is 3 hr. 50 min. 23 sec. by Hari Roka (Nepal) in 2000, and the fastest time for a woman is 4 hr. 35 min. 4 sec. by Anna Frost (New Zealand) in 2009.

First woman to climb Mount Everest Junko Tabei (Japan) reached the summit of Mount Everest on May 16, 1975.

HO CHI MINH CITY, VIETNAM (10°46'N 106°41'E): The **largest T-shirt** measured 187 ft. 7 in. (57.19 m) long and 134 ft. 1 in. (40.88 m) wide. The T-shirt was made by OMO Safe Detergent in Ho Chi Minh City, Vietnam, and displayed on March 9, 2006.

FIRST PEOPLE TO CLIMB EACH OF THE 8,000ERS

The 8,000ers are the 14 mountains on Earth that rise to more than 26,247 ft. (8,000 m) above sea level. They are all located in the Himalayan and Karakoram mountain ranges in Asia. Reinhold Messner (Italy) became the **first person to climb all of the 8,000ers** when he summited Lhotse on the Nepal-Tibet border on October 16, 1986, having begun his quest in June 1970—a total of 16 years 3 months 19 days. By the end of 2009, only 18 people had completed the feat. The ★ **fastest person to climb all 8,000ers** is Jerzy Kukuczka (Poland), who took 7 years 11 months 14 days to complete the feat, between October 4, 1979, and September 18, 1987. (source for table: www.8000ers.com)

MOUNTAIN	HEIGHT	DATE	EXPEDITION NATIONALITY	FIRST TO CLIMB (nationality as Expedition unless stated)
Everest	29,028 ft. (8,848 m)	May 29, 1953	British	Edmund Hillary (New Zealand), Tenzing Norgay (India/Sherpa)
K2	28,251 ft. (8,611 m)	July 31, 1954	Italian	Achille Compagnoni, Lino Lacedelli
Kangchenjunga	28,169 ft. (8,586 m)	May 25, 1955	British	George Band, Joe Brown
Lhotse	27,939 ft. (8,516 m)	May 18, 1956	Swiss	Fritz Luchsinger, Ernst Reiss
Makalu	27,837 ft. (8,485 m)	May 15, 1955	French	Jean Couzy, Lionel Terray
Cho Oyu	26,863 ft. (8,188 m)	May 19, 1954	Austrian	Josef Jöchler, Herbert Tichy, Pasang Dawa Lama (India/Sherpa)
Dhaulagiri I	26,794 ft. (8,167 m)	May 13, 1960	Swiss	Kurt Diemberger (Austria), Peter Diener (Germany), Ernst Forrer, Albin Schelbert, Nawang Dorje (Nepal/Sherpa), Dorji (Nepal/Sherpa)
Manaslu	26,781 ft. (8,163 m)	May 9, 1956	Japanese	Toshio Imanishi, Gyalzen Norbu (India/Sherpa)
Nanga Parbat	26,656 ft. (8,125 m)	July 3, 1953	Austro-German	Hermann Buhl (Austria)
Annapurna I	26,545 ft. (8,091 m)	June 3, 1950	French	Maurice Herzog, Louis Lachenal
Gasherbrum I	26,509 ft. (8,080 m)	July 5, 1958	American	Andrew Kauffman, Peter Schoening
Broad Peak	26,414 ft. (8,051 m)	June 9, 1957	Austrian	Hermann Buhl, Kurt Diemberger, Marcus Schmuck, Fritz Wintersteller
Gasherbrum II	26,362 ft. (8,035 m)	July 7, 1956	Austrian	Josef Larch, Fritz Moravec, Johann Willenpart
Shisha Pangma	26,335 ft. (8,027 m)	May 2, 1964	Chinese	Hsu Ching, Chang Chun-yen, Wang Fu-zhou, Chen Sam, Cheng Tien-liang, Wu Tsung-yue, Sodnam Doji, Migmar, Trashi, Doji, Yonten

REACH FOR THE SKIES

First aircraft flight over the North Pole Roald Amundsen (Norway) made the first verified flight over the North Pole on May 12, 1926, in the airship *Norge*. Amundsen was accompanied on the flight from Spitzbergen, Norway, to Alaska, U.S.A., by 15 crew members, including Umberto Nobile (Italy), the airship's designer and pilot, American explorer Lincoln Ellsworth, and Oscar Wisting (Norway), a polar explorer who was also the helmsman.

NORTH!: Ivan André Trifonov (Austria) flew a one-man Thunder and Colt Cloudhopper balloon over the geographic North Pole on April 20, 1996. . . .

★**FASTEST ELECTRIC AIRCRAFT** On June 12, 2009, Maurizio Cheli (Italy) piloted the electrically powered SkySpark light aircraft at the World Air Games 2009 in Turin, Italy. During the eight-minute flight, Cheli achieved a record-breaking maximum speed of 155 mph (250 km/h).

SOUTH!: . . . On January 8, 2000, Trifonov ballooned over the geographic South Pole, Antartica. He is the first man to achieve both feats.

HONG KONG, CHINA (22°18'N 114°12'E): The **world's longest escalator system** is Hong Kong's Central Hillside Escalator Link. The 2,624-ft.-long (800-m) system carries commuters between the Mid-Levels district and Central Market on Hong Kong Island.

EXTRA! Want to look even farther afield? Check out the space chapter, from p. 1.

★ MOST TANDEM JUMPS BY ONE INSTRUCTOR IN 24 HOURS Harold "Chip" Bowlin, with his passenger Kristine Gould (both U.S.A.), achieved 103 tandem parachute jumps in 24 hours, the record for a single instructor. The attempt was undertaken in Zephyrhills Skydive City, Florida, U.S.A., on April 14–15, 2009.

★First landing on an aircraft carrier Flying a Sea Vampire of the Royal Navy registration LZ551/G, Eric "Winkle" Brown (UK) became the first person to land and take off a jet aircraft from an aircraft carrier (HMS *Ocean*) on December 3, 1945.

★First corps of military balloonists The French Army established a corps of balloonists—known as the Aérostiers—on April 2, 1794. The corps was a reconnaissance unit that used its elevated position to plot the location of the enemy on the battlefield.

★ GREATEST VERTICAL DISTANCE FREEFALLING IN 24 HOURS The greatest accumulated vertical distance covered while freefalling in 24 hours is 63.38 miles (102 km) and was achieved by the Nagual Freefly Team—Daniele Fraternali, Cristian Giorgi, and Alessandro Mitrugno (all Italy)—in Fano, Italy, on June 28, 2009.

BANDAR SERI BEGAWAN, BRUNEI (4°53'N 114°56'E): The **most countries to participate in an international military tattoo** is 13 at the Brunei Darussalam International Tattoo 2006, which was organized by the Ministry of Defence and the Royal Brunei Armed Forces at the Hassanal Bolkiah National Stadium in Bandar Seri Begawan, Brunei, from July 29, to August 1, 2006.

QUIZ!: In 1911, Norway's Roald Amundsen became the **first man to reach the south pole**. What other polar record did he achieve 15 years later? See p. 543 for the answer.

★**FASTEST HANG GLIDER**
Dustin Martin (U.S.A.) completed a circuit of a 62.14-mile (100-km) triangular course in a hang glider at an average speed of 30.45 mph (49 km/h). A U.S. national hang-gliding team member, Martin completed his flight over Zapata, Texas, U.S.A., on July 26, 2009, in his Wills Wing T2C 144.

☆**Farthest flight by a paraglider (female)** Kamira Pereira (Brazil) flew her paraglider 201.63 miles (324.5 km) in a straight line west from Quixada, Brazil, on November 14, 2009. In doing so, she beat her own record of 200.7 miles (323 km), which she had set just six days earlier.

☆**Heaviest item airlifted** A power plant generator weighing 206.7 tons (187.6 tonnes) was airlifted by an Antonov Airlines 225 "Mriya" aircraft at Frankfurt Hahn Airport in Frankfurt, Germany, on August 11, 2009.

★**Largest civilian formation flight** A record 37 Van's RV Aircraft led by Stu McCurdy (U.S.A.) flew in different close formations during the Air-Venture09 Airshow in Oshkosh, Wisconsin, U.S.A., on July 28–29, 2009.

★**OLDEST SOLO PILOT HELICOPTER FLIGHT** Peter Chantler (UK) completed a solo helicopter flight over Rosebank Farm in Tarporley, UK, on April 8, 2009, at the age of 83 years 2 months and 11 days.

"Once you've learned the skills, your muscles remember."
Peter Chantler (above)

First flight over Everest On April 3, 1933, two aircraft, a Houston-Westland and a Westland-Wallace—both open-cockpit biplanes fitted with Bristol Pegasus SIII engines—made the first manned flights over Mount Everest (29,029 ft.; 8,848 m), the **highest mountain in the world**. The aircraft took off from Lalbalu aerodrome, near Purnea, India, crewed by Colonel L.V.S. Blacker and Squadron Leader Lord Clydesdale in one and Flight Lieutenant D. F. MacIntyre and S. R. Bonnet (all UK) in the other.

The flight cleared the mountain by a reported 100 ft. (30.48 m). Close-range photographs of Everest proved the achievement.

★ **First public demonstration of a steerable lighter-than-air craft** On September 24, 1852, engineer Henri Giffard (France) traveled 16.7 miles (27 km), from Paris to Trappes (both France), in his hydrogen-filled dirigible. He controlled the aircraft using a tiny steam engine, and maintained a speed of just 3 mph (5 km/h).

★ **Longest hot-air balloon flight by a female team** On September 8, 2009, Dr. Ann Webb and Dr. Janet Folkes (both UK) set a new world record for the longest balloon flight by an all-female team, breaking the previous record of 60 hr. 12 min. by just over nine hours. They set the record during the annual Coupe Aéronautique Gordon Bennett.

Fastest time to fly a helicopter around the world (eastbound) Simon Oliphant-Hope (UK) flew around the world in a time of 17 days 14 hr. 2 min. 27 sec., at an average speed of 55.2 mph (88.9 km/h), in an MD Hughes HU/50-MD500E single-engined helicopter from June 3–21, 2004. His start and finishing point was Shoreham, West Sussex, UK.

Highest flight by an airship David Hempleman-Adams (UK) flew a Boland Rover A-2 airship over Rosedale, Alberta, Canada, reaching an altitude ratified by the Fédération Aéronautique Internationale (FAI) at 21,699 ft. (6,614 m) on December 13, 2004.

Longest time flying an airship In November 1928, Hugo Eckener (Germany) flew the Graf Zeppelin for 71 hours, covering a total of 3,967 miles (6,384.5 km), between Lakehurst, New Jersey, U.S.A., and Friedrichshafen, Germany. This is the longest nonstop flight by an airship, both in distance and duration.

ALL AT SEA

Atlantic ocean The **first person to row any ocean solo** is John Fairfax (UK), who rowed the Atlantic east to west in *Britannia* from January 20 to July 19, 1969. He and Sylvia Cook (UK) were also the **first team to row the Pacific Ocean**, in *Britannia II*, between April 26, 1971, and April 22, 1972.

John Fairfax also holds the record for the **first person to row two oceans**.

★FIRST TANDEM ROW ACROSS THE INDIAN OCEAN Guy Watts and Andrew Delaney (both UK) rowed across the Indian Ocean aboard their boat *Flying Ferkins* in 102 days 13 hr. 40 min. between April 19 and July 30, 2009. Guy and Andrew's incredible achievement secured the pair Guinness World Records recognition for the **first** and the ★**fastest tandem row across the Indian Ocean.**

PERTH, AUSTRALIA (31°57'S 115°51'E): The **longest line of footprints** consisted of 15,200 foot marks and measured 14,711 ft. (4,484 m) at an event arranged by WA Newspapers in Perth, Australia, on December 10, 2005.

**★ FASTEST NORTH SEA
CROSSING BY A DOUBLE SEA
KAYAK (CANOEING)** On July 4,
2009, Ian Castro and Simon
Worsley (both UK) crossed the
North Sea in a double kayak in
17 hr. 53 min. They began in
Southwold, UK, and ended in
Zeebrugge, Belgium. The pair
also achieved the **fastest
North Sea crossing in single
sea kayaks:** 24 hr 20 min.,
ending on August 28, 1999.

The **youngest person to sail the Atlantic Ocean solo** is David Sandeman
(UK), who, in 1976, sailed between Jersey, UK, and Newport, Rhode Island,
U.S.A., aged 17 years 176 days.

David's boat was the 35-ft.-long (10.67-m) *Sea Raider,* and his voyage
lasted 43 days. *Guinness World Records does not endorse or sanction any
attempts under the age of 16 for this category.*

Indian ocean The ★ **first row across the Indian Ocean by a four-
man-strong team** was completed by team Row 4 Charity—Phil McCorry,
Matt Hellier, Ian Allen, and Nick McCorry (all UK)—who completed the
journey aboard the *Bexhill Trust Challenger* between April 19 and June 26,
2009.

The ★ **first row across the Indian Ocean by a female team of four** was
by the Ocean Angels—Sarah Duff, Fiona Waller, Elin Haf Davis, and
Joanna Jackson (all UK)—who made the crossing from April 19 to July 6,
2009, in the *Pura Vida*.

The Ocean Angels quartet completed their trip in 78 days—making it the
★ **fastest row across the Indian Ocean by a team of four (female)**.

The ★ **fastest row across the Indian Ocean** took 58 days 15 hr. 8 min.,
between April 28 and June 25, 2009. The feat was accomplished by team Pirate Row—Angela Madsen, Doug Tumminello, Brian Flick (all U.S.A.);
Helen Taylor, Paul Cannon, Ian Couch, Simon Chalk (all UK); and Bernard
Fissett (Belgium)—in their boat *Aud Eamus.* The trip also gave them another record—see p. 202!

EXTRA! If we've whetted your appetite for adventure, turn to p. 183 for more amazing feats of endurance.

★ **FIRST CROSSING OF THE INDIAN OCEAN (TEAM)** The eight-strong team Pirate Row—comprising one Belgian, four Britons, and three Americans—rowed across the Indian Ocean between April 28 and June 25, 2009, in their craft, *Aud Eamus*.

Pacific ocean Mick Dawson and Chris Martin (UK) were the ★ **first team to row the Pacific Ocean (west to east)**. They made the journey from Choshi, Japan, to the Golden Gate Bridge, San Francisco, California, U.S.A., aboard their craft, *Bojangles*, in 189 days 10 hr. 39 min., between May 8 and November 13, 2009.

Born on February 19, 1947, Peter Bird (UK) was the ★ **youngest person to row solo (east to west) across the Pacific Ocean** in his boat, *Hele-on-Britannia*. He left San Francisco, U.S.A., on August 23, 1982, and arrived at the Great Barrier Reef, Australia, on June 14, 1983, at the age of 36 years 114 days. In doing so, he also became the **first person to row the Pacific Ocean solo**.

....

BEIJING, CHINA (39°54'N 116°24'E): The Imperial Palace in the center of Beijing, China, covers a rectangle measuring 3,150 x 2,460 ft. (960 x 750 m) over an area of 178 acres (72 ha). It is the **largest palace** on Earth. The outline survives from the construction of the third Ming emperor, Yongle (1402–24).

....

WATER: At 64,186,000 miles^2 (166,241,000 km^2), the Pacific Ocean is about twice the size of the Atlantic (33,420,000 miles^2; 86,557,000 km^2).

FASTEST ATLANTIC CROSSING WALK ON WATER Rémy Bricka (France) "walked" across the Atlantic Ocean between Tenerife, Canary Islands, and Trinidad on 13-ft. 9-in.-long (4.2-m) skis in 59 days, from April 2 to May 31, 1988. He covered 3,502 miles (5,636 km), towing a platform housing supplies and essentials, such as a water still. Rémy is also a seasoned musician, and has produced a string of albums and singles since the 1970s.

WORLD: Approximately 70% of the earth's surface is covered by water—around 138,000,000 miles^2 (360,000,000 km^2).

The **fastest solo row (west to east) across the Pacific Ocean** is 134 days 12 hr. 15 min., by Gerard d'Aboville (France). He departed from Choshi, Japan, on July 11, 1991, and arrived in Ilwaco, Washington, U.S.A., on November 21, 1991, after covering 6,200 nautical miles (7,134 miles; 11,482 km).

The raft *Nord*, captained by Andrew Urbanczyk (U.S.A.), sailed from Half Moon Bay, California, U.S.A., to the Pacific island of Guam, a straight-line distance of 5,110 nautical miles (5,880 miles; 9,463 km), in 136 days from August 26, 2002, to January 28, 2003. This represents the **longest nonstop journey by raft**.

English channel The **fastest swim of the English Channel**, and the **fastest swim of the England-France route**, is 6 hr. 57 min. 50 sec. and was achieved by Petar Stoychev (Bulgaria), who crossed from Shakespeare Beach, Dover, UK, to Cap Gris Nez, France, on August 24, 2007.

On May 24, 2007, Micha Robyn (Belgium) achieved the ★ **fastest crossing of the English Channel by waterski**, in 29 min. 26 sec.

The **oldest person to swim the English Channel** was George Brunstad (U.S.A., b. August 25, 1934), who was aged 70 years 4 days when he completed the crossing, in a time of 15 hr. 59 min., on August 29, 2004.

Simon Paterson (UK) traveled underwater from France to England with an air hose attached to a pilot boat in 14 hr. 50 min. on July 28, 1962, the **fastest time to swim the English Channel underwater**.

The ★ **fastest crossing of the English Channel by a single canoe/kayak** is 2 hr. 59 min., by Ian Wynne (UK), between Shakespeare Beach, Dover, UK, and Cap Gris Nez, France, on October 5, 2007.

HUMAN SOCIETY

CONTENTS

THAT'S LIFE

UNICEF

After World War II, children in Europe were at great risk of famine and disease, so the United Nations Children's Fund (UNICEF) was created in December 1946 to provide them with food, clothing, and health care. Today, the organization provides humanitarian aid to children in developing countries worldwide.

WHO?: In July 2009, the population of Afghanistan was estimated at 28,395,716, of whom 43.6% are aged between 0 and 14 years. (Male, 6,343,611; female, 6,036,673.)

★**MOST DANGEROUS COUNTRY IN WHICH TO BE BORN** According to the UNICEF Annual Report *The State of the World's Children*, Afghanistan is the worst country in which a child can be born. The infant mortality rate in the country is 257 deaths for every 1,000 live births. Apart from the danger posed by military operations against Taliban insurgents, the lack of access to clean water and growing insecurity in the country often make it impossible to carry out vital life-saving vaccination programs against diseases such as poliomyelitis and measles. Afghanistan also has the world's ★**lowest adult life expectancy: 43.8 years.**

WHERE?: Afghanistan is situated in Southern Asia, north and west of Pakistan and east of Iran. It has an area of 251,827 miles^2 (652,230 km^2), which is slightly smaller than Texas, U.S.A.

EXTRA! Turn to pp. 216–220 for more on Nations & Politics.

Most prolific mother The greatest recorded number of children born to one mother is 69, to the first wife of Feodor Vassilyev (Russia). In 27 pregnancies between 1725 and 1765, she gave birth to 16 pairs of twins, seven sets of triplets, and four sets of quadruplets. Only two of the children failed to survive their infancy.

This mother also holds the records for giving birth to the most sets of twins and the most sets of quadruplets.

Most sets of triplets Maddalena Granata (Italy, 1839–1886) gave birth to 15 sets of triplets during her lifetime.

Most generations born on the same day Five families hold the record for having four generations born on the same day: Ralph Betram Williams (U.S.A., b. July 4, 1982), Veera Tuulia Tuijantyär Kivistö (Finland, b. March 21, 1997), Maureen Werner (U.S.A., b. October 13, 1998), Jacob Camren Hildebrandt (U.S.A., b. August 23, 2001), and Mion Masuda (Japan, b. March 26, 2005) all share their birthday with a parent, grandparent, and great-grandparent.

☆ **LONGEST MARRIAGE** Herbert Fisher (U.S.A., b. June 10, 1905) and Zelmyra Fisher (U.S.A., b. December 10, 1907) were married on May 13, 1924, in North Carolina, U.S.A. They had been married for 85 years, 10 months, and 8 days as of March 21, 2010.

SILVER SURFERS: For tips on a long, healthy marriage, follow Herbert and Zelmyra's twitter feed at http://twitter.com/longestmarried.

TAINAN, TAIWAN (22°59'N 120°11'E): The **largest display of lanterns** in a single venue numbered 47,759, at an event organized by Tainan County Government at Solar City in the "Prayer for Peace" area of Tainan Science Park in Tainan, Taiwan, on February 24, 2008.

MOST ALBINO SIBLINGS All four children of Canada's Mario and Angie Gaulin—Sarah (b. 1981), Christopher (b. 1983), Joshua (b. 1987), and Brendan (b. 1989)—were born with the rare genetic condition oculocutaneous albinism. Their father also has the condition, and their mother carries the gene. Pictured at left are the family's three brothers.

Most twins born on the same day There are only two verified examples of a mother producing two sets of twins with coincident birthdays. The first is that of Laura Shelley (U.S.A.), who gave birth to Melissa Nicole and Mark Fredrick Julian Jr. on March 25, 1990, and Kayla May and Jonathan Price Moore on the same date in 2003. The second is that of Caroline Cargado (U.S.A.), who gave birth to Keilani Marie and Kahleah Mae on May 30, 1996, and Mikayla Anee and Malia Abigail on the same date in 2003.

☆ **Most couples married in 24 hours** A total of 163 couples were married, one after the other, at the Singapore Botanic Gardens in Singapore on September 20, 2009.

☆ **Largest vow-renewal ceremony** On June 20, 2009, 1,087 married couples amassed at Miami University in Oxford, Ohio, U.S.A., for the "Miami Merger Moment," a wedding-vow-renewal event that formed part of the university's Alumni Weekend.

MANILA, THE PHILIPPINES (14°35'N 120°58'E): On May 22, 1998, the Central Bank of Manila, in the Philippines, issued a special commemorative 100,000-peso legal-tender banknote, measuring 8½ x 11 in. (22 x 33 cm), printed by Giesecke Devrient of Munich, Germany. It is the **largest legal banknote**, in terms of size.

★ MOST "MULTIPLES" IN ONE CLASS The 2009–10 tenth-grade class (left) at J. J. Pearce High School in Richardson, Texas, U.S.A., boasts 10 sets of twins and one set of triplets. Having 10 sets of twins in one academic year is also a record, shared with the 7th grade of the 2006–07 year at Raymond J. Grey Jr. High School in Acton, Massachusetts, U.S.A. At the Louis Marshall School in Brooklyn, New York City, U.S.A., there were 29 sets of twins for the 1999–2000 school year (the most twins in one school).

★ MOST SETS OF MIXED TWINS Lightning struck twice for mixed-race parents Dean Durrant (UK, of West Indian descent) and Alison Spooner (UK) when, in March 2009, Alison delivered her second set of mixed twins: Leah and Miya. In 2001, she gave birth to mixed twins—the dark-skinned Hayleigh and fair-skinned Layren.

ODDS: A mixed-race couple has a 1-in-500,000 chance of having a set of mixed twins, but no statistics exist for Leah and Miya—two sets is such a rare occurrence!

SHANGHAI, CHINA (31°12'N 121°30'E): The world's **highest library** is located on the 60th story of the JW Marriott Hotel at Tomorrow Square in Shanghai, China, at 757 ft. 6 in. (230.9 m) above street level. Membership is available to the public, and the 103 shelves in the library contain an ever-expanding collection of Chinese and English books.

EXTRA! For more bizarre body records, visit "Skin Deep" on pp. 115–119.

★**FIRST ZERO-GRAVITY WEDDING** On June 23, 2009, Erin Finnegan and Noah Fulmor (both U.S.A.) wed in zero gravity in a modified Boeing 727-200. Weightlessness was achieved by flying the plane in repeated dives from 36,000 ft. (10,970 m) to 24,000 ft. (7,315 m).

☆**Longest bridal veil** A wedding veil measuring 11,017 ft. (3,358 m) long was worn by Sandra Mechleb at her wedding to Chady Abi Younis (both Lebanon) in Arnaoon, Lebanon, on October 18, 2009. The veil was longer than 140 tennis courts laid end to end.

★**Smallest age differential in a married couple** The married couple with the smallest known age difference is Allan Ramirez (b. December 19, 1980, 12:14 p.m.) and Elizabeth Ramirez (b. December 19, 1980, 12:16 p.m.) of Texas, U.S.A., who were born just two minutes apart. They were married on November 4, 2000, in Plantersville, Texas, U.S.A.

☆**Most expensive divorce** When media mogul Rupert Murdoch and his wife Anna (both Australia) divorced in 1999—after 32 years of marriage—he agreed to let his ex-wife have $1.7 billion worth of his assets as well as $110 million in cash. He remarried soon after.

DEATH

★**Oldest known catacombs** The first burial chambers to be referred to directly as catacombs were those beneath San Sebastiano ad Catacumbas (aka Sebastiano fuori le mura) in Rome, Italy, which was built in the early 4th century. There are many such tombs along the Via Appia (Appian Way)—the ancient road that leads from Rome to Brindisi—as burials were considered Christian and outlawed within the walls of Rome.

QUIZ!: On average, how many graves did Johann Heinrich Karl Thime dig in his 50-year career? See p. 543 for the answer.

☆**LARGEST GATHERING OF ZOMBIES** The Big Chill music festival in Ledbury, Herefordshire, UK, was swamped by 4,026 zombies on August 6, 2009. The living dead were taking part in filming for the forthcoming Film4/Warp Films production *I Spit on Your Rave*. Set nine years in the future, the movie stars comedian Noel Fielding (UK) as a zombie king in a Britain wiped out by a virus.

★**Largest automated tomb facility** The six-story Kouanji Buddhist Temple in Tokyo, Japan, is an automated tomb facility that, as of January 1, 2010, houses 6,850 human remains. Square marble boxes—which can contain the cremated remains ("cremains") of up to nine relatives—are accessed by visitors using a swipe card that identifies the location of the remains and delivers them via a conveyor-belt system. Each burial costs around Y800,000 ($8,800).

Largest communal tomb A communal tomb housing 180,000 World War II dead on Okinawa, Japan, was enlarged in 1985 to accommodate another 9,000 bodies thought to be buried on the island.

Farthest resting place On July 31, 1999, America's *Lunar Prospector* spacecraft crashed into the Moon after 18 months of successful mission operations. Incorporated into this orbiter was a small (1.5-in.; 3.8-cm) polycarbonate container holding 1 oz. (28.3 g) of the remains of the pioneering planetary scientist Dr. Eugene Shoemaker (U.S.A.). Wrapped around the container was a piece of foil inscribed with some of Shoemaker's work.

TAIPEI, TAIWAN (25°02'N 121°38'E): The **largest gathering of twins** took place in Taiwan on November 12, 1999, when 3,961 pairs converged on the square of Taipei City Hall. The twins came from as far away as the UK, Germany, India, and the U.S.A., and ranged in age from one month to 88 years.

CATACOMB

Underground tomb or burial chamber, suspected to derive from the Latin *cata tumbas*—"among the tombs."

★ **LARGEST OSSUARY** The skeletal remains of 6 million people lie, neatly arranged, in subterranean catacombs—aka ossuaries or charnel houses—beneath the streets of Paris, France. The city is riddled with an estimated 186 miles (300 km) of tunnels and pathways, of which 3 acres (nearly 11,000 m²) are packed tightly with the bones of those reinterred from the city's overflowing cemeteries in the late 1700s.

LARGEST MASS CREMATION In December 1997, at a temple in Smut Scom, Thailand, tons of bones (including 21,347 skulls) were cremated to mark the end of urban burials in Bangkok, the overcrowded Thai capital. The bones represented unclaimed remains from a Chinese cemetery in Bangkok.

SHENYANG, CHINA (41°47'N 123°27'E): A brush measuring 18 ft. 4 in. (5.6 m) long and 6 ft. 9 in. (2.06 m) wide—the **largest calligraphy brush**—was used by calligrapher Zhang Kesi (China) to paint the Chinese character for "long" (which means "dragon") at the China International Horticultural Exposition on May 6, 2006.

LARGEST FUNERALS The funeral of India's charismatic C. N. Annadurai (above right, d. Feb 3, 1969), a Chennai Chief Minister, was attended by 15 million people, according to police sources.

- The queue at the grave of the popular Russian singer Vladimir Visotsky (d. July 28, 1980) stretched for 6 miles (10 km).

Largest live TV audience The worldwide TV audience for the funeral of Diana, Princess of Wales (UK, 1961–97) on September 6, 1997, at Westminster Abbey, London, UK, was watched by an estimated global audience of 2.5 billion.

Largest virtual funeral In October 2005, an avid computer gamer known only as Snowly (China) indulged in a three-day nonstop marathon of the massively multiplayer online role-playing game *World of Warcraft* (Blizzard, U.S.A.). While attempting a particularly challenging task in the game, Snowly died of fatigue in the real world. More than 100 gamers visited a virtual cathedral inside the game, where a service was held in her memory.

★ **MOST EXPENSIVE GHOSTS** Two vials supposedly containing the exorcized spirits of an old man and a young girl were sold at an online auction in March 2010 for NZ $2,830 (U.S. $1,990). New Zealander Avie Woodbury claimed to have enlisted the help of an exorcist and a Ouija board to contact and trap the spirits in July 2009.

GENEROUS SPIRITS: Proceeds from the sale of the expensive spirits—trapped in bottles with holy water—will go to an animal charity...once the exorcist's fee has been paid.

★ LONGEST-RUNNING FESTIVAL OF THE DEAD In one form or another, Día de los Muertos (Day of the Dead) in Mexico has been celebrated in this part of the world for more than 3,500 years. To honor their dead, and the goddess Mictecacihuatl (the "Lady of the Dead"), the Aztecs and other Meso-Americans would perform rites and rituals, often involving skulls. Today the tradition continues on November 1 and 2 each year, with the emphasis on partying and celebrating with the family, often in flamboyant costumes and masks.

Fastest hearse Joe Gosschalk (Australia) covered a quarter-mile in his 1979 Ford LTD P6 hearse in 13.7 sec. at 98 mph (158 km/h) at Willowbank Raceway in Queensland, Australia, on June 10, 2005. The hearse has a 351-cu-in. (5.7-liter) engine with nitrous oxide boost. Its license plates read "Undead."

Longest career as a grave digger It is recorded that Johann Heinrich Karl Thieme, sexton of Aldenburg, Germany, dug 23,311 graves during a 50-year career. After his death in 1826, his understudy dug *his* grave!

PYONGYANG, NORTH KOREA (39°00'N 125°30'E): The world's **longest train journey without changing trains** is one of 6,346 miles (10,214 km) from Moscow, Russia, to Pyongyang in North Korea. One train a week makes the journey by this route, which includes sections of the famous Trans-Siberian line. It is scheduled to take 7 days 20 hr. 25 min.

NATIONS & POLITICS

★**Largest country without an airport** With an area of 180 miles^2 (468 km^2) and a population of 71,822, Andorra is the largest country without an airport. Visitors wishing to travel there by air are advised to fly to Barcelona and take a bus the rest of the way.

☆**Most corrupt country** According to Transparency International's most recent Corruption Perceptions Index, in 2009 Somalia scored 1.1 on its 10-point corruption scale. By contrast, New Zealand rated as the ☆**least corrupt country** with a score of 9.4.

★**Country with most political armed groups** On January 7, 2010, an independent commission in the Philippines began work on disbanding politicians' private armies. According to the Philippines's Defense Secretary Norberto Gonzales, there are 132 armed groups, many led by politicians, totaling some 10,000 armed individuals spread throughout the country. Such private armies are typically used to assist the official security forces and to defend communities endangered by communist or Muslim separatist guerrillas, but are also often used to maintain local politicians in power by intimidating rivals, voters, and journalists.

★**LEAST STABLE STATE** Somalia has lacked an effective central government since 1991, when the previous president was overthrown. Since Ethiopian troops left Somalia in January 2009, its stability rating has fallen further, according to *Jane's Intelligence Review*.

SEOUL, SOUTH KOREA (37°33'N 126°59'E): The **first cloned dog to survive birth** was Snuppy, an Afghan hound puppy, created by Hwang Woo-Suk (South Korea) and his team of scientists at Seoul National University (SNU) in South Korea, and born by caesarean section on April 25, 2005.

☆ **HIGHEST DEATH RATE FROM AIDS (COUNTRY)** In 2007, incidence of AIDS-related deaths in Zimbabwe reached a shocking 1,060 people per 100,000 population. An estimated 15.3% of Zimbabwe's population is living with AIDS, but drought, famine, and a poor economy have all made matters worse.

★ **COUNTRIES MOST THREATENED BY INUNDATION** The collection of reef islands and atolls (such as Funafuti Atoll, above) that constitute the low-lying nations of Tuvalu and the Maldives are under imminent threat of disappearing under the waves due to a combination of factors, including rising sea levels due to global warming. At their highest elevations, Tuvalu and the Maldives are 16 ft. 3 in. (5 m) and 8 ft. (2.4 m) above sea level, respectively.

☆ **LONGEST-REIGNING LIVING MONARCH** Born on December 5, 1927, King Bhumibol Adulyadej, King Rama IX of the Chakri dynasty of Thailand, ascended to the throne on June 9, 1946, following the death of his older brother. His formal coronation did not take place until May 5, 1950, and he has since reigned without interruption for more than 63 years.

★ **Largest march against illegal drugs** The "Grand BIDA March" against illegal drugs included 332,963 people and was held in Manila, in the Philippines, on March 21, 2009.

Largest opium producer Despite a reduction in recent years, Afghanistan still had the largest opium harvest in 2008, according to United Nations statistics, with an 8,480-ton (7,700-tonne) crop, worth $3.4 billion in the illegal heroin trade.

★ **Largest opium seizure** According to the 2009 report of the United Nations Office on Drugs and Crime (UNODC), Afghanistan's eastern neighbor Iran seized 941,698 lb. (427,147 kg) of opium in 2007, a figure that constitutes 84% of all opium seizures worldwide in that year.

KAGOSHIMA, JAPAN (31°36'N 130°33'E): The **largest sliding doors** are 221 ft. 4 in. (67.46 m) high, 88 ft. 5 in. (26.95 m) wide, and 8 ft. 2 in. (2.5 m) thick, and weigh 882,000 lb. (400 tonnes) each. They are fitted to the vehicle assembly building at the Japan Aerospace Exploration Agency's (JAXA) Tanegashima Space Center in Kagoshima, Japan.

★**LONGEST-SERVING DEMOCRATIC HEAD** Lee Kuan Yew was Prime Minister of Singapore from 1959 to 1990—a total of 31 consecutive years. Despite leaving power, Kuan Yew remains an important political figure in Singapore and is "Minister Mentor" to the current Prime Minister, his son Lee Hsien Loong.

Iran also registered the largest seizures of heroin and morphine in 2007, with 56,394 lb. (25,580 kg)—representing 28% of the global total.

★**Largest donor of foreign aid** The U.S.A. donated $21.7 billion worth of aid to foreign countries in 2007, according to figures published by *The Economist*. The ★**largest recipient of foreign aid** in 2007 was Iraq, which received $9.1 billion.

★**Most human rights activists killed** The 2010 Human Rights Watch World Report revealed that eight murders were perpetrated against human rights supporters in Russia during 2009.

★**LAST SPEAKER OF BO** Bo, the tongue of the Bo tribe of the Andaman Islands in the Bay of Bengal, is said to have emerged 10,000 years ago. In January 2010, it ceased to be a living language when its last native speaker, Boa Sr (pictured at left), died.

☆**Highest natural population increase** The population of the East African state of Niger is currently estimated to grow 3.73% between 2010 and 2015, largely thanks to the country's high fertility rate. It's estimated that there will be 6.86 children for each woman of childbearing age during the same period.

CONFLICT

☆**Largest Army** According to 2008 estimates published in the CIA World Factbook, the manpower available for military service in China is 375,009,345 people, with 218,459,000 active military personnel.

★**Largest scuttling of ships** On November 27, 1942, the French fleet in Toulon, France, was scuttled on the orders of the French Admiralty to avoid their capture by German forces. Of the 73 ships sunk in the action, 57 were major vessels. Only three submarines managed to escape Toulon and join up with the Allies.

★**Youngest serviceman to die in World War II** On February 5, 2010, on what would have been his 83rd birthday, Reginald Earnshaw (UK) was

☆**HIGHEST AWARD FOR ANIMAL GALLANTRY** Introduced in 1943 by Maria Dickin (UK), the founder of the People's Dispensary for Sick Animals (PDSA), the Dickin Medal is the highest honor for animals serving in a military conflict. On February 24, 2010, an eight-year-old black Labrador named Treo became the latest animal to be awarded the medal in recognition of the numerous lives he had saved in Afghanistan sniffing out and locating roadside bombs.

☆ **MOST DANGEROUS COUNTRY FOR THE MEDIA** According to the International Federation of Journalists, 74 journalists have been killed in the Philippines since 2002, with 36 being killed in 2009, in the ongoing bloody conflict between the Moro Islamic Liberation Front (MILF) separatists and government forces.

named by the Commonwealth War Graves Commission as the youngest serviceman to have been killed in World War II. He had lied about his age in order to join the British Royal Navy, claiming to be 15 years old, and went on to serve as a cabin boy. Reginald was killed on July 6, 1941, at the age of 14 years 152 days—just five months after joining up—when his ship, the *SS Devon*, was attacked by a German aircraft.

☆ **Oldest living World War I veteran** Frank Woodruff Buckles was born in Harrison County, Missouri, U.S.A., on February 1, 1901, and became the oldest surviving World War I veteran on July 28, 2009, aged 108 years 168 days. Mr. Buckles served as an ambulance driver in the Army from 1917 to 1919; he is also the last of 4.7 million Americans who served during the conflict.

★ **Most people killed by Friendly fire** During their 1788 campaign against the Turks, the Austrian Army crossed a bridge at Karansebes, Turkey. An advance guard of cavalrymen stopped to buy alcohol from local

☆ **LARGEST CONTRIBUTOR TO UN PEACEKEEPING FORCES** As of February 28, 2010, Bangladesh is the largest contributor of uniformed personnel to UN peacekeeping missions, with a total of 10,852 blue-hatted personnel deployed worldwide.

KOBE, JAPAN (34°41'N 135°12'E): The **most books written in one year** by an individual is six by Shinichi Kobayashi (Japan), who wrote and published the novels between October 1, 2007, and September 15, 2008.

LONG . . .: The **longest war** that could be described as continuous was the Thirty Years War fought between the Holy Roman Empire and various European countries from 1618 to 1648.

★ **MOST LAND-MINED COUNTRY** According to the United Nations, Afghanistan now shares with Iraq the record for the most mined country in the world, with an estimated total of 10,000,000 mines each. In Afghanistan, more than 60 Afghans fall victim to land mines every month.

peasants. The infantrymen bringing up the rear wanted a share of the booze. When the cavalry refused, the infantry tried to frighten them, firing their rifles in the air. The surrounding Austrian forces were confused by this and opened fire on their colleagues, causing the utility horses at the rear to stampede. The fighting raged for hours, resulting in more than 10,000 dead and injured Austrians.

★ **Largest contributor to the UN peacekeeping budget** The UN's Peacekeeping budget between July 1, 2009, and June 30, 2010, is $7.9 bil-

. . . SHORT: The **shortest war** was fought between Britain and Zanzibar (now part of modern Tanzania). it lasted from 9:00 a.m. to 9:45 a.m. on August 27, 1896 and ended in a swift British victory.

OSAKA, JAPAN (34°40'N 135°30'E): The **longest monorail** is the Osaka Monorail, in Osaka, Japan, which has a total length of 13.8 miles (22.2 km). Fully operational since August 1997, its main line runs between Osaka International Airport and Hankyu Railway Minami Ibaraki Station.

★ SMALLEST ARMY The smallest and oldest standing army is the Pontifical Swiss Guard in the Vatican City, which was created in its current form on January 21, 1506, and had 110 active guards as of 2006. Swiss Guardsmen must be single Swiss-Catholic men taller than 5 ft. 8 in. (1.7 m).

lion. The largest single contributor to this figure is the U.S.A., which donates 27.17% of the total; next donor is Japan, which provides 12.53% of the total peacekeeping budget.

★ Most people deployed in peacekeeping operations According to the Stockholm International Peace Research Institute (SIPRI), a total of 187,586 people were deployed on peacekeeping missions in 2008. Military forces accounted for 166,146 of those deployed. The largest peace operation occurred—not surprisingly—in Afghanistan.

FIRST CONFIRMED SURVIVOR OF TWO NUCLEAR ATTACKS Tsutomu Yamaguchi (Japan) was in Hiroshima, Japan, on a business trip on August 6, 1945, when U.S. forces dropped the "Little Boy" atomic bomb on the city, killing 140,000 people. Suffering burns to his upper body, Tsutomu returned to his hometown of Nagasaki on August 8. The next day, the U.S. Army dropped "Fat Boy" on the city, killing a further 73,000 people. Tsutomu again managed to survive with minor injuries, despite living within 3 km (1.8 miles) of ground zero each time. .

CRIME

☆ **Largest speeding fine** In January 2010, an unnamed Swiss millionaire was given a record fine by the regional court in St. Gallen, Switzerland, of 307,496 Swiss Francs ($290,000) for speeding. He was caught driving his red Ferrari Testarossa 35 mph (57 km/h) faster than the legal speed limit allowed. The huge fine was based on the driver's wealth, which was assessed at 24 million Swiss Francs ($22.7 million), and the fact that he was a repeat traffic offender.

☆ **Most murders** According to the 10th United Nations Survey of Crime Trends and Operations of Criminal Justice Systems, covering the period of 2005–06, India has the greatest number of murders of any of the 86 countries listed in the report. It had a total of 32,481 homicides in 2006.

★ **Largest backlog of court cases** According to an annual report for the Delhi High Court, India, by Chief Justice A. P. Shah, there is such a

★ **WORST WAR CRIMINAL CONVICTED IN THE 21ST CENTURY** Kang Kek Ieu, or "Comrade Duch," ran the Tuol Sleng prison in Cambodia, southeast Asia, when the country was under the control of Pol Pot's regime. Between 1977 and 1979, of the 15,000 people who entered the prison, only around 15 emerged alive. This figure makes Kang Kek Ieu the worst war criminal convicted in the 21st century.

ADELAIDE, AUSTRALIA (34°55'S 138°36'E): The record for the **most jokes told in an hour** is held by Anthony Lehmann (Australia), who cracked 549 jokes against the clock at the Rhino Room club, Adelaide, South Australia, on May 25, 2005.

WORST PHOTOFIT . . . ? A contender for worst photofit was considered in early 2010, but was rejected by GWR, as it actually achieved its purpose. The extremely basic picture of an alleged murderer—drawn for Bolivian police by a neighbor of the victim, Rafael Vargas, who was stabbed seven times—has led to two arrests so far.

★ **HIGHEST PRISON RIOT DEATH TOLL** The war for supremacy between different drug cartels in Mexico, which saw more than 5,400 people killed in 2008, has been carried into Mexican jails. At least 83 prisoners were killed and many more injured in a number of riots during a six-month period covering part of 2008 and part of 2009. The trend appears to have continued into 2010, with the latest riot on January 20, 2010, when at least 23 inmates of rival drug trafficking gangs in a prison in the northern Mexican state of Durango were killed.

backlog of cases that it could take the court 466 years to clear. The court hears cases in an average time of 4 min. 55 sec., but it has 700,000 cases waiting to be heard out of a national backlog reported by the United Nations Development Programme to be in the order of 20 million. The court has 629 civil cases and about 17 criminal cases pending that are more than 20 years old.

☆ **Most prisoners on death row** According to Amnesty International's Annual Report 2009, the country with the most prisoners awaiting execution in 2008 is Pakistan, with more than 7,000—almost one-third of the estimated 24,000 on death row around the world. In the same year, Pakistan executed at least 36 people and reportedly sentenced 236 to death.

QUIZ!: How old was the oldest person to be accused of murder? See p. 543 for the answer.

☆ **LARGEST PRISON** Housing about 5,000 inmates but with a total capacity of 6,750, the Twin Towers Correctional Facility in Los Angeles, U.S.A., has a 1.5-million-ft.^{2} (140,000-m^2) floor area and is situated on a 10-acre (4-ha) site. In 2004, it cost around $50 million a year to run—$61.21 a day for each inmate.

★ **Largest passport forgery** On May 8, 2009, Mandip Sharma (India) and Brando Sibayan (Philippines) received jail terms of four years each from a UK court for running the largest known passport forgery factory. On searching a property in Leicester, UK, officers from the Border Agency found up to 4,000 counterfeit passports for several EU countries.

★ **Oldest person accused of murder (female)** A postmortem examination determined that Elizabeth Barrow (U.S.A.), aged 100, had been strangled in her nursing home in Massachusetts, U.S.A., on September 24,

★**OLDEST CRIMINAL GANG (AVERAGE AGE) In March 2009, a group of British criminals with an average age of 57 (the oldest being 83) pleaded guilty to counterfeiting charges and were sentenced to a total of 13 years. They had been able to produce a finished batch of notes worth £800 ($1,600) in just half an hour.**

2009. The accused is Laura Lundquist (U.S.A.), the victim's roommate, who is 98 years old and suffers from dementia.

★**First judicial single-drug execution** On December 8, 2009, convicted murderer Kenneth Biros was executed in Ohio, U.S.A., using a single large injection of anesthetic. It is the first time that a single injection has been used in a legal judicial execution in a democratic state. Normally, a mixture of three drugs is used.

☆**Most prisoners** According to data from the International Centre for Prison Studies at King's College, London, UK, the U.S.A. has 2.3 million

YOKOHAMA, JAPAN (35°27'N 139°38'E): The world's **tallest lighthouse** is the steel "Marine Tower" at Yamashita Park in Yokohama, Japan, at 348 ft. (106 m) high. It has a visibility range of 20 miles (32 km), and an observatory located 328 ft. (100 m) above ground.

EXTRA! For the latest defense technology, shoot to pp. 392–397.

prisoners behind bars, of whom 1,610,446 were sentenced prisoners at the end of 2008. China, with four times the population of the U.S.A., has 1.6 million prisoners. The ☆ **country with the least prisoners**, out of a list of 218 countries for which data was available, was San Marino, with only one.

★ **Largest fine** In September 2009, U.S. pharmaceutical giant Pfizer Inc. and its subsidiary Pharmacia & Upjohn Company Inc. agreed to pay $2.3 billion, the largest-ever health-care fraud settlement, to resolve criminal and civil liability arising from the illegal promotion of certain pharmaceutical products. Of the total, Pfizer will pay a $1.195 billion fine—the largest criminal fine in U.S. history.

☆ **Highest bail set** In New York, U.S.A., on October 16, 2009, bail for the billion-dollar hedge fund owner Raj Rajaratnam (Sri Lanka) was set at a record $100 million after his arrest on criminal charges for alleged insider trading.

★ **Longest jury deliberation** In a 1992 lawsuit in Long Beach, California, U.S.A., which took 11 years and 6 months to reach trial, Shirley and Jason McClure (U.S.A.) accused city officials of violating the U.S. Fair Housing Act by conspiring to prevent them from opening a chain of residential homes. The jury deliberated for four and a half months, and eventually awarded the McClures $25.5 million in damages.

WEALTH & COMMERCE

☆ **Richest person (present day)** Mexico's Carlos Slim Helú's estimated worth of $53.5 billion sees him top the 2010 *Forbes* list of the world's billionaires.

Slim has amassed a fortune that includes fixed-line telephone assets and a construction conglomerate, plus stakes in financial group Inbursa, Bronco Drilling, Independent News & Media, Saks, and New York Times Co. He increased his wealth by $18.5 billion in 2009, which helped knock Bill Gates (U.S.A.) off the top spot.

....

KAWASAKI, JAPAN (35°31'N 139°42'E): The world's **shortest escalator** is the moving walkway at Okadaya More's Shopping Mall at Kawasaki-shi, Japan, which has a vertical height of 2 ft. 8 in. (83.4 cm). The escalator was installed by Hitachi Ltd.

....

OOH!: The Orapa diamond mine, Botswana, is the world's largest by area. It covers 0.45 miles² (1.18 km²) and in 2003 produced 16.3 million carats (3,260 kg) of diamonds.

★**LARGEST LOSS OF PERSONAL FORTUNE** The collapse of the world's economy saw a decline in many fortunes, but none more dramatic than that of Anil Ambani (India). By March 2009, he had lost an estimated $32 billion—76% of his fortune—owing to the crumbling value of shares in his companies Reliance Power, Reliance Communications, and Reliance Capital.

☆**Richest woman** Christy Walton (U.S.A.), former daughter-in-law of deceased Wal-Mart founder Sam Walton, has a fortune estimated by *Forbes* at $22.5 billion. Her sister-in-law Alice Walton (U.S.A.) is runner-up, with $19.5 billion.

★**LARGEST LOTTERY PRIZE FUND** Spain's Christmas lottery, nicknamed "El Gordo" (Fat One), is a Christmas tradition in the country and is the world's biggest lottery in terms of the total sum paid out. The 2009 lottery showered €2.3 billion ($3.3 billion) on its winners. The top prize went to the 1,950 lucky ticket holders, who won €300,000 ($430,797) each.

OW!: In the financial year ending 2009, the world's 1,125 billionaires lost an estimated $1.4 trillion among them.

CASH

The word "cash" comes from the French word *caisse,* meaning "money box."

LARGEST PRIVATELY OWNED YACHT The *Eclipse*, which is owned by Chelsea Football Club (UK) owner Roman Abramovich (Russia), measures 560 ft. (170 m) long and was constructed by German shipbuilding company Blohm + Voss.

The price of the yacht is estimated at $485 million. It is equipped with two helicopter pads, 11 luxurious guest cabins, a mini-submarine, and its own missile-defense system.

INSTANT EXPERT

• The world's ★ **first dollar billionaire** was John D. Rockefeller (U.S.A., 1839–1937). He made his fortune in the oil business and was worth an estimated $1.4 billion.

• It is estimated that Rockefeller's wealth would be the equivalent of $210 billion today (measured as a percentage of GDP), which would make him, arguably, **the richest person ever.**

• Rockefeller gave away the vast majority of his wealth to worthy causes.

QUIZ!: Who did Carlos Slim Helú replace as the world's richest man? See p. 544 for the answer.

★LARGEST FIND OF ANGLO-SAXON TREASURE Metal detectorist Terry Herbert (UK) found more than 1,500 gold and silver pieces, estimated to date from the 7th century, in a farmer's field in Staffordshire, UK. The find, announced on September 24, 2009, included at least 650 items of gold, weighing more than 11 lb. (5 kg), and 530 silver objects, weighing more than 2.2 lb. (1 kg).

★Largest decline in billionaires in one year The financial year ending in late 2009 saw billionaires melting away like snow in spring. According to *Forbes*'s annual list, the world lost 332 billionaires, leaving just 793 of these rare creatures compared to 1,125 in the previous year.

☆Wealthiest university Harvard University, located in Cambridge, Massachusetts, is America's oldest university (established in 1636) and is also the world's wealthiest. When assessed in June 2009, Harvard's endowment was $26 billion, down from $36.9 billion the previous year.

DID YOU KNOW?

In 2009, New York City, U.S.A., regained the title of ☆ **city with the most billionaires** from Moscow, Russia. There are currently 55 members of the Big Apple billionaires club.

TRIVIA

The world's highest average net income in relation to cost of living is earned by the citizens of Zürich, Switzerland.

TOKYO, JAPAN (35°41'N 139°46'E): The Tower Belcon is a concrete-conveying robot that was completed in 1998. It is the world's **largest robot,** measuring 231 ft. (70.5 m) high, with a 250-ft. (76.5-m) boom, and can deliver 6,356 ft.^{3} (180 m^3) of concrete an hour. It was designed and manufactured by Mitsubishi Heavy Industries, Tokyo, Japan.

☆ **LARGEST CORPORATE BANKRUPTCY** On September 15, 2008, U.S. investment bank Lehman Brothers Holdings Inc. filed for bankruptcy to the tune of $613 billion, having succumbed to the subprime mortgage crisis that started the worldwide recession in 2008.

★ **Largest deposit lost** In 2008, Mikhail Prokhorov (Russia) agreed to pay €390 million ($528.9 million) for the villa *Leopolda de Villefranche-sur-Mer*, owned by heiress Lily Safra (Brazil), and located outside Nice, France. Prokhorov withdrew from the sale in 2009, losing his €40-million ($54.2-million) deposit in the process.

Largest life insurance policy July 2010 marked the 20th anniversary of Peter Rosengard's (UK) record insurance sale. In 1990, he sold the largest-ever single life insurance policy for $100 million on the life of a well-known U.S. entertainment industry figure. Incredibly, he made the sale during a cold call from a telephone booth!

CONSUMPTION & WASTE

☆ **Largest producer of energy (country)** China produces more energy annually than any other nation, with 1,749 Mtoe (million tonnes of oil equivalent) as of 2006.

☆ **Largest consumption of energy per head** The people of Qatar each consumed an average of 48,627 lb. (22,057 kg) in 2006. Iceland was in second place with 31,387 lb. (14,237 kg) per head, while the U.S.A., which is the greatest annual consumer of energy, is 10th on the list with 17,125 lb. (7,768 kg).

☆**LARGEST PRODUCER OF CARBON DIOXIDE EMISSIONS (COUNTRY) According to a report compiled by the Netherlands Environmental Assessment Agency, as of 2006 the country responsible for the greatest carbon dioxide emissions is China, which produced 6,200 million tonnes of CO_2 compared with 5,800 million tonnes produced by the U.S.A. By comparison, the UK produced 600 million tonnes.**

☆**Highest carbon dioxide emissions per capita** Citizens of Kuwait emitted 40.6 tons (36.9 tonnes) of carbon dioxide per person in 2005.

★**First climigration** In 2009, Alaskan human rights lawyer Robin Bronen coined the word "climigration" to describe the forced migration of people resulting from climate-induced ecological changes in a community's environment.

☆**LARGEST CONSUMER OF ENERGY The country that consumes more energy than any other is the U.S.A., which was shown to have used 2,321 Mtoe (million tonnes of oil equivalent) in 2006, the latest year for which records exist.**

Bronen used the term in a report on Alaskan indigenous communities who were having to relocate due to climate change. The Intergovernmental Panel on Climate Change (IPCC) has estimated that there will be 150 million such "climate refugees" seeking new homes by 2050.

★**Largest island evacuation as a result of climate change** In 1995, more than 500,000 inhabitants of Bhola Island, Bangladesh, were forced to evacuate when rising seas, attributed to climate change, threatened to flood the island.

★**Greenest city** Masdar City in Abu Dhabi, UAE, designed by the British architect firm Foster and Partners, is the world's first city designed to be zero-carbon and zero-waste. All of its power is generated from renewable resources, and all waste material is recycled. Automobiles are banned

LARGEST PLASTIC BAG SCULPTURE A sculpture of a globe made of 17,773 plastic bags measuring 36 ft. 1 in. (11 m) in circumference was revealed at the Ministerio de Medio Ambiente in Madrid, Spain, by the charity InspirAction, to promote recycling and environmental issues, on December 12, 2009.

SAPPORO, JAPAN (43°00'N 141°21'E): The **most consecutive league games scoring hat tricks** by a soccer player in a national top division is four by Masashi Nakayama (Japan) for Jubilo Iwata in the Japanese League—First Stage between April 15 and 29, 1998.

EXTRA! For a different kind of consumption, look at extreme cuisine on p. 246.

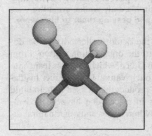

LONGEST-SURVIVING GREENHOUSE GAS Of all the gases emitted by mankind that add to global warming, the longest lived is the refrigerant gas tetrafluoromethane. It can last for 50,000 years in the atmosphere.

in favor of electric, driverless, underground vehicles, so the city's projected 50,000 citizens should leave no carbon footprint.

★**Most steel cans collected in one month** South African recycling venture Collect-a-Can collected 2,122,238 steel cans weighing 146,210 lb. 7 oz. (66,319.95 kg) from schools across South Africa between October 1 and 31, 2009, in an initiative to promote the recycling of cans in the country.

★**Largest collection of clothes to recycle** On August 12, 2009, at Union Station, Washington, D.C., U.S.A., *National Geographic Kids* magazine announced that it had collected 33,088 pairs of jeans for recycling through its denim drive event.

☆**MOST TREES PLANTED IN AN HOUR (TEAM)** A team of 100 people planted 26,422 trees at Gransha Park, Derry, UK, on December 5, 2009. BBC Breathing Places achieved the feat in partnership with Conservation Volunteers NI, Western Health & Social Care Trust, Northern Ireland EA, and Derry City Council.

MELBOURNE, AUSTRALIA (37°48'S 144°57'E): The **most expensive cricket bat** was Sir Donald Bradman's bat, used in his debut Test, which sold for A$145,000 (U.S. $121,945) at Leski Auctions, Melbourne, Australia, on September 24, 2008. The bat was used only in Bradman's debut test match in the 1928/29 Ashes series.

☆ **MOST BOTTLES RECYCLED BY A DOG** A Labrador called Tubby, owned by Sandra Gilmore of Pontnewydd, Torfaen, UK, has helped recycle an estimated 26,000 plastic bottles during the past six years by collecting them on his daily walks, crushing them, and passing them to his owner.

All the denim collected will be donated to the organization Cotton. From Blue to Green, which recycles jeans into UltraTouch Natural Cotton Fiber Insulation, a product that is used to help build houses in places that have been damaged by hurricanes and other natural disasters.

It takes about 500 pairs of jeans to recycle enough denim to insulate one average-size house.

AMERICAN HEROES

AMELIA EARHART On May 20–21, 1932, Amelia Earhart became the **first woman** (and second person) **to make a solo transatlantic flight** when she piloted her Lockheed Vega from Harbour Grace in Newfoundland, Canada, to Londonderry, Northern Ireland, UK, in 13 hr. 30 min.

MICHAEL JORDAN The NBA's **highest point-scoring average** for players exceeding 10,000 points is 30.1 by Michael Jordan, who scored 32,292 points in 1,072 games for the Chicago Bulls (1984–98) and the Washington Wizards (2001–03).

EXTRA! For the latest records from America's "favorite pastime," see p. 438.

STEPHEN SONDHEIM Recipient of the **most Tony Awards won by a composer** (seven), Stephen Sondheim (b. 1930) is also the greatest living Broadway lyricist (for *West Side Story* and *Gypsy*, among others) and composer (credits include *Company*, *Follies*, *Sweeney Todd*, and *Into the Woods*).

OPRAH WINFREY Undoubtedly the ★ **most powerful person in television** (11 places ahead of Dr. Phil and 13 ahead of David Letterman!), Oprah Gail Winfrey (b. 1954) is also the **highest paid TV personality** ($275 million earned in 2008–09, thanks to her TV and radio shows, magazine, and Oprah Winfrey Network). A self-made billionaire (worth $2.3 billion as of September 2009), the philanthropist/actress/producer is arguably the most influential woman in the world.

NYC FIREFIGHTERS The **single largest loss of firefighters** occurred on September 11, 2001, when 341 New York City Fire Department staff—plus two paramedics—who attended the World Trade Center attacks died. In all, 411 emergency workers lost their lives.

HOBART, TASMANIA, AUSTRALIA (42°53'S 147°19'E): The Rostrum Clubs of Tasmania, together with members of the Tasmanian community totaling 725 people, debated the motion "Tasmania's greatest asset is its people" for 29 days 4 hr. 3 min. 20 sec., from November 2 to December 1, 1996, on the lawns of Hobart's Parliament House in Tasmania, Australia. This represents the **longest debating marathon**.

BARACK: Chief among our heroes is Barack Obama (b. 1961), who made history in 2009 by becoming the **first black American president**.

APOLLO 11 CREW Neil Alden Armstrong and Edwin "Buzz" Aldrin became the **first men on the moon** on July 21, 1969. The third man in the Apollo 11 team—Michael Collins (Italy/U.S.A.)—remained behind in the command module *Columbia.*

OBAMA: He's also the **first U.S. president to have regular email access**, and he rides in the **most secure presidential limousine**.

WALT DISNEY The Disney brothers Roy (1893–1971) and Walter (1901–66) might have been cofounders of the world's **largest theme park operator**, but it's Walt whose name lives on as a synonym for fun. He holds the record for the **most Oscar nominations (64)**, and between 1942 and 1950, he was nominated every single year, also a record. In addition, he holds the record for the **most Oscar wins (26)**, and in 1953, he was awarded the **most Oscar wins in a year (4)**.

RONALD REAGAN In a poll of 2.4 million Americans conducted by AOL and the Discovery Channel in 2005, 40th U.S. President Ronald Reagan was voted the **greatest American of all time**. His two terms in office (1981–89) are associated with the end of the Cold War and economic prosperity, a period of much-needed stability following the Vietnam War.

BILL GATES William Gates III, who is worth an estimated $40 billion, was the **richest person alive** from 1995 to 2010, excluding 2007. In 2009, he and his wife donated $3.8 billion to the Bill and Melinda Gates Foundation, the world's **richest charitable group**.

SYDNEY, AUSTRALIA (33°51'S 151°12'E): The Panasonic IMAX Theatre at Darling Harbour, Sydney, Australia, holds the **largest fixed projection screen** in the world, measuring 117 x 97 ft. (35.72 x 29.57 m). It opened in September 1996 and can seat 540 people.

MICHAEL No list of iconic Americans would be complete without the King of Pop himself, Michael Jackson. Check out our special tribute to the legend on p. 350.

JOHN F. KENNEDY John Fitzgerald Kennedy (1917–63), Democratic victor in the 1960 U.S. presidential election, was, at age 43, the **youngest man ever to win the American presidency.** He was also the ★ **youngest U.S. president to die in office,** when he was assassinated on November 22, 1963. An advocate of civil rights, JFK remains one of the most popular figures in the White House, having survived the Bay of Pigs debacle and the Cuban Missile Crisis.

BILLIE-JEAN KING Between 1961 and 1979, Billie-Jean King (b. 1943) achieved the **most Wimbledon victories by a woman,** winning 20 titles (six singles, 10 women's doubles, and four mixed doubles)—a record she shares with Martina Navratilova (U.S.A., b. Czechoslovakia).

CHESLEY B. SULLENBERGER Although there have been previous incidents of commercial airliners ditching in which 100% of the passengers have survived, the **largest number of survivors** in such a scenario was the 155 passengers and crew involved in the ditching of U.S. Airways Airbus A320 Flight 1549 from LaGuardia into the Hudson, by Captain Chesley B. "Sully" Sullenberger, on January 15, 2009.

MADONNA: And for her enduring appeal, her constant reinvention, her decadence, and her endless string of hit albums, singles, and tours, hats off to the material girl—see p. 347.

"BABE" RUTH During his career, George Herman "Babe" Ruth (1895–1946) hit 714 homers from 8,399 times at bat: a success rate of 8.5% and the **highest home run percentage in MLB history.** He also hit the longest home run—575 ft. (175 m) for the Yankees against the Detroit Tigers on July 18, 1921.

MARTIN LUTHER KING JR. On August 28, 1963, civil rights leader Martin Luther King Jr. (1929–68) led more than 250,000 demonstrators down the Mall in Washington, D.C., to promote equal civil rights for all Americans—the **largest racial-equality rally** ever held. From the steps of the Lincoln Memorial, King delivered his legendary "I have a dream" speech.

MORE AMERICAN HEROES

These pages are a warm tribute to those great Americans who hold Guinness World Records. Here are some more candidates worthy of inclusion in any American Hall of Fame:

Franklin Delano Roosevelt, "FDR" (1882–1945)	*32nd President of the United States (1933–45)*	Led the country through economic depression and World War II; only president elected to more than two terms
Abraham Lincoln (1809–65)	*16th President of the United States (1861–65)*	Preserved the Union through the Civil War; abolished slavery; Gettysburg Address
David "Davy" Crockett (1786–1836)	*Frontiersman, soldier, folk hero*	Tennessee Member of House of Representatives; fought for independence of Texas; killed at the Alamo
George Washington (1732–1799)	*1st President of the United States (1789–97)*	"Father of Our Country," Commander-in-Chief of colonial armies in American Revolution, stabilized country after political chaos
Jonas Salk (1914–95)	*Virologist*	Developed polio vaccine (announced April 12, 1955)

MOST EXPENSIVE

☆**Drawing by an old master** *Head of a Muse* by Raphael (Italy, 1483–1520) sold for £29,200,000 ($46,700,000) at Christie's, London, UK, on December 9, 2009.

Ice-cream maker The G Series ice-cream makers launched by Nitro-Cream (U.S.A.) are customized and signed by the artists Robert Kennedy and Ward Goodell, and sell for $75,000. The G Series uses liquid nitrogen to create desserts almost instantly by mixing the cold nitrogen—which turns into gas at -321°F (-196°C)—directly with the ice-cream or sorbet mixture.

★**Music single** A rare seven-inch copy of the unreleased 1965 single "Do I Love You (Indeed I Do)" by Frank Wilson (U.S.A.) sold for $39,294 in April 2009 to a buyer who wishes to remain anonymous.

★**Chocolate bar** A Wispa Gold bar covered in edible gold leaf was created by Cadbury (UK) in 2009 to celebrate its comeback after six years. The chocolate treat—which usually sells for 55p (82¢)—is available to buy from Selfridges in London, UK, for £961.48 ($1,441).

☆ **DIAMOND PER CARAT** A 7.03-carat fancy vivid-blue modified rectangular brilliant-cut diamond sold for a record per-carat price of $1,375,938 at Sotheby's in Geneva, Switzerland, on May 12, 2009.

★ **CITY COMMUTE** Based on an average downtown commuter journey by the most popular public means, London is the most expensive city for commuters, averaging £2.62 ($4.33) per single journey. The results were drawn from Mercer's Worldwide Cost of Living 2009.

BRISBANE, AUSTRALIA (27°28'S 153°01'E): The world's **oldest koala sanctuary** is the Lone Pine Koala Sanctuary in Brisbane, Queensland, Australia. It currently houses the **largest number of koalas in captivity**, with 137 koalas.

EXTRA! To find out more about the world's richest and poorest, flip back to p. 228.

★ **BED** The K.mooi Crystal Noir Limited Edition bed created by Maxxa International Limited (China) is covered with 802,903 CRYSTALLIZED™ Swarovski crystals and is on sale for RMB 3,000,000 ($440,000). It was first unveiled at the 100% Design show in Shanghai, China, on October 15, 2009.

★ **Suit** It took Alexander Amosu (UK) more than 80 hours—and 5,000 stitches—to create a suit from gold thread and the wool of Himalayan pashmina goats, Arctic musk oxen, and Peruvian vicuñas. The suit, finished with nine 18-carat-gold-and-pavé-set-diamond buttons, sold for $113,000 in April 2009 and was delivered to the buyer in an armored Land Rover.

☆ **Rough diamond** Petra Diamonds Ltd (UK) sold a 507.9-carat rough diamond—the 19th largest gem ever discovered—for $35.5 million to the Chow Tai Fook Jewellery Co. Ltd (Hong Kong) on February 26, 2010. The stone, named the Petra Heritage, weighed just over 3.3 oz. (100 g) and is as big as a chicken's egg. It was found in September 2009 in South Africa's Cullinan mine.

☆ **Wall calendar** A wall calendar titled *Still Missing Still Missed* was sold for £20,000 ($30,000) at an auction held on January 27, 2010, in London, UK. The auction was in aid of three charities: Missing Children Europe; Missing People; and Madeleine's Fund: Leaving No Stone Unturned, the charity established to find Madeleine McCann (UK), who went missing during a family holiday in Portugal on May 3, 2007. The fund-raiser was held on the 1,000th day of Madeleine's disappearance, and the calendar—which was bought by Duncan Mackay (UK)—featured a variety of drawings made by Madeleine and her siblings, Sean and Amelie.

DOLLAR

From the Low German *Thal/Thaler,* meaning "valley." In the 15th century, silver was mined in a place called Joachim's Thal; the coins minted from this silver were known as Thalers.

MOVE: In 2003, Ronaldo moved from Sporting Lisbon (Portugal) to Manchester United (England) for a modest €12.2 million ($15.3 million).

☆ **SOCCER PLAYER** **The highest transfer fee for a player is a reported €80 million ($131.86 million) for Cristiano Ronaldo (Portugal) by Real Madrid (Spain) to English Premiership club Manchester United on July 1, 2009. According to Spanish newspaper *El Mundo*, Ronaldo cost Real Madrid 57 times his own weight in gold!**

☆ **LETTER** **A letter written by George Washington in 1787 to his nephew Bushrod Washington, urging adoption of the country's new constitution, sold for $3,200,000 on December 5, 2009, at Christie's, New York, U.S.A.—the highest price ever paid for a single signed letter.**

MOVIES: Ronaldo—aka Cristiano Ronaldo dos Santos Aveiro—was named after U.S. President Ronald Reagan, his father's favorite movie actor!

INVERCARGILL, NEW ZEALAND (46°25'S 168°18'E): Despite his Hungarian (and therefore landlocked) ancestry, Mike Rácz set the record for the **fastest time to open 100 oysters**, taking just 2 min. 20.07 sec.—a rate of one oyster every 1.4 seconds—at Invercargill, New Zealand, on July 16, 1990.

☆ **SCULPTURE SOLD AT AUCTION**
Alberto Giacometti's (Switzerland) bronze sculpture titled *Walking Man I* (1960) sold to an anonymous bidder at Sotheby's in London, UK, for a record £65,000,000 ($104,300,000) on February 3, 2010. The sculpture stands 6 ft. (1.82 m) tall.

☆ **Hotel suite** The Royal Penthouse Suite at the President Wilson Hotel in Geneva, Switzerland, costs $65,000 per day, although for that price you do get access to 18,000 ft.^{2} (1,670 m^2) of space, plus views of Mont Blanc (through 2-in.-thick [6-cm] bullet-proof windows), a private cocktail lounge, a Jacuzzi and fitness center, and a conference room.

★ **Spa package** On sale at the Vitality Show in London's Earls Court, UK, in March 2010: spa therapy for £5,000 ($7,560). Included was a hot-rock spinal massage using diamonds, a 24-carat-gold facial wrap, a chocolate body wrap, and a caviar-and-coffee hair wash.

COST!: Ten years ago, another Giacometti held the **most expensive sculpture** record—his *Grande Femme Debout* 1 sold at Christie's for $14 million.

EXTREME CUISINE

THE CHOMP-IONS

FOOD	MOST EATEN IN 1 MIN.	WHO
After Eight Thin Mints (no hands)	8	Ashrita Furman (U.S.A.) James Graham Boyd (UK)
Bananas (peeled & eaten)	6	Robert Godfrey (U.S.A.)
Brussels sprouts	31	Linus Urbanec (Sweden)
Garlic cloves	22	Ashrita Furman (U.S.A.)
Cockroaches	5	Alexis Chambon (France)
Ferrero Rocher (chocolates)	8	Chris Vollmershausen (Canada)
Jaffa Cakes	8	Gustav Schulz (Germany)
Jalapeño chilis	16	Alfredo Hernandes (U.S.A.)
Gelatin (Jell-O)	16 oz. (455 g)	Ashrita Furman (U.S.A.)
M&Ms (with chopsticks)	42	Fero Andersen (Germany)
Meatballs	27	Nick Marshall (UK)
Sausages	8	Stefan Paladin (NZ)

	MOST EATEN IN 3 MIN.	
Doughnuts (jelly)	6	Lup Fun Yau (UK)
Doughnuts (powdered)	5	Christopher "Big Black" Boykin (U.S.A.)
Grapes (with teaspoon)	151	Ashrita Furman (U.S.A.)
Hot dogs	6	Takeru Kobayashi (Japan)
Oysters	233	Colin Shirlow (UK)
Corn kernels (with cocktail stick)	236	Ian Richard Purvis (UK)

☆ **LARGEST SERVING OF HUMMUS** On May 10, 2010, 300 Lebanese chefs prepared a serving of hummus that weighed 59,992 lb. (23,130 kg) in Ain Saadeh, northeast of Beirut. The dish, which beat the previous effort from neighboring Israel, required 22,046 lb. (10 tons) of chickpeas.

QUIZ!: On May 2, 2007, Lup Fun Yau (UK) set a new record for the **most jelly doughnuts eaten in three minutes**. But how many did he eat? See p. 544 for the answer.

MOST PIZZA ROLLS The ☆**most continuous pizza rolls across the shoulders in 30 seconds** using 20 oz. (567 g) of dough is 37 by Tony Gemignani (U.S.A.) at the Mall of America, Minneapolis, Minnesota, U.S.A., on April 20, 2006, for the Food Network channel.

Most expensive . . .

★**Fishsticks:** In 2004, Barry Coutts's Bistro in Aberdeen, UK, added to their menu haute cuisine fishsticks—made with smoked halibut, king scallops, crayfish, monkfish (goosefish), and Beluga caviar—at a cost of £100 ($167.58) each.

★**Bottle:** Tequila Ley .925 sold a Platinum & White Gold Tequila bottle to a private collector in Mexico City, Mexico, on July 20, 2006, for $225,000.

★**Cherries:** In October 2007, Nick Moraitis (Australia) paid A$35,000 (U.S. $31,771) to Variety, the children's charity of New South Wales, for a box of cherries sold by Sydney Markets, Australia.

★**Cognac:** A 1788 bottle of Vieux Cognac sold at auction by the Tour d'Argent restaurant (France) in December 2009 raised €25,000 ($35,364).

★**First cocktail** In September 2005, archaeochemist Patrick McGovern from University of Pennsylvania, U.S.A., announced the discovery of 5,000-year-old earthenware from the banks of the Tigris, between Iran and Iraq, containing traces of tartaric acid, honey, apple juice, and barley.

☆**Largest pie fight** Shaw Floors in Grapevine, Texas, U.S.A., organized a pie fight among 434 employees on January 7, 2010. The flan fighters flung a total of 1,200 chocolate, apple, and cherry pies at a Shaw sales meeting to demonstrate the stain resistance of a premium nylon carpet.

CHRISTCHURCH, NEW ZEALAND (43°31'S 172°37'E): The **most participants in a snowboard race** was 88 at an event organized by The Rock FM and Mount Hutt at Mount Hutt in Christchurch, New Zealand, on October 6, 2007.

BANANA

They don't grow on trees—the banana plant is actually one of the world's biggest herbs!

☆ **MOST EGGS HELD IN ONE HAND** Zachery George (U.S.A.) held 24 eggs in one hand at the Subway restaurant in Parsons, West Virginia, U.S.A., on March 21, 2009. As stipulated in the guidelines, Zachery had 30 seconds to position all the eggs in his hand and then held them there for 10 seconds.

Fastest time to . . .

★ **Carve a turkey:** Paul Kelly (UK) carved a turkey in 3 min. 19.47 sec. at Little Claydon Farm, Essex, UK, on June 3, 2009.

Pluck a turkey: Vincent Pilkington (Ireland) plucked a turkey in 1 min. 30 sec. on November 17, 1980.

★ **Most custard pies in the face** James Kerley "pied" Damien Bignell (both Australia) with 46 custard pies in a minute on the set of *Australia Smashes Guinness World Records* at the Warringah Mall in Sydney, Australia, on January 15, 2010.

★ **Most ice-cream scoops stacked on one cone** Terry Morris (New Zealand) balanced 25 scoops of ice cream on a single cone on the set of *NZ Smashes Guinness World Records* at Sylvia Park shopping mall, Auckland, New Zealand, on September 20, 2009.

☆ **MOST BANANAS SNAPPED (ONE MINUTE)** Graheme Celledoni (Australia) snapped a total of 96 bananas in half, using only his hands, at the Innisfail Society Show in Queensland, Australia, on July 9, 2009.

WELLINGTON, NEW ZEALAND (41°17'S 174°46'E):

Wellington, North Island, New Zealand, with a population of 179,436, is the **most southerly capital city** of an independent country.

☆ **MOST COCONUTS SMASHED WITH ONE HAND IN ONE MINUTE** Nut cracker Muhamed Kahrimanovic (Germany, pictured) crushed 82 coconuts by hand during the Vienna Recordia event in Vienna, Austria, on September 27, 2009. In a similar event held in Malaysia on June 21, 2009, Ho Eng Hui (Malaysia) pierced four coconuts with his right index finger—the ★ **most coconuts pierced by finger in one minute.**

☆ **Most pancakes made (eight hours)** A total of 175 volunteers from Batter Blaster (U.S.A.) used 37 griddles to prepare a record 76,382 pancakes on May 9, 2009—and serve them to 20,000 people for breakfast—on the Great Lawn of the Centennial Olympic Park in Atlanta, Georgia, U.S.A. Each recipient paid $1 toward two charities: Homeless and Hosea Feed the Hungry.

★ **Most naans made (one hour)** A team of five from the Indian Ocean restaurant in Ashton-under-Lyne, UK, made 640 naans on September 29, 2009.

★**Largest display of tequila** The Tequila Regulatory Council of Mexico displayed a record 1,201 varieties of tequila at Hospicio Cabañas, Guadalajara, Mexico, on November 6, 2009.

Tallest . . .
☆**Poppadom stack:** A freestanding tower of 1,052 poppadoms (thin and crispy Indian flatbreads) measured 4 ft. 11 in. (1.51 m) at the Curry Lounge in Nottingham, UK, on July 22, 2009.
☆**Sugar cube tower:** Paul Van den Nieuwenhof (Belgium) took 2 hr. 12 min. to build a record-breaking 6-ft.-2-in.-tall (1.9-m) tower from 1,753 sugar cubes on November 12, 2009.

ENORMOUS NOSH

FANTASTIC FEASTS

LARGEST . . .	RECORD	ORGANIZER/VENUE	DATE
★Birth feast	*819*	Council of Utrecht/ Vinkenburgstraat, the Netherlands	Jan. 24, 2009
Breakfast (cooked)	*18,941*	The Cowboy Breakfast Foundation, San Antonio, U.S.A.	Jan. 26, 2001
Breakfast (noncooked)	*27,854 in 1 hr.*	Nutella/Arena AufSchalke, Gelsenkirchen, Germany	May 29, 2005
Coffee morning (multi-venue)	*576,157*	Macmillan Cancer Relief (UK)	Sep. 26, 2003
Picnic (single-venue) *(see also p. 167)*	*22,232*	Modelo/Parque da Bela Vista, Lisbon, Portugal	Jun. 20, 2009
Tea party (multi-venue)	*280,246*	The Cancer Council/ 6,062 locations across Australia	May 26, 2005

....

AUCKLAND, NEW ZEALAND (36°51'S 174°47'E): On February 19, 1998, the four main power cables to downtown Auckland, New Zealand, failed, in the **longest peacetime blackout**. The disruption lasted for 66 days, affected 7,500 business and residential customers, and cost businesses some NZ $300 million (U.S. $156 million).

....

☆ **LARGEST DISH OF MUSSELS** A mussels dish weighing 4.07 tons (3,692 kg) was prepared for the public in the streets of Taranto, Italy, on August 1, 2009.

WHAT? • Mussels: 7,275 lb. 4 oz. • Red tomatoes: 661 lb. 6 oz. • Garlic: 66 lb. 2 oz. • Salt: 6 lb. 10 oz. • Olive Oil: 330 lb. 11 oz. • Pepper: 44 lb. 2 oz. • Parsley: 44 lb. 2 oz. • Wine: 33 gal. • Bread croutons: 661 lb. 6 oz.

WHO?: The fishy dish was organized by the shopping mall Mongolfiera and Coop Estense and the "Societa" Sviluppo Commerciale in Taranto, Italy.

☆ **LARGEST CUPCAKE** A colossal cupcake weighing 1,315 lb. (596.47 kg) was made by Global TV Concepts (U.S.A.) during the second annual Think Pink Rocks charity concert at Mizner Park in Boca Raton, Florida, U.S.A., on October 3, 2009.

LONGEST BAR The 405-ft. 10-in. (123.7-m) counter in the Beer Barrel Saloon at Put-in-Bay, South Bass Island, Ohio, U.S.A., is fitted with 56 beer taps and features 160 bar stools, and is the longest continuous bar in the world.

LARGEST . . .

★**Crab cake** The largest crab cake on record weighed 253 lb. (114.75 kg) and was made by Special Olympics Maryland in conjunction with Handy International and Graul's Market (all U.S.A.) in Hampden, Maryland, U.S.A., on June 13, 2009.

★**Fishstick** A 16-ft.-6-in.-long (2-m) fishstick weighing 299 lb. 13 oz. (136 kg) was prepared by Michael Gorich (Germany) in Bremerhaven, Germany, on January 22, 2009.

★**LARGEST "FULL ENGLISH" BREAKFAST** A "full English" on the menu at Mario's Cafe Bar in Bolton, Lancashire, UK, weighs on average 6 lb. 7 oz. (2.9 kg) and costs £10.95 ($17.87). The melee of bacon, sausages, eggs, bread, mushrooms, blood sausage, beans, and tomatoes is free if eaten within 20 minutes.

★**Fudge** On June 29, 2009, William Nicklosovich and Peppermint Jim Crosby (both U.S.A.) made a slab of fudge weighing 5,200 lb. (2.35 tonnes) at Lansing Community College West Campus, Delta Township, Michigan, U.S.A.

★**Haggis** The national dish of Scotland, haggis, is a sausage of minced offal with oatmeal, beef suet, and spices. The largest ever weighed 1,234 lb. 9 oz. (560 kg)—about the same as a Jersey cow—and was made by the Mauchline Burns Club in Ayrshire, UK, in May 2009.

★**Halva** A halva—a Middle Eastern dessert—weighing 8,402 lb. (3,811 kg) was created by the Nazareth Halva Factory in Israel on October 14, 2009. It contained an estimated 20 million calories!

★**Lollipop** On August 27, 2009, Ashrita Furman (U.S.A.) and members of the New York Sri Chinmoy Centre created a 25-ft.-tall (7.62-m) lollipop weighing 6,514 lb. (2.95 tonnes)—equal to 165,070 regular lollipops!

LARGEST CHOCOLATE RABBIT A chocolate rabbit weighing in at 6,172 lb. 15 oz. (2,800 kg) was made by Supermercados Imperatriz Ltda and Nestlé FoodServices (both Brazil) in São José, Santa Catarina, Brazil, on March 30, 2009.

HONOLULU, HI, U.S.A. (21°18'N 157°49'W): On December 19, 1992, local citizens made a 14,550-ft. (4,434-m) paper lei at the Hyatt Regency Waikiki, Honolulu, Hawaii, U.S.A.—the **largest artificial garland**.

☆**Meatball** A meatball weighing 222 lb. 8 oz. (100.92 kg) was created by Nonni's Italian Eatery in Concord, New Hampshire, U.S.A., on November 1, 2009.

★**Meat stew** A stew weighing 5,132 lb. 15 oz. (2,328.2 kg), containing 2,854 lb. (1,294.6 kg) of lamb meat (from an estimated 75 lambs), was cooked in Badajoz, Spain, on October 25, 2009.

★**Mojito** The largest glass of mojito—a Cuban cocktail of rum, sugar, mint, and lime juice—contained 156 gal. (713 liters) and measured 4 ft. 4 in. (1.34 m) tall and 4 ft. 1 in. (1.25 m) at its widest. It was made by the bar-ristorante Sirio in Spotorno, Savona, Italy, on August 28, 2009, and required at least 200 lb. (90 kg) of limes.

☆**Porridge** The largest bowl of porridge weighed 378 lb. 15 oz. (171.9 kg) and was prepared by Mornflake Oats (UK) at the Lowry Theatre, Salford, UK, on September 10, 2009. The 55 lb. 1 oz. (25 kg) of porridge oats and 32.9 gal. (150 liters) of water was sufficient to cater for 830 individual servings.

☆**Soup** DENK Communicatie prepared a 5,863-gal. (26,658-liter) vegetable soup in Poeldijk, the Netherlands, on May 16, 2009.

LONGEST . . .

★**Garlic bread** A garlic bread measuring 12 ft. 6 in. (3.81 m) was baked by Cole's Quality Foods in Muskegon, Michigan, U.S.A., on June 12, 2009.

★**Sausage chain** On June 28, 2009, at Gelsenkirchen, Germany, more than 10,000 Fleischwurst sausages were linked in a 4,921-ft.-3-in.-long (1,500-m) chain. The **fastest man to run 1,500 m**—Hicham El Guerrouj (Morocco)—would take 3 min. 26 sec. to run from end to end!

★**Rice noodle** A 1,800-ft.-2-in. (548.7-m) noodle—as long as five football fields—was unveiled at Taipei County Hakka Museum, Taiwan, on December 28, 2008.

....

ANCHORAGE, AK, U.S.A. (61°13'N 149°53'W): The **fastest-moving major glacier** is the Columbia Glacier, between Anchorage and Valdez in Alaska, U.S.A. In 1999, its average rate of flow was measured at 115 ft. (35 m) per day.

....

COLLECTORS' ITEMS

☆**Bottled water labels** Lorenzo Pescini of Florence, Italy, had a collection of 8,650 different bottled water labels from 185 different countries of 1,683 different springs, as of January 12, 2009. He started his collection in 1992.

☆**Bus tickets** Ladislav Šejnoha (Czech Republic) had 200,000 bus tickets from 36 countries as of September 30, 2008.

★**Calendars** Yakov L. Kofman (U.S.A.) had put together a collection of 16,552 different calendars as of October 26, 2008. His collection began in 1945.

★ **SMURF MEMORABILIA** Stephen Parkes (UK) began collecting Smurfs as a child, when they were sold by a chain of filling stations across the UK. As of January 28, 2010, his collection totals 1,061 and includes Christmas Smurfs, Easter Smurfs, Smurfs dressed as historical figures, and Smurfs doing almost every occupation you can imagine. And he's still collecting....

....

FAIRBANKS, AK, U.S.A. (64°50'N 147°42'W): The Pan-American Highway, the **longest motorable road**, starts at Fairbanks, Alaska, U.S.A., and stretches to Santiago, Chile; it then turns eastward to Buenos Aires, Argentina, and terminates in Brasilia, Brazil—a distance of more than 15,000 miles (24,140 km).

....

☆**Movie cameras** Since 1960, Richard LaRiviere (U.S.A.) has built up a collection of 894 movie cameras. The oldest is a 1907 Darling with a hand crank.

★**Hearts** Dr. Diana Reser (Switzerland) has collected 775 heart-shaped motifs and items since becoming a cardiac surgeon in 2006.

☆**Trolls** Sophie Marie Cross (UK) began collecting trolls in 2003 and, as of December 3, 2009, had amassed a set of 633 unique items.

NEW COLLECTIONS

ITEM	COLLECTOR	QUANTITY	DATE ACHIEVED
★ *Airline boarding passes*	Miguel Fernandez (Spain)	1,020	Aug. 2009
★ *Banknotes*	Anil Bohora (India)	10,025	Jan. 2009
★ *Cachaça bottles*	Messias Soares Cavalcante (Brazil)	12,800	Aug. 2009
★ *Casino chips and tokens*	Bruce and Sue Wunder (both U.S.A.)	554	May 2009
★ *Chicken memorabilia*	Cecil and Joann Dixon (both U.S.A.)	6,505	June 2006
★ *Christmas brooches*	Adam Wide (UK)	1,329	June 2009
★ *Cow memorabilia*	Denise Tubangui (U.S.A.)	2,261	Oct. 2009
★ *Hedgehog memorabilia*	Bengt W. Johansson (Sweden)	468	Nov. 2009
★ *Joker playing cards*	Tony De Santis (Italy)	8,520	Mar. 2009
★ *Kappa (Japanese river sprite) memorabilia*	Tatsuo Kitano (Japan)	7,845	June 2009
★ *Millstones*	He Hengde (China)	39,052	July 2009
★ *Oil lamps*	Gerd Bonk (Germany)	356	Nov. 2009
★ *Panda memorabilia*	Miranda Middleton (U.S.A.)	1,175	Jan. 2009
★ *Stamps (postal covers)*	Joshua Steinberg (UK)	6,037	Nov. 2004
★ *Sugar packets*	Pavlina Yotkova (Bulgaria)	3,384	Apr. 2009
★ *Surfboards*	Donald Dettloff (U.S.A.)	647	Nov. 2009
★ *Tea-bag holders*	Mimi Wilfong (U.S.A.)	116	June 2009

QUACK!: As of May 28, 2008, Mary Brooks (U.S.A.) had 1,285 items of Donald Duck memorabilia. She has been collecting for more than 30 years.

☆ **MICKEY MOUSE MEMORABILIA** As of December 11, 2008, Janet Esteves (U.S.A.) had collected 2,760 different Mickey Mouse items. Janet started her collection in 1960, when she was a child. Her father made regular business trips to California and would bring back Disney products for her.

★ **SOAPS** Carol Vaughan (UK) has collected 1,331 individual soap bars since 1991. She is always on the lookout for new, unusual soaps—though, of course, she never uses items in her collection to wash with....

D'OH!: Cameron Gibbs (Australia) had amassed a total of 2,580 different Simpsons items, as of March 20, 2008.

CLASSIC COLLECTIONS

ITEM	COLLECTOR	QUANTITY	DATE ACHIEVED
☆ Airsickness bags	Niek Vermeulen (Netherlands)	6,016	Jan. 2010
☆ Barbie dolls	Bettina Dorfmann (Germany)	7,246	Feb. 2010
Bells	Myrtle B. Eldridge (U.S.A.)	9,638	Mar. 2005
Board games	Brian Arnett (U.S.A.)	1,345	Feb. 2007
☆ Bookmarks	Frank Divendal (Netherlands)	103,009	Feb. 2010
☆ Candles	Véronique Salmont (France)	2,119	June 2009
☆ Clocks	Jack Schoff (U.S.A.)	1,509	Feb. 2010
☆ Coffeepots	Robert Dahl (Germany)	13,267	Sep. 2009
☆ Colored vinyl records	Alessandro Benedetti (Italy)	1,507	Mar. 2010
"Do Not Disturb" signs	Jean-François Vernetti (Switzerland)	10,000	June 2009
☆ Hats	Roger Buckey Legried (U.S.A.)	100,336	Mar. 2010
☆ Ladybird memorabilia	Carine Roosen (Belgium)	3,531	Sep. 2009
☆ Magic sets	Manfred Klaghofer (Austria)	2,401	Feb. 2010
☆ Masks	Gerold Weschenmoser (Germany)	5,385	Mar. 2010
☆ Mobile (cell) phones	Carsten Tews (Germany)	1,563	Feb. 2010
☆ Model cars	Nabil Karam (Lebanon)	22,222	Nov. 2009
☆ Pencils	Vladimir Jindra (Czech Republic)	11,068	Nov. 2009
☆ Registration (license) plates	Shahin Ebrahim Mohajer (Oman)	561	May 2009
☆ Rubber ducks	Charlotte Lee (U.S.A.)	5,429	Feb. 2010
☆ Santa Claus memorabilia	Jean-Guy Laquerre (Canada)	23,947	Feb. 2010
☆ Sports mascots	Adina and Falk Hinneberg (both Germany)	874	Feb. 2010
Stickers for bumpers	Bill Heermann (U.S.A.)	4,131	Apr. 2009
Teapots	Tang Yu (China)	30,000	Oct. 2008
☆ Toothbrushes	Grigori Fleicher (Russia)	1,320	Nov. 2008
☆ Yo-yos	John "Lucky" Meisenheimer (U.S.A.)	4,586	Feb. 2010

TOYS & GAMES

LARGEST PARTY GAMES

★ **Old MacDonald Had a Farm** A record 332 people played the largest game of "Old MacDonald Had a Farm" on the set of *Lo Show dei Record*, in Milan, Italy, on April 25, 2009.

☆ **Head, shoulders, knees, and toes** A mammoth 1,461 participants from Gladesmore Community School and Crowland Primary School got together to play the largest game of "Head, Shoulders, Knees, and Toes" at Markfield Park, Tottenham, London, UK, on October 23, 2009.

☆ **If You're Happy and You Know It** During the SkyFest family festival held in Edinburgh, UK, on September 6, 2009, 755 people took part in the largest-ever game of the children's favorite "If You're Happy and You Know It."

☆ **Musical statues** A record 987 people tried to keep very still when the music stopped as they took part in the largest game of musical statues at an event organized by Sir Thomas Boteler Church of England High School in Latchford, Warrington, UK, on July 10, 2009.

☆ **MOST SIMULTANEOUS CHESS GAMES** Morteza Mahjoob (Iran) played 500 games of chess simultaneously against different opponents at the Engelab Sports Complex in Tehran, Iran, on August 13–14, 2009. Only 13 of his opponents beat him.

SITKA, AK, U.S.A. (57°03'N 135°19'W): Guy German of Sitka, Alaska, U.S.A., climbed up a 100-ft. (30.5-m) fir spar pole and back down to the ground in 24.82 seconds—the **fastest fir tree climb**—at the World Championship Timber Carnival in Albany, Oregon, U.S.A., on July 3, 1988.

STACK!: The **largest number of dominoes stacked on one single piece** was 1,002, achieved by Maximilian Poser (Germany) in Berlin, Germany, on February 6, 2009.

★FASTEST JENGA TOWER Mitchell Bettell (UK) built 10 levels on a Jenga tower in 43.94 seconds at the GWR Live! event held at Butlins, Bognor Regis, UK, on August 26, 2009.

☆**Musical bumps** On July 15, 2009, 348 people gathered at St. Thomas of Aquin's High School in Edinburgh, UK, to play the largest-ever game of musical bumps.

Musical chairs On August 5, 1989, the largest game of musical chairs began with 8,238 participants at the Anglo-Chinese School in Singapore. Three and a half hours later, 15-year-old Xu Chong Wei (Singapore) was left sitting on the last chair.

★LARGEST GAME OF DODGEBALL San Diego State University (U.S.A.) organized a game of dodgeball for 450 participants at the Aztec Recreation Center in San Diego, California, U.S.A., on September 5, 2009.

SPIRAL!: The **largest number of dominoes toppled in a spiral** was 28,800, by Maximilian Poser (Germany) in Berlin, Germany, on April 14, 2009.

★ **GREATEST DISTANCE TRAVELED BY A RADIO-CONTROLLED MODEL VEHICLE ON A SET OF BATTERIES** A battery-operated radio-controlled model vehicle in the shape of a robot pedaling a three-wheeled cycle covered 14.742 miles (23.726 km) using just one set of Panasonic Evolta batteries in Le Mans, France, on August 5–6, 2009.

EXTRA! For video game records, take a look at p. 291.

SCHOOL FAVES

★ **Longest hopscotch game** A hopscotch game measuring 15,762 ft. (4,804.55 m)—equal in length to about 45 soccer pitches—was created by Victory Baptist Church in cooperation with Toms Shoes (both U.S.A.) in Ladd Landing, Kingston, Tennessee, U.S.A., on September 26, 2009.

WHITEHORSE, YT, CANADA (60°43'N 135°03'W): On October 22, 2000, in the city of Whitehorse in the Yukon Territory of Canada, 210 dogs pulled a sled attached to a weight of 145,302 lb. (65,910 kg), the **heaviest weight pulled by a dog sled team**. The vehicle reached a top speed of 9 mph (15 km/h) and traveled a distance of six blocks.

LEGO

The name LEGO is an abbreviation of the two Danish words *leg godt,* meaning "play well."

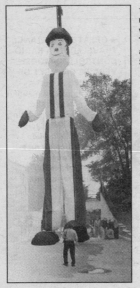

☆**LARGEST MARIONETTE** A marionette measuring 58 ft 5.5 in. (17.82 m) in height was presented by the Villa Marconi Long-Term Care Centre as the mascot to the annual Ital-Fest in Ottawa, Canada, on September 6, 2008.

☆**Fastest game of hopscotch** Ashrita Furman (U.S.A.) completed a game of hopscotch in 1 min. 8 sec. in New York City, U.S.A., on December 29, 2009.

★**Largest game of tag** On April 29, 2009, 465 people took part in a game of tag at an event organized by Marcia LeVatte (Canada) in Sherwood Park, Canada.

★**Largest game of He Loves Me, He Loves Me Not** On the set of *Lo Show dei Record*, in Milan, Italy, on April 18, 2009, 331 people picked petals off daisies in a game of He Loves Me, He Loves Me Not.

★**LARGEST LEGO HOUSE** A full-scale LEGO house measuring 15 ft. 4 in. (4.69 m) high, 30 ft. 9 in. (9.39 m) long, and 18 ft. 10 in. (5.75 m) wide was built by 1,200 volunteers and television presenter James May (UK) for the program *James May's Toy Stories* in Dorking, UK, on September 17, 2009. In all, 2.4 million LEGO bricks were used in the construction.

CLASSIC TOYS

☆ **Longest slot car track** A fully working slot car track measuring 2.953 miles (4.752 km) was built by James May (UK) and 300 volunteers at Brooklands, UK, on August 16, 2009.

★ **Most Rubik's cubes solved underwater** David Calvo (Spain) solved four Rubik's Cubes while holding his breath underwater in Madrid, Spain, on January 16, 2009.

☆ **Longest model train** An HO (that is, 1:87.1) scale model train measuring 892 ft. 3 in. (271.97 m) made up of eight locomotives and 2,212 cars was constructed by Miniature Wunderland in Hamburg, Germany, on July 25, 2008.

☆ **Largest simultaneous yo-yo** On March 13, 2009, a group of 662 people "yo-yo'd" together at an event organized by CTC Kingshurst Academy in Birmingham, UK.

ROUTE 66

Running nearly 2,500 miles (4,020 km) from Santa Monica on the west coast to the Windy City of Chicago, Route 66 is an inherent part of American folklore. Inspired by this historic highway, GWR takes you on a record-breaking road trip. . . .

1. SANTA MONICA–IRWINDALE (CA), 36.7 MILES The first leg of the journey takes us from the starting point at Santa Monica to the Irwindale Speedway to ride the **fastest monowheel**. Designed by Kerry McLean, this is no ordinary unicycle: powered by a 340 cc snowmobile engine generating 40 hp (30 kW), it can reach up to 57 mph (91.7 km/h)!

2. IRWINDALE–SAN DIMAS (CA), 10.1 MILES From Irwindale to San Dimas should take just 15 minutes by car, so pop on over and say hello to Bert, the world's **highest-ranking camel** (he's officially a Reserve Deputy Sheriff!).

3. SAN DIMAS–LAKE HAVASU CITY (AR), 270 MILES It's just a four-and-a-half-hour drive to see London Bridge . . . in Arizona? Yes, it's the record for the **farthest distance to move a bridge**. The British bridge was auctioned in 1962 to Robert McCulloch (U.S.A.) for $2,460,000 and dismantled and moved 5,300 miles (8,530 km) to Arizona!

4. LAKE HAVASU CITY–WINSLOW (AR), 270 MILES We continue on another four hours or so to Coon Butte (or Barringer Crater), the **largest meteor crater in the Americas**. Discovered in 1891, near Winslow, Arizona, it's 4,150 ft. (1,265 m) wide and 575 ft. (175 m) deep.

5. WINSLOW–ALBUQUERQUE (NM), 269 MILES Another four hours on and you'll come to the New Mexico capital of Albuquerque, where, if you time your trip correctly, you'll witness the International Balloon Fiesta and the **largest combined ascent of hot-air balloons**. The biggest-ever launch took place on October 7, 2000, when 329 balloons took to the skies in the space of an hour.

....

JUNEAU, AK, U.S.A. (58°21'N 134°30'W): In a 24-hour period between July 20 and 21, 2005, Isabel Bush (U.S.A.) skipped an incredible 151,036 jumps of a rope in Juneau, Alaska, U.S.A.—the **most skips in 24 hours**.

....

6. ALBUQUERQUE–OKLAHOMA CITY (OK), 541 MILES After a nine-hour drive, you'll be grateful for Carl C. Magee's (U.S.A.) invention: the **first parking meter** was installed on Park and Robinson Avenues, Oklahoma City, Oklahoma, on July 19, 1935.

7. OKLAHOMA CITY–SHAWNEE (OK), 39 MILES A 40-minute detour is worth the drive to see the world's **largest pair of bib overalls**. They boast an 8-ft. (2.46-m) inseam, a 15-ft. (4.54-m) waist, and buttons 8 in. (20.3 cm) wide!

VANCOUVER, BC, CANADA (49°15'N 123°06'W): The world's **largest orchestra** consisted of 6,452 musicians from the Vancouver Symphony Orchestra and music students from throughout British Columbia. The ensemble played "Ten Minutes of Nine" for 9 min. 44 sec. at BC Place Stadium, Vancouver, Canada, on May 15, 2000, conducted by Maestro Bramwell Tovey (UK).

8. SHAWNEE–CUBA (MO), 417 MILES From Oklahoma, you can hook up with I-44 East or, more enjoyably, join the original "historic" Route 66 and ride it most of the way to Cuba, MO, and the largest rocking chair. At 42 ft. 1 in. (12.83 m) tall and 20 ft. 3 in. (6.17 m) wide, you can't miss it!

9. CUBA–ST. LOUIS (MO), 83 MILES No trip to St. Louis should be without a visit to the biggest thing you can see for miles around: the 630-ft.-tall (192-m) stainless-steel Gateway Arch, the world's tallest commemorative monument. It was completed in 1965, cost $29 million to build, and celebrates the westward expansion after the Louisiana Purchase of 1803.

10. ST. LOUIS–CHICAGO (IL), 298 MILES So, 2,231 miles and 37 hours of solid driving later and we're here, two blocks from Lake Shore Drive, at the John Hancock Center, the highest residential apartments in the world. From 1,127 ft. (343.5 m) and 100 stories up, you can almost see all the way back toward Santa Monica!

ANIMAL MAGIC

CONTENTS

BARKING MAD

EXTRA! For more canine champions, simply turn the page. . . .

★ **Most dogs in fancy dress** A total of 123 dogs took to the runway for the "101 Chihuahua Fashion Show" in the downtown of Oosterhout, the Netherlands, on May 3, 2009. To qualify for this record, each dog had to be dressed for the occasion and walk at least one length of the platform with their owner by their side, as per Guinness World Records guidelines.

★ **First airplane crash caused by a dog** At 2:20 p.m. on November 29, 1976, an unrestrained German shepherd dog on board a Piper 32-300 Air Taxi operated by Grand Canyon Air interfered with the controls, causing the airplane to crash. The dog perished along with the pilot and lone passenger.

This is the first and, to date, only known accident in which a pet has caused the crash of an aircraft.

☆ **LONGEST TONGUE ON A DOG** The longest recorded canine tongue measures 4.5 in. (11.43 cm) and belongs to Puggy, a Pekingese owned by Becky Stanford (U.S.A.). The record-breaking muscle was measured at Avondale Haslet Animal Clinic in Texas, U.S.A., on May 8, 2009.

PORTLAND, OR, U.S.A. (45°31'N 122°40'W): The world's **smallest park** is Mill Ends Park on a safety island on SW Front Avenue, Portland, Oregon, U.S.A. The park is a circle of 24 in. (60.96 cm) in diameter, which is an area of 452.16 in.^{2} (2,917.15 cm^2).

LOW!: the **shortest dog living** measures just 4 in. (10.16 cm) tall. turn to page 275 find out more about this pint-sized pooch!

DID YOU KNOW?

• A dog's noseprint is as unique as a human fingerprint!

• Humans have 5 million smell (olfactory) cells; dogs have 220 million!

TRIVIA

Dogs sweat in just one place: between their paw pads. When they need to cool down, they hang out their tongues!

★**Most expensive kennel** In 2008, UK architect Andy Ramus designed a £250,000 ($384,623) kennel—nicknamed Barkingham Palace—complete with high-tech gadgets, such as a plasma TV and a retina-controlled dog door.

Fastest canine rat catcher In the 1820s, a 26-lb. (11.8-kg) "bull and terrier" dog named Billy killed 4,000 rats in 17 hours, a remarkable achievement considering that he was blind in one eye. His most notable feat was the killing of 100 rats in 5 min. 30 sec. at the Cockpit in Tufton Street, London, UK, on April 23, 1825. He died on February 23, 1829, at the age of 13 years.

LOUDEST BARK The loudest bark by a dog measured 108 dB and was produced by a white German shepherd dog named Daz, owned by Peter Lucken (UK), in Finsbury Park, London, UK, on June 15, 2009.

LOWER!: the **smallest dog ever** was a fist-sized, dwarf Yorkshire terrier owned by Arthur Marples (UK). Full grown, it stood 2.8 in. (7.11 cm) tall.

Animal Magic

★ **MOST FRISBEES CAUGHT AND HELD** Edward Watson's (U.S.A.) dog Rose can catch seven flying discs, thrown one at a time, and hold them all in her mouth at once!

Deepest scuba dive by a dog You've heard about the doggy paddle, but what happens when you take this to an extreme? Dwane Folsom (U.S.A.) regularly takes his dog, Shadow, scuba diving off the coast of Grand Cayman Island, going as deep as 13 ft. (4 m). Shadow wears a diving suit comprising a helmet, weighted dog jacket, and breathing tube connected to his owner's air tank.

INSTANT EXPERT

• According to biologist Dr. Raymond Coppinger, there are an estimated 400 million dogs in the world!

• Dogs were the first animals to be domesticated.

• The scientific name for dog is *Canis lupus familiaris,* referring to a domesticated form of gray wolf.

• In some countries, dog meat is acceptable fare, with *Animal People* newspaper estimating that a total of 13–16 million dogs are eaten in Asia every year.

TACOMA, WA, U.S.A. (47°14'N 122°26'W): The **largest school reunion** involved 3,299 former pupils of Stadium High School, Tacoma, Washington, U.S.A., who attended the centennial event on September 16, 2006.

Longest journey home by a lost dog The farthest distance a lost pet dog has walked in order to find his way home is 2,000 miles (3,218 km). Jimpa, a Labrador/boxer cross, turned up at his old home in Pimpinio, Victoria, Australia, after walking across the entire country. His owner, Warren Dumesney (Australia), had taken the dog with him 14 months earlier but lost him when he worked on a farm at Nyabing, Western Australia. During Jimpa's trek, the dog negotiated the almost waterless Nullarbor Plain.

Longest time on death row for a dog A dog named Word was held on doggy death row for a total of eight years and 190 days. Word, a Lhasa apso owned by Wilton Rabon of Seattle, Washington, U.S.A., was initially incarcerated at the Seattle Animal Control Shelter, U.S.A., on May 4, 1993, following two biting incidents. He was later released on November 10, 2001, and transported to the Pigs Peace Sanctuary in Washington, U.S.A. Word ended his days as a seeing eye dog to a visually impaired potbellied pig!

Largest dog wedding The record for the largest dog "wedding" ceremony was achieved by 178 dog couples who sealed their marriage at the Bow Wow Vows event at the Aspen Grove Lifestyle Center in Littleton, U.S.A., on May 19, 2007.

FASTEST TIME TO POP 100 BALLOONS BY A DOG The fastest time to pop 100 balloons by a dog is 44.49 seconds by Anastasia (a Jack Russell terrier), owned by Doree Sitterly (U.S.A.), on the set of *Live with Regis and Kelly* in Los Angeles, U.S.A., on February 24, 2008.

SAN FRANCISCO, CA, U.S.A. (37°46'N 122°25'W): Alvin Karpis, known as "Public Enemy No.1," was the **longest serving prisoner on Alcatraz**. He was imprisoned on the infamous island from August 1936 to April 1962, before being transferred to USP McNeil Island.

EXTRA! Find more peculiar pets on pp. 274–278.

★ **FASTEST SPEED ON A SKATEBOARD BY A DOG** Meet Tillman, the skateboarding, body-boarding, surfing action dog. The California-based bulldog loves to board, and set a new Guinness World Record—at X Games 15 in Los Angeles, no less—as the fastest skateboarding dog! Tillman's average time across a two-way 100-m (328-ft.) stretch in a parking lot was 19.678 seconds.

....

SEATTLE, WA, U.S.A. (47°36'N 122°19'W): The **tallest cut Christmas tree** was a 221-ft. (67.36-m) Douglas fir (*Pseudotsga menziesii*) at Northgate Shopping Center in Seattle, Washington, U.S.A., in December 1950.

....

Hardiest dog On April 15, 2003, a mixed-breed named Dosha slipped out of her home in Clearlake, California, U.S.A., only to be run over by a truck. A concerned police officer decided to end her pain and shot her in the head; she was then sealed in a bag and placed in a freezer at an animal center. Two hours later, staff at the clinic looked inside the freezer—and found Dosha alive and sitting up!

Largest solid object swallowed by a dog Kyle, a collie/Staffordshire bull terrier, who was 18 in. (45.7 cm) long at the time, swallowed a 15-in. (38-cm) bread knife in December 2000. The knife was stuck in his stomach, pointing toward his throat. The dog was taken to the People's Dispensary for Sick Animals in Leeds, UK, where Dr. Ann Draper carefully removed the knife.

Kyle now lives a normal life back at home with owner Eva Oliver (UK). Let's hope he sticks to a more sensible diet from now on!

PETS

★ **Earliest domesticated cat** The oldest archaeological evidence of the domestication of the cat dates back 9,500 years. The bones of a cat were discovered in the neolithic village of Shillourokambos on Cyprus.

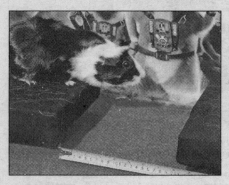

★ **FARTHEST JUMP BY A GUINEA PIG** The longest leap by a guinea pig was achieved by Diesel (left), who cleared a gap of 8.07 in. (20.5 cm) in London, UK, on July 27, 2009. The highest jump by a guinea pig was achieved by Puckel Martin, who jumped 7.8 in. (20 cm), on March 16, 2003.

OAKLAND, CA, U.S.A. (37°49'N 122°16'W): On January 11, 1935, Amelia Earhart (U.S.A.) made the **first successful solo flight from Hawaii to North America**, setting off from Wheeler Field, Honolulu, Hawaii, U.S.A., to Oakland Airport California, U.S.A. The flight lasted 18 hours and covered 2,400 miles (3,860 km).

SMALLEST LIVING DOG
The smallest dog living, in terms of height, is a long-haired female Chihuahua named Boo Boo, who measured 4 in. (10.16 cm) tall on May 12, 2007. Boo Boo is owned by Lana Elswick of Raceland, Kentucky, U.S.A.

Most intelligent dog breed Research by Stanley Coren (U.S.A.), professor of psychology at the University of British Columbia—and the polling of professional dog obedience judges—reveals the smartest dog breed to be the Border collie, followed by the poodle and German shepherd.

★**Longest jump by a rabbit** The world record for the longest rabbit jump is 9 ft. 9.6 in. (3 m) and was achieved by Yabo, handled by Maria Brunn Jensen (Denmark), on June 12, 1999, in Horsens, Denmark. That's some bunny hop. . . .

★**NEWEST BREED OF CAT** Finally recognized as an official cat breed in 2002, though it was first reported in Toronto, Canada, in the mid-20th century, the hairless sphynx cat can trace its origin to a number of cats with a recessive gene that causes hairlessness.

FUR!: The sphynx cat does not have any fur, but its skin is the same coloration as fur and also features the usual cat marking patterns, such as solid, tabby, or tortie!

☆Highest rate of pet ownership (country) The country with the highest rate of pet ownership per household as of 2010 is Australia, with more than 60% of households having at least one animal as a companion (typically a cat or dog) and 83% of Australians having owned a pet at some point in their life.

Longest ears on a rabbit Nipper's Geronimo, an English lop owned by Waymon and Margaret Nipper (U.S.A.), has ears that were measured at 31.125 in. (79 cm) in a complete span on November 1, 2003, at the American Rabbit Breeders Association National Show in Wichita, Kansas, U.S.A.

★TALLEST DOMESTIC CAT Scarlett's Magic, an F1 Savannah cross owned by Kimberly and Lee Draper (U.S.A.), measured 16.48 in. (41.87 cm) tall on December 17, 2009.

PURR!: The F1 Savannah is a first-generation serval (wild cat)/domestic cat hybrid, which is considered a domesticated cat by the International Cat Association (TICA).

SACRAMENTO, CA, U.S.A. (38°33'N 121°28'W): The **longest table tennis doubles marathon** lasted 101 hr. 1 min. 11 sec. and was carried out by Lance, Phil, and Mark Warren and Bill Weir (all U.S.A.) in Sacramento, California, U.S.A., on April 9–13, 1979.

☆ **LONGEST RABBIT**
Darius, a Flemish giant rabbit owned by Annette Edwards (UK, pictured with her big bunny), was found to be 4 ft. 3 in. (129 cm) long when measured for an article in the UK's *Daily Mail* newspaper on April 6, 2010.

Smallest rabbit Both the Netherlandish and Polish dwarf breeds of rabbit have a weight range of 2 lb. to 2 lb. 7 oz. (0.9–1.13 kg). In 1975, Jacques Boulance of Coulommiere, France, announced a new hybrid of these two breeds weighing just 13.9 oz. (396 g).

Oldest dog ever The greatest recorded age for a dog is 29 years 5 months for an Australian cattle dog named Bluey, owned by Les Hall (Australia). Bluey was obtained as a puppy in 1910 and lived until November 14, 1939.

Oldest cat ever Born on August 3, 1967, Creme Puff lived with her owner, Jake Perry, in Austin, Texas, U.S.A., until August 6, 2005—an amazing 38 years 3 days!

Oldest goldfish ever In 1956, seven-year-old Peter Hand of Carlton Minniot, North Yorkshire, UK, won a goldfish (which he named Tish) at a fairground stall. For the next 43 years, Peter's parents, Hilda and Gordon, cared for Tish until the fish died in 1999.

EXTRA! GWR's tour around our incredible living planet starts on p. 51.

☆ **TALLEST LIVING DOG** Giant George is a Great Dane who measured 43 in. (1.092 m) tall on February 15, 2010. The huge hound weighs 245 lb. (111 kg) and is owned by David Nasser of Tucson, Arizona, U.S.A.

Oldest caged gerbil A Mongolian gerbil called Sahara, born in May 1973 and belonging to Aaron Milstone of Lathrup Village, Michigan, U.S.A., died on October 4, 1981, at age 8 years and 4.5 months.

Smallest breed of domestic hamster The Roborovski (*Phodopus roborovskii*) typically grows to a length of 1.5–2 in. (4–5 cm). These hamsters originate from Mongolia and northern China.

Most toes on a cat Jake, a male ginger tabby cat owned by Michelle and Paul Contant (both Canada), had 28 toes—seven per paw—with each toe having its own claw, pad, and bone structure, on September 24, 2002.

....

LOS ANGELES, CA, U.S.A. (34°03'N 118°15'W): The first movie shot in Hollywood was *In Old California* (U.S.A., 1910), which was filmed in Los Angeles in 1907 by a Chicago production that had moved to California to take advantage of the state's sunnier weather.

....

ZOOS & SANCTUARIES

Oldest zoo The **earliest known collection of animals** was established at modern-day Puzurish, Iraq, by Shulgi, a 3rd-dynasty ruler of Ur from 2097 B.C. to 2094 B.C. In the early 13th century, English monarch King John began the most extensive animal collection of the medieval era, which was housed in the Tower of London.

The ☆ **oldest continuously operating zoo** is the Tiergarten Schönbrunn, part of the Schönbrunn Palace in Vienna, Austria. Created in 1752 by order of Holy Roman Emperor Francis I, initially as a crown menagerie, it was first opened to the public in 1779. The first elephant born in captivity was born here in 1906.

Largest zoo In terms of numbers of different species in captivity, the largest zoo is the Zoologischer Garten Berlin (Berlin zoological garden), also the first zoo in Germany, which opened on August 1, 1844. The 86-acre (35-ha) site currently houses 14,000 animals from 1,500 different species, and receives some 2.6 million visitors each year.

Aquariums Sea Life in Brighton, East Sussex, UK, is the world's ★ **oldest aquarium**, dating back to 1872. Combining Victorian architecture with modern-day, high-tech exhibits, it contains more than 150 species of marine life, which are exhibited in 57 separate displays.

☆ **LONGEST SNAKE** Fluffy, a reticulated python (*Python reticulatus*), lives in Columbus Zoo and Aquarium, Powell, Ohio, U.S.A. When measured on September 30, 2009, she was found to be more than 24 ft. (7.3 m) long. The **longest snake ever** was found in Indonesia in 1912 and measured 32 ft. 9.5 in. (10 m).

In terms of water volume, the Georgia Aquarium in Atlanta, Georgia, U.S.A., is the **largest aquarium**, with 8 million gal. (30.28 million liters) of fresh and salt water. The attraction opened in November 2005, covers 500,000 ft.² (51,096 m²), and contains 120,000 fish and animals from 500 species. It has 60 different habitats, the largest of which contains 6.2 million gal. (23.47 million liters) and was designed to house whale sharks.

★**Largest walk-in aviary** Part of Singapore's Jurong Bird Park—the world's largest bird park, with 8,000 birds—the world's largest walk-in aviary is the African Waterfall Aviary, containing more than 1,500 free-flying birds belonging to more than 50 different species.

GORILLA: The **greatest height recorded for a primate** in the wild is 6 ft. 5 in. (1.95 m) for a mountain bull gorilla found in the eastern Congo in May 1938.

GORILLA: The **largest mammal to build a nest** is the African gorilla (*Gorilla gorilla*), which grows up to 6 ft. (1.8 m) tall and weighs up to 500 lb. (227 kg).

☆**OLDEST GORILLA IN CAPTIVITY** Colo (b. December 22, 1956), the first gorilla ever born in captivity, currently lives in Columbus Zoo in Powell, Ohio, U.S.A. She has now reached the grand old age of 53 years.

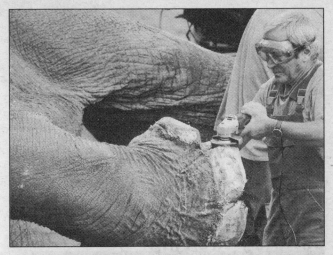

★ **LARGEST PEDICURES** Elephants in captivity are the largest animals to receive pedicures. Pictured above is a (sedated) 39-year-old Asian elephant named Boy, receiving a pedicure from a German vet on May 23, 2009, at Kiev Zoo, Ukraine.

★ **MOST GIRAFFE OFFSPRING BORN IN CAPTIVITY** Denisa, a female giraffe living in the Safari Park zoo in Ramat Gan, Israel, has given birth to a record 11 offspring. She is pictured with her latest, in July 2009.

Largest litter of tigers On April 15, 1979, eight tigers were born at Marine World Africa U.S.A., Redwood City, California, U.S.A., to a Bengal tiger (*Panthera tigris tigris*) named Baghdad. This is the greatest recorded number of tigers born in captivity at once.

DOWN ON THE FARM

Largest farm The farm owned by Laucídio Coelho (Brazil) in Mato Grosso, Brazil, covered 3,360 miles^2 (8,700 km^2) and supported 250,000 cattle at the time of Coelho's death in 1975. The smallest U.S. state, Rhode Island, would fit into the farm three times.

★**First moose farm** The first farm devoted to the domestication and rearing of the moose (*Alces alces*)—the world's **largest species of deer**—is the Kostroma Moose Farm (established 1963) in Kostroma Oblast, Russia. It includes 10 to 15 milk-producing moose cows, with more than 800 moose having lived on the farm during its existence.

★**Largest ant farm** An ant farm measuring 3 ft. 11 in. x 2 ft. 11 in. x 3 in. (1.2 x 0.9 x 0.08 m) and housing between 200 and 300 ants was unveiled on December 28, 2008, by Colgate Palmolive Ltd as part of a toothpaste advert on the side of a bus stop in Singapore.

☆**Most horns on a sheep** Both ewes and rams of the Jacob sheep—a rare breed produced in both the U.S.A. and UK—typically grow two or four horns; however, some six-horned specimens have been recorded.

SPOKANE, WA, U.S.A. (47°39'N 117°25'W): On April 17, 2001, James David (U.S.A.) performed a continuous 130-m (425-ft. 3-in.) skid on his bicycle on a flat surface at the Spokane Raceway Park, Washington, U.S.A.—the **longest continuous skid on a bicycle**.

MENTAL!: A "mantle" of bees is a giant cluster of bees that forms a protective layer around the queen. By wearing the queen in a locket, an individual can encourage a mantle of bees to form around themselves!

☆ **HEAVIEST MANTLE OF BEES** On March 9, 2009, at the Indian Agriculture Research Institute in New Delhi, India, Vipin Seth (India) was covered by a mantle of bees weighing 136 lb. 4 oz. (61.4 kg) and comprising an estimated 613,500 bees.

☆**SMALLEST COW** Swallow, a Dexter cow owned by Martyn and
Caroline Ryder (both UK)—pictured here with Freddie, a full-size British
shorthorn—was measured at 33.5 in. (85 cm), from rear foot to hind, at
Pike End Farm, Rishworth, Halifax, UK, on July 22, 2009.

SAN DIEGO, CA, U.S.A. (32°46'N 117°09'W): The **highest wave**
dependent on just weather or climate was calculated at 112 ft. (34 m) from
trough to crest. It was measured from the USS *Ramapo* traveling from
Manila in the Philippines to San Diego, California, U.S.A., on the night of
February 6–7, 1933.

★ OLDEST LIVING SHEEP Lucky, a Dorset cross owned by Delrae and Frank Westgarth (both Australia) of Lake Bolac, Australia, was born on April 25, 1986.

DID YOU KNOW?

The date November 17, 2010, marks the 30th anniversary of the **Fastest turkey pluck:** Vincent Pilkington (Ireland) plucked a bird in 1 min. 30 sec.

TRIVIA

Vincent also killed 100 turkeys in 7 hr. 32 min. on December 15, 1978—an average of one every four-and-a-half minutes!

FASTER!: The **fastest time to shear a single sheep** is 45.41 seconds, also by Dwayne Black (Australia) in Sydney, New South Wales, Australia, on April 17, 2005.

EXTRA! Want even more tall tales? why not try pp. 111–115 on for size.

LARGEST HORN CIRCUMFERENCE The African ankole watusi breed of cattle are famed for their thick horns. For **steers**, Lurch (pictured) is the record holder, with a horn 37.5 in. (95.25 cm) in circumference. For **bulls**, C. T. Woodie takes the title with a 40.75-in. (103.5-cm) horn.

★**Most prolific chicken** The highest authenticated rate of egg-laying is 371 eggs in 364 days, laid by a White Leghorn (No. 2988) in an official test conducted by Prof. Harold V. Biellier and ending on August 29, 1979, at the College of Agriculture, University of Missouri, U.S.A.

☆**Oldest living pig** The oldest pig is Oscar, who turned 20 years old on October 29, 2009. He lives with his owner, Stacy Leigh Kimbell (U.S.A.), in Dallas, Texas, U.S.A.

TIJUANA, MEXICO (32°31'N 117°02'W): The world's **largest Caesar salad** was prepared by Canirac—the Tijuana Restaurateurs Chamber of Commerce—on October 20, 2007. A team of 160 people prepared the 7,246-lb. (3.287-tonne) salad, which was unveiled in Tijuana, Baja California, Mexico.

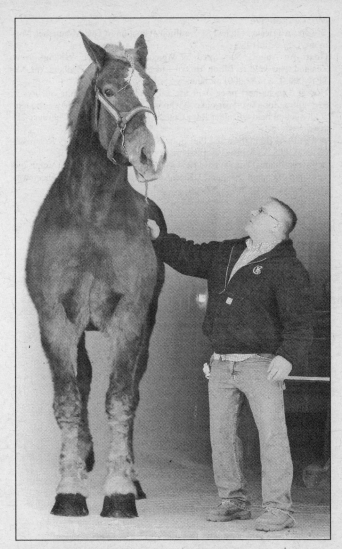

☆TALLEST HORSE Big Jake, a nine-year-old Belgian gelding horse, measured 20 hands 2.75 in. (82.75 in.; 210.19 cm), without shoes, at Smokey Hollow Farms in Poynette, Wisconsin, U.S.A., on January 19, 2010.

Most expensive . . .

☆**Cow:** A Friesian fetched $1.3 million at auction in East Montpelier, Vermont, U.S.A., in 1985.

Goat: An Angora buck bred by Waitangi Angoras of Waitangi, New Zealand, was sold to Elliott Brown Ltd of Waipu, New Zealand, for NZ $140,000 (U.S. $82,600) on January 25, 1985.

Horse: The highest price paid for a Thoroughbred at public auction is $16 million for a two-year-old colt who had yet to even race. He was bought at an auction held at Calder Race Course, Florida, U.S.A., on February 28, 2006.

★**Pig:** E. A. Bud Olson and Phil Bonzio paid $56,000 to Jeffrey Roemisch of Texas, U.S.A., for Bud, a crossbred barrow, on March 5, 1983.

★**Sheep:** Jimmy Douglas paid £231,000 ($369,000) for an eight-month-old Texel tup in Lanark, Scotland, UK, in August 2009. This valuable sheep was purchased for breeding purposes.

POPULAR CULTURE

CONTENTS

SLOW!: *Avatar* was in production for so many years that each frame of the movie (¹⁄₂₄th of a second) took an average of 47 hours to shoot!

☆**HIGHEST BOX-OFFICE MOVIE GROSS** James Cameron's (Canada) sci-fi extravaganza *Avatar* (U.S.A./UK, 2009) sailed past his own *Titanic* (U.S.A., 1997) to become the biggest movie in box-office history, grossing $2.05 billion worldwide as of February 2010. *Avatar*— starring Sam Worthington (UK) and Zoe Saldana (U.S.A.), pictured, top—is the ★**first movie to gross more than $2 billion** and makes Cameron the director of the ★**most movies to gross more than $1 billion**. It also claims the record for the ★**fastest-selling Blu-ray disc**, with 2.7 million copies purchased in its first four days on sale in North America alone. For more *Avatar* achievements, see page 292.

FAST!: The movie crossed the $1 billion mark in a record 17 days— a vast improvement on the 197 days that it took *The Dark Knight* to achieve the same gross.

AVATAR RECORDS

RECORD	NOTES	DATE
☆ Highest-grossing movie	Beating *Titanic* (U.S.A., 1997)	Jan. 26, 2010
☆ Fastest to $500 million	Achieved in 32 days; *Titanic* took 45 days	Jan. 19, 2010
☆ Highest-grossing PG-13	Beating *Titanic* (U.S.A., 1997)	Mar. 1, 2010
☆ Highest-grossing 3D movie	Beating *Up* (U.S.A., 2009, now in 3rd place) and staying ahead of *Alice in Wonderland* (U.S.A., 2010, in 2nd place)	Mar. 1, 2010
☆ Highest-grossing sci-fi movie	$2.69 billion (£1.80 billion)	Mar. 1, 2010
★ Highest-grossing New Year's Day	Took $25.2 million (£16.8 million)	Jan. 1, 2010
★ Largest motion-capture project	Three years of motion-capture by Giant Studios (Los Angeles, U.S.A.)	NA
★ Largest area to be motion-captured	The Kong stage (Wellington, NZ): 150 x 80 x 40 ft. (45 x 24 x 12 m)	NA
★ Most actors motion-captured for a movie	Giant Studios captured 80 people	NA
★ First 3D movie to win Best Cinematography Oscar	*Avatar* (U.S.A., 2010)	Mar. 7, 2010

VIDEO GAMES

☆**Best-selling video game** With lifetime sales of 45.7 million copies between its launch in 2006 and May 2009, the best-selling video game of all time is Nintendo's *Wii Sports*, which came bundled with the Wii console.

★**Best-selling rhythm game series** *Guitar Hero* (RedOctane, 2005) had seen total sales of more than 32 million units between November 2005 and June 2009.

☆**LARGEST POKÉMON COLLECTION** Lisa Courtney (UK) was found to have 12,113 different items of Pokémon memorabilia when Guinness World Records examined her collection on June 13, 2009.

BOISE, ID, U.S.A. (43°37'N 116°13'W): The **longest alpenhorn** is 78 ft. 9 in. (24.02 m) long and weighs 183 lb. (83 kg). Built from spruce by Swiss-born Peter Wutherich, it took over a year and a half to complete.

DRAW DISTANCE

The distance in a 3D scene that is still drawn by the game engine.

☆ **HIGHEST REVENUE GENERATED BY AN ENTERTAINMENT PRODUCT IN 24 HOURS** *Call of Duty: Modern Warfare 2* (Activision, 2009) generated $401 million in sales within the first 24 hours of its worldwide launch on November 11, 2009. This is the greatest amount ever generated on a first day of sale by an entertainment product, outstripping any movie, music, or previous video-game launch.

☆ **MOST DETAILED VIDEO-GAME CHARACTER** With a character model that consists of 32,816 rendered polygons during gameplay, the most detailed video-game character is Lara Croft in her *Tomb Raider: Underworld* (Eidos Interactive, 2008) incarnation.

MEXICALI, MEXICO (32°40'N 115°28'W): The **largest flour taco** in the world weighed 1,654 lb. (750 kg) and was made by the city of Mexicali and Cocinex SA de CV, in Mexicali, Baja California, Mexico, on March 8, 2003.

★ **LONGEST RACING GAME MARATHON** Rolf Loraas, Hans Moe, Alexander Moerk, Lars-Christian Klingstroem, Per Helge Fagermoen, Benny Charles Fredstad, Benjamin Ward, Jan Dalan, and Joachim Olsen (all Norway) played *Need for Speed Shift* (EA, 2009) for 25 hours at Oslo City, Oslo, Norway, on September 18–19, 2009.

★ **Best-selling console real-time strategy game** Of the current generation of consoles, the best-selling real-time strategy game is *Halo Wars* (Microsoft, 2009), which had achieved global sales of 1.21 million as of May 2009.

★ **Highest cash prize awarded in a fan mod tournament** The Sendi Mutiara Multimedia Grand National DotA Tournament, which took place in Kuala Lumpur, Malaysia, on November 22–23, 2008, had a prize fund of 120,000 Malaysian ringgits ($35,000). The tournament welcomed

LAS VEGAS, NV, U.S.A. (36°10'N 115°08'W): The **highest gross gaming revenue** generated by the casinos and entertainment complexes of a city in a year is $7,673,134,286 by Las Vegas, Nevada, U.S.A., in 2000.

★ LONGEST SOCCER GAME MARATHON A group of gamers, supported by online gaming leagues website Stryxa.com, recorded the longest marathon playing a soccer video game when they played *FIFA 10* (EA Sports, 2009) for 24 hours at Victoria Station, London, UK, on January 27–28, 2009.

World Record attempt
24 hour football
gaming marathon

competitors from seven countries, who competed on the *Warcraft III* mod "Defense of the Ancients." Team Ehome from China emerged as overall champions of the competition, pocketing RM36,000 ($10,500) in cash along with other prizes.

★ Fastest-selling multiplatform role-playing game (RPG) Bethesda's *Fallout 3* sold more than 4.7 million copies in its first week on sale from October 28 to November 4, 2008.

☆ Fastest-selling PC game Released on November 13, 2008, *World of Warcraft* expansion pack *Wrath of the Lich King* (Activision Blizzard) sold around 2.8 million copies in 24 hours, and 4 million copies in its first month.

★ Most powerful flight simulator Described as "a next generation military simulation synthetic environment," the *Simusphere HD World*, produced by Link Simulation and Training (U.S.A.) for clients including the United States Air Force (USAF), is the most powerful flight simulation system in the world. The USAF version simulates an F-16 fighter jet and runs on 120 dual-core PCs, each of which contains a $400 graphics card, allowing for 10,000 onscreen objects to be displayed simultaneously.

★ First concert held in a real and a virtual space simultaneously
On June 2, 2009, U.S. punk-pop band The Dares (Ben Peterson, Matt Peterson, and Martin Lascano) performed the first music concert to take place in both the real world and in a virtual space. The gig was held on a stage at E3 2009 in the Los Angeles Convention Center, California, U.S.A., and simultaneously online in *Free Realms* (Sony, 2009). The Dares' set list included the *Free Realms* theme "It's Your World."

CALGARY, AB, CANADA (51°02'N 114°03'W): The **longest journey of the Olympic torch within one country** was for the XV Winter Olympic Games in Canada in 1988. The torch arrived from Greece at St. Johns, Newfoundland, Canada, on November 17, 1987, and was transported a total distance of 11,222 miles (18,060 km).

★Longest draw distance in a racing game Codemasters' *FUEL* boasts a draw distance of 24.8 miles (40 km), the longest in a simulation racing game. *FUEL's* racing environment is inspired by the North American wilderness. The landscape, which is modeled from satellite data and rendered by the game engine, is battered by weather effects, including blizzards, tsunamis, and tornadoes.

PUBLISHING

☆**Largest single-volume biography** Between 1996 and 2007, Dr. A. V. S. Raju (India) wrote a biography chronicling the life of Sri Sathya Sai Baba (India), a popular religious figure and spiritual teacher. The single bound book consists of 32 volumes.

★Most banned book of the year The book most frequently reported to the American Library Association's (ALA) Office for Intellectual Freedom in 2008—and each year since 2006—is *And Tango Makes Three* by Justin Richardson and Peter Parnell (both U.S.A.). The award-winning book—which recounts the true tale of two male penguins who raise a baby penguin—attracted the most complaints from parents and school officials for its promotion of a "homosexual lifestyle."

Most Nobel prizes for literature (country) The country that claims the most outright or shared Nobel prizes awarded for literature is France, with 13.

★Youngest recipient of the Nobel Prize for literature Poet and author Rudyard Kipling (UK, 1865–1936) won the Nobel prize for literature

★HIGHEST DAILY ENGLISH-LANGUAGE NEWSPAPER CIRCULATION *The Times of India*, owned by the Sahu Jain family (India), has an average daily circulation of 3,146,000 according to the latest figures from the World Association of Newspapers and the Audit Bureau of Circulations.

EDMONTON, AB, CANADA (53°34'N 113°31'W): The world's **longest crude oil pipeline** is the Interprovincial Pipe Line Inc. (now Enbridge Pipelines) installation, which spans the North American continent from Edmonton, Alberta, Canada, through Chicago to Montreal: a distance of 2,353 miles (3,787.2 km).

★**OLDEST PLAYBOY MODEL** Model and presenter Patricia Paay (Netherlands, b. April 7, 1949) posed for the Christmas edition of *Playboy Netherlands* on December 10, 2009, at the age of 60.

in 1907 at the age of 42, in recognition of his "power of observation, originality of imagination, virility of ideas."

★**First woman to win the Nobel Prize for literature** Selma Lagerlöf (Sweden, 1858–1940) was awarded the Nobel prize for literature in 1909 for the "lofty idealism, vivid imagination and spiritual perception that characterize her writings."

★**Most audiobooks published for one author** L. Ron Hubbard (U.S.A.) has had 185 audiobooks published as of April 21, 2009.

★**Longest audiobook** Published on August 1, 2008, by Tokyo Shigesato Itoi Office K K (Japan), the audiobook *50 Lectures* by Takaaki Yoshimoto (Japan) has a running time of 115 hr. 43 min.

Longest novel *A la recherche du temps perdu* by Marcel Proust (France) contains around 9,609,000 characters (each letter counts as a character; so do spaces). The title translates as *In Search of Lost Time,* and the first of seven volumes appeared in 1913.

★**Oldest printing and publishing house** Cambridge University Press is the oldest printing and publishing house in the world. It was founded on a royal charter

THICKEST BOOK The entire collection of Agatha Christie's (UK) *Miss Marple* detective stories—a grand total of 12 novels and 20 short stories—was published as one single volume by HarperCollins on May 20, 2009. The capacious compendium is 12.67 in. (322 mm) thick.

☆ **LARGEST POP-UP BOOK**
The largest pop-up book measures 3 ft. 8 in. (1.13 m) by 3 ft. (92 cm) and weighs 42 lb. (19 kg). It is an outsize version of *The Pop-Up Story of Delray Beach* by Roger Culberston (U.S.A.) and illustrated by Al Margolis. The book contains six pop-up spreads illustrating the experiences of residents and visitors to the city of Delray Beach, Florida, U.S.A.

granted to the university by Henry VIII in 1534 and has been operating continuously as a printer and publisher since the first Press book was printed in 1584.

☆ **Richest author** According to *Forbes*, J. K. Rowling (UK), author of the Harry Potter series, has grossed more than $1 billion for her novels and from related earnings. Rowling is one of only five self-made female billionaires, and the ★ **first billion-dollar author**. The seven Potter books have sold 400 million copies around the world and are published in 55 languages, including Latin and ancient Greek.

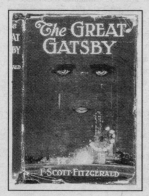

★ **MOST BANNED CLASSIC NOVEL**
Topping the American Library Association's list of most banned or "challenged" classic novels is *The Great Gatsby* (1924) by F. Scott Fitzgerald. The Baptist College in Charleston, South Carolina, U.S.A., challenged the book because of "language and sexual references" as recently as 1987.

★**LARGEST ATLAS** The 350-year-old Klencke Atlas was presented to Charles II, King of England, on his restoration in 1660. Created by Dutch merchant Yohannes Klencke, the atlas features 41 maps on 39 sheets, and is 5 ft. 10 in. (1.78 m) tall, 3 ft. 5 in. (1.05 m) wide, and 4 in. (11 cm) thick.

☆**Most books typed backward** Using a computer and four blank keyboards, and without looking at the screen, Michele Santelia (Italy) has typed backward 68 books (3,663,324 words; 20,680,060 characters; 24,154 pages; 266,741 paragraphs; 516,498 lines) in their original languages, including *The Odyssey*, *Macbeth*, The Vulgate Bible, *Guinness World Records 2002*, and the Dead Sea scrolls (in Ancient Hebrew).

Santelia's most recent book typed backward and in the English language is *Life of Abraham Lincoln* (956 pages; 160,311 words; 919,124 characters; 2,810 paragraphs; 16,944 lines). He started typing it on January 20, 2009, and finished it on June 16, 2009.

PHOENIX, AZ, U.S.A. (33°26'N 112°104'W): Best Western International Inc. is the world's **biggest hotel chain**, with more than 4,000 hotels in 82 countries and territories under its banner. The company, which is based in Phoenix, Arizona, U.S.A., says it has 308,640 rooms available in its establishments, which, although part of the Best Western group, are independently owned and operated.

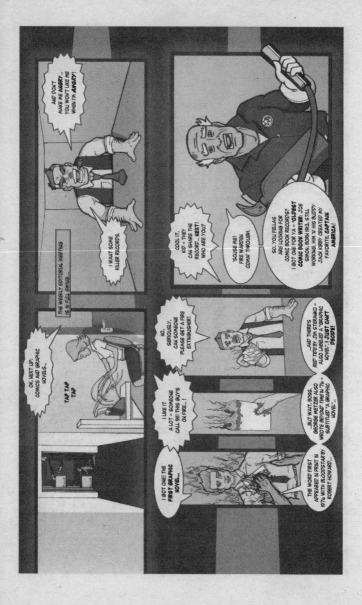

WHAT'S ON TV

☆ Most watched TV series (2009)
Global: The most popular TV show continues to be the medical drama *House* (Fox). According to ratings agency Eurodata TV Worldwide, the show—starring Hugh Laurie (UK) as the unconventional maverick Dr. Gregory House—was seen by more than 81.8 million viewers in 66 countries.
UK: The final of *Britain's Got Talent* was seen by nearly 18 million viewers.
Europe: The *Eurovision Song Contest* 2009 clocked up an impressive 122 million viewers.
U.S.A.: *NCIS* (NBC) season 7 episode "Reunion" averaged 21.37 million viewers.

☆ Most watched TV
2009: The funeral of Michael Jackson (U.S.A.) on July 7, 2009, was watched by a global audience of 2–3 billion.
Sports event: According to the BBC, English Premier League soccer games are broadcast to more than 600 million homes in 202 countries.

★ Most time-shifted TV show According to 2009 figures from Nielsen, the most "time-shifted" primetime show of the year was *Battlestar Galactica* (SYFY), which enjoyed a 59.4% increase in viewing figures as a result. Time-shifting involves recording TV shows on digital video recorders (DVRs) or storing them via premium TV services such as TiVo.

★ LONGEST-RUNNING MEDICAL DRAMA *Casualty* (BBC, 1986–present) is the world's most enduring primetime medical drama series. Only the hospital-based soap opera *General Hospital* (ABC, 1963–present)—now the world's ☆ longest-running daytime soap opera with the demise of *As the World Turns* (CBS, 1956–2010)—has been broadcast for a longer period.

TUCSON, AR, U.S.A. (32°12'N 110°55'W): Dayton C. Fouts of Tucson, Arizona, had the **longest career as Santa Claus**, having played the role every year from 1937 until 1997. He first appeared as Santa for 55 years in Harvey, Illinois, and continued the tradition in Tucson, with his last event at a Tucson Boys Chorus concert.

Popular Culture

☆ **Longest-running soap opera on TV** It was announced in 2009 that *As the World Turns* (CBS, 1956–2010) would be canceled by September 2010, meaning that the UK's *Coronation Street* (ITV, 1960–) would become the world's longest-running soap opera. Actor William Roach (UK) would then become the ☆ **longest-serving soap actor**, having debuted as Ken Barlow in episode 1.

☆ **Highest paid**

Actor: Charlie Sheen (U.S.A.) was estimated to earn $800,000 per episode of *Two and a Half Men* (CBS, 2003–present).

Actress: Katherine Heigl (U.S.A.)—Izzie Stevens in *Grey's Anatomy* (ABC, 2005–present)—earned $200,000 per show.

SASKATOON, SK, CANADA (52°10'N 106°38'W): The **longest eyelash on a dog** measured 5.35 in. (13.6 cm) on November 27, 2004, and belonged to Prince Albert, a Lhasa apso owned by Sandra Daku of Saskatoon, Saskatchewan, Canada.

IDOL: Cowell produced the "Got Talent" and "X Factor" franchises—two of the fastest-selling TV formats ever. "Talent" was the only show to be no.1 in the UK and U.S.A. at the same time.

☆ **HIGHEST-EARNING PRIMETIME TV STARS** While Oprah reigns supreme as the highest-earning TV personality (see below), the *Forbes* Celebrity 100 list identifies Simon Cowell (UK) and Tyra Banks (U.S.A.) as the highest-earning *primetime* celebrities. In the 12 months between June 2009 and June 2010, talent judge Cowell earned an estimated $75 million, while supermodel-turned-host Banks made $30 million.

☆ **HIGHEST-EARNING CELEBRITY** Between June 2009 and June 2010, Oprah Winfrey (U.S.A.) earned an estimated $275 million, thanks to her monthly magazine, her radio contract, her production company Harpo, and the debut of the Oprah Winfrey Network.

"The only people who never tumble are those who never mount the high wire."

Oprah Winfrey

☆ **HIGHEST-RATED TV SHOWS (CURRENT) Three shows can boast to be the most critically acclaimed series currently on TV. The third season of *Mad Men* (Lionsgate/AMC, pictured left), *Sons of Anarchy* (FX), and *Modern Family* (ABC) all scored 86/100 on the critical aggregation site metacritic.com.**

EMMY AWARDS

★**Most wins** The televised Oscars (Academy Awards) ceremony has been nominated for 195 Primetime Emmy awards, winning a record 46 times.

★**Most wins for a variety, music, or comedy series** *The Daily Show with Jon Stewart* (Comedy Central) has won the Emmy for Outstanding Variety, Music, or Comedy series for a record seven consecutive years.

★**Youngest actress to win a lead acting Emmy** In 2007, at the age of 23, America Ferrara (U.S.A., b. April 18, 1984) was voted the Outstanding Lead Actress in a Comedy Series for her portrayal of Betty Suarez in *Ugly Betty* (ABC)—the youngest person to win a lead acting Emmy award.

★**Nominations—most in one year**
Variety show: *Saturday Night Live* (NBC)—13 nominations in 2009.
Comedy show: *30 Rock* (NBC)—22 nominations in 2009.
Drama: *NYPD Blue* (ABC)—27 nominations in 1994.
Miniseries: *Roots* (ABC)—37 nominations in 1977.

★**Most daytime Emmys won** The Public Broadcasting Service's *Sesame Street* has won a record 122 Daytime Emmys since 1984.

75 YEARS OF BROADCAST TV

Although experimental services had operated across the world from the 1920s, the television broadcasting age as we recognize it began at 3 p.m. on November 2, 1936 in London, UK, when the BBC launched the world's **first regular television broadcasts**.

> *"Good afternoon, ladies and gentlemen. It is with great pleasure that I introduce you to the magic of television. . . ."*
> **Leslie Mitchell, first words spoken on TV**

1936: First TV host Radio personality Leslie Mitchell is the first of three TV hosts that also includes Jasmine Bligh and Elizabeth Cowell (all UK), the **first female TV hosts**.

1936: First black performers Buck and Bubbles (U.S.A.), an energetic vaudeville comedy dance act, are guests on *Variety* (UK), one of the shows broadcast on the first day of service.

1936: First magazine show *Picture Page* (UK), a variety and chat show, runs daily from day one, hosted by Joan Millar (Canada), who becomes the world's **first TV star**.

1936: First TV drama On day five, excerpts from the West End play *Marigold* by L. Allen Harker and F. R. Pryor (both UK) are broadcast.

1937: First children's series *For the Children* (UK) debuts at 3 p.m. on April 24 and runs until 1950 (with a break for World War II); episodes last 10 minutes.

1937: FIRST REGULAR TV CHEF Marcel Boulestin (France, left) begins hosting *Dish of the Month* (UK) on October 15.

1938: First TV sci-fi aired—an adaptation of *R.U.R. (Rossum's Universal Robots)*, a play in the Czech language by Karel Čapek; also the world's **first depiction of robots**.

1939: First regular U.S. programming Franklin D Roosevelt (U.S.A.) opens the 1939 New York World's Fair (April 30), relayed to the nation via a high-def telecast.

1939–46: BBC TV suspended for the duration of World War II.

1940: First ice hockey (February 25) and **first basketball game** (February 28) aired.

Popular Culture

1941: First TV advert NBC's WNBT station (U.S.A.) promotes a Bulova watch on June 27.

1949: First Emmy Awards The TV equivalent of the Oscars is first aired on January 25.

1951: First regular color broadcast On June 25, CBS broadcasts the first color images from five stations on the U.S. east coast . . . to a virtually nonexistent audience, as so few color TV sets exist!

1951: First use of TV detector vans in the UK to trace TV license evaders.

1952: Longest-running soap opera Procter & Gamble Productions' *Guiding Light* (CBS, U.S.A.) first airs on June 30, and is the world's longest-lived soap until it finishes in 2009.

1953: The CBS system fails; RCA's system adopted as industry standard in the U.S.A.

1954: First coast-to-coast color transmission (U.S.A.) RCA's broadcasting wing (NBC) airs first countrywide color transmission on January 1, 1954, with the Tournament of Roses Parade from Pasadena, California.

1954: First network series regularly shown in color: NBC sitcom *The Marriage* debuts.

1954: First in-vision weather report is shown with anchor George Cowling (UK) standing in front of a projected map.

1957: *The Sky at Night* **(BBC) introduces the Brits to the monocled Patrick Moore (UK, left), who continues to host the show, making him the most enduring TV host.**

1958: First actor to die on live TV is Gareth Jones (UK) during an ITV production of *Armchair Theatre*.

1958: *Blue Peter*, the **longest-running children's magazine program**, debuts on BBC1.

1960: Debut of record-breaking soap *Coronation Street* (see p. 305).

1963: First murder on live TV takes place as John F. Kennedy's assassin, Lee Harvey Oswald (U.S.A.), is shot and killed by Jack Ruby (U.S.A.).

1963: Longest-running sci-fi show—*Doctor Who*—receives its first airing on November 12.

1965: First use of the f–word on TV is on November 13, 1965, by literary agent Kenneth Tynan (UK) during a satirical discussion show titled *BBC3*.

1969: The first Moon landing becomes the **most watched live TV event**, drawing in 600 million viewers—a fifth of the world population at the time.

1973: First fly-on-the-wall documentary series, *An American Family*, airs to 10 million viewers.

1975: BBC introduces the classic weather symbols as we know them today.

1976: *The Muppet Show* airs in the UK on September 5, then in the U.S.A. on September 27; it goes on to become the world's **most popular show**, watched by 300 million viewers in 103 countries.

1976: The BBC formally launches its CEEFAX teletex service.

1977: First "gaffe" show *It'll Be Alright on the Night* (ITV, UK) features host Denis Norden (UK) revealing the gaffes or "bloopers" filmed while making television shows.

1979: First use of satellite data for TV weather reports.

1981: MTV launches in the U.S.A.

1983: Largest TV audience (U.S.A.) The final episode of *M*A*S*H* (CBS, left) is transmitted on February 28, 1983, to 60.3% of all households in the U.S.A.; it is watched by some 125 million people.

1985: Live Aid takes place in London, UK, and Philadelphia, PA, U.S.A., and is watched by 1.5 billion TV viewers worldwide, making it the world's **largest simultaneous charity rock concert** in terms of viewers.

1986: More than 30 million people tune in as Den divorces Angie in *EastEnders* (BBC, UK) on Christmas Day—the **highest-ever viewing figures for a series in the UK**.

1993: The **first computer-generated 3D models** on TV are the spacecraft conceived for *Babylon 5* (PTEN, U.S.A.).

1996: At its peak of popularity, *Baywatch* (NBC, U.S.A.) becomes the **most widely viewed TV series** ever, with an estimated weekly audience of more than 1.1 billion in 142 countries in 1996.

1999: Helen Hunt, the star of *Mad About You* (NBC, U.S.A.), becomes the **highest-paid TV actress**, with an estimated salary of $31 million.

2000: Darva Conger (U.S.A.) and Rick Rockwell (U.S.A.) celebrate the **first reality TV marriage** on *Who Wants to Marry a Multimillionaire?* (Fox, U.S.A.).

2004: A four-minute feature film made by director Baz Lurhmann (Australia) advertising Chanel No. 5 perfume becomes the world's **most expensive television advertisement**, costing $33 million to produce. It starred Nicole Kidman (Australia) as a Marilyn Monroe–style actress who is pursued by the paparazzi.

2006: The **most watched live sporting event on television** is the 2006 FIFA World Cup held in Germany. FIFA claimed that the tournament was seen by 30 billion (non-unique) viewers.

2009: The **most hours on U.S. television** is 16,343 by presenter Regis Philbin (U.S.A.), whose career spans 50 years.

2010: According to *Forbes*, the ★ **most powerful person in television** is Oprah Winfrey (U.S.A.). Winfrey is also the ☆ **highest-paid TV personality,** having earned $275 million in 2008–09, thanks to her extensive media empire. The philanthropist/actress/producer is arguably the most influential woman in the world.

COP & CRIME SHOWS

★**First armchair detective series** The first time the police used TV to appeal for help in a murder case was in Germany in 1938, and the first "missing person" appeal was made on October 3, 1943, by New York police. The first regular series to enlist the help of the public to solve real-life crimes was *Police 5* (LWT, 1962–92), hosted by Shaw Taylor (UK).

★**LONGEST-RUNNING COP SHOW (BY EPISODE)** At the time of going to press (April 2010), *The Bill* (ITV, 1983–2010) had an episode count of 2,389. *The Bill* finally ended on August 31, 2010, and racked up 2,405 episodes.

★ MOST SUCCESSFUL COP FRANCHISE (CURRENT) While *Z-Cars* holds the absolute record, in terms of shows currently on air, the franchise winner is *Law & Order* (NBC, 1990–present)—which includes *Criminal Intent, Special Victims Unit* (pictured are stars Mariska Hargitay and Ice-T, both U.S.A.), and the now defunct *Trial by Jury* and *Conviction*)—with more than 915 episodes to date.

★ First crime show on TV *Telecrime* (BBC, 1938–39)—later known as *Telecrimes* (1946)—challenged TV viewers to unravel crimes before the police and featured the **★ first TV police detective**, Inspector Holt (played by J. B. Rowe, UK). He was assisted by Sgt. Carter (Richard George, UK), **★ TV's first cop sidekick**.

★ Longest-running cop show (by date) Germany's *Der Alte* ("The Old Fox") has run on ZDF since 1977. The UK's longest-running cop shows are ITV's *Taggart* and *The Bill*, which have been running since 1983. The U.S.A.'s longest-running cop show is *Law & Order* (NBC), which began in 1990.

★ FIRST FEMALE TV COP STAR *Decoy* (aka *Police Woman: Decoy*), a U.S. series syndicated in 1957–58, starred Beverly Garland (U.S.A.) as undercover policewoman Patricia "Casey" Jones. Britain's first female-led cop show was *The Gentle Touch* (ITV, 1980–84), starring Jill Gascoigne as Detective Inspector Maggie Forbes (pictured at left).

ALBUQUERQUE, NM, U.S.A. (35°06'N 106°36'W): The first **Hot-air Balloon World Championships** were held in Albuquerque, New Mexico, U.S.A., from February 10 to 17, 1973.

FRANK COLUMBO Peter Falk (U.S.A.) is the ★ **most enduring cop actor**, having portrayed the shambling detective Lieutenant Columbo from *Prescription Murder* (NBC, 1968) to 2003's *Columbo Likes the Nightlife* (ABC).

JANE MARPLE The ★ **most TV depictions of Miss Marple**, Agatha Christie's silver sleuth, is 12, shared by Brit actresses Joan Hickson (*Miss Marple*, BBC, 1984–92, pictured far left) and Geraldine McEwan (*Marple*, ITV, 2004–09, left).

GEORGE DIXON The ★ **most prolific TV cop** was PC George Dixon (Jack Warner, UK) in *Dixon of Dock Green* (BBC, 1955–76), who appeared in 431 episodes.

'ELLO: The **first actor to play Hercule Poirot on TV** was James L. Sullivan (UK) in the **first Agatha Christie TV adaptation**: *The Wasp's Nest* (BBC, 1937).

HERCULE POIROT The ★ **most depictions of Hercule Poirot on TV** is 60 and counting by David Suchet (UK), who has gone on record saying he hopes to film the entire canon (84 stories) by his 65th birthday in May 2011.

LAW: Perry Mason was the creation of real-life lawyer Erle Stanley Gardner (U.S.A., 1889–1970), who featured his fictional attorney in around 80 novels.

PERRY MASON The ★ **most murders solved on TV** is at least 297 by the defense attorney Perry Mason (Raymond Burr, U.S.A., 1917–93) in *Perry Mason* (CBS, 1957–66) and the *Perry Mason TV Movies* (NBC, 1985–93).

ORDER: Perry mason has appeared in novels, short stories, radio serials, comic books, TV series, TV movies, daytime soaps, and even a book of poetry!

TELE-MENTARY: The first actor to portray Sherlock Holmes on TV was Louis Hector (U.S.A.) in an experimental NBC (U.S.A.) production in 1937.

SHERLOCK HOLMES The most depictions of Sherlock Holmes on TV is 41 by Jeremy Brett (UK, pictured) in the ITV series that ran from 1984 to 1994. The first Holmes TV series—*Sherlock Holmes* (BBC, 1951)—starred Alan Wheatley (UK).

★ **Most successful cop show franchise** *The Bill* (see p. 311) gave rise to a total of three spin-off series. They were: *Burnside*, 2000; *Beech Is Back*, 2001; and *MIT: Murder Investigation Team*, 2003–05, giving a combined episode count of 2,413 (as of April 2010). The final combined total is 2,429.

The **most successful non-soap cop show** ever was *Z-Cars* (BBC, 1962–78), which ran to 799 episodes. With its spin-offs *Softly Softly* (1966–69), *Softly Softly: Task Force* (1969–76), *Barlow at Large* (1971–73), *Barlow* (1974–75), *Jack the Ripper* (1973), and *Second Verdict* (1974), it had a combined episode count of more than 1,100. The **most successful non-soap cop show (current)** is *Law & Order* (see p. 312).

★ **Highest-rated cop show** According to metacritic.com, *The Sopranos* remains the most popular "crime" show among TV reviewers, garnering a score of 96/100; *The Wire*, which could be considered more truly a "cop" show—being more about police than criminals—comes in at second place with a metascore of 89/100.

The cop/crime show that most wowed reviewers in 2009 was the FBI-based *White Collar* (USA Network/Fox) with a score of 78/100.

EL PASO, TX, U.S.A. (31°47'N 106°25'W): El Paso Diablos Baseball Club, Texas, U.S.A., made the world's **largest pecan pie** on May 22, 1999. The pie weighed 41,586 lb. (18.863 tonnes) and measured 50 ft. (15.24 m) in diameter when measured at Cohen Stadium.

SCI-FI & FANTASY TV

★ **First recorded sci-fi TV show** While early TV shows were broadcast live (see *Captain Video*, p. 319), the first sci-fi series to be prerecorded was *Rocky Jones, Space Ranger* (U.S.A., syndicated, 1953). Recorded shows made for better sets and effects—particularly important for the science-fiction genre.

Longest-running TV sci-fi See *Doctor Who*, pp. 322–325, and *Smallville*, 319.

★ **First sci-fi sitcom on TV** The animated series *The Jetsons* (ABC, U.S.A.) debuted in 1962. *My Favorite Martian* (CBS, U.S.A., 1963–66) was the ★ **first live-action sci-fi sitcom**. The show followed the exploits of a Martian "exo-anthropologist" (played by Ray Walston, U.S.A.) who crash-lands on Earth and is rescued by a newspaper reporter (played by Bill Bixby, U.S.A.), who passes him off to friends and the authorities as his uncle. It ran for three seasons.

★ **First fantasy sitcom** *Topper* (CBS, then ABC, later NBC; all U.S.A.) ran from 1953 to 1956. It was based on Thorne Smith's novels (previously made into movies) about the staid Cosmo Topper, whose life takes an unexpectedly lively turn after he is haunted by a fun-loving couple who had lived in his house before their deaths.

★ **MOST SUCCESSFUL SCI-FI TV ADAPTATION** Paramount's (U.S.A.) 2009 movie "rebooting" of the *Star Trek* TV show (NBC, U.S.A., 1966–69, above right) took in $385,494,555 globally— the biggest box-office gross for a live-action TV adaptation.

PRINCE ALBERT, SK, CANADA (53°12'N 105°45'W): The record for the **most trees planted in a day by an individual** is held by Ken Chaplin (Canada), who single-handedly planted 15,170 red pine seedlings in one day near Prince Albert, Saskatchewan, Canada, on June 30, 2001.

★ **HIGHEST-RATED SCI-FI MINISERIES** "Children of Earth" (UK, 2009), the third season of the BBC's sci-fi miniseries *Torchwood* (UK), received a review score of 80/100 on metacritic.com. This made it the highest-rated sci-fi miniseries of 2009, ahead of the reimagined version of *The Prisoner* (AMC/ITV, UK).

★**First superhero on TV** Superman was the first comicbook superhero to appear in his own television series. *The Adventures of Superman* (U.S.A., syndicated, 1952) starred George Reeves (U.S.A.) as the Man of Steel and was sponsored by Kellogg's.

★**Most prolific sci-fi TV writers** Rodman "Rod" Serling (U.S.A.)—creator and narrator of *The Twilight Zone* (CBS, U.S.A., 1959–64)—wrote 92 episodes (out of 156) of the successful sci-fi anthology show.

Babylon 5 (PTEN) creator Joe Straczynski (U.S.A.) also wrote 92 (out of 110) episodes of his CGI-heavy sci-fi show.

★**Most sci-fi TV spin-offs** The Japanese series *Ultraman* (United Artists/ Tokyo Broadcasting System, 1966–67) spawned 30 spin-off series and several movies. Unlike *King Kong* (U.S.A., 1933), which used stop-motion animation, *Ultraman* was made using miniature buildings and an actor wearing a monster costume who moved around the diminutive set, creating havoc.

The technique subsequently became a standard for Japanese monster movies (*kaiju*).

BEING: A dark comedy series by the BBC, *Being Human* achieved a rating of 79/100 on the review aggregation site metacritic.com.

☆ **HIGHEST-RATED FANTASY-/SCI-FI SHOW** *Being Human* (BBC)—the tale of a werewolf, vampire, and ghost living together in suburban Britain—was the most critically acclaimed sci-fi show of 2009, according to an average of review scores on metacritic.com.

HUMAN: The hit 2009 show stars Russell Tovey, Aidan Turner, and Leonora Crichlow (pictured left to right) as a werewolf, vampire, and ghost, respectively.

DENVER, CO, U.S.A. (39°44'N 104°59'W): A peak reading of 128.7 dBA was recorded during the Denver Broncos vs. New England Patriots NFL game at the 76,123-seat Mile High Stadium, Denver, Colorado, U.S.A., on October 1, 2000—the **loudest crowd roar at a sports stadium**.

★ FIRST SCI-FI SERIAL The first regular sci-fi serial on TV was *Captain Video and His Video Rangers* (Dumont, U.S.A., June 1949–April 1955). Set in the year 2254, it followed the exploits of Captain Video (played by Richard Coogan, U.S.A.), an inventor and "Master of Science." It aired nightly—live—at 7 p.m.

☆ **Longest-running sci-fi TV SHOW (current)** *Smallville* (The WB, U.S.A., 2001–), based on the DC Comics character Superman, has aired continuously since October 16, 2001. The last sci-fi show to reach its 10th anniversary was *Stargate SG-1* (Sony/MGM, Canada/U.S.A., 1997–2007).

The original run of *Doctor Who* (BBC, 1963–89) has the absolute record for **most consecutive sci-fi episodes ever**. (For more details, see pp. 322–325.)

Most expensive costume from a TV series sold at auction The Superman suit from the 1955 series *The Adventures of Superman* (U.S.A.) sold for $129,800 at the Profiles in History auction in Los Angeles, U.S.A., on July 31, 2003. It was one of two costumes from the series worn by George Reeves.

CLONE WARS *Star Wars: The Clone Wars* (Lucasfilm Animation/Warner Bros. TV, 2008–present) is the ★ **highest-rated sci-fi animation on TV**, with an average review of 64/100 on metacritic.com on its release. The CGI series has expanded the scope of the "galaxy far, far away" and taken the *Star Wars* story in new directions down darker, more mature paths.

DOCTOR WHO

☆ **Longest-running sci-fi TV show** *Doctor Who* (BBC, UK) has chalked up 769 episodes as of June 2010, encompassing 212 storylines, including a full-length TV movie. This total does not include spoofs, spin-offs, or webisodes. The number is 770 if you include the new Christmas special.

★ **Most successful sci-fi TV show** Based on longevity, DVD sales, views on BBC's iPlayer, and publishing spin-offs, *Doctor Who* is the most successful science-fiction program on TV. This eclipses the original *Star Trek* series, which has had numerous spin-offs (such as *The Next Generation* and *Voyager*) that are not a genuine continuation of the same show.

★ **Most prolific doctor** In terms of the **TV shows**, Tom Baker (UK) starred in 173 episodes (seasons 12–18), more than any other actor. A former monk, Baker was working on a building site when he received the call

from the BBC. Famous for his Doctor's lengthy scarf and wild hair, he revitalized the series and lasted seven years.

In terms of **total output**—including audiobooks, TV shows, DVDs, novels, and comics—the busiest Doctor was the tenth (David Tennant, UK), with more than 342 appearances.

TV's ★ **least prolific Doctor** was the eighth (Paul McGann, UK), who appeared just once, in a 1996 TV movie. Across all media, the fewest appearances to date were made by the ninth Doctor (Christopher Eccleston, UK), with only 25 outings.

DID YOU KNOW?

The *Doctor Who* Appreciation Society, which began in May 1976, is the longest-running *Doctor Who* fanclub.

PUEBLO, CO, U.S.A. (38°16'N 104°37'W): The Pueblo Levee Project in Pueblo, Colorado, U.S.A., produced the **largest mural**, measuring 178,200 ft.^{2} (16,554.8 m^2). The mural doesn't depict a single image—it is made up of images provided by a wide variety of artists.

★ **LONGEST-RUNNING TV TIE-IN**
Doctor Who Magazine launched (as *Doctor Who Weekly*) on October 11, 1979, and went monthly at issue 44. The magazine's tenure is all the more remarkable for the fact that for 16 years of its 31-year run there was no TV series in production!

★ **DEAREST DALEK**
The most money paid for a Dalek prop at auction was £36,000 ($61,930) by the now-defunct company Indeprod in 2005 for this "Dalek Supreme," first seen on screen in the 1970s.

WHO?: Pictured with the Dalek Supreme is June Hudson (UK), who provided costumes for several episodes of *Doctor Who* in the 1980s.

WHO'S WHO IN *DOCTOR WHO*?

WILLIAM HARTNELL (1963–66)   **PATRICK TROUGHTON (1966–69)**   **JON PERTWEE (1970–74)**   **TOM BAKER (1974–81)**

PETER DAVISON (1981–84)   **COLIN BAKER (1984–86)**   **SYLVESTER McCOY (1987–89, 1996)**   **PAUL McGANN (1996)**

CHRISTOPHER ECCLESTON (2005)   **DAVID TENNANT (2005–10)**

INTERVIEW: MATT SMITH—THE ELEVENTH DOCTOR . . .

Guinness World Records entered the TARDIS for a chat with the new Doctor and asked how he felt being cast as the eleventh Time Lord.

How does it feel to be the eleventh Doctor?
It's a real privilege to join such a successful show; it's a bit like joining Manchester Utd. It's good to be part of something strong, and long may it continue. Plus, I couldn't have inherited the role from a nicer man. I guess it's like anything, really—the more you do something, the less daunting and intimidating it becomes.

**MATT SMITH
(2010–)**

Was there a defining moment during filming when it finally sunk in that you are THE DOCTOR?
I don't know. The Doctor has such a wealth of cultural history and carries such a depth of emotion and duty; initially I didn't know how to digest it all. I just got on with the nuts and bolts of what I had to do. . . . There was a scene when I was standing on the roof in the first episode, shouting, "I am the Doctor!" . . .

New Doctor, new TARDIS. What's it like?
It's like a Ferrari, Lamborghini, and Porsche all molded into one! I am quite clumsy, though, so I kept breaking parts of the console and the poor production team had to keep fixing it. The TARDIS is a magic concept, and it provides a constant source of adventure for both the Doctor and the viewers.

Where would you like the TARDIS to take you if you could go anywhere?
I would definitely travel back in time to see the dinosaurs, and then I'd get the TARDIS to take me to the bottom of the sea to the lost city of Atlantis.

FACT

The 11 Doctors have all been portrayed by British actors. . . .

Doctor Who

★ **Youngest Doctor** The latest incarnation of the Doctor is Matt Smith (UK, b. October 28, 1982), who was 26 when he filmed his first scenes as the Time Lord.

The ★ **oldest Doctor** was William Hartnell (UK), who played the part from the age of 55 to 57. He last reprised the role in 1973, aged 65.

★ **Longest-serving assistant** James Robert McCrimmon (played principally by Frazer Hines, UK), companion of the second Doctor, appeared in 115 episodes between 1966 and 1969, making him the longest continually serving assistant on screen. The only character to make more appearances other than a Doctor was Brigadier Sir Alistair Gordon Lethbridge-Stewart, portrayed by actor Nicholas Courtney (UK).

★ **Most popular story** "The Caves of Androzani" (1984) received an average user review of 9.3/10 on IMDb.com, and was voted by readers of *Doctor Who Magazine* as the best ever story. The epic tale recounts the last days of the fifth Doctor (Peter Davison, UK), who, by the end of the serial, is poisoned and forced to regenerate—into the sixth Doctor (Colin Baker, UK)—to save his life. The classic four-parter narrowly beat the 2007 episode "Blink," starring the tenth Doctor, David Tennant.

★ **LARGEST FICTION SERIES** The official *Doctor Who* books—including novels, novelizations of TV episodes, and "quick reads"—represent the longest licensed fictional series based on one principal character. Some 472 titles have appeared since the mid-1960s.

MONTERREY, NL, MEXICO (25°40'N 100°18'W): The longest hot dog measured 375 ft. 0.7 in. (114.32 m) and was made by Empacadora Ponderosa (Mexico) in Monterrey, Mexico, on September 27, 2008.

★HUGO AWARDS The Hugo Awards are presented annually by the World Science Fiction Convention for science fiction and fantasy work (*statue pictured left*). In the category of Best Dramatic Presentation, Short Form—which includes dramatic productions of 90 minutes or less—*Doctor Who* storylines have been nominated 10 times—the ★most Hugo Award nominations for Best Dramatic Presentation, Short Form.

In addition, writer Steven Moffat has won a record three awards for his *Doctor Who* stories "The Empty Child"/"The Doctor Dances" (2006), "The Girl in the Fireplace" (2007), and "Blink" (2008). Moffat's three consecutive wins is also a record in this category.

TOONS & ANIMATION

FIRST . . .

Animated movie The first movie to use the stop-motion technique—to give the illusion of movement to inanimate objects—was Vitagraph's *The Humpty Dumpty Circus* (U.S.A., 1897). Albert E. Smith (U.S.A.) borrowed his daughter's toy circus and succeeded in animating acrobat and animal figurines by shooting them in barely changed positions one frame at a time.

The ★ **first 2D animation** was J. Stuart Blackton's (U.S.A., b. UK) *Humorous Phases of Funny Faces* (U.S.A., 1906), a series of caricatures drawn in white chalk on a blackboard, shot one frame at a time, then wiped clean and redrawn.

> *"I would rather entertain and hope that people learned something than educate people and hope they were entertained."*
> **Walt Disney**

MEXICO CITY, MEXICO (19°24'N 99°07'W): A total of 18,000 people volunteered to collectively pose in the **largest naked photo shoot** in Zocalo Square, Mexico City, Mexico, for photographer Spencer Tunick (U.S.A.) on May 6, 2007.

FIRST PRIME-TIME ANIMATION *The Flintstones* (ABC, U.S.A., 1960–66)—a cartoon about a "modern Stone Age family"—premiered on the evening of September 30, 1960. The show was designed to appeal to the entire family, not just children.

Full-length feature cartoon *El Apóstol* (Argentina, 1917), a political satire by Quirino Cristiani (Argentina), comprised 58,000 drawings and ran for 70 minutes.

Cartoon "talkie" Max Fleischer's (Austria) animated short *Come Take a Trip in My Airship* (U.S.A., 1924), based on the song of the same name and directed by his brother Dave Fleischer (U.S.A.), opened with the animated figure of a woman speaking some patter as the lead-in to the song.

★Full-color cartoon The first Technicolor cartoon to be commercially released was Disney's *Flowers and Trees* (U.S.A., 1932), a "Silly Symphonies" short that became the **★ first cartoon to win an Oscar**.

CG images The Disney movie *Tron* (U.S.A., 1982) was the first major motion feature to fully utilize computer-generated (CG) animation. The movie's setting, inside a video game, was ideal inspiration for computer animators.

CG character The first character in a full-length feature film to be entirely computer-generated was a stained-glass knight that comes to life and steps down from a window in *Young Sherlock Holmes* (U.S.A./UK, 1985). It was designed by John Lasseter (U.S.A.), who would later go on to establish Pixar.

UP!: You would need 13 million helium balloons to lift the average 1,600-ft.^{2} (150-m^2) home off the ground! In the movie, Carl uses just 20,622 balloons.

★ **HIGHEST-GROSSING 3D ANIMATION** Disney/Pixar's *Up* (U.S.A., 2009) has earned more than $507 million at the global box office from its opening on May 29, 2009. The animated feature tells the story of an old man's dream to visit South America—which he does by tethering thousands of helium balloons to his home and flying there!

★ **MOST "ANNIE" NOMINATIONS** The Annie Awards have been presented by the International Animated Film Association in Los Angeles, California, U.S.A., since 1972 and celebrate the best in animation. Three movies have had a record 16 nominations, each winning 10 awards: *The Incredibles* (U.S.A., 2004), *Wallace & Gromit: The Curse of the Were-Rabbit* (UK, 2005), and *Kung Fu Panda* (U.S.A., 2008).

SAN ANTONIO, TX, U.S.A. (29°32'N 98°28'W): The **largest concentration of bats** found anywhere in the world is that of the Mexican free-tailed bat (*Tadarida brasiliensis*) in Bracken Cave, San Antonio, Texas, U.S.A., where up to 20 million females and offspring gather.

☆**LONGEST-RUNNING SITCOM** The longest-running sitcom by episode count—and the ☆**longest-running animation series**—is *The Simpsons* (Fox, U.S.A.), at 452 episodes and counting. It first aired on December 17, 1989, and, during its 20th season (2008–09), overtook the 435 episodes of former record holder *The Adventures of Ozzie and Harriet* (ABC, U.S.A., 1952–66).

★**Feature-length animated movie** In 1996, animator John Lasseter received a Special Achievement Academy Award for his "inspired leadership of the Pixar *Toy Story* (U.S.A., 1995) team resulting in the first feature-length computer animated film."

Anime to win an oscar *Sen to Chihiro no Kamikakushi*, aka *Spirited Away* (Japan, 2001), is the first anime to win an Oscar, for Best Animated Feature, in 2003. At 124 minutes, Hayao Miyazaki's (Japan) film is also the longest movie to win in this category.

Animation to be nominated for best foreign language film *Vals Im Bashir*, aka *Waltz with Bashir* (Israel/Germany/France/U.S.A., 2008), was nominated for Best Foreign Language Film at the 2009 Academy Awards. The movie, directed by Ari Folman (Israel), tells the story of an ex-soldier piecing together his memories of an Israeli Army mission in the first Lebanon war, which began in June 1982.

HIGHEST-GROSSING . . .

Animation *Shrek 2* (U.S.A., 2004), produced by DreamWorks Animation and directed by Adam Adamson and Vicky Jenson, took in $920.6 million at

---

INSTANT EXPERT

• Aardman Animations' *Wallace & Gromit: The Curse of the Were-Rabbit* (UK, 2005) used 6,272 lb. (2.84 tonnes) of plasticine!

• *Snow White and the Seven Dwarfs* (U.S.A., 1937) was the **first movie with an official soundtrack**.

• The Japanese anime *Soreike! Anpanman*, written by Takashi Yanase (Japan), boasts the ★ **most characters in an animation series**, with 1,768 different characters as of June 2009.

• *The Jungle Book* (U.S.A., 1967) was the last movie Walt Disney personally oversaw.

---

the global box office, making it the fourth biggest movie of all time. The *Shrek* franchise is also the most successful animated movie series ever.

The **highest-grossing animation adjusted for inflation** is Walt Disney's *Snow White and the Seven Dwarfs* (U.S.A., 1937), which took in $184.9 million at the global box office, equivalent to about $1.6 billion in today's money.

★**Opening weekend** *Shrek the Third* (U.S.A., 2007) grossed $322,719,944 at the domestic box office over its opening weekend, beginning on May 18, 2007.

Of this total, $47,077,497 was grossed on Saturday, May 19—the ☆**highest-grossing day for an animation**—and $38,426,991 was earned on Friday, May 18—the ☆**highest-grossing opening day for an animation**.

★**Stop-motion animation** *Chicken Run* (UK, 2000), produced by the Bristol, UK–based animation studios Aardman Animations, cost just $67 million to make but recouped $224.8 million at the international box office.

BLOCKBUSTERS

HOLMES: Sherlock Holmes is the ☆ **most frequently recurring character on-screen.** He has been portrayed by some 81 actors in more than 217 films.

SHERLOCK HOLMES *Sherlock Holmes* (U.S.A./Germany, 2009), directed by Guy Ritchie (UK), set a new U.S. box-office record for ★ **highest-grossing Christmas Day movie**, earning $24.6 million* on Friday, December 25, 2009.

HORROR: With a box-office gross of $296,596,319 to March 24, 2010, *New Moon* (see p. 330) is the most successful movie in both vampire and werewolf genres.

THE DARK KNIGHT Despite losing almost all of its records to *Avatar* (see p. 291), *The Dark Knight* (U.S.A., 2008) is still the ☆ **highest-grossing movie in its opening weekend**, having taken $158 million from Friday, July 18, to Sunday, July 20, 2008.

THE TWILIGHT SAGA: NEW MOON In November 2009, the *Twilight* sequel *New Moon* (U.S.A., 2009) eclipsed *The Dark Knight* to achieve the ☆ **highest opening-day gross** of $72.7 million in the U.S.A.

AVATAR Now officially the ☆ **most successful movie in history**—at least in terms of box-office takings—James Cameron's (Canada) *Avatar* (U.S.A./UK, 2010) achieved the box-office triple, topping first the foreign chart (January 23, 2010), then the world chart (January 25, 2010), and finally the domestic (February 2, 2010).

THE HANGOVER The surprise hit of 2009 was Todd Phillips's (U.S.A.) road movie *The Hangover* (U.S.A., 2009), which quickly became the ★ **highest-grossing R-rated comedy**, grossing $467.3 million at the global box office.

SAW III The ★ **highest-grossing Halloween movie** is *Saw III* (U.S.A., 2006) the third installment of the Jigsaw Killer franchise, which had taken $33.6 million by October 31, 2006. Globally, the threequel was the most successful of the series.

HARRY POTTER VI Harry Potter installment *The Half-Blood Prince* (UK/U.S.A., 2009) had the ☆ **highest-grossing worldwide opening**, raking in $394 million up to the end of its first domestic weekend in July 2009.

AT THE MOVIES

☆ **Largest movie theater screen (drive-in)** The famous outdoor water-filming facility at Pinewood Studios in Middlesex, UK, was, in 2009, converted into a giant drive-in theater with a screen measuring a record 240 x 60 ft. (73.1 x 18.3 m). The screen opened on Halloween 2009.

☆ **Highest-grossing . . .**
Director: Topping the list of Hollywood's highest-grossing directors is Steven Spielberg (U.S.A.), whose motion pictures have earned a whopping $3.76 billion in box office receipts.

As a producer, Spielberg is responsible for generating $5.03 billion, making him the ☆ **highest-grossing producer**, too.
☆ **Screenwriter:** The 15 movies written by George Lucas (U.S.A.) have grossed a lifetime combined total of $3.33 billion.

☆ **Highest earner in Hollywood** Michael Bay, director of *Transformers: Revenge of the Fallen* (U.S.A., 2009), earned an estimated $125 million in 2009 thanks to his blockbuster movie release, a share of the merchandising and DVD rights, and a few back-end production deals.

★ FIRST BEST ACTRESS OSCAR WON FOR DEPICTING A BEST ACTRESS Cate Blanchett (Australia, pictured) won the 2005 Best Actress Oscar for depicting Best Actress Academy Award winner Katherine Hepburn (U.S.A.) in *Aviator* (2004).

AUSTIN, TX, U.S.A. (30°17'N 97°45'W): Rob Williams of Austin, Texas, U.S.A., chose an unconventional method to make a Bologna, cheese, and lettuce sandwich—complete with sliced tomatoes, mustard, mayo, and olives on cocktail sticks—in 1 min. 57 sec. on November 10, 2000. His record? The **fastest time to make a sandwich using only the feet**.

RAZZIES

The Golden Raspberry Awards, set up in 1981 by John Wilson (U.S.A.)
to "salute the worst that Hollywood has to offer." The anti-Oscars!

MOST BANKABLE STARS The Hollywood actor giving the best value for money is Shia LaBeouf (U.S.A.); in 2009, the star of *Transformers* and *Indiana Jones 4* made $160 for every $1 he was paid. The most bankable actress, according to *Forbes*, is *King Kong* star Naomi Watts (UK), who made $44 per $1 paid.

☆ **Least bankable actor** Thanks to flop *Land of the Lost* (U.S.A., 2009), Will Ferrell (U.S.A.) floats to the top of the list of most overpaid actors. The movie cost $100 million to make but made just $65 million and is the latest in a run of bad luck for Ferrell. On average, for every $1 he is paid, he returns just $3.29 at the box office, according to *Forbes*.

☆ **Least bankable actress** In the same list is Drew Barrymore (U.S.A.), whose $1 fee will see a return of $7.43 (£4.66)—the lowest return on investment for an actress.

DID YOU KNOW?

There are 11 categories in the Golden Raspberry Awards (Razzies), including Worst Picture and Worst New Star.

TRIVIA

Bill Cosby (U.S.A.) became the ★ **first Razzie winner to collect the prize in person** in 1987.

OKLAHOMA CITY, OK, U.S.A. (35°28'N 97°32'W): The **longest chain of pipe cleaners** measured 10,459 ft. (3.18 km) and was made by Oklahoma Children's Cancer Association at the Children's Hospital OU Medical Center in Oklahoma City, Oklahoma, U.S.A., on February 14, 2007.

☆**HIGHEST-EARNING MOVIE STARS** Once again, Harry Potter leads Daniel Radcliffe and Emma Watson top the chart of Hollywood's highest-earning stars. Emma earned $10 million apiece for the last two Potter movies, while Daniel secured $20 million per movie plus a $1 million bonus for licensing and royalties.

☆**First winner of a Best Actress Oscar and a Worst Actress Razzie in the same year** Sandra Bullock (U.S.A.) won Worst Actress at the 2009 Golden Raspberry Awards for *All About Steve* (U.S.A., 2009) and turned up in person to accept the trophy the day before she won the Academy Award for Best Actress in *The Blind Side* (U.S.A., 2009).

☆**Highest-grossing series** The Harry Potter franchise has, in only six movies, earned $5.39 billion at the worldwide box office, ahead of *Star Wars* ($4.32 billion; £2.81 billion) and James Bond ($4.82 billion). The last movie in the series—*Deathly Hallows*—will be delivered in two instalments.

OSCARS

☆**Most acting nominations** With a nomination for her role as cook Julia Child in *Julia & Julie* (U.S.A., 2009), Meryl Streep notched up her 16th Oscars nod (having won two).

★**First fictional character to be Oscar nominated** Donald Kaufman, a fictitious character in Spike Jonze's (U.S.A.) *Adaptation* (U.S.A., 2002), was nonetheless nominated for Best Adapted Screenplay along with his (real) "brother" Charlie Kaufman (U.S.A.) at the 2003 Oscars. Both

WICHITA, KA, U.S.A. (37°41'N 97°20'W): The **largest stitched teddy bear** measures 55 ft. 4 in. (16.86 m) in length and was constructed by Dana Warren (U.S.A.). The bear was completed on June 6, 2008, and displayed at the Exploration Place in Wichita, Kansas, U.S.A.

★ **FIRST FEMALE TO WIN A BEST PICTURE ACADEMY AWARD** When Kathryn Bigelow's (U.S.A., above left) *Hurt Locker* (U.S.A., 2008, above right) won Best Picture at the 2010 Academy Awards ceremony, it marked the first time that a female director had won an Oscar in this category. "There should be more women directing," said Bigelow. "There's just not the awareness that it's really possible. It is."

characters appeared in the movie—both played by Nicolas Cage (U.S.A.)— and both are credited as writers, yet only Charlie exists!

Worst Oscar percentage Sound mixer Kevin O'Connell (U.S.A.) has had 20 Oscar nominations without a win—the longest losing streak in Oscars history.

★ **Best Oscars percentage** Sound editor Mark Berger (U.S.A.) has the best "score" at the Oscars with 100%—he has had four wins from four nominations: *Apocalyse Now* (U.S.A., 1979), *The Right Stuff* (U.S.A., 1983), *Amadeus* (U.S.A., 1984), and *The English Patient* (U.S.A., 1996).

SEXIST?: Bigelow was also the first woman to be awarded the Directors Guild of America Award for Outstanding Achievement in Feature Film.

WINNIPEG, MB, CANADA (49°54'N 97°08'W): The **longest recorded heart stoppage** is a minimum of 3 hr. 40 min. in the case of Jean Jawbone (Canada), who at the age of 20 was revived by a team of 26 using peritoneal dialysis in the Health Sciences Centre, Winnipeg, Manitoba, Canada, on January 8, 1977.

★ **MOST MULTI-DISCIPLINE TECHNICAL OSCARS** Richard Taylor (NZ), effects supervisor at Weta Workshops in Wellington, New Zealand, has won technical Oscars across a record three disciplines: Visual Effects for *King Kong* (NZ/U.S.A./Ger, 2005), and Costume Design and Makeup for *The Return of the King* (U.S.A./NZ/Ger, 2003).

3D CINEMA

FIRST . . .

★ **Demonstration of 3D film: 1915** An audience at the Astor Theater in New York City, U.S.A., donned red-and-green glasses for the first time to view test reels of 3D footage. Produced by Edwin S. Porter and William E. Waddell (both U.S.A.), the footage depicted, among other things, dancing girls and the Niagara Falls—the first images seen using the anaglyph 3D process.

★ **3D Feature: 1922** Harry K. Fairhall and Robert F. Elder (both U.S.A.) used two cameras and two projectors—"set at a distance from each other equal to the average distance between the human eyes"—to premiere Nat

★ **MOST ANIMATED 3D FEATURES RELEASED IN A SINGLE YEAR** Hollywood embraced 3D cinema in a big way in 2009, with the major studios releasing a grand total of 10 animated 3D features during the year. While most of these animations were new, *Toy Story 3D* (U.S.A., 2009) was a double feature of the first two movies remastered to be a 3D experience.

SPEX: The red-and-blue-lens 3D glasses are now a thing of the past. instead, Today's "polarized" filters split the image into horizontal and vertical strips.

★ **MOST EXPENSIVE 3D ANIMATION** The 2009 3D performance-capture version of *A Christmas Carol* (U.S.A.), directed by Robert Zemeckis (U.S.A.), cost $200 million to produce. One of the first of the new wave of 3D blockbusters, it went on to gross $323,555,899 globally.

Deverich's (U.S.A.) stereoscopic movie *The Power of Love* (U.S.A., 1922) in front of an invited audience at the Ambassador Hotel Theater in Los Angeles, U.S.A., on September 27, 1922. It was the first and only feature-length application of Fairhall and Elder's new technology. The movie is now lost, sadly.

★ **3D screening to a paying audience: 1922** Research by historian Daniel L. Symmes suggests that the documentary short *Movies of the Future* (U.S.A., 1922), directed by William Van Doren Kelley (U.S.A.), was the first stereoscopic print shown to a paying audience. The 14-minute movie explored this nascent film technology and was shown at the Rivoli Theater in New York City, U.S.A., in 1922.

45.6 MILLION

Computing hours required to make *Monsters vs. Aliens* (that's 1.9 million complete days, or 5,205 years!).

DALLAS, TX, U.S.A. (32°46'N 96°48'W): The **tallest freestanding house of cards** measured 25 ft. 9 in. (7.86 m) and was built by Bryan Berg (U.S.A.) on October 16, 2007, in Dallas, Texas, U.S.A., as part of the annual State Fair.

QUIZ!: Which animated movie was the first to be produced in stereoscopic 3D? Find out the answer on p. 544.

★ **FIRST ANIMATED FEATURE PRODUCED IN STEREOSCOPIC 3D** Until *Monsters vs. Aliens* (U.S.A., 2009), animated movies were converted to 3D after completion; *MvA*, however, was "shot" in a stereoscopic format from the beginning, an expensive "premium" process that added $15 million to the budget.

★ **3D movie to be nominated for an Oscar: 1936** A short experimental movie titled *Audioscopiks* (U.S.A., 1935), filmed using the Norling-Leventhal 3-Dimensions process—an anaglyph technique devised by John Norling and Jacob Leventhal (both U.S.A.)—received Academy Award recognition in the category "Best Short Subject, Novelty."

The eight-minute reel showcased the 3D effect with a ladder being pushed out of a window, a sliding trombone, a woman on a swing, and someone throwing a baseball.

3D talkie: 1936 Sante Bonaldo's production *Nozze Vagabonde* (*Beggar's Wedding*, Italy, 1936), starring Italians Leda Gloria and Ermes Zacconi, was the first movie to offer 3D polarizing glasses and a synchronized soundtrack.

3D movie in color: 1952 *Bwana Devil* (U.S.A., 1952), written and directed by Arch Oboler (U.S.A.), promised viewers "The Miracle of the Age!!! A LION in your lap. A LOVER in your arms!" Audiences—who had to wear colored filter glasses—flocked to the cinema to witness the spectacular tale of two man-eating lions.

Despite a poor critical reception, the movie grossed $95,000 in its first week from just two theaters.

★ **3D movie by a major studio: 1953** Columbia Pictures became the first big studio to venture into the 3D movie market with their release of *Man in the Dark* (U.S.A., 1953) on April 9, 1953. The movie—a remake of the 1936 film noir *The Man Who Lived Twice* (U.S.A.)—was rushed out to capitalize on the 3D craze, and wowed audiences with scenes in which spiders, fists, and dead bodies loomed out of the screen.

★ **3D movie . . .**
In French (1953): *Soirs de Paris* (France, 1953), directed by Jean Laviron (France), ran for 85 minutes.
In Japanese (1953): *Tobidashita Nichi Yôbi*, aka *Runaway Sunday* (Japan, 1953), was a supporting movie lasting just 11 minutes.
In Indian (1983): *Chhota Chetan* (India, 1983, aka *My Dear Kuttichathan*), was a children's fantasy movie.

MISCELLANY

★ **Highest budget-to-box-office ratio for a 3D movie** To date, the most successful 3D movie in terms of its profitability is *The Stewardesses* (U.S.A., 1969), directed by Al Silliman (U.S.A.). A pioneering, single-camera 3D system was devised to keep the total budget just over $100,000. An adult movie, it grossed upward of $30 million at the box office.

★ **Biggest 3D opening weekend** Tim Burton's (U.S.A.) *Alice in Wonderland* (U.S.A., 2010) grossed an unprecedented $116.1 million in the U.S.A. on March 5–7. Its nearest 3D rival, *Avatar* (U.S.A., 2009), took a "mere" $77 million in its opening weekend.

★ **FIRST 3D MOVIE WITH STEREO SOUND** Warner Bros., the second major Hollywood studio to enter the 3D market and the first to do so in full color, released *House of Wax* (1953) with stereo sound.

FARGO, ND, U.S.A. (46°53'N 96°48'W): The **largest baseball bat** measures 13 ft. 5 in. (4.08 m) with a circumference of 40 in. (101.6 cm). Known as "Big Bruce," it is made from white ash—the same material as Major League Baseball bats—and is owned by the Fargo-Moorhead RedHawks baseball club (Fargo Baseball LLC) of Fargo, North Dakota, U.S.A.

TOP 10

	MOVIE	WORLDWIDE GROSS TO FEB. 2010 (MILLIONS)*	YEAR RELEASED
1	*Avatar* (Fox)	$2,376 m	2010
2	*Ice Age: Dawn of the Dinosaurs* (Fox, above)	$884 m	2009
3	*Up* (Buena Vista)	$723 m	2009
4	*Alice in Wonderland* (Walt Disney Pictures)	$660 m	2010
5	*Monsters vs. Aliens* (Paramount/DreamWorks)	$381 m	2009
6	*A Christmas Carol* (Buena Vista)	$323 m	2009
7	*Chicken Little* (Buena Vista)	$314 m	2005
8	*Bolt* (Buena Vista)	$308 m	2009
9	*G-Force* (Buena Vista)	$285 m	2009
10	*Journey to the Center of the Earth* (Warner Bros./New Line)	$241 m	2009

Source: boxofficemojo.com   *figures as of May 3, 2010

THAT'S SHOWBIZ

Here at *Guinness World Records*, our researchers don't just stick to scientific journals and research papers for record-worthy content—it's also our responsibility to monitor the fashion and celebrity news in order to bring you the most up-to-date showbiz records.

So, what have we discovered this year? Well, Johnny Depp (U.S.A.) topped the *People* magazine poll of ☆ **sexiest men alive** for the second time this year, while the magazine revealed the ★ **most beautiful person** to be actress Christina Applegate (U.S.A.).

•••

OMAHA, NE, U.S.A. (41°15′N 96°00′W): The **longest straight "hole in one" golf putt** was the tenth (1,338 ft.; 447 yd.; 408 m) at Miracle Hills Golf Course, Omaha, Nebraska, U.S.A., by Robert Mitera (U.S.A.) on October 7, 1965.

•••

In the power stakes, Brad Pitt (U.S.A.) returns as the ☆ **most powerful actor**, thanks in part to his Oscar-nominated role in *Benjamin Button* (U.S.A., 2008), but largely to endless tabloid news of his family life and stories about his humanitarian activities. No surprise, then, that 2009's ☆ **most powerful actress** was Pitt's partner, Angelina Jolie (U.S.A.)!

In surveys of magazine and online polls regarding the ★ **most infamous female celebrity**, one name repeatedly floats to the surface: Lindsay Lohan (U.S.A.). *Forbes* and E-Poll named her the "most infamous," while others were less kind, focusing on the troubled actress's private life as well as her unfortunate movie choices. Runners-up included singer Amy Winehouse (UK) and Miss California Carrie Prejean (U.S.A.).

MOST INFAMOUS FEMALE CELEBRITY Li-lo's movie *I Know Who Killed Me* (U.S.A., 2007) won a record eight Golden Raspberries—including two Worst Actress awards for Lohan's two roles.

. . . AND MALE CELEBRITY Alex Rodriguez (U.S.A.) has had better years. Since his revelations about drug abuse during the 2000s, the New York Yankees No.13—and multiple world-record holder—has had a bad press. "Slugger turned tabloid tragedy," said *Forbes*, who listed A-Rod as their No.1 ★ most infamous male celebrity, thanks to his steroid use, his high-profile divorce, and his higher-profile affair with Madonna!

PLUS . . . : A-Rod: *The Many Lives of Alex Rodriguez*, an unauthorized biography, also accuses the star of cheating during ball games.

☆ **Most searched-for female** Singer Lady Gaga (U.S.A., aka Stefani Joanne Angelina Germanotta)—was the most searched-for female online in 2009, according to Google, the **largest search engine**.

Did you know: Lady Gaga adapted her stage name from the Queen hit song "Radio Ga Ga."

☆ **Most searched-for male** The untimely death of Michael Jackson (U.S.A., 1958–2009)—first announced virally—sent you online in your millions, making him the most searched-for male in 2009.

Did you know: Jackson achieved more world records *after* his death than he did when he was alive! See p. 350 for more of his posthumous record-breaking feats.

☆**Highest-earning primetime TV star** From June 1, 2008, to June 1, 2009, *X Factor* and *American Idol* judge Simon Cowell (UK) earned $75 million.

★**Most powerful sports star** Despite the controversial end to his year, golfing legend Tiger Woods (U.S.A.) earned an impressive $103 million in 2009, and topped the 2010 *BusinessWeek* Sports Power 100 list.

The ★**richest fashion designer is Giorgio Armani (Italy, left).** Clothes, watches, perfumes, homeware, and hotels all bear his name . . . a fantastic achievement for a medical school dropout who's now worth a record $5.3 billion!

"You can think you've made it and yet the next day's press will always be waiting for you!"
Giorgio Armani, the world's richest fashion designer

★**MOST SEARCHED-FOR CELEBRITY WEDDING** The wedding of the year—if Google's hit tracker is anything to go by—was that of reality TV star Khloé Kardashian and the LA Lakers' Lamar Odom (both U.S.A.) on September 27, 2009. It ranked the highest on the Google zeitgeist list of celeb weddings.

PLUS . . . : The reality TV show *Keeping up with the Kardashians* debuted in the U.S.A. in October 2007 and follows the lives of Los Angeles socialites.

★ **MOST TRUSTED CELEBRITY** In a survey conducted by E-Poll Market Research for business magazine *Forbes*, respondents were asked to rate the "trustworthiness, awareness, and appeal" of celebrities. Top of the list was actor James Earl Jones (U.S.A.)—the velvety voice behind NBC's Olympic coverage and the CNN tagline (and *Star Wars*'s less-than-trustworthy Darth Vader!).

EXTRA! For more online stats, facts, and world records, turn to p. 408.

234,901 FOLLOWERS   4,649,421 FOLLOWERS

CELEBRITY TWEEPS* Actor Ashton Kutcher (U.S.A., above center) is ahead in the celeb Twitter battle, as the ★ **first tweep with more than 1 million followers**. The ★ **most searched-for tweep of 2009**? Singer/actress Miley Cyrus (U.S.A., above left), according to Google.

*Tweeps

People (peeps) who use Twitter

HOUSTON, TX, U.S.A. (29°45'N 95°22'W): The **largest audience to attend a film premiere** was 23,930 people at the opening of *Brewster McCloud* (U.S.A., 1970) at the Houston Astrodome in Houston, Texas, U.S.A., on December 5, 1970.

EXTRA! Who are the biggest record-breakers in the music industry? Find out on pp. 345–351.

POWER COUPLES

COUPLE	COMBINED EARNINGS (JUNE 1, 2008– JUNE 1, 2009)
1 *Shawn "Jay-Z" Carter & Beyoncé Knowles (both U.S.A., below right)*	$122 m
2 *Harrison Ford & Calista Flockhart (both U.S.A.)*	$69 m
3 *Brad Pitt & Angelina Jolie (both U.S.A.)*	$55 m
4 *Will & Jada Pinkett Smith (both U.S.A.)*	$48 m
5 *David & Victoria Beckham (both UK, below left)*	$46 m
6 *Ellen DeGeneres & Portia de Rossi (both U.S.A.)*	$36 m
7 *Tom Hanks & Rita Wilson (both U.S.A.)*	$35.5 m
8 *Jim Carrey & Jenny McCarthy (both U.S.A.)*	$34 m
9 *Tom Cruise & Katie Holmes (both U.S.A.)*	$33.5 m
10 *Chris Martin (UK) & Gwyneth Paltrow (U.S.A.)*	$22 m

Source: *Forbes*

KANSAS CITY, KS, U.S.A. (39°06'N 94°34'W): The **oldest baseball player** is Leroy Robert "Satchel" Paige (U.S.A., 1906–82), who pitched for the Kansas City Athletics in Kansas City, U.S.A., at 59 years 80 days on September 25, 1965.

MUSIC

CHART-TOPPERS

★**Most simultaneous U.S. Hot 100 hits by a female** On November 14, 2009, 19-year-old U.S. country singer Taylor Swift became the first female artist to have eight tracks simultaneously on the U.S. Hot 100. On that chart she also became the first artist to have five tracks simultaneously enter the Top 30.

★**21st century's top-selling album act (U.S.A.)** Rapper Eminem (U.S.A.) was the biggest-selling album act in the U.S. in the first 10 years of the century, with sales of 32,241,000.

★ **Most new entries on UK album chart** On the September 19, 2009, chart, 16 albums by The Beatles (UK) entered the UK Top 75. This included four in the Top 10— a record for a group.

☆ **MOST WEEKS ON UK CHART IN ANY YEAR** In 2009, Lady Gaga (U.S.A.) clocked 154 chart weeks in the UK Top 75 (with 90 of these in the Top 40), mainly thanks to her hits "Just Dance," "Poker Face," "Paparazzi," and "Bad Romance."

HIT!: Lady Gaga was born Stefani Joanne Angelina Germanotta on March 28, 1986. She has sold more than 11 million albums and more than 35 million digital singles.

☆ **MOST SUCCESSIVE WEEKS AT TOP OF U.S. HOT 100** The Black Eyed Peas (U.S.A.) spent 26 successive weeks at No.1 on the U.S. Hot 100 in 2009. After 12 weeks at the summit, their "Boom Boom Pow" was replaced by "I Gotta Feeling," which stayed at the top for 14 weeks.

★ **Most charted teenager (U.S.A.)** The 16-year-old singer/actor Miley Cyrus (U.S.A.) scored her 29th U.S. Hot 100 chart entry on November 7, 2009, with "Party in the U.S.A." She has had hits under her own name and as Hannah Montana.

☆ **Most successful first week UK album sale** Released on November 23, 2009, Susan Boyle's (UK) *I Dreamed a Dream* sold 411,820 copies in its first week in the UK (133,599 on the first day)—the biggest weekly UK sale of any solo singer's album.

★ **FASTEST-SELLING ALBUM BY A FEMALE (UK)** Susan Boyle's (UK) debut album *I Dreamed a Dream*, released in November 2009, sold more than a million copies in just 21 days. It was the biggest-selling album in the UK in 2009, and a clip of her singing the title song for the first time on UK TV's *Britain's Got Talent* was the most watched YouTube clip in 2009.

☆ **BIGGEST JUMP TO NO.1 (UK)** Pixie Lott's (UK) single "Boys and Girls" broke the record for a jump within the Top 75 to the No.1 spot in the UK on September 19, 2009, when it climbed there from No.73.

★**MOST SIMULTANEOUS HITS ON UK SINGLES CHART DEBUT** On the chart dated January 23, 2010, the cast of the U.S. TV series *Glee* (U.S.A.) made their UK chart debut with five tracks simultaneously entering the UK Top 75.

☆**Most successive album entries at no.1 (U.S.A.)** On June 6, 2009, Eminem's (U.S.A.) album *Relapse* gave him his fifth successive U.S. album chart entry at No.1. This equaled the record set between 1998 and 2003 by fellow rapper DMX (U.S.A.).

☆**Female with most album no.1s (UK)** Madonna (U.S.A.) has had 11 UK No.1 albums. Her latest chart-topper came with *Celebration* on October 3, 2009. She is also the **biggest-selling female album act of the 21st century (UK)**, with sales of 6.68 million to October 2009.

★**Female with most album no.1s (U.S.A.)** Barbra Streisand (U.S.A.) had her ninth No.1 album in the U.S.A. on October 17, 2009, aged 67. She is also the first artist to have a No.1 album in five different decades.

DIGITAL HITS

★**Most downloaded acts in a year (U.S.A.)** In 2009, Lady Gaga (U.S.A.) broke the record for female acts by selling 11.1 million downloads in the U.S.A.. The Black Eyed Peas (U.S.A.) broke the record for a group, with 10.3 million downloads.

☆**Fastest-selling digital track (UK)** Californian alternative hard rock band Rage Against the Machine's 1993 recording "Killing in the Name" entered the UK singles chart at No.1 on December 26, 2009. It was available only as a download, and in its first week it sold 502,672 copies.

★**Biggest-selling digital album act (U.S.A.)** In July 2009, British band Coldplay became the first act to sell more than a million digital albums in the U.S.A..

> **ALBUM:** Susan Boyle was age 48 when her album I *Dreamed a Dream* debuted at No.1 in the U.S. and UK. She is the ★**oldest artist to reach No.1** on these charts with a debut.

★ **TOP-SELLING FEMALE RECORDING ARTIST** Madonna (U.S.A.) holds the record for album sales up to December 2009 of 75 million in the U.S.A. and 200 million abroad.

★ **Most simultaneous top 20 entries on U.S. digital chart** On November 14, 2009, Taylor Swift (U.S.A.) became the first act to have five tracks ("Jump Then Fall," "Untouchable," "Other Side of the Door," "Superstar," and "Come in with the Rain") enter the Top 20 of the U.S. digital chart simultaneously.

★ **First 3D broadcast on the Internet** British rock trio Keane were the first act to make a 3D broadcast on the Internet. They sang five songs in a 20-minute set from Studio Two at Abbey Road, London, UK. In 2006, Keane also released the **first USB stick single**, "Nothing in My Way."

☆ **Most singles sold in a year (UK)** In 2009, an unprecedented 152.7 million "singles" were sold in the UK, with a record 98% of them being downloaded tracks. It was the first year since 1967 that more singles were sold in the UK than albums.

> *"It's a great honor to visit the Guinness World Records offices. I love the book."*
>
> **Michael Jackson, October 14, 2006**

SPRINGFIELD, MO, U.S.A. (37°11'N 93°17'W): The **longest distance cycled backward on a unicycle** was set by Steve Gordon (U.S.A.), who covered a distance of 109.4 km (68 miles) in Springfield, Missouri, U.S.A., on June 24, 1999.

TOP EARNERS

★ **Most successful tour (solo artist)** Madonna's (U.S.A.) Sticky & Sweet tour (August 23, 2008–September 2, 2009) grossed $408 million.

★ **Top-grossing country act** Kenny Chesney (U.S.A.) is the top-grossing country music performer of the 21st century. Since 2002, he has sold 7 million tickets to his shows and grossed almost $500 million.

★ **Biggest and most expensive top 40 box set (U.S. & UK)** The 16-CD box set *The Beatles in Stereo*, which sold for $243.98, entered the U.S. album chart at No.15 on September 26, 2009. One week earlier, it had entered the UK chart at No.24—it sold there for £172 ($265).

★ **MOST SUCCESSFUL REALITY TV GIRL GROUP** Girls Aloud (UK/Ireland) formed on the reality TV show *Pop Stars: The Rivals* in 2002, and have gone on to have 20 Top 10 singles as of January 2009, including a female record 17 consecutive Top 10 hits from December 2002 to December 2007.

★ **HIGHEST-GROSSING CONCERT MOVIE** The release of Michael Jackson's rehearsals for the *This Is It* tour on October 28, 2009, grossed $250 million. It opened simultaneously in 250,000 movie theaters around the world and took in $200 million in its first two weeks.

EXTRA! For more movie marvels, turn to pp. 332, 336, and 340.

MINNEAPOLIS, MN, U.S.A. (44°58'N 93°15'W): The **quietest place** in the world is the Anechoic Test Chamber at Orfield Laboratories, Minneapolis, Minnesota, U.S.A. Ultra-sensitive tests performed on January 21, 2004, gave the lab a background noise reading of -9.4 dBA (decibels, A-weighted).

MICHAEL JACKSON, 1958–2009 Before his untimely death on June 25, 2009, at the age of 50, Michael Joseph Jackson (U.S.A.) was probably the most famous living human being on the planet. A multiple Guinness World Record holder—he received eight in his lifetime for his chart achievements, album sales, earnings, and charity donations—Michael's contribution to the arts was immeasurable. And remarkably, the record breaking continued after his passing.

In the year of his death, a record **11.3 million tracks** by the artist were downloaded in the U.S.A., and **2.8 million albums** were sold in the UK. From his death to the end of November 2009, he sold **7 million albums**, **10.2 million downloaded tracks**, and **1.3 million DVDs** in the U.S.A. The first morning after his death saw more than **1 million YouTube plays** of "Beat It," and in the first week **2.6 million Michael Jackson down-loads** were sold in the U.S.A.

★ **HIGHEST-GROSSING SOLO TOUR OF AUSTRALIA** U.S. singer P!nk (born Alecia Moore) grossed $80 million for her 58 arena shows in Australia, which were seen by 660,000 people in the summer of 2009.

Highest annual earnings ever for a pop star In 1989, Michael Jackson (U.S.A.) topped the *Forbes* list as the highest paid entertainer, with annual earnings of $125 million. This record is still unbroken 21 years later.

YOUNG & OLD

☆**Oldest no.1 singles act (UK)** Sir Tom Jones (UK) was 68 years 9 months old when he sang on "Barry Islands in the Stream" with Vanessa Jenkins, Bryn West, and Robin Gibb (all UK). A charity single, the track topped the UK chart on March 21, 2009.

★**Youngest country "Entertainer of the Year"** In 2009, 19-year-old Taylor Swift (U.S.A.) became the youngest artist to receive the Country Music Association's (CMA) highest award, Entertainer of the Year. In that year, her 43 shows took in $23.7 million gross and her album *Fearless* outsold all others in the U.S.A.

☆**Oldest UK chart-topper and record spans of no.1s** On May 9, 2009, Bob Dylan (U.S.A.) topped the UK album chart with *Together Through Life*, which made the 67-year-old the oldest act to top the UK chart with a newly recorded album. It was his first No.1 for 38 years 7 months, and increased his span of studio-recorded No.1 albums to 44 years and 1 month—also both records.

THEATER & CLASSICAL ARTS

> *"You can't stop my happiness, 'cuz I like the way I am! And you just can't stop my knife and fork when I see a Christmas ham!"*
> **Edna Turnblad in *Hairspray***

★**Most prolific theater producer** Theater impresario Howard E. Pechet (Canada) produced 485 plays at 10 different venues across Canada, between January 1975 and July 2008.

ST. PAUL, MN, U.S.A. (44°57'N 93°06'W): The **tallest ice building** was an ice palace completed in January 1992, using 18,000 blocks of ice, at St. Paul, Minnesota, U.S.A., during the Winter Carnival. Built by TMK Construction Specialties Inc., it was 166 ft. 8 in. (50.8 m) high and contained 10.8 million lb. (4,900 tonnes) of ice.

SMALLEST PROFESSIONAL THEATER Founded in 2004, the Theatre Lilli Chapeau, in Miltenberg, Germany, has a maximum capacity of 27 seats. The theater performs around 70 shows per year, and the only performer to have graced its stage is Lilli Chapeau, aka Celine Bauer (pictured at right).

☆**Most flamenco taps in a minute (male)** José Miguel Fernández Pintado (Spain) performed 814 flamenco taps in one minute on the set of *Lo Show dei Record* in Rome, Italy, on April 1, 2010.

Fastest pantomime horse (female) Samantha Kavanagh and Melissa Archer (both UK, front and rear, respectively) ran 328 ft. (100 m) in 18.13 seconds as a pantomime horse at an event organized by the advertising agency Claydon Heeley Jones Mason at Harrow School, Middlesex, UK, on August 18, 2005.

The record for the ☆**fastest pantomime horse (male)** is held by Shane Crawford and Adrian Mott (both Australia), who ran 100 m in 12.045 seconds outside the set of *The Footy Show* in Melbourne, Victoria, Australia, on July 30, 2009.

The ★**fastest pantomime horse (mixed)**—Nafi Baram and Kathleen Rice (both UK, front and rear, respectively)—ran 100 m in 16.37 seconds at the Battersea Millennium Arena, London, UK, on November 30, 2006.

☆ **MOST TONYS FOR A PLAY** *The Coast of Utopia* by playwright Tom Stoppard (UK) won a record seven Tony Awards in 2007. A trilogy of plays—*Voyage*, *Shipwreck*, and *Salvage*—lasting nine hours in total and embracing a 33-year timespan, *The Coast of Utopia* explores the subject of change as experienced by a huge cast of around 70 real-life Russian writers, politicians, philosophers, and journalists.

ST. LOUIS, MO, U.S.A. (38°37′N 90°11′W): The site of the Louisiana Purchase Exposition in St. Louis, Missouri, U.S.A., in 1904 covered 1,271.76 acres (514.66 ha), making it the **largest fair**. There was an attendance of 19,694,855.

EXTRA! Turn back to pp. 340–345 for all the top showbiz records.

★ **LONGEST-RUNNING PLAY** The longest continuously run show in the world is *The Mousetrap* by Dame Agatha Christie (UK, 1890–1976), with 23,940 performances as of May 10, 2010, at St. Martin's Theatre in London, UK. The play opened on November 25, 1952, at the Ambassadors Theatre, London, and moved after 8,862 performances to the St. Martin's Theatre next door on March 25, 1974. Pictured above is the cast from the 58th annual performance.

Fastest theatrical production The cast and crew of Dundee University Musical Society in association with Apex Productions produced and performed *Seven Brides for Seven Brothers* at the Gardyne Theatre, Dundee, UK, at 7:30 p.m. on September 27, 2003—23 hr. 30 min. after first receiving the script. The production time included all auditions, casting, rehearsals, publicity, rigging, stage and set design, and construction time.

☆ **Largest audience for a comedian** German comedian Mario Barth performed in front of an audience of 67,733 people at the Olympiastadion, Berlin, Germany, on July 12, 2008.

NEW ORLEANS, LA, U.S.A. (29°58'N 90°04'W): The **longest recorded boxing fight** with gloves was between Andy Bowen and Jack Burke (both U.S.A.) at New Orleans, Louisiana, U.S.A., on April 6–7, 1893. It lasted 110 rounds, 7 hr. 19 min. (9:15 p.m.–4:34 a.m.), and was declared a "no contest" (later changed to a draw).

★ **MOST TONY AWARDS WON FOR BEST ACTRESS IN A MUSICAL**
Angela Lansbury (UK, above left) has won four Tony Awards (out of four nominations) in the category of Best Performance by a Leading Actress in a Musical for *Mame* (1966), *Dear World* (1969), *Gypsy* (1975), and *Sweeney Todd* (1979). The ★ most Tony awards for a male actor in a musical is three, by Hinton Battle (U.S.A., above right), who won for *Sophisticated Ladies* (1981), *The Tapdance Kid* (1984), and *Miss Saigon* (1991), all in the category of Featured Role in a Musical.

☆ **Largest simultaneous performance of one show** The most widespread simultaneous performance of a show was organized by Stagecoach Theatre Arts and achieved by 66 performances of *Glad Rags* in the UK, Ireland, and Germany at 4:15 p.m. on December 6, 2008.

☆ **Most ballet dancers "en pointe"** A total of 220 ballet dancers successfully stood "en pointe" (meaning on the tips of their toes) for a minute at the Youth America Grand Prix (U.S.A.) 10th Anniversary Gala at New York City Center in Manhattan, New York City, U.S.A., on April 22, 2009.

☆ **Most theatrical appearances on a single night** Pendem Krishna Kumar (India) appeared in nine different scripted roles in nine different theater productions in Suryapet, India, on July 9, 2009.

★ **MOST TONY AWARDS FOR PLAYING THE OPPOSITE SEX** Only two actors have ever won a Tony Award for playing someone of the opposite sex: Mary Martin (U.S.A.) for playing the title role in *Peter Pan* in 1956 and Harvey Fierstein (U.S.A., left) for his depiction of Edna Turnblad in *Hairspray* in 2003.

ART & SCULPTURE

LARGEST . . .

☆**Drawing** The largest pencil drawing by one artist—*My journey of life, where I meet people of different color, birds, trees, etc . . . and the life goes on*—is 1,500 ft. (457.20 m) long and 20 in. (50.8 cm) wide, and has an overall surface area of 2,490 ft.^{2} (231.33 m^2). It was completed by Jainthan Francis (U.S.A.) and measured in Sayreville, New Jersey, U.S.A., on June 21, 2009.

☆**Anamorphic pavement art** To mark the launch of *Ice Age 3* on DVD in the UK in November 2009, Twentieth Century Fox Home Entertainment asked German artist Edgar Mueller to paint a 3,423-ft.^{2} (318-m^2) anamorphic reproduction of the movie's poster on the pavement outside London's

Westfield Shopping Centre. In the U.S.A., Fox promoted the movie with an ice statue of the character Scrat. Its height made it, briefly, a record holder, but today the world's ☆**tallest ice sculpture** is a 53-ft. 2.58-in.-tall (16.22-m) piece created by the People's Government of Yichun city, China, on January 19, 2010.

☆ **LONGEST PAINTING BY NUMBERS**
The world's longest painting by numbers measures 3,147 ft. 5 in. (959.35 m) long and is titled *Birds and Wetlands*. It was created by 2,041 participants at an event organized by the Hong Kong Wetland Park and was staged at their premises in Hong Kong, China, on October 17, 2009.

ANAMORPHIC

A work of art that seems distorted from most angles, but will appear normal when seen from a particular viewpoint.

MEMPHIS, TN, U.S.A. (35°07'N 89°58'W): The letter M installed on the Great Mississippi River Bridge in Memphis, Tennessee, U.S.A., is 1,800 ft. (550 m) long—making it the **longest neon sign**. It comprises 200 high-intensity lamps.

★ **LARGEST SAND ART** The largest artwork created from sand—and the ★ largest freehand drawing—is 3.02 miles (4.86 km) in diameter and contains 1,000 individual circles. Jim Denevan (U.S.A., above right) made the artwork in the Black Rock Desert, Nevada, U.S.A., in May 2009 in seven days, etching the sand with a rake and using chains dragged behind a vehicle.

☆ **Finger painting** A finger painting measuring 22,619.51 ft.^{2} (2,101.43 m^2) was created by 3,242 students in Hong Kong, China, on November 26, 2009.

★ **Shuttlecock mosaic** A shuttlecock mosaic measuring 326.95 ft.^{2} (30.375 m^2) was created by Fuqiang Zhao (China) on August 2, 2009. It comprised 5,236 individual shuttlecocks and depicted two interlaced hearts and the words "Show the love with shuttlecocks, be together forever."

☆ **Bead mosaic** The largest bead mosaic measures 72.33 ft.^{2} (6.72 m^2) and was realized by Cao Zhitao (China) at an event organized by the Fuxin Municipal Government in Fuxin City, Liaoning Province, China, on October 25, 2009. The mosaic contained more than 30,000 agate beads.

☆ **Painting by numbers** The largest painting by numbers measures 26,493 ft.^{2} (2,461.3 m^2) and was created by 960 students from Mingren Elementary School in Tongliao City, Inner Mongolia, China, on September 30, 2009.

★ **OLDEST FIGURATIVE SCULPTURE** The Venus of Hohle Fels is the name given to a female figurine carved from a mammoth tusk and dated to *c.* 33,000 B.C. It was discovered in the Hohle Fels ("Hollow Rock") cave near Ulm in Baden-Württemberg, Germany, in September 2008 by Nicolas Conard and a team from the University of Tübingen, Germany.

★ LARGEST RUBIK'S CUBE MOSAIC Five artists from the art collective Cube Works Studio in Toronto, Canada, re-created *The Last Supper* by Leonardo da Vinci . . . from 4,050 Rubik's cubes! The miraculous "cube-ist" mosaic measures 17 ft. (5.18 m) by 8 ft. 6 in. (2.59 m), weighs 1,102 lb. (500 kg), and was finally completed on October 23, 2009.

★ Ground-based digital lunar mosaic On April 4, 2009, 11 amateur astronomers (all UK) used a telescope owned by broadcaster Patrick Moore (UK) to capture 288 images of the Moon. These were then digitally stitched together to make a lunar mosaic 87.4 megapixels in size.

★ Confetti mosaic Nikki Douthwaite (UK) made a mosaic consisting of 587,000 hole-punched dots measuring 10 ft. 1 in. x 6 ft. 10 in. (3.07 x 2.08 m) in February–June 2008.

☆ Mural (solo) Ernesto Espiridion Rios Rocha (Mexico) single-handedly created a mural covering 18,066 ft.² (1,678 m²) in Mazatlán, Mexico, on October 6, 2009.

LONGEST . . .

☆ Painting The longest painting measures 16,256 ft. 6 in. (4,955 m) long and was created by 8,000 school students (all Bahrain) at an event organized by the Ministry of Education in Manama, Bahrain, on December 13, 2009. The theme of the painting was "life in Bahrain."

★ Pavement art Chalk pavement art measuring 18,372 ft. 8 in. (5,600 m) long and 6 ft. 6 in. (2 m) wide was created by 5,000 students from Jena, Germany, on June 5, 2009.

THUNDER BAY, ON, CANADA (8°22'N 89°14'W): Despite having an artificial leg, Terry Fox (Canada, 1958–81) managed to raise Can. $24.7 million (U.S. $20.7 million) on a charity run from St. John's, Newfoundland, to Thunder Bay, Ontario. This represents the **largest amount of money raised in a charity walk or run**. He finished in 143 days, from April 12, to September 2, 1980, and covered 3,339 miles (5,373 km).

LARGEST MODELING BALLOON SCULPTURE John Cassidy (U.S.A.) used 434 modeling balloons to make a biplane that measured 192 in. (490 cm) wide and 147 in. (375 cm) long on September 25, 2009.

☆**Cartoon strip** The students, teachers, and members of Vasavi Vidhyalaya Matriculation School, Trichy, India, created a continuous 1,971-ft. 8-in. (601-m) cartoon strip. It was measured in Tamil Nadu, India, on January 25, 2010.

MISCELLANY

★ **Least valuable art collection in a public museum** The Museum of Bad Art's (MOBA) collection in Boston, Massachusetts, U.S.A., has the lowest value of any public museum's art collection. Its 573 works are worth a total of just $1,197.35.

★ **Oldest painting on a wall** In October 2006, the French archaeological mission at Dja'de al-Mughara—a Neolithic settlement on the Euphrates River near Aleppo, Syria—identified walls of a house that bore a series of geometric paintings. Measuring 25.1 ft.² (2 m²), the wall paintings date from *c.* 9,000 B.C.

EXTRA! For more outsized endeavors, turn to pp. 370, 378, and 384.

☆**LARGEST INFLATABLE SCULPTURE** Gulliver has a volume of 63,252.45 ft.³ (1,791.11 m³) and measures 196 ft. 10 in. x 65 ft. 7 in. x 22 ft. 11 in. (60 x 20 x 7 m) in size. It was presented and measured in Taipei, Taiwan, on July 20, 2009.

ENGINEERING AND TECHNOLOGY

CONTENTS

ARCHITECTURE

CAR: The plush interior decor is based on the days of the railroad Pullman cars, which were popular from the mid-19th century.

★ **HEAVIEST LIMOUSINE** *The Midnight Rider* is a tractor-trailer limousine that weighs 50,560 lb. (22,933 kg), and is 70 ft. (21.3 m) long and 13 ft. 8 in. (4.1 m) high. This mighty motor features three lounges and a separate bar, and can accommodate 40 passengers served by a crew of four. It was designed by Michael Machado and Pamela Bartholemew (both U.S.A.) in California, U.S.A., and began operation on September 3, 2004.

BAR: The bar contains air-suspension seats for a smooth ride, satellite TV and large movie screens, and an internal phone system with four outside lines!

EXTRA! Turn to pp. 397–400 for more vehicle records.

★ **HIGHEST OBSERVATION DECK** A glass observation deck 1,568 ft 1 in. (477.96 m) above street level is located on the 100th floor of the Shanghai World Financial Center in Pudong, China. The mixed-use skyscraper also houses the world's ☆ highest hotel—the Park Hyatt Shanghai occupies floors 79 to 93.

★ **Largest reinforced concrete cement flat roof span** The Satsang Hall within the Govind Devji's Temple in Jaipur, India, has a reinforced concrete cement flat roof with a single span of 119 ft. (36.27 m). It was designed by N M Roof Designers Ltd, and the hall was dedicated to the public on July 23, 2009.

★ **Largest revolving restaurant** Bellini is an Italian and international cuisine restaurant located on the 45th floor of Mexico City's World Trade Center. The establishment opened in 1994 and has an area of 11,244.58 ft.^{2} (1,044.66 m^2).

Largest hotel lobby The lobby at the Hyatt Regency in San Francisco, California, U.S.A., is 350 ft. (107 m) long, 160 ft. (49 m) wide, and, at 170 ft. (52 m), is the height of a 15-story building. The lobby has 300,000 cascading lights and features trees, a stream, and a fountain.

☆ **LARGEST SHOPPING MALL** The Dubai Mall in Dubai, UAE, has an internal floor area of 5.9 million ft.^{2} (548,127 m^2) over four levels. It houses 1,200 retail outlets and more than 160 food and drink outlets, and opened on November 4, 2008.

MILWAUKEE, WI, U.S.A. (43°03'N 87°57'W): Detective Lieutenant Andrew F. Anewenter (U.S.A., b. January 12, 1916) holds the record for the **longest-serving police officer**. He worked for the Milwaukee (Wisconsin) Police Department for 61 years, from June 1, 1942, until his retirement on May 15, 2003.

HIGH!: The record-breaking Burj Khalifa (see below) also holds the title for the ★ **building with the most floors,** at 160 storys!

☆ **TALLEST BUILDING** The Burj Khalifa (formally Burj Dubai) opened on January 17, 2009, in Dubai, UAE. It topped out at a record-breaking 2,717 ft. (828 m), making it not only the tallest man-made structure on Earth but also the ☆ **tallest building ever.**

RISE!: Dubai is home to a range of other impressive structures, including The Rose Rayhaan, the ☆ **tallest hotel,** standing at 1,092 ft. 6 in. (333 m).

★ **LARGEST STEEL STRUCTURE** Designed by Swiss architects Herzog & de Meuron, the Beijing Olympic Stadium, also known as the Bird's Nest, cost $423 million to construct and has a floor space of 2,777,088 ft.^{2} (258,000 m^2) on a 51-acre (21-ha) site. The main body of the stadium is a saddle-shaped elliptic steel structure weighing 42,000 tons (38,100 tonnes).

> *"In China, a bird's nest is very expensive, something you eat on special occasions."*
> **Architect Li Xinggang explains the origins of the stadium's nickname**

Largest airport passenger terminal The Hong Kong International Airport passenger terminal building is 0.8 miles (1.3 km) long and covers 5,920,150 ft.^{2} (550,000 m^2). It has a capacity of 45 million passengers a year, arriving on 460 flights every day, and cost $20 billion to build. The baggage hall alone is as big as Yankee Stadium in New York City, U.S.A.

★ **Tallest steel structure** Willis Tower (formerly Sears Tower) in Chicago, Illinois, U.S.A., is a 1,451-ft.-tall (442-m), 108-story office skyscraper constructed from steel. The building's design includes nine steel-unit square tubes in a 3 x 3 arrangement, with a 75 x 75 ft. (22 x 22 m) footprint. Completed in 1974, it has 4.56 million ft.^{2} (423,637 m^2) of floor space.

CHICAGO, IL, U.S.A. (41°52'N 87°37'W): The **longest recorded operation** lasted for 96 hours and was performed on February 4–8, 1951, in Chicago, Illinois, U.S.A., on Mrs. Gertrude Levandowski (U.S.A.) for the removal of an ovarian cyst.

★ **LARGEST DEPARTMENT STORE** Built by Shinsegae Co. Ltd and opened on June 26, 2009, the Shinsegae ("New World") Centum City Department Store in Busan, South Korea, covers an area of 3.16 million ft.² (293,905 m²), beating the previous record holder, the famous Macy's store in New York City, U.S.A., by more than 1.022 million ft.² (95,000 m²).

★ **Tallest concrete structure** Completed in 2009, the 92-story Trump International Hotel & Tower in Chicago, Illinois, U.S.A., tops out at 1,170 ft. (360 m), or 1,389 ft. (423 m) including the building's spire. Designed by Skidmore, Owings, and Merrill, the complex features 486 residential apartments and a 339-room hotel, and is the world's tallest formwork concrete structure.

Highest concentration of theme hotels There are more than 16 theme hotels on the Strip in Las Vegas, Nevada, U.S.A. Themes include the skylines of Paris and New York, Treasure Island, and Venice. Las Vegas boasts an incredible 120,000 hotel rooms, nearly one for every four of its inhabitants.

Largest retractable stadium roof Completed in June 1989, the roof of the SkyDome, home of the Toronto Blue Jays baseball team, located near the CN Tower in Toronto, Canada, covers 8 acres (3.2 ha), spans 685 ft. (209 m) at its widest, and rises to 282 ft. (86 m). It weighs 12,125 tons (11,000 tonnes) and takes 20 minutes to open fully. When retracted, the entire field and 91% of the seats are uncovered.

••

NASHVILLE, TN, U.S.A. (36°10'N 86°47'W): Dan Runte (U.S.A.) reached a speed of 69.3 mph (111.5 km/h) in B*igfoot* 14 on September 11, 1999, at Symrna Airport, Nashville, Tennessee, U.S.A., the **highest speed ever recorded in a monster truck**.

••

Largest residential palace The palace (Istana Nurul Iman) of HM the Sultan of Brunei in the capital Bandar Seri Begawan is the largest residence in the world, with a floor space of 2,152,780 ft.² (200,000 m²), 1,788 rooms, and 257 lavatories.

ROLLER COASTERS

☆**Most track inversions** *Colossus* at Thorpe Park, Chertsey, Surrey, UK, turns riders upside down a total of 10 times during each 2,789-ft. (850-m) run. The ride has a maximum height of 98 ft. (30 m) and a top speed of 40 mph (65 km/h). The inversions include a vertical loop, a twin cobra roll, a twin corkscrew, and five heart rolls. The *Tenth Ring Roller Coaster* of Chimelong Paradise in Guangzhou, China, also holds the record, but is a duplicate of *Colossus*.

FASTEST

★**Absolute** See *ring°racer*, p. 367.

★ **MOST EXPENSIVE** *Expedition Everest* was opened by Disney for $100 million in 2006 after six years of research and construction. The concept is a train journey through the Himalayas that uses a shortcut via Forbidden Mountain, wherein lies the fearsome Yeti—an enormous 22-ft.-tall (6.7-m) audio-animatronic beast controlled by 19 actuators and covered in 1,000 ft.² (93 m²) of fur.

COSTLY: The ★ **most expensive roller coaster** just in terms of pure steel is Steel Dragon 2000 in Mie, Japan, which cost $50 million in 2000. For the priciest roller coaster, including sets and extras, see above.

★ **FASTEST (ABSOLUTE)** The *ring°racer* Formula One–themed coaster at the Nürburgring racetrack in Nürburg, Germany, features a pneumatic launch system that blasts riders to 134.8 mph (216.9 km/h) in a breathtaking 2.5 seconds—twice as fast as a Formula One car.

★ **4th dimension** This type of coaster features cars that sit on either side of the track and spin about a horizontal axis. The ★ **first 4th dimension coaster** was *X* at Six Flags Magic Mountain, in 2002, but the ★ **fastest** is *Eejanaika* at Fuji-Q Highland in Fujiyoshida, Yamanashi, Japan, which reaches 78.3 mph (126 km/h).

Flying *Tatsu* at Six Flags Magic Mountain in Valencia, California, U.S.A., is the fastest flying coaster—that is, its riders travel with their backs parallel to the track to give the impression of flight. It reaches speeds of 62 mph (99.7 km/h). At 170 ft. (51.8 m) high, it is also the world's **tallest flying coaster**.

Shuttle A shuttle coaster is one that does not complete a full circuit and must therefore travel out and back. The speed record for this category of coaster is shared by *Superman the Escape* at Six Flags Magic Mountain, Valencia, California, U.S.A., and *Tower of Terror* at Dreamworld, Gold Coast, Australia. Both opened in 1997, and both register a top speed of 100 mph (161 km/h).

☆ **Suspended** The speed record for suspended coasters—in which the riders hang from the track and pivot from side to side, emphasizing the track's banks and turns—is shared between *Vortex* at Canada's Wonderland in Vaughan, Ontario, Canada, and *Ninja* at Six Flags Magic Mountain in Valencia, California, U.S.A. Both can reach 55 mph (88.5 km/h).

TALLEST

Absolute *Kingda Ka*, see *Tallest Absolute* (p. 370).

....

MONTGOMERY, AL, U.S.A. (32°21'N 86°16'W): Ed Long of Montgomery, Alabama, logged 64,396 hr. 55 min. of flying time between May 1933 and June 1999—the **most flying hours by a pilot**. A large portion of the seven years (in total) he was airborne was spent patrolling power lines for the Alabama Power Company.

....

★ **4th dimension** At 249 ft. 4 in. (76 m) tall, *Eejanaika* at Fuji-Q Highland in Yamanashi Prefecture, Japan, is the loftiest of the 4th dimension coasters. The 2-min. 10-sec. ride opened at a cost of just over Y3.5 billion ($35 million).

Flying *Tatsu*, see *Fastest Flying Coaster, p. 367*.

Shuttle *Superman the Escape* at Six Flags Magic Mountain, Valencia, California, U.S.A., opened in 1997 at a height of 415 ft. (126.5 m).

★ **Suspended** *Vortex* at Wonderland in Vaughan, Ontario, Canada, reaches a peak of 91 ft. (27.7 m), making it the world's tallest suspended ride.

☆ **FASTEST (WOODEN)** *Colossos* at Heide-Park Soltau in Lower Saxony, Germany, reaches a peak speed of 74.6 mph (120 km/h). It is also the tallest operating wooden coaster at 196 ft. 10 in. (60 m).

INDIANAPOLIS, IN, U.S.A. (39°47'N 86°09'W): The **first Indy 500 winner** was Ray Harroun (U.S.A.), driving the Marmon Wasp, on May 30, 1911. Ray maintained an average speed of 120.06 km/h (74.602 mph) throughout the race.

TOP 10 FASTEST

	SPEED	COASTER	PARK	LOCATION	DATE
*	134.8 mph	*ring°racer*	Nürburgring	Nürburg, Germany	2009
1	128 mph	*Kingda Ka*	Six Flags Great Adventure	Jackson, New Jersey, U.S.A.	2005
2	120 mph	*Top Thrill Dragster*	Cedar Point	Sandusky, Ohio, U.S.A.	2003
3	106.9 mph	*Dodonp*	Fuji-Q Highland	Fujiyoshida, Yamanashi, Japan	2001
4	100 mph	*Superman the Escape*	Six Flags Magic Mountain	Valencia, California, U.S.A.	1997
		Tower of Terror	Dreamworld	Coomera, Australia	1997
5	95 mph	*Steel Dragon 2000*	Nagashima Spa Land	Nagashima, Kuwana Mie, Japan	2000
6	93 mph	*Millennium Force*	Cedar Point	Sandusky, Ohio, U.S.A.	2000
*	90 mph	*Intimidator 305 (above)*	Kings Dominion	Doswell, Virginia, U.S.A.	2010
7	85 mph	*Goliath*	Six Flags Magic Mountain	Valencia, California, U.S.A.	2000
		Phantom's Revenge	Kennywood	West Mifflin, Pennsylvania, U.S.A.	1991
		Titan	Six Flags Over Texas	Arlington, Texas, U.S.A.	2001
8	83.9 mph	*Furius Baco*	PortAventura Park	Salou, Tarragona, Spain	2007
9	82 mph	*Xcelerator*	Knott's Berry Farm	Buena Park, California, U.S.A.	2002
10	80.8 mph	*Fujiyama*	Fuji-Q Highland	Fujiyoshida, Yamanashi, Japan	1996
		Thunder Dolphin	Tokyo Dome City	Bunkyo Tokyo, Japan	2003

*Source: Roller Coaster Database * Unopened at time of going to press*

TALLEST (ABSOLUTE)
Kingda Ka at Six Flags Great Adventure in New Jersey, U.S.A., reaches a height of 456 ft. (139 m). It opened in spring 2005 and at the time was the world's fastest coaster.

LOUISVILLE, KY, U.S.A. (38°15'N 85°45'W): The Grawemeyer Award for Music Composition from the University of Louisville in Kentucky, U.S.A., is the world's **greatest prize money for writing music**, with a value of $200,000 (£160,000).

STEEPEST

☆**Absolute** *Mumbo Jumbo* at Flamingo Land Theme Park & Zoo in Malton, UK, has an angle of descent of 112°. The 98-ft.-tall (30-m) ride was opened on July 4, 2009, at a cost of £4 million ($6.3 million). The extreme drop exerts a maximum force of 4 g.

Wooden *El Toro* at Six Flags Great Adventure, New Jersey, U.S.A., has a drop of 76°. The 4,400-ft. (1,341-m) ride lasts 1 min. 43 sec., reaching speeds of 75 mph (120 km/h). It towers 188 ft. (57.3 m) above the theme park at its tallest point.

☆**Shuttle** The steepest angle of descent on a shuttle-style coaster is 90°, a record currently held by at least 14 different rides. The most recent shuttle-style coaster to open was the 196-ft. (60-m) *Aftershock* at the Silverwood Theme Park in Athol, Idaho, U.S.A., which had relocated from Six Flags Great America in Gurnee, Illinois, U.S.A.

BIG ENGINEERING

☆**Largest man-made excavation** The Bingham Canyon Copper Mine near Salt Lake City, Utah, U.S.A., is the world's largest manmade excavation. More than 5.9 billion tons (5.4 billion tonnes) of rock have been excavated from it since 1906. Visible from space, it measures 2.5 miles (4 km) across and 0.75 miles (1.2 km) deep and has been called "the richest hole on Earth."

As of 2004, more than 16.9 million tons (15.4 million tonnes) of copper have been produced from the mine, as well as 23 million oz. (652 million g) of gold and 190 million oz. (5.3 billion g) of silver.

★**Longest drilled oil well** The world's longest drilled oil well is BD-04-A, with a total length of 40,320 ft. (12,289 m). It was completed in May 2008 by Maersk Oil Qatar and Qatar Petroleum, in the Al-Shaheen offshore oil field off the coast of Qatar. The well includes a horizontal section measuring 35,770 ft. (10,902 m).

☆**HEAVIEST WEIGHT LIFTED BY CRANE** A barge, ballasted with water and weighing a hefty 44,385,667 lb. (20,133 tonnes) was lifted by the "Taisun" crane at Yantai Raffles Shipyard, Yantai, China, on April 18, 2008.

★**Largest excavation by hand** Jagersfontein Mine near Jagersfontein, South Africa, is an open-pit mine that has provided some of the largest diamonds ever discovered. It operated as a mine from 1888 until 1971, first as an open mine and then as an underground mine. The Jagersfontein Mine was dug by hand to a depth of 660 ft. (201 m) between 1888 and 1911. The area of the opening measures 48.55 acres (19.65 ha).

★**Farthest manmade leaning tower** The "Capital Gate" has an inclination of 18 degrees and is 524 ft. 11 in. (160 m) high. It was designed by Global Architects RMJM (Dubai) and was completed in Abu Dhabi, United Arab Emirates, on January 4, 2010.

Tallest bridge The 8,070-ft.-long (2,460-m) Millau Viaduct across the Tarn Valley, France, is supported by seven concrete piers, the tallest of which measures 1,095 ft. 4.8 in. (333.88 m) from the ground to its highest point.

★**Largest lake created by a nuclear explosion** On January 15, 1965, the Soviet Union detonated a 140-kiloton nuclear device underneath a dry bed of the Chagan River, Kazakhstan. Part of the Soviets' Nuclear Explosions for the National Economy program, the raised rim of the resulting crater dammed the river, allowing the creation of a reservoir, now known as Lake Chagan. It has a volume of around 3,531,000 ft.^{3} (100,000 m^3).

....

CINCINNATI, OH, U.S.A. (39°08'N 84°30'W): The **largest gathering of scarecrows in one location** is 3,311. All were on display at the Cincinnati Horticultural Society's Cincinnati Flower and Farm Fest on Coney Island, Cincinnati, Ohio, U.S.A., on October 12, 2003.

....

★**LARGEST FLOOD DEFENSE** The Delta Works off the coast of Holland is a huge series of dams, locks, sluices, storm surge barriers, and dikes designed to protect low-lying areas of the country from the sea. Construction began in 1950 and ended in 1997 with the completion of the Maeslantkering and the Hartelkering barriers. The Delta Works contain some 10,250 miles (16,495 km) of dikes and around 300 structures.

ATLANTA, GA, U.S.A. (33°45'N 84°23'W): Willie Jones (U.S.A.) was admitted to Grady Memorial Hospital, Atlanta, Georgia, U.S.A., on July 10, 1980, with heatstroke on a day when the temperature reached 90°F (32.2°C). His temperature was found to be 115.7°F (46.5°C)—the **highest known body temperature**.

★**Tallest hospital** Guy's Tower at Guy's Hospital in London, UK, is 468 ft. (142.6 m) tall. It was completed in 1974 and has 34 stories.

Tallest boat lift The Strépy-Thieu boat lift on the Canal du Centre, Hainaut, Belgium, uses a counterweight system to carry boats a vertical distance of 240 ft. (73.15 m) from its upstream and downstream sections. The two boxes, or caissons, that each boat enters are 367 x 39 ft. (112 x 12 m) and weigh between 7,936 and 9,259 tons (7,200–8,400 tonnes), depending on the current water level. It takes seven minutes for the vertical journey to be completed.

★**Tallest transmission tower** At Jiangyin, Jiangsu Province, China, two electricity transmission towers stand on opposite banks of the Yangtze River at 1,137 ft. (346.5 m) tall. Their height allows the power lines to span the river, which is 7,556 ft. (2,303 m) wide at this point. Another tower, on the Damaoshan Mountain in Zhoushan city, China, will be 1,213 ft. (370 m) tall when it is completed in 2010.

★**Widest canal** The Cape Cod Canal, which crosses the land that connects Cape Cod to mainland Massachusetts, U.S.A., was constructed between 1909 and 1916. It is 17.4 miles (28 km) long and 540 ft. (164.6 m) wide. It is a segment of the Atlantic Intracoastal Waterway, which runs for 3,000 miles (4,800 km) along the American east coast.

☆ **TALLEST CHIMNEY DEMOLISHED BY EXPLOSIVES** The Westerholt Power Plant in Gelsenkirchen-Westerholt, Germany, was a coal power plant constructed in the 1960s and decommissioned in 2005. Its chimney, or smokestack, was constructed in 1997 and was 1,104 ft. (337 m) high—the tallest in Germany at that time. It was demolished using explosives on December 3, 2006.

EXTRA! For more aeronautical records, turn back to pp. 196–200.

MOST SPACIOUS BUILDING The Boeing Company's main assembly plant in Everett, Washington, U.S.A., has a volume of 472 million ft.^{3} (13.4 million m^3) and a floor area of 98.3 acres (39.8 ha). Boeing's 747, 767, and 777 aircraft are assembled there.

★**LARGEST AUTOCLAVE** An autoclave is typically used to sterilize medical or laboratory instruments. In August 2006, ASC Process Systems (U.S.A.) announced it had built an autoclave with an internal volume of 82,000 ft.^{3} (2,321 m^3). It is designed to process components of the Boeing 787 Dreamliner passenger aircraft by subjecting them to temperatures of up to 450°F (232°C) and pressures of up to 10.2 bar.

Most expensive object on Earth The Itaipu hydroelectric dam on the Paraná River between Brazil and Paraguay cost $27 billion to build in 1984 ($35.93 billion today), which makes it the priciest object on Earth. Only the International Space Station (ISS) has cost more as a single project.

ROAD & RAIL

ROAD

Deadliest place to travel by road According to findings from its first report on global road safety, the World Health Organization states that Eritrea, in Africa, is the deadliest place to travel by road in terms of deaths caused by road traffic accidents. There were 48 deaths per 100,000 people in 2007.

★ **LONGEST ICE ROAD** Canada's Tibbitt to Contwoyto Winter Road was first used in 1982 to supply mines in the Northwest Territories. Open from January to the end of March, the ice road is rebuilt annually. It is 353 miles (568 km) long, 308 miles (495 km) of which traverses frozen lakes.

★ **FASTEST JET-POWERED TRAIN** The M-497 was a prototype experimental train powered by two General Electric J47–19 jet engines. It was developed and tested in 1966 in the U.S.A. and was able to reach a top speed of 183 mph (296 km/h).

OAK RIDGE, TN, U.S.A. (36°00'N 84°15'W): The **largest electrical current** was achieved in April 1996 by scientists at Oak Ridge National Laboratory, U.S.A., who sent a current of 2 million amperes per square centimeter down a superconducting wire.

★ **OLDEST STACK INTERCHANGE** The Four Level Interchange in Los Angeles, California, U.S.A., features, as its name suggests, four layers of multilane road and was first opened to the public in 1953. The interchange links U.S. Route 101 to State Route 110 using a free-flowing design to help minimize L.A.'s notorious congestion.

☆**Longest underwater road tunnel** The Tokyo Bay Aqua-Line is a combination of bridge and tunnel that spans Tokyo Bay, Japan. The tunnel section is 31,440 ft. (9,583 m) long and was opened in 1997.

★**Largest national road network** The U.S.A. has 4,017,661 miles (6,465,799 km) of roads, of which 2,615,870 miles (4,209,835 km) are paved. China is in second place with 2,226,817 miles (3,583,715 km) of roads.

★**Oldest "magic roundabout"** Ring junctions were first designed by the Road Research Laboratory (UK) in order to ease traffic congestion at busy junctions. The first opened in Swindon, UK, in 1972. Nicknamed the "Magic Roundabout," it consists of five mini-roundabouts connected to-

★**OLDEST SUBWAY TUNNEL** The Atlantic Avenue Tunnel beneath Brooklyn, U.S.A., was built over a period of seven months in 1844. Running for 2,517 ft. (767 m), it is 21 ft. (6.4 m) wide and 17 ft. (5.2 m) high. The tunnel was the first in the world built underground in order to improve urban congestion, public safety, and rail operations. It operated until 1861, when the ends were sealed off, and was rediscovered in 1981.

KNOXVILLE, TN, U.S.A. (35°58'N 83°55'W): FORDISC is the world's **most complete database of the human skeleton**. Established by the University of Tennessee's "Body Farm," it allows data captured from decomposing bodies to be organized and analyzed by forensic anthropologists.

> **CHUFF!:** The official speed of the *Fairy Queen* is 25 mph
> (40 km/h), although it is capable of going much faster than this.

gether in a circle, allowing traffic to move in both directions around the main central island.

RAIL

★**Longest subway by total length** The London Underground, London, UK, has a combined length of around 250 miles (400 km) of track, as well as 270 stations. Some 45% of it is underground. With its first section opening in 1863, the London Underground is also the **oldest subway system** in the world.

☆**Largest national rail network** The U.S.A. has some 140,695 miles (226,427 km) of rail. Second place belongs to Russia, with 54,156 miles (87,157 km) of track.

OLDEST STEAM LOCOMOTIVE IN USE The *Fairy Queen* was built in 1855 by Kitson Thompson Hewitson of Leeds, UK. Brought back into service in October 1997 hauling a twin-car train between Delhi Cantonment, Delhi, and Alwar, Rajasthan, India, the train now provides a popular service to tourists.

> **CHUFF!:** The *Fairy Queen* was restored and made fully functional in 1966. When not in use, it is kept at the Indian National Railway Museum in New Delhi.

☆ **HIGHEST RAILROAD STATION** The Tanggula Railroad Station in Tibet is the highest in the world at 16,627 ft. (5,068 m) above sea level. The unstaffed station on the Qingzang Railroad opened on July 1, 2006, and has a 0.77-mile-long (1.25-km) platform.

Smallest armored train During World War II, the 15-in.-gauge (381-mm) Romney, Hythe & Dymchurch Railway, which runs between Hythe and Dungeness along the coast of Kent, UK, was requisitioned by the British government for use in the war effort. Roughly a quarter of the size of UK standard-gauge trains, a steam locomotive and several passenger cars were given steel armor for wartime use.

Fastest steam locomotive The London North Eastern Railway "Class A4" No. 4468 *Mallard* hauled seven passenger cars at a speed of 125 mph (201 km/h) between Grantham, Lincolnshire, and Peterborough, Cambridgeshire, UK, on July 3, 1938.

Heaviest haul railroad On April 8, 2008, the Fortescue Metals Group (Australia) completed 155 miles (250 km) of single-track railroad capable of running 1.53-mile-long (2.5-km) trains carrying a gross load of 42,328 tons (38,400 tonnes) of ore.

BIG STUFF

LARGEST . . .

★ **Backpack/rucksack** A backpack/rucksack 9 ft. 10 in. (3 m) tall and 9 ft. 8 in. (2.95 m) wide, adorned with the character Lulu Caty, was manufactured by Lulu Caty (Rainbow Max Co., China) and unveiled in Dubai, UAE, on October 10, 2009.

....

DETROIT, MI, U.S.A. (42°20'N 83°03'W): The longest measured home run in a Major League Baseball game is 193 m (634 ft.), by Mickey Mantle (U.S.A.) for the New York Yankees against the Detroit Tigers at Briggs Stadium, Detroit, Michigan, U.S.A., on September 10, 1960.

....

EXTRA! Can't get enough big stuff? No problem—turn to p. 384 to find more scaled-up records.

☆ **LARGEST SPORTS SHOE**
A sports shoe measuring 13 ft. 1 in. (4 m) long, 5 ft. 2 in. (1.6 m) wide, and 5 ft. 6 in. (1.7 m) high was created by Launch Group (UK) in Cardiff, UK, in March 2009. It was made on behalf of supermarket chain Tesco's support for Cancer Research UK's Race for Life.

★ **Christmas star ornament** Measuring 103 ft. 8 in. (31.59 m) tall, the largest Christmas star ornament was constructed by Apple A Day Properties (India) and unveiled in Kochi, Kerala, India, on December 31, 2009. The giant festive decoration was created to celebrate the building of a new music academy in the city.

☆ **Cup of tea** Mercy Health Center of Fort Scott, Kansas, U.S.A., made a cup of tea measuring 7.92 ft. (2.41 m) in diameter, 1.96 ft. (0.6 m) in height, and with a volume of 660 gal (3,000 liters). The giant cuppa was unveiled on September 26, 2009.

★ **LARGEST SCREWDRIVER**
Thomas Blackthorne (UK) owns the world's largest screwdriver. It has an acrylic handle that measures 7.6 in. (19.5 cm) at its widest point and is 19.6 in. (50 cm) long. The steel shaft is 1 in. (25 mm) thick and projects a farther 20 in. (51 cm), making the overall length 39.7 in. (101 cm).

☆**LONGEST USABLE GOLF CLUB**
Measuring 13 ft. 5 in. (4.09 m) in length, the longest usable golf club was created and used by Denmark's Karsten Maas. The club was used to drive a ball a distance of 403 ft. 6 in. (123 m) on a Trackman device at the Bella Center, Copenhagen, Denmark, on January 24, 2009.

☆**Fan** A fan measuring 27 ft. 10 in. (8.48 m) long and 17 ft. (5.18 m) in height when fully opened was created by Goods of Desire (G.O.D.) and was unveiled at the G.O.D. Peak Galleria store in Hong Kong, China, on August 20, 2009. The fan was made from wood and paper and operated just like a standard-size fan of that construction.

☆**LARGEST WARDROBE** Jan Bilý (Czech Republic) and his company Art-Style created a wardrobe that measures 19 ft. 10 in. (6.06 m) high, 13 ft. 4 in. (4.07 m) wide, and 4 ft. 11 in. (1.5 m) deep. The wardrobe, which has two doors, was presented and measured in Prague, Czech Republic, on September 10, 2009.

COLUMBUS, OH, U.S.A. (39°59'N 82°59'W): Working on the basis that a joke must have a beginning, a middle, and an end, the **longest joke-telling marathon** was achieved by Mike Hessman of Columbus, Ohio, U.S.A., who told 12,682 jokes in 24 hours on November 16–17 1992.

☆ **LONGEST RIDEABLE SURFBOARD** A surfboard measuring 30 ft. 10 in. (9.42 m) long was successfully ridden by Rico De Souza (Brazil, pictured) at Solemar Beach, Espirito Santo, Brazil, on June 12, 2009.

The largest surfboard ever was made by Nev Hyman (Australia) and is 39 ft. 4 in. (12 m) long, 9 ft. 10 in. (3 m) wide, and 11.8 in. (30 cm) thick. It was launched in Queensland, Australia, on March 5, 2005.

★ **Glass of spritzer** A spritzer with a volume of 109 gal. (500 liters) was created by the Hungarian Wine Marketing Agency in Budapest, Hungary, on June 20, 2009. It was made by combining 54 gal. (250 liters) each of Neszmely Rose wine and soda water.

☆ **Golf tee** Students of Jerry Havill's Team Problem Solving Course at Bay de Noc Community College in Escanaba, Michigan, U.S.A., built a giant golf tee that measured 26 ft. 8 in. (8.13 m) long with a head diameter of 35 in. (88.9 cm), and a shaft width of 13.87 in. (35.24 cm). It was unveiled on July 23, 2009.

☆ **Pom-pom** A pom-pom measuring 3 ft. (91.4 cm) high and 10 ft. 5 in. (320 cm) across was created by the creative arts department at Self Unlimited in Kent, UK, on June 30, 2009.

LARGEST BEACH BALL An inflatable beach ball measuring 41 ft. 3 in. (12.59 m) in diameter was made by Westtoer (Belgium), and displayed in Liège, Belgium, on August 8, 2009.

★ **LARGEST HIGH-DEFINITION TV SCREEN** A Diamond Vision High Definition LED television screen measuring 35 ft. 8.4 in. x 352 ft. 9 in. (10.88 x 107.52 m) was unveiled on January 28, 2010, at Meydan Racecourse, Dubai, UAE. The world-beating screen, which has a total surface area of 12,591.83 ft.² (1,169.82 m²), was created by the Mitsubishi Electric Corporation (Japan) for the Meydan City Corporation, which is based in Dubai.

TAMPA, FL, U.S.A. (27°58'N 82°28'W): In May 1994, Howard Jenkins, from Tampa, Florida, U.S.A., discovered that $88 million (£62 million) had been transferred mistakenly into his bank account. Although he initially withdrew $4 million (£2.8 million), his conscience got the better of him and he returned the $88 million in full. At least he got into the record books, for making the **largest cash return**. . . .

☆**Poster** A 139 ft. 9 in. x 207 ft. (42.6 x 63.1 m) poster was created by Alpiq (Switzerland) and presented and measured at the Cleuson Dam near Nendaz, Switzerland, on February 8, 2010. The poster is a greeting to Swiss athletes at the Winter Olympics in Vancouver, Canada.

★**Santa hat** Measuring a whopping 50 ft. 9 in. (15.47 m) long and 27 ft. (8.23 m) wide, the largest Santa hat was created by children from the Chill Youth Club (all Norway). The festive headgear, which took a total of three months to construct, was presented in Fredrikstad, Norway, on December 9, 2008.

☆**LARGEST CARD STRUCTURE** Bryan Berg (U.S.A.) completed a playing card structure measuring 34 ft. 1.05 in. (10.39 m) long, 9 ft. 5.39 in. (2.88 m) tall, and 11 ft. 7.37 in. (3.54 m) deep at the Venetian Macao-Resort-Hotel in Macau, China, on March 10, 2010. The structure, which was made of 218,792 cards, was a replica of the Macau skyline.

LARGEST . . .

OBJECT	DIMENSIONS	RECORD HOLDER	DATE ACHIEVED
☆ *Ballpoint pen*	11 ft. 11 in. (3.63 m) long	Biswaroop Roy Chowdhury (India)	March 29, 2009
☆ *Canned food structure*	115,527 cans	Disney VoluntEARS (U.S.A.)	February 11, 2010
☆ *Cardboard box*	20 ft. 1.2 in. (6.12 m) wide; 46 ft. 1.2 in. (14.05 m) long; 9 ft. 0.3 in. (2.75 m) tall	Chegg.com (U.S.A.)	September 19, 2009
☆ *Ceramic plate*	6,327 lb. 4 oz. (2,870 kg) in weight; 19 ft. (5.8 m) in diameter	Joe Kabalan and the Association of Lebanese Industrialists (both Lebanon)	October 14, 2009
☆ *Chair*	98 ft. 5 in. (30 m) tall	XXXLutz and Holzleimbauwerk Wiehag GmbH (both Austria)	February 9, 2009
☆ *Chess set*	Board: 19 ft. 4 in. (5.89 m) on each side King: 47 in. (119 cm) tall; 1 ft. 2 in. (37.4 cm) wide	Medicine Hat Chess Club (Canada)	May 27, 2009
★ *Chinowa*	36 ft. 1 in. (11 m) in diameter	Aichiken Gokokujinjya (Japan)	June 28, 2009
☆ *Chopsticks*	27 ft. 6 in. (8.4 m)	Wakasa Chopsticks Industry Cooperative (Japan)	March 22, 2009
★ *Cup of hot chocolate*	84.07 gal (318.23 liters)	City of St. Thomas (Canada)	December 22, 2009
★ *Cup of soft drink*	1,213.5 gal (4,593.7 liters)	People's Government of Jiagedaqi District, China	August 6, 2009
★ *Cushion*	33 ft. 0.8 in. x 33 ft. 0.8 in. (10.08 x 10.08 m)	Shanghai Konglong Textile Ornaments Co., Ltd (China)	May 29, 2009
☆ *Dog biscuit*	231 lb. 7 oz. (105 kg)	Warner Bros. Entertainment UK and the Canine Cookie Company (both UK)	October 5, 2009
☆ *Flag (draped)*	467,206.99 ft.^{2} (43,404.95 m^2)	Grace Galindez-Gupana (Philippines)	April 11, 2009
☆ *Flute*	10 ft. 7 in. (3.25 m) long; 1.97 in. (5 cm) in diameter	Fushun Youth and Children Palace (China)	July 14, 2009
☆ *Soccer shirt*	234 ft. 1 in. x 259 ft. 8 in. (71.35 x 79.15 m)	AVEA (Turkey)	April 5, 2009
★ *Fresh flower garland*	1.3 miles (2.2 km) long	The people of Peiting (Germany)	July 19, 2009
★ *Glow stick*	9 ft. 10 in. (3 m) tall; 7.87 in. (20 cm) in diameter	KNIXS GmbH (Germany)	June 29, 2009

		RECORD	DATE
OBJECT	DIMENSIONS	HOLDER	ACHIEVED
☆ Handwoven carpet	10,279 ft.² (955 m²)	Samovar Carpets & Antiques (Kuwait)	November 1, 2009
★ Horseshoe	1 ft. 10 in. (56 cm) long; 2 ft. (61.5 cm) wide	Caritas Tagesstätte Krumbach (Austria)	June 21, 2008
★ Impossible bottle	15.8 gal (60 liters)	Aidano Dallafiora (Italy)	August 24, 2009
☆ Inflatable sofa	67 ft. 3 in. (20.5 m) long; 26 ft. 9 in. (8.10 m) wide; 26 ft. 5 in. (8.1 m) tall	Jacobs Krönung (Germany)	April 14, 2009
★ Javelin	94 ft. 7 in. (28.83 m) long; 11 in. (30 cm) in diameter	Vattenfall (Germany)	July 31, 2009
★ Model aircraft by wingspan	49 ft. 2 in. (15 m) wingspan	Markus Stadelmann (Switzerland)	May 8, 2009
☆ Postcard	524.74 ft.² (48.75 m²)	Deutsche Post (Germany) and Toyota Cars (Japan)	August 10, 2009
☆ Punching bag	22 ft. 10 in. (6.97 m) tall; 3 ft. 2 in. (98 cm) wide; 1,763 lb. (800 kg) in weight	Helio Dipp Jr. and Cintia Schmitt (both Brazil)	March 28, 2009
☆ Scissors	7 ft. 7 in. (2.31 m) from tip to handle	Neerja Roy Chowdhury (India)	August 16, 2009
★ Sheet of handmade paper	45 ft. 7 in. x 22 ft. 7 in. (13.9 m x 6.9 m)	Made for Masaki Takahashi and Kazuki Maeda (both Japan)	August 19, 2009
☆ Shopping bag (made from paper)	13 ft. 8 in. x 21 ft. 8 in. x 5 ft. 10 in. (4.18 m x 6.62 m x 1.79 m)	Kaufland (Romania)	May 18, 2009
☆ Shower	100 ft. (30.48 m) long; 40 ft. (12.19 m) wide; 10 ft. (3.04 m) tall	PertPlus and Chicago firefighters (both U.S.A.)	July 9, 2009
★ Sky lantern	38 ft. 3 in. (11.68 m) high; 32 ft. 9 in. (10 m) wide; 30 ft. 6 in. (9.3 m) deep; 38,360.2 ft.³ (1,086.24 m³) in volume	Jhon Freddy Daza, Eyder Burbano, and Rene Muñoz (all Colombia)	January 11, 2009
★ Ten Commandments tablet	700.08 ft.² (65.04 m²)	Grace Galindez-Gupana (Philippines)	April 11, 2009
★ Trousers	40 ft. (12.19 m) long; 26 ft. (7.92 m) waist	Rishi S. Thobhani from R.S.T. International Limited (UK)	May 23, 2009

MITT: The **largest baseball mitt** measures 26 ft. (8 m) high, 32 ft. (9.7 m) wide, and 12 ft. (3.6 m) deep, and weighs 20,000 lb. (9,070 kg).

☆ **LARGEST GARDEN GNOME** A giant garden gnome measuring 17 ft. 8 in. (5.41 m) tall was made by the company PHU MALPOL (Poland) and presented in Nowa Sol, Poland, on June 2, 2009. It was built from fiberglass-covered polystyrene.

★**Trumpet** Benny J. Mamoto (Indonesia) built a playable trumpet measuring 104 ft. 11.8 in. (32 m) long with a bell of 17 ft. (5.20 m) in diameter, and 22 ft. 3.7 in. (6.8 m) in circumference. It was displayed in Tondano, North Sulawesi, Indonesia, on October 31, 2009.

MAT: Using 70,000 beer mats, Sven Goebel (Germany) built a structure measuring 9 ft. 10 in. (3 m) tall and 16 ft. 4 in. (5 m) wide in Germany on August 16, 2004.

GREENVILLE, SC, U.S.A. (34°50'N 82°23'W): The **largest group of carol singers** consisted of 7,514 participants and took place at Bob Jones University, South Carolina, U.S.A., on December 3, 2004.

LONGEST . . .

☆**Abacus** An abacus measuring 43 ft. 0.14 in. (13.11 m) was presented at an event organized by the Development & Reform Commission of Fuxin Municipal Government in Fuxin city, Liaoning Province, China, on October 25, 2009.

☆**Couch** Fancy a nice long sit down? You could do worse than choose the world's longest couch, which was measured at 2,920 ft. 9 in. (890.25 m) in Sykkylven, Norway, on June 14, 2009. The super-size sofa, which was manufactured by 20 local furniture factories, was put together and displayed across the span of the Sykkylven bridge.

★**Tablecloth** A tablecloth measuring 3,776 ft. 10.74 in. (1,151.2 m) long and 5 ft. 3 in. (1.6 m) wide was made by Green Development Ltd (Poland) and unveiled in Żyrardów, Poland, on June 13, 2009.

☆**Walk-through Horror House** The Cutting Edge Haunted House in Fort Worth Texas, U.S.A., had a walk-through measured at 2,261 ft. 0.9 in. (689.17 m) long on September 12, 2009.

☆**Wedding dress train** Watters Inc. (U.S.A.) created a wedding dress train 7,829 ft. 6 in. (2,386.44 m) long. It was measured in Round Mountain, Texas, U.S.A., on December 19, 2009.

★**Wooden chain** Markley B. Noel (U.S.A.) created a wooden chain measuring 487 ft. 6 in. (148.59 m) long in Kalamazoo, Michigan, U.S.A., on October 2, 2009.

☆**Longest balloon chain** A balloon chain measuring 2.92 miles (4.77 km) long was constructed by customers of the shopping mall Belforte (Italy). The chain, which used 42,000 balloons, was displayed and measured in Serravalle, Italy, on July 12, 2009.

★**Longest chain of Fire hoses** Verband Bernischer Gemeiden and Gebäudeversicherung Bern organized the connection of the longest chain of fire hoses, which carried water a distance of 34.8 miles (56 km) between Frutigen and Bern, Switzerland, on September 19, 2003.

☆**Largest sandal** Created in December 2003 by Nelson Jimenez Florez (Colombia), the largest sandal measures 21 ft. 7 in. (6.6 m) long, 6 ft. 6 in. (2 m) wide, and 11 ft. 5 in. (3.5 m) high and was designed on behalf of Diseos Ruddy, Bucaramanga, Colombia.

☆**Largest Handbag** A handbag created by Picard and Klar in Offenbach, Germany, measured 16 ft. 4 in. (5 m) tall, 21 ft. 3 in. (6.5 m) long, and 8 ft. 2 in. (2.5 m) deep in June 2001.

★Largest ·packaged product display A display of promotional Kleenex tissue boxes measuring 10,228.54 ft.³ (289.64 m³) was constructed by Al-Mansouriya Consumers Trading Co. and Olayan Kimberly-Clark (both Kuwait) at The Sultan Center, Kuwait, on March 7, 2010.

★Longest wooden bench A 2,011-ft.-6-in.-long (613.13-m) bench was built by a group of people from Osieczna (Poland) and unveiled in Szlachta, Poland, on August 27, 2005.

☆Largest garden spade An 11-ft.-10-in.-tall (3.61-m) spade with a 1-ft.-11-in.-wide (59.8-cm) blade was manufactured by Rollins Bulldog Tools Ltd (UK) and presented in Wigan, UK, on December 7, 2009.

☆Largest button-down shirt On June 25, 2009, Walbusch (Germany) presented a button-down shirt 214 ft. 6 in. (65.39 m) long, with a chest of 172 ft. 11 in. (52.72 m) and sleeves of 78 ft. 8 in. x 51 ft. 3 in. (23.98 m x 15.64 m). The gargantuan garment was measured at the LTU Arena, in Düsseldorf, Germany.

ALTERNATIVE ENERGIES

★Oldest alternative fuel In medieval Europe, *c.* 1500, the overuse of wood for burning led to general shortages and deforestation. Around this time, Europeans began to burn coal instead of wood, the first time in history that an alternative fuel was adopted because of shortages of conventional fuel.

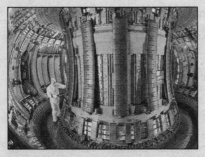

★ LARGEST TOKAMAK
With a radius of 9 ft. 8.5 in. (2.96 m) and a plasma volume of 3,500 ft.³ (100 m³), the Joint European Torus in Culham, Oxfordshire, UK, is the largest operating tokamak in the world. Tokamaks use a magnetic field to confine plasma and are used for experiments in nuclear fusion.

HAVANA, CUBA (23°08'N 82°23'W): The **trial with the largest attendance** was recorded when 51-year-old Major Jesus Sosa Blanco was tried for 108 murders on January 22–23, 1959. At one point, 17,000 people were present in the Havana Sports Palace, Cuba.

★ **LARGEST PHOTOVOLTAIC POWER PLANT** The Olmedilla Photovoltaic Park in Olmedilla, Spain, uses around 162,000 solar panels to generate a maximum of 60 megawatts on a sunny day. Completed in September 2008, it can provide enough electricity to power around 40,000 homes.

★**Largest hydroelectric wave-power device** In November 2009, Aquamarine Power (UK) launched Oyster, a 213-ton (194-tonne) device bolted to the seabed off the Orkney Islands, UK. It consists of a simple mechanical hinged flap that, at 33 ft. (10 m) below the sea's surface, oscillates with passing waves and drives hydraulic pistons that power a turbine. This demonstration model is designed to supply around 315 kilowatts of power.

Hydro power remains the **largest contributor to renewable energy**, reaching a capacity of 770 gigawatts in 2007.

★ **LARGEST SOLAR-POWERED BUILDING** In December 2009, China unveiled an office building in Dezhou, Shangdong province, that meets almost all of its energy needs with its solar-paneled roof. The building covers 807,000 ft.² (75,000 m²) and contains research facilities, display areas, and a hotel.

★ **FIRST CLEAN COAL POWER STATION** In September 2008, a new prototype power plant went online at The Schwarze Pumpe power station, Spremberg, Germany. It is the first in the world to use the CCS technique—carbon capture and storage, which means it captures the CO_2 emissions produced from burning coal, preventing them from entering the atmosphere.

★ **Highest-altitude wind generator** In December 2007, a wind generator designed to supply power to a gold mine became operational in the Veladero mine in San Juan, in the Andes mountain range, Argentina. Built by DeWind (Germany) and owned by Barrick (Canada), the hub of the generator is 13,484 ft. (4,110 m) above sea level.

On March 11, 2009, strong winds across Spain allowed the country's wind power infrastructure to generate some 11,180 megawatts, 40% of all of its national electricity requirements—the ★ **highest percentage of power generated by wind**.

★ **Most electricity produced from a kite** In 2008, scientists at Delft University of Technology, the Netherlands, successfully tested a kite-powered electricity-generating system known as Laddermill. The concept involves a kite being raised upward by the wind, with the strings of the kite attached to a generator on the ground. The test involved a single kite with an area of 107 ft.^{2} (10 m^2) that was able to generate 10 kw of electricity while in flight—enough to power approximately 10 homes. The researchers believe that in time they could generate 100 megawatts of electricity this way, enough for up to 100,000 homes.

....

CLEVELAND, OH, U.S.A. (41°29'N 81°40'W): The Cleveland Convention Center, Ohio, U.S.A., hosted the White Elephant Sale (instituted 1933)—the **largest ever jumble sale**—on October 18–19, 1983. In total it raised $427,935.21.

....

WIND: The world's first wind farm was built in 1980, and located on Crotched Mountain, New Hampshire, U.S.A. Its 20 turbines could produce 30 kilowatts each.

★LARGEST OFFSHORE WIND FARM The Horns Rev 2 offshore wind farm was officially inaugurated on September 17, 2009. Located in a shallow region of the North Sea, off the coast of Denmark, it comprises 91 turbines, each with a maximum capacity of 2.3 megawatts, giving a total of 209 megawatts at peak production.

POWER: The U.S.A. is the greatest producer of wind power, with about 2% of its electricity produced in this way. It is hoped that this figure will rise to 20% by 2030.

★ Largest source of Helium 3 Helium 3 is an isotope of helium that is a strong candidate as fuel for nuclear fusion. It is produced by the Sun and streams off into space as part of the solar wind. Helium 3 exists only as a trace on Earth but, on the Moon, with its lack of atmosphere and magnetic field, the solar Helium 3 atoms directly strike and embed themselves into the lunar soil. The isotope was discovered on the Moon by *Apollo* astronauts, and scientists estimate there could be 1.1 million tons of it spread across the lunar surface—enough to power the whole world's energy needs for thousands of years.

★ First osmotic power plant In November 2009, a prototype osmotic power plant went online on the banks of the Oslo fjord in Norway. It generates power using osmosis, which occurs naturally when two solutions of different concentrations meet each other at a semi-permeable membrane. The pressure difference generated as one liquid passes through the membrane can be converted to electricity.

In this prototype power station, the two liquids used are salt water from the sea and fresh water from runoff into the sea. The station's initial capacity is around 4 kilowatts, enough to heat a large kettle, but scientists hope that this can be increased to 25 megawatts by 2015.

★ Fastest automobile powered by biogas Jürgen Hohenester (Germany) reached a speed of 226.55 mph (364.6 km/h) in a biogas-powered automobile at the ATP testing facilities in Papenburg, Germany, on April 3, 2009. The technology was developed by TÜV Rheinland's Competence Center for Alternative Fuels.

DEFENSE TECHNOLOGY

★ First use of playstations as military training equipment The British Royal Navy is the first service organization to use Sony PlayStations for military use. Marine engineering technicians have been provided with the PlayStations to enable them to use study packages produced by the Maritime Warfare School at HMS *Collingwood*, Fareham, UK. So far, the school has bought 230 consoles, in recognition of the arrival of a generation that no longer naturally studies from books.

....

JACKSONVILLE, FL, U.S.A. (30°19'N 81°39'W): The **greatest basketball goal-shooting demonstration** was by Ted St. Martin (U.S.A.), who scored 5,221 consecutive free throws at Jacksonville, Florida, U.S.A., on April 28, 1996.

....

RECORD-BREAKING C-5M SUPER GALAXY The largest aircraft in the U.S. Air Force, the Lockheed Martin C-5M Super Galaxy, set 41 aviation records on September 13, 2009, in a flight from Dover Air Force Base, Delaware, U.S.A. Of these, 33 were new records and eight were updates of existing records. The principle flight record set was a world altitude record of 41,188 ft. (12,554 m) obtained in 23 min. 59 sec. while carrying a 176,610 lb. (80,108 kg) payload.

★**LARGEST AIRCRAFT "GRAVEYARD"** The 309th Aerospace Maintenance and Regeneration Group (aka "The Boneyard," above) is a U.S. Air Force storage facility where old planes are salvaged for parts or made ready for service again. Located on the Davis-Monthan Air Force Base in Tucson, Arizona, U.S.A., the 4-mile^2 (10.3-km^2) site accommodates around 4,000 aircraft.

DID YOU KNOW?

The L115A3 Long Range Rifle (see p. 394) is designed to achieve a first-round hit at 1,968 ft. (600 m) and harassing fire out to 3,608 ft. (1,100 m).

TRIVIA

The rifle's heavy 8.59 mm bullets are less likely to be deflected in flight.

EXTRA! for more military hardware records, turn back to pp. 220–223.

★ **LONGEST CONFIRMED SNIPER KILL** **Confirmed by GPS, Craig Harrison (UK) of the UK's Household Cavalry killed two Taliban insurgents from a distance of 1.54 miles (2.47 km) in November 2009. It took the 8.59 mm rounds almost three seconds to hit their targets, which were 3,000 ft. (914 m) beyond the recommended range of the L115A3 sniper rifle (picture above). A third shot took out the insurgent's machine gun.**

★ **Deadliest UAV** The Predator C Avenger Unmanned Aerial Vehicle is capable of 460 mph (740 km/h) at 60,000 ft. (18,288 m) for up to 20 hours. The ability to carry 3,000 lb. (1,360 kg) of weapons and its stealthy design—there are no sharp angles between surfaces in order to reduce its radar signature—make it the world's deadliest UAV to date. Its first flight was on April 4, 2009.

★ **Most advanced robotic snake for military operations** The Israeli Defense Ministry has developed a 6-ft. (1.8-m) robotic snake that can be fitted with video and audio equipment. Operated from a laptop, it is used to advance on the ground into hostile environments to collect information. It also has applications for locating survivors in disaster areas or after terrorist attacks.

★ **Smallest robotic minesweeper** Engineers at the Massachusetts Institute of Technology (MIT) in Massachusetts, U.S.A., have designed small robots, smaller than a cigarette lighter, based on the Atlantic razor clam (*Ensis directus*). The clam is one of nature's best diggers, able to burrow about 0.3 in. (1 cm) per second. Used in conjunction with seabed-penetrating sonar to locate sea mines, the robotic clam can be deposited next to the mine in order to detonate it.

EXTRA! For epic-scale engineering records, turn back to pp. 370–374.

★**Smallest flight-deck printer**
The world's smallest flight-deck printer is the ToughWriter 5, used to print in-flight text and graphics. It is 7.3 in. (185 mm) deep and weighs less than 9 lb. (4 kg).

★**Oldest serving military warship**
Built in the Netherlands, the VMF *Kommuna* is a 2,500-ton (2,267-tonne) catamaran salvage vessel that entered service in 1915 and is still serving in the Russian Navy today, employed to recover small submarines and submersibles. It is considered more cost-effective to keep the ship operational than to fund and build a replacement.

★**Largest airship** Built by Zeppelin Luftschifftechnik GmbH Germany and owned by the U.S. company Airship Ventures Inc., *Eureka* has a length of 246 ft. (75 m). Airships are used nowa-

★**FIRST USE OF QUAD BIKES IN COMBAT** A total of 200 upgraded quad bikes have been ordered for UK forces in Afghanistan. They will be used to deliver vital combat supplies and are fitted with dual stretchers to evacuate two casualties at a time, thereby speeding up emergency treatment.

days for surveillance, research, sightseeing, and advertising. Plans are under way to make a geostationary airship platform for military intelligence and reconnaissance applications.

★**MOST NUCLEAR WEAPONS** As of May 2010, Russia had 4,650 operational warheads out of a stockpile of 12,000, according to the Federation of American Scientists. Pictured at left is a Topol-M intercontinental ballistic missile, displayed in Moscow's Victory Day Parade in May 2009.

> **DOWN:** HMS *Astute* can purify water and air, and is therefore able to circumnavigate the globe without resurfacing.

★ **SUBMARINE WITH BIGGEST "EARS"** HMS *Astute* is a nuclear-powered attack submarine currently undergoing sea trials for the UK's Royal Navy. It has the biggest "ears" of any sonar system in service today. The Type 2076 sonar is reported to be able to detect ships leaving New York harbor while lying in the English Channel, 3,452 miles (5,556 km) away.

> **DOWN:** The submarine's nuclear reactor will not need to be refueled during its expected 25-year service.

★ **Longest flight by solar-powered spy plane** Between July 28 and 31, 2008, *Zephyr*, a solar-powered, high-altitude, long-endurance (HALE) unmanned aerial system (UAS), achieved a record flight of 82 hr. 37 min. *Zephyr* is launched by hand, and flies on solar power generated by amorphous silicon arrays that cover the 75-ft. (22.8-m) wings. By night, it is powered by a lithium-sulfur battery that is charged during the day. Made of carbon fiber weighing less than 100 lb. (30 kg), it is designed to carry military surveillance payloads and operate at altitudes of 60,000 ft. (18,288 m) at speeds of up to 70 mph (112 km/h).

SAVANNAH, GA, U.S.A. (32°04'N 81°05'W): The **highest speed recorded on an aquabike** (PWC) is 76.172 mph (122.79 km/h) over a measured kilometer by Forrest Smith (U.S.A.) on a modified Yamaha GP1200R at Savannah, Georgia, U.S.A., on July 5, 2002.

★ **Newest littoral combat ship** The U.S. Navy commissioned the USS *Independence* littoral ("close-to-shore") combat ship, LCS-2, into service on January 16, 2010. Although it is the second vessel in the LCS class, it is the first of a new type of ship based on a three-hulled design and built of aluminum. Manufactured by General Dynamics and Austal (U.S.A.), it can carry a crew of 75 and accommodate two MH-60S Seahawk helicopters. It is 379 ft. (115.5 m) long and has a top speed of around 44 knots (50.6 mph; 81.4 km/h).

★ **Most expensive single weapon system** The USS *Ronald Reagan*, the CVN 76 class nuclear-powered aircraft carrier, is, with its crew, armament, 85 aircraft, and other defense and communication systems, the most costly operational weapon system in the world. Its total cost was around $4.5 billion.

MEGA MOTORS

★ **Fastest 0–60 mph acceleration by a four-seater production automobile** A Nissan GT-R achieved an acceleration of 0–60 mph in 3.5 seconds while completing a lap of the Nürburgring circuit in Nürburg, Germany, on April 17, 2008.

☆ **Highest vehicle mileage** A 1966 Volvo P-1800S owned by Irvin Gordon of East Patchogue, New York, U.S.A., had covered in excess of 2,721,000 miles (4,379,033.78 km) by by August 2009. The automobile, still driven on a daily basis, covers more than 100,000 miles (160,000 km) per year, thanks in part to being driven to numerous auto shows and events in the U.S.A. and Europe.

☆ **HIGHEST AVERAGE SPEED IN A STEAM AUTOMOBILE** On August 26, 2009, Don Wales (UK) achieved a Fédération Internationale de l'Automobile (FIA)-approved average speed of 139.84 mph (225.05 km/h) over two one-kilometer runs in the *Inspiration Streamliner* at Edwards Air Force Base in California, U.S.A.

MIAMI, FL, U.S.A. (25°47'N 80°13'W): On November 8, 1996, one-hour-old Cheyenne Pyle (U.S.A.) became the **youngest ever patient to undergo a transplant** when she received a donor heart at Jackson Children's Hospital, Miami, Florida, U.S.A.

SMALLEST AND LOWEST AUTOMOBILES The ★smallest automobile is 41 in. (104.14 cm) high and 26 in. (66.04 cm) wide and was measured on May 8, 2009. The ★lowest automobile is 19 in. (48.26 cm) from the ground. Perry Watkins (UK) created both cars.

★FASTEST AMPHIBIOUS CAR With an engine based on the LS Corvette power train, the WaterCar Python is the fastest amphibious vehicle in the world. It has a top speed of 60 mph (96 km; 52 knots) on water and can perform a 0–60 mph acceleration in 4.5 seconds on land. The Python is hand-built to order, and prices start from $200,000.

HORSEPOWER

A measurement of power, originally to compare the output of steam engines against the power of draft (heavy labor) horses.

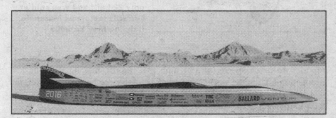

☆**FASTEST ELECTRIC CAR** The highest average speed achieved for an electric vehicle is 303.025 mph (487.672 km/h) over a two-way flying kilometer by *Buckeye Bullet 2*, designed and built by engineering students at The Ohio State University (U.S.A.) at the university's Center for Automotive Research (CAR) and driven by Roger Schroer (U.S.A.) at the Bonneville Salt Flats, Utah, U.S.A., on September 25, 2009. The hydrogen fuel cell streamliner is nicknamed "La Jamais Contente" in tribute to the first vehicle to go faster than 60 mph (100 km/h) in 1899.

☆**Most expensive car** The greatest price ever paid for a car is $17,275,000 (£12,000,000) for a 1963 Ferrari 250 GT, of which only 36 were ever made. It was sold to TV presenter Chris Evans (UK) on May 14, 2010.

★**Most expensive "veteran" automobile** The highest amount paid for a London to Brighton Run veteran (i.e., pre-1905) automobile is £3,521,500 ($7,242,916), for the oldest surviving Rolls-Royce, numbered 20154. The two-seater, 10-hp automobile was sold to an anonymous British collector in London, UK, on December 3, 2007.

PITTSBURGH, PA, U.S.A. (40°26'N 79°58'W): The **first brain cell transplant** was performed by a team of doctors from the University of Pittsburgh Medical Center, Pennsylvania, U.S.A., on June 23, 1998. The aim of the operation was to reverse the damage that had been caused to 62-year-old Alma Cerasini (U.S.A.) by a stroke.

Fastest production motorcycle The Suzuki GSX1300R Hayabusa is reported to reach speeds of 194 mph (312 km/h), making it the fastest production bike in the world. Named after a Japanese peregrine falcon, the 474-lb. (215-kg) Hayabusa is powered by a 1,298 cc (72.2 cu. in.) engine with four valves per cylinder.

Fastest caravan tow by a production automobile A Mercedes Benz S600 driven by Eugene Herbert (South Africa) reached a speed of 139.113 mph (223.881 km/h) towing a standard caravan at Hoedspruit Air Force Base, South Africa, on October 24, 2003.

Fastest production automobile The Ultimate Aero TT Super Car, made by Shelby Supercars (U.S.A.), achieved two-way timed speeds in excess of 256.14 mph (412 km/h) on Highway 221, Washington, U.S.A., on September 13, 2007. It can go from 0 to 60 mph in just 2.78 seconds.

Lightest car Louis Borsi (UK) has built and driven a 21-lb. (9.5-kg) car with a 2.5 cc engine. It is capable of 15 mph (25 km/h) at top speed.

TOP TECH

★ **Most secure mouse** The Fujitsu PalmSecure mouse may look like a regular three-button optical mouse, but it features a CIA-level security device to prevent unauthorized use: a palm-vein biometric sensor. As you place your hand over the mouse, the sensor reads the unique pattern of veins on your palm and, if there is a match, grants you access to the cursor. It retails for ¥20,500 ($220).

CHARLESTON, SC, U.S.A. (32°47'N 79°56'W): The U.S. Civil War Confederate ship H.L. *Hunley* was the **first submarine ever to sink another vessel during wartime**, when she successfully torpedoed the Union Navy's *Housatonic* off Charleston Harbor, South Carolina, U.S.A., on February 17, 1864.

★ THINNEST X10 ZOOM DIGITAL CAMERA
Casio's 12.1-megapixel Exilim EX-H10 digital camera is, at just under 1 in. (24.3 mm) thick, the slimmest digital camera with a x10 optical telephoto zoom. At just 5.78 oz. (164 g), it is also among the lightest. It can take 100 pictures a day for 10 days without needing to be charged.

★ THINNEST LCD TV LG Korea has created a fully hi-def (1,920 x 1,080 pixel) liquid-crystal display panel that is a mere 0.10 in. (2.6 mm) thick. The 42-in. (106-cm) screen uses an ultraslim LED backlighting system, and the entire unit weighs just 9 lb. 4 oz. (4.2 kg).

EXTRA! experience the cutting-edge of science on pp. 404–408.

★ MOST EXPENSIVE TELEVISION The PrestigeHD Supreme Rose TV, made from 61 lb. (28 kg) of 18-carat rose gold inset with 72 brilliant 1-carat flawless diamonds, costs $2,250,000.

★ Lightest touchscreen cell phone The modu-t (right), which weighs a mere 1.94 oz. (55.1 g), is manufactured by modu Ltd (Israel) and was launched at the Mobile World Congress in Barcelona, Spain, on February 15, 2010. The phone is 1.83 x 2.95 x 0.43 in. (46.5 x 75 x 11 mm) in size.

★ Smallest mp3 player No bigger than a couple of sugar cubes, the Micro Sport MP3 player (right) boasts a 4-GB memory, full stereo sound through its two earbuds, and a rechargeable battery.

★ Most powerful vacuum cleaner The handheld Dyson DC31 vacuum cleaner is powered by a digital motor that spins at 104,000 rpm. That's five times faster than the engine of a Formula One racing car, and ten times faster than a standard commercial airliner!

☆ Fastest sms Sonja Kristiansen (Norway) wrote a 160-character text message in 37.28 seconds at Oslo City Shopping Center in Oslo, Norway, on November 14, 2009.

★ Best-selling iPad app At the time of going to press (April 2010), Apple had just launched their much-anticipated iPad. This tablet computer sold at least 300,000 units on its first day (although some early estimates place this figure as high as 700,000), with 1 million apps downloaded.

To date, the biggest-selling paid-for app is Pages, which is a word-processing program.

The most downloaded free app for the iPad as of April 2010 is iBooks—an ebook reader and shopfront with which the user can browse for (and download) tens of thousands of books, many of them free.

Be sure to look out for **Guinness World Records: At Your Fingertips**, *a free iPad lite app that showcases record-breaking achievements.*

★ MOST COMPACT ELECTRIC BIKE Weighing in at 22 lb. (10 kg), and folding down to just 6 x 23.5 x 23.5 in. (15 x 60 x 60 cm)—smaller than most folding bicycles—the YikeBike is the most compact folding electric bicycle on the market. The "mini-farthing" design is based on the "penny farthing" bicycle of *c.*1870.

★ FIRST 3D CAMCORDER On January 7, 2010, Panasonic unveiled the world's first professional-use 3D camcorder, equipped with double lenses that can record high-definition movies on an SD memory card. The twin-lens camera was demonstrated during a press preview at the company's plant in Amagasaki city in Hyogo prefecture, western Japan. The retail price? $21,000.

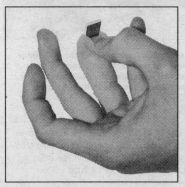

FIRST USB PROSTHETIC In May 2008, Finnish computer programmer Jerry Jalava lost part of a finger in a motor-cycle accident. Instead of a regular fingertip prosthetic, Jalava had a 2-GB USB memory stick made, allowing him to carry data around with him constantly.

CUTTING-EDGE SCIENCE

★**Highest laser energy shone onto a single target** In June 2009, scientists at the National Ignition Facility at Lawrence Livermore National Laboratory in California, U.S.A., began operating the array of 192 powerful lasers designed to research nuclear fusion. The lasers are focused on a fingernail-sized container known as a hohlraum that will eventually contain a pellet of hydrogen fuel for fusion experiments. On January 27, 2010, researchers fired the laser array for a few billionths of a second and delivered one megajoule of energy onto the target. This is equivalent to the explosion caused by 0.44 lb. (0.2 kg) of TNT.

★**Deepest underground lab** SNOLAB, 1.2 miles (2 km) below ground in Sudbury, Ontario, Canada, is best known for housing the Sudbury Neutrino Observatory. The observatory was created to study neutrinos—weakly interacting particles—using the rock above it to filter out cosmic radiation. This ensured that only neutrinos, which easily penetrate matter, were observed.

☆**FASTEST COMPUTER** The Jaguar supercomputer at the Oak Ridge National Laboratory in Oak Ridge, Tennessee, U.S.A., became the world's fastest in November 2009 after an upgrade. Built by Cray Inc. (U.S.A.), it is capable of 1.759 petaflops (quadrillion floating point operations per second).

PANAMA CITY, PANAMA (8°59'N 79°31'W): The **longest ever journey on an aquabike** is 10,729 miles (17,266.69 km), by Adriaan Marais and Marinus du Plessis (both South Africa), who arrived in Panama City, Panama, after 95 days of navigation, on September 19, 2006.

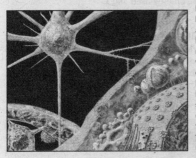

★ FIRST EVIDENCE OF EVOLUTION WITHOUT DNA In January 2010, scientists at the Scripps Research Institute, California, U.S.A., reported that they had witnessed evidence of evolution occurring in the lifeless, DNA-less proteins known as prions (artwork shown at left). They exhibited signs of adapting to new environments and following the rules of natural selection. Prions are associated with 20 different diseases of the brain in humans and animals.

★ SHORTEST WAVELENGTH LASER The Linac Coherent Light Source (LCLS) at the SLAC National Accelerator Laboratory, Stanford, California, U.S.A., is an X-ray laser capable of producing X-ray laser radiation at a wavelength of just 0.15 nanometers. Visible light that the human eye can see ranges from around 390 to 750 nanometers.

TORONTO, ON, CANADA (43°39'N 79°23'W): The **tallest free-standing tower** (as opposed to a guyed mast) in the world is the $63-million CN Tower in Toronto, Canada, which rises to 1,815 ft. 5 in. (553.34 m). Excavation began on February 12, 1973, and the tower topped out on April 2, 1975.

EXTRA! Prefer science fiction to science fact? Turn to pp. 316–319.

☆ **Largest known prime number** On August 23, 2008, the latest giant number discovered by the Great Internet Mersenne Prime Search project was announced. It is a Mersenne prime, which means it can be written as 2^n-1, where "n" is a power; $2^{43112609}-1$ contains some 12,978,189 digits. As a prime number, it can be divided only by itself and 1.

☆ **Highest energy operational accelerator** On March 19, 2010, scientists at the Large Hadron Collider in Geneva, Switzerland, announced that they had used the particle accelerator to produce two beams of protons with energies of 3.5 tera electron volts. (One electron volt equals the kinetic energy gained by an electron when it is accelerated by one volt. "Tera" means "trillion.")

☆ **Slowest light** In January 2010, a team of U.S. scientists reported that they had "frozen" light to a standstill for 1.5 seconds using a form of supercold matter known as a Bose-Einstein condensate.

★ MOST WATER-REPELLENT MANMADE MATERIAL In February 2010, scientists at the University of Florida, U.S.A., announced that they had created an almost perfect water-repellent, or hydrophobic, surface. They used sheets of polypropylene and a mold to create tiny irregular "hairs" on the surface of the sheets, which resemble the microscopic structure of hairs on some water-walking arthropods.

HUNTINGDON, WV, U.S.A. (40°30'N 78°01'W): The longest interval between birth of twins is held by Peggy Lynn (U.S.A.), of Huntingdon, West Virginia, U.S.A., who gave birth to a baby girl, Hanna, on November 11, 1995. She did not deliver the other twin, Eric, until February 2, 1996, 84 days later, at the Geisinger Medical Center, Danville, Pennsylvania, U.S.A.

☆ **HEAVIEST ELEMENT** Copernicium, with an atomic number of 112, is the heaviest element officially recognized to date. It was first created on February 9, 1996, at the Gesellschaft für Schwerionenforschung (GSI, left) in Darmstadt, Germany, and officially named copernicium on February 19, 2010.

☆ **Highest manmade temperature** In February 2010, scientists at Brookhaven National Laboratory's Relativistic Heavy Ion Collider on Long Island, New York, U.S.A., announced that they had smashed together gold ions at nearly the speed of light, briefly forming an exotic state of matter known as a quark-gluon plasma. This substance is believed to have filled the universe just a few microseconds after the Big Bang. During the experiment the plasma reached temperatures of around 4 trillion°C, some 250,000 times hotter than the center of the Sun.

Lowest manmade temperature A team of scientists at the Massachusetts Institute of Technology (MIT), Cambridge, Massachusetts, U.S.A., led by Professor Aaron E. Leanhardt, managed to produce a temperature of 450 picokelvin above absolute zero by cooling down a Bose-Einstein condensate. Details of their research first appeared in *Science* magazine on September 12, 2003.

★ FIRST VIRUS-POWERED BATTERY In April 2009, scientists at MIT in Massachusetts, U.S.A., announced that they had used genetically engineered viruses to build the positive and negative ends of a lithium ion battery. In tests, the new battery technology can be charged up more than 100 times before deteriorating.

★ First homogeneous self-righting shape The Gömböc is a mathematical shape first theorized in 1996 and proven in 2006 by Hungarian scientists Péter Várkonyi and Gábor Domokos. It is a three-dimensional shape that is mono-monostatic, convex, and homogeneous, i.e., with equal density throughout. It is characterized by its properties of balance in that it has two equilibria, one stable and one unstable.

INTERNET

☆ Oldest .com Symbolics.com was registered by computer manufacturer Symbolics Inc. (U.S.A.) on March 15, 1985, making it the world's oldest .com url. Symbolics.com is still registered and active today, and was bought by XF.com in 2009.

★ First tweet Twitter was invented by Jack Dorsey (U.S.A.) in 2006. Users can post messages ("tweets") of up to 140 characters, which are sent to their subscribers. The first tweet was posted by Dorsey at 9:50 p.m. PST on March 21, 2006, and read "just setting up my twittr."

★ Largest botnet In December 2009, an operation by Spanish police and the FBI closed down a network of more than 13 million PCs that had been infected with viruses. This so-called "Mariposa botnet" was designed to steal credit card data, passwords, and account information. It had infected machines in 190 countries, spreading via USB sticks, spammed links, and a vulnerability in Internet Explorer.

....

ROCHESTER, NY, U.S.A. (43°09'N 77°41'W): On October 16, 1976, Kathy Wafler (U.S.A.) peeled an apple in 11 hr. 30 min., resulting in a peel length of 172 ft. 4 in. (52.51 m)—the **longest unbroken apple peel**, at Long Ridge Mall, Rochester, New York, U.S.A.

....

MEME: An idea that possesses some quality that makes people want to share it with each other—such as a joke, or a YouTube video. On the internet, memes are said to grow and be transmitted "virally."

☆**GREATEST MEMES** According to MSNBC, the top Internet meme (above left) of 2009 was Kanye West's antics during the MTV Video Music Awards in New York City, U.S.A., on September 13, when he grabbed the mic from award-winner Taylor Swift and announced that Beyoncé should have won. West's outburst led to the "Ima let you finish" meme. In second place was the "Crasher Squirrel," in which Melissa Brandts and her husband, Jackson, were taking a photo of themselves using a timer. During the shot, a squirrel popped up in front of the camera.

★**FIRST TWEET FROM SPACE** On October 21, 2009, U.S. astronauts Nicola Scott and Jeff Williams took part in a live "tweetup" from the International Space Station with around 35 members of the public at NASA Headquarters, Washington, D.C., U.S.A.

WIKIPEDIA
The Free Encyclopedia

★ **Fastest-selling top-level domain** The .me domain is the Internet country code for Montenegro, located in southeastern Europe, which first became an independent state in June 2006. Registration for .me domains was made available on July 16, 2008. By January 2010, more than 320,000 .me domains had been sold, making it the fastest-selling top-level domain in the history of the Internet. The suffix is popular due to its attractiveness for social networking websites.

☆ **Largest Internet exchange** Of the exchanges that make their data public, the largest by traffic is the Deutscher Commercial Internet Exchange in Frankfurt, Germany. As of March 2010, it had a maximum throughput of 1,994 gigabits/sec. (The term "throughput" refers to the amount of work processed in a given time.)

☆ **Most Internet users (country)** According to www.internetworld stats.com, China had approximately 360,000,000 Internet users by September 2009, 26.9% of its population.

★ **Most viewed online video ad** As of August 19, 2009, the advertisement for Evian Roller Babies had been watched 25,687,416 times via online video sites.

★ **FIRST FLASHMOB** "Flashmobs" are sudden gatherings of people in a public place at a set time to engage in a brief and usually pointless activity. The first notable flashmob, organized by Bill Wasik (U.S.A.), occurred in May 2003 in New York City, U.S.A., though police had received a tip-off. The second attempt, also by Wasik, was more successful: on June 3, 2003, nearly 100 people gathered around a $10,000 rug at Macy's department store in New York City (left).

★ **LARGEST AUDIENCE FOR AN INTERNET CONCERT** On October 25, 2009, U2's set at the Rose Bowl, Pasadena, U.S.A., was streamed live on YouTube. It was watched over the Web by nearly 10 million people.

AWARD: U2 (Ireland) have won a record 22 Grammys, the **most for any group**. They have also won seven BRIT awards, more than any other group.

NASSAU, THE BAHAMAS (25°03'N 77°20'W): Sir Etienne Dupuch of Nassau, Bahamas, was editor-in-chief of *The Tribune* from 1919 to 1972 and contributing editor until his death on August 23, 1991, a total of 72 years. His is the **longest editorship** on record.

☆ **MOST SONGS DOWNLOADED FROM ONE COMPANY** On February 25, 2010, the 10 billionth song was downloaded from iTunes, Apple's online music store: "Guess Things Happen That Way," a 1958 hit by Johnny Cash. To mark the event, the lucky downloader, Louie Sulcer (U.S.A.), received a $10,000 iTunes gift card from Apple.

★ **Largest online quiz** Five hundred employees of DKV Seguros, Spain, took part in an online quiz in Saragoza, Spain, on September 9, 2009.

☆ **Longest LAN party** On April 11–12, 2009, a nonstop local area network (LAN) party lasting 40 hours was completed by 274 gamers during Cyber Fusion 2009 at the Multimedia University in Cyberjaya, Malaysia.

TOP 10 MOST VIEWED (2009)

	ARTIST, SONG TITLE/FILM	FORMAT	VIEWS
1	Soulja Boy Tellem: "Crank Dat (Soulja Boy)"	Music Video	722,438,268
2	*Twilight Saga: New Moon* (preview)	Film	639,966,996
3	Beyoncé: "Single Ladies (Put a Ring on It)"	Music Video	522,039,429
4	Michael Jackson: "Thriller"	Music Video	443,535,722
5	"The Gummy Bear Song"	Music Video	394,327,606
6	Lady Gaga: "Poker Face"	Music Video	374,606,128
7	Lady Gaga: "Bad Romance"	Music Video	360,020,327
8	Timbaland: "Apologize" (feat. OneRepublic)	Music Video	355,404,824
9	Susan Boyle: *Britain's Got Talent*	TV	347,670,927
10	*Twilight* (preview)	Film	343,969,063

Source: Visible Measures Internet Research Company

SPORTS

CONTENTS

ACTION SPORTS

☆ **MOST GRAND SLAM TITLES** When Roger Federer (Switzerland, pictured) clinched his fourth Australian Open title by defeating Andy Murray (UK) 6–3 6–4 7–6 (13–11) on January 31, 2010, he recorded his 16th Grand Slam singles title, **the greatest number of Grand Slam singles tennis titles won by a man.** Federer's first Grand Slam win had come at Wimbledon: he triumphed over Mark Philippoussis (Australia) at the London, UK, tournament on July 6, 2003.

As well as six Wimbledon grass court Slam victories, Federer has won four Australian Open titles, five U.S. Open titles and, in 2009, won his first French Open title, beating Robin Söderling (Sweden) in the final.

EXTRA! For more fabulous feats and daring deeds, don't forget stunts on pp. 133–170.

AQUABIKE

- On October 11, 1996, Cory A. Wimpheimer (U.S.A.) recorded a time of 17.76 seconds to complete an International Jet Sports Boating Association (IJSBA) Pro Runabout 785 slalom course on Lake Havasu, Arizona, U.S.A. This represents the ☆**fastest time** in which this course has been completed.
- The ★**most wins of the IJSBA Pro Runabout 1200 World Championships** is five by Chris MacClugage (U.S.A.) who claimed titles in 1999, 2001–02, 2004, and 2005.
- Based in Monaco, the Union Internationale Motonautique (UIM) is the governing body for the sports of powerboating and aquabiking. Gimmi Bosio (Italy) holds the record for the ★**most wins of the UIM Aquabike Pro Runabout 1200 World Championship**, with two titles, in 2001–02. The ★**most wins of the UIM Pro Ski World Championship** is also two, with Kevin Laigle (France) claiming the top spot in 2002 and 2004.

PARAGLIDING

- Nicole Fedele (Italy) paraglided 102.2 miles (164.6 km) from Sorica, Slovenia, to Piombada, Italy, and back on August 19, 2009, to secure the record for the ★**farthest paragliding out-and-return distance (female)**.
- The record for the ★**farthest paragliding out-and-return distance (male)** is held by Aljaz Valic, who flew 161.3 miles (259.7 km), departing from and returning to Soriska Planina, in his Slovenian homeland, on July 20, 2006.

ON A WING AND A PRAYER With an impressive six titles to his name between 1985 and 1999, Jerzy Makula (Poland) has the ★**most wins of the World Glider Aerobatic Championships**, a competition organized by the Gliding Commission of the Fédération Aéronautique Internationale (FAI).

....

WASHINGTON, D.C., U.S.A. (38°53'N 77°02'W): The Library of Congress in Washington, D.C., U.S.A., is the **largest library** in the world. Its shelves contain more than 128 million items, including approximately 29 million books, 2.7 million recordings, 12 million photographs, 4 million maps, and 57 million manuscripts.

....

☆ **FARTHEST DYNO WALL CLIMB** Dynamic ("dyno") moves involve climbers flinging themselves from one handhold to the next. Nicky de Leeuw (Netherlands) achieved a distance of 9 ft. 2 in. (2.80 m) in Eindhoven, the Netherlands, on June 14, 2009. The ☆ **farthest distance achieved by a woman in Dyno climbing** is 6 ft. 5 in. (1.98 m) by Anne-Laure Chevrier (France) on the set of *Lo Show dei Record* in Milan, Italy, on April 17, 2009.

• The team of Toby Colombe and Cefn Hoile (both UK) achieved a distance of 104 miles (167.3 km) in setting the record for the ★ **farthest paragliding out-and-return distance by a team** when gliding from Sorica in Slovenia and back on July 26, 2009.

• The ☆ **farthest flight by a paraglider (male)** was made by Nevil Hulett (South Africa) who paraglided a distance of 312.5 miles (502.9 km) from Copperton, South Africa, on December 14, 2008.

BUNGEE

• The ★ **highest bungee dive into water** was recorded by action sports enthusiast Zhang Di (China), who performed a dive into water from a height of 164 ft. (50 m) in Quindao City, Shandong Province, China, on November 15, 2006.

• The **highest bungee jump from a building** is 652 ft. 10 in. (199 m) by A. J. Hackett (New Zealand), who leaped off a platform at 764 ft. 5 in. (233 m) on the Macau Tower, Macau, China, on December 17, 2006. This meant that Hackett came within 111 ft. 6 in. (34 m) of the ground at the lowest point of his jump.

AWESOME AQUA-BATICS! Lee Stone (UK, left) and Alessander Lenzi (Brazil) share the honor of the ★ **most wins of the Union Internationale Motonautique (UIM) Aquabike Pro Freestyle Class World Championship**, with three wins apiece. Lenzi won the title from 2003 to 2005, and Stone took the top spot from 2006 to 2008.

LIMA, PERU (12°02'S 77°01'W): The **longest harp marathon** by an individual lasted for 24 hr. 30 min. and was achieved by Laurita Pacheco (Peru) at the Bolivar Hotel, Lima, Peru, on May 20–21, 2004.

AIR: Ian Metcher (Australia) was 85 years old when he won an aerobatics title in 2001, making him the **oldest competitive aerobatic pilot**.

★ **MOST SURFERS ON A WAVE** A total of 110 surfers rode a single wave at the Earthwave Beach Festival, Muizenberg Beach, Cape Town, South Africa, on October 4, 2009, at an event to raise awareness of climate change.

WAKEBOARDING

• The ★ **longest wakeboarding ramp jump (male)** is a 49-ft.-2-in. (15-m) attempt by Jérôme Macquart (France), which was filmed as part of *L'Été De Tous Les Records*, in Argelès-Gazost, France, on July 14, 2004.

• In wakeboarding, the term "superman" describes the situation when boarders are completely lifted off the surface of the water, higher than head height, and assume a stretched pose (with the wakeboard attached to their feet). Jérôme Macquart performed an unprecedented five "supermans" in 30 seconds at Biscarrosse, France, on July 14, 2005. This feat represents the ★ **most wakeboarding "supermans" in 30 seconds**.

• Aged 63 years 227 days when she competed in the Battle of Bull Run Wakeboard Tournament at Smith Mountain Lake, Virginia, U.S.A., on July 25, 2009, Linda Brown (U.S.A., b. December 10, 1945) is the ★ **oldest competitive wakeboarder**.

WATER: Nuno Gomes (South Africa) performed a record 1,044-ft.-deep (318.25-m) scuba dive in the Red Sea off Dahab, Egypt, on June 10, 2005.

KINGSTON, JAMAICA (17°59'N 76°48'W): The **highest maiden Test century** is 365 not out by Sir Garfield St. Aubrun Sobers (Barbados) for the West Indies against Pakistan at Kingston, Jamaica, on February 27–28, and March 1, 1958.

★ **MOST KITE SURFING CHAMPIONSHIPS (FEMALE)** When it comes to kite surfing, few can compare to Kristin Boese (Germany, left). Between 2005 and 2008, she won nine kite surfing world championship titles!

AEROBATICS

• Daredevil pilot Joann Osterud (Canada) flew upside down for 4 hr. 38 min. 10 sec. on a flight from Vancouver to Vanderhoof, Canada, on July 24, 1991, to record the **longest inverted flight (aerobatics)**.

• Svetlana Kapanina (Russia) has recorded the ☆ **most wins of the women's Aerobatics World Championships**, having won the women's overall competition an unprecedented six times, in 1996, 1998, 2001, 2003, 2005, and 2007.

• No single male pilot has dominated the World Championships in quite the way that Svetlana Kapanina has in the women's event. The ☆ **most wins of the men's Aerobatics World Championships** is two, achieved by two pilots, Petr Jirmus (Czechoslovakia) in 1984 and 1986, and Sergei Rakhmanin (Russia) in 2003 and 2005.

OTTAWA, ON, CANADA (12°02'S 77°01'W): The **largest naturally frozen ice rink** is the Rideau Canal Skateway in Ottawa, Canada. It is 4.8 miles (7.8 km) long and has a total maintained surface area of 1.782 million ft.² (165,621 m²).

★ **LONGEST MOUNTAINBOARD RACE** With a course that stretches 6.95 miles (11.18 km) down Palomar Mountain, San Diego County, California, U.S.A., the annual Nate Harrison Grade Race is a true mountainboard endurance test. Four victories over the event's six-year history make Kris Kidwell (U.S.A.) the king of the mountain.

KITE SURFING

• The ☆**longest journey kite surfing (male)** is 178.50 nautical miles (205.41 miles; 330.58 km) by Steen Carstens (Denmark), who traveled from Sprogo, Denmark, to Lysekil, Sweden, on August 17, 2009. The **longest continuous kite surfing journey (female)** was 115.4 nautical miles (132.80 miles; 213.72 km) by Andreya Wharry (UK) between Watergate Bay, UK, and Dungarven, Ireland, on September 7, 2005.

• The **youngest kite surfing world champion (female)** is Gisela Pulido (Spain, b. January 14, 1994) who won her first Kiteboard Pro World Tour (KPWT) world title on November 4, 2004, aged 10 years 294 days.

AMERICAN FOOTBALL

★ **Most kickoff returns for touchdowns in an NFL game** There have been seven occasions on which an NFL player has scored two touchdowns from a kickoff return: Timmy Brown for Philadelphia Eagles against Dallas Cowboys on November 6, 1966; Travis Williams for Green Bay Packers against Cleveland Browns on November 12, 1967; Ron Brown for L.A. Rams against Green Bay Packers on November 24, 1985; Tyrone Hughes for New Orleans Saints against LA Rams on October 23, 1994; Chad Morton for New York Jets against Buffalo Bills on September 8, 2002; Devin Hester for Chicago Bears against St. Louis Rams on December 11, 2006; Andre Davis for Houston Texans against Jacksonville Jaguars on December 30, 2007; and Ted Ginn Jr. for Miami Dolphins against New York Jets (all teams and players U.S.A.) on November 1, 2009.

★ **Most catches in an NFL game** Brandon Marshall (U.S.A.) made a record 21 catches in a single NFL game, playing as wide receiver for the Denver Broncos against the Indianapolis Colts (both U.S.A.) in Indianapolis, Indiana, U.S.A., on December 13, 2009. Marshall totaled 200 yards across his 21 receptions, two of which were for touchdowns.

★ **OLDEST SUPER BOWL PLAYER** Aged 42 years 11 days, placekicker Matt Stover (U.S.A.) became the oldest player in Super Bowl history when he made an appearance for the Indianapolis Colts (U.S.A.) in Super Bowl XLIV on February 7, 2010. The game, which was played at the Sun Life Stadium, Miami Gardens, Florida, U.S.A., saw the Colts lose to the New Orleans Saints (U.S.A.) 31–17.

★ **Most combined yards from scrimmage in an NFL season** Chris Johnson (U.S.A.) recorded 2,509 combined yards from scrimmage playing for the Tennessee Titans (U.S.A.) from September 10, 2009, to January 3, 2010.

★ **Highest completion percentage in an NFL game** Kurt Warner (U.S.A.) recorded a completion percentage of 92.3% playing as quarterback for the Arizona Cardinals (U.S.A.) in a 31–17 win over the Jacksonville Jaguars (U.S.A.) on September 20, 2009.

☆ **Most pass completions in an NFL career** Brett Favre (U.S.A.) has made 6,083 pass completions in his career playing for the Atlanta Falcons, Green Bay Packers, New York Jets, and Minnesota Vikings (all U.S.A.) between 1992 and 2009, the most pass completions in an NFL career by a quarterback.

Favre's career has also seen him record the ★ **most postseason passing yards in an NFL career**, with 5,855 yards. He broke the record with 310 passing yards on January 24, 2010, while quarterbacking the Minnesota Vikings in a 31–28 loss to the New Orleans Saints (both U.S.A.) in the NFC Championship Game.

....

PHILADELPHIA, PA, U.S.A. (39°57'N 75°10'W): The United States mint facility located in Philadelphia, Pennsylvania, U.S.A., is the **largest mint in the world**. Constructed during the period 1965–69 on Independence Mall, the Philadelphia Mint covers 11.5 acres (4.7 ha).

....

EXTRA! Flip forward to p. 438 for all the latest baseball records.

★ **HIGHEST PUNTING AVERAGE (CAREER)** Shane Lechler (U.S.A.) has played for the Oakland Raiders (U.S.A.) in the NFL since the 2000 season, in which time he has attained the highest career punting average of 47.3 yards per game.

★ **Most touchdown passes in one quarter of a game** Tom Brady (U.S.A.) made the most touchdown passes in one quarter of an NFL game when he threw for five touchdowns playing for the New England Patriots against the Tennessee Titans (both U.S.A.) at Gillette Stadium, Foxborough, Massachusetts, U.S.A., on October 18, 2009. Brady also holds the record for the **most touchdown passes in a season**, with 50 touchdown passes thrown during the 2007 season.

DID YOU KNOW?

Peter Baroody (U.S.A.) watched a complete National Football League (NFL) match at all 31 NFL stadiums in the U.S.A. in just 107 days, from September 5 to December 22, 2002.

TRIVIA

Neil Rackers (U.S.A.) scored a record 40 field goals playing for the Arizona Cardinals in the 2005 NFL season.

JERSEY CITY, NJ, U.S.A. (41°26'N 74°08'W): Dorothy Allison, from Jersey City, New Jersey, U.S.A., assisted police in more than 5,000 cases as a law enforcement psychic, a figure that represents the **most crime cases worked on by a psychic.**

MOST KICKOFF RETURNS FOR TOUCHDOWNS (CAREER) Wide receiver/return specialist Joshua Cribbs (U.S.A.) has made eight returns for touchdowns in his NFL career playing for the Cleveland Browns (U.S.A.) since 2005.

★**Most touchdowns by a tight end in an NFL season** Vernon Davis (U.S.A.) scored 13 touchdowns playing for the San Francisco 49ers (U.S.A.) as tight end in the 2009 season, matching the 2004 record set by Antonio Gates (U.S.A.) of the San Diego Chargers (U.S.A.).

Most points scored by an individual in a single game Ernie Nevers (U.S.A.) scored 40 points for the Chicago Cardinals vs. the Chicago Bears (both U.S.A.) on November 28, 1929. Nevers scored six touchdowns and kicked four extra points in a game that the Cardinals won 40–6. The next highest individual total is 36 points.

A DECADE OF SUCCESS Peyton Manning (U.S.A.) was one of the standout American sportsmen of the Noughties, a decade in which he racked up a host of world records. Playing for the Indianapolis Colts (U.S.A.) from 2000 to 2009, Manning achieved the ★ **most passing touchdowns in a decade**, with 314, and also the ★ **most passing yards in a decade**, with 42,254. In that period, Manning also achieved the ★ **most wins of the NFL Most Valuable Player award**, with four wins, in 2003, 2004, 2008, and 2009.

★ **HIGHEST COMPLETION PERCENTAGE (SEASON)** Quarterback Drew Brees (U.S.A.) registered a 70.62% completion percentage playing for the New Orleans Saints (U.S.A.) in the 2009 season, an NFL record.

★ **First person to return an opening kickoff for a touchdown in the Super Bowl** Playing for the Chicago Bears against the Indianapolis Colts (both U.S.A.) in Super Bowl XLI, Devin Hester (U.S.A.) became the first player in Super Bowl history to return the opening kickoff for a touchdown, at Dolphin Stadium in Miami Gardens, Florida, U.S.A., on February 4, 2007. Despite posting the best start in the history of the Super Bowl, the Bears went on to lose the game 29–17.

Hester also jointly holds the record for the ★ **longest play in NFL history**, which he set when he returned a missed field goal 108 yards for a touchdown playing for the Chicago Bears against the New York Giants (both U.S.A.) on November 12, 2006. The score equaled the feat of Hester's Chicago Bears teammate Nathan Vasher (U.S.A.), who returned a missed field goal 108 yards for a touchdown against the San Francisco 49ers (U.S.A.) at Soldier Field, Chicago, Illinois, U.S.A., on November 13, 2005.

★ **MOST REGULAR SEASON WINS** The Chicago Bears (U.S.A.) have won 693 regular season games, the most by a team in NFL history, since competing in the inaugural NFL season in 1920.

NEW YORK CITY, NY, U.S.A. (40°43'N 74°00'W): The **underground system with the most stations** is the New York City subway, with 468 stations (277 of which are underground) in a network that covers 230 miles (370 km). It serves an estimated 4.5 million passengers per day.

COLTS CLASSICS The Indianapolis Colts (U.S.A.) recorded 23 consecutive wins from November 2, 2008, to December 17, 2009, the ☆most consecutive wins in NFL history. The winning streak came at the end of a successful 10-year period for the Colts, whose 115 wins from 2000 to 2009 stand as the ☆most NFL game wins in a single decade.

★First NFL team to score touchdowns on interception, kickoff, and punt returns in the same game The Minnesota Vikings (U.S.A.) became the first NFL team in history to score touchdowns on interception, kickoff, and punt returns in the same game, against the New York Giants (U.S.A.), in Giants Stadium, New York, U.S.A., on November 13, 2005.

Highest Super Bowl attendance A crowd of 103,985 saw Super Bowl XIV between the Pittsburgh Steelers and the L.A. Rams (both U.S.A.) at the Rose Bowl, Pasadena, California, U.S.A., on January 20, 1980.

☆LARGEST NFL ATTENDANCE An unprecedented crowd of 105,121 spectators watched the Dallas Cowboys play the New York Giants (both U.S.A.) at the Cowboys Stadium in Arlington, Texas, U.S.A., on September 20, 2009. The game, which marked the opening of the stadium, saw the Giants win 33–31.

TROY, NY, U.S.A. (42°43'N 73°41'W): The darkest manmade substance is a low-density carbon nanotube array created by Rensselaer Polytechnic Institute and Rice University (both U.S.A.). The substance demonstrated reflectance of 0.045%.

Sports Illustrated

THE BUCCANEERS COME ABOARD

Tampa Bay's Steve Spurrier

WORST START BY AN NFL FRANCHISE In 1976, the Tampa Bay Buccaneers (U.S.A.) marked their first year in the NFL by losing their first 26 regular games, over two seasons. The streak was ended by a 33–14 win over the New Orleans Saints (U.S.A.) on December 11, 1977.

First undefeated regular season

The New England Patriots (U.S.A.) scored a 16–0 record in 2007, becoming the first NFL team to achieve an undefeated regular season since the league went to a 16-game schedule in 1978.

Highest regular season score The Washington Redskins (U.S.A.) scored 72 points against the New York Giants' (U.S.A.) 41 at Washington, U.S.A., on November 27, 1966. The aggregate score of 113 is also a record.

★Most consecutive NFL game wins to start a career (head coach) Jim Caldwell (U.S.A.) started his career as head coach with the Indianapolis Colts (U.S.A., see also p. 426) with 14 consecutive wins from September 13, 2009, to December 17, 2009, the best start to a coaching career in NFL history.

Highest aggregate score in a Super Bowl When the San Francisco 49ers beat the San Diego Chargers (both U.S.A.) 49–26 in Super Bowl XXIX, they posted the highest aggregate score of any Super Bowl. The game, which was played on January 29, 1995, at Joe Robbie Stadium in Miami, Florida, saw the 49ers become the first team to win five Super Bowls. It was also the first Super Bowl between two teams from the same state.

Highest score in a non-NFL game Georgia Tech from Atlanta, Georgia, U.S.A., scored 222 points, including a record 32 touchdowns, against Cumberland University, Lebanon, Tennessee, U.S.A., on October 7, 1916. Georgia Tech is one of the most successful college football teams.

Most consecutive postseason victories by an NFL team The New England Patriots (U.S.A.) won 10 consecutive NFL postseason games from 2001 to 2006. During this time, they captured three Super Bowls in four seasons.

☆Highest postseason winning percentage by an NFL head coach NFL coaching legend Vince Lombardi (U.S.A.) registered a postseason mark of nine wins and one loss as coach of the Green Bay Packers (1961–67)—a .900 win percentage.

★ **HIGHEST-SCORING POSTSEASON NFL GAME On January 10, 2010, a playoff game between the Arizona Cardinals and the Green Bay Packers (both U.S.A.) ended in a 51–45 victory to the Cardinals. The 96-point total is an NFL postseason record.**

Largest comeback in a championship game On January 21, 2007, the Indianapolis Colts (U.S.A.) overcame a 21–3 deficit and won the American Football Conference championship game over the New England Patriots (U.S.A.) 38–34, pulling off the biggest comeback in conference championship game history.

★ **Most points scored in an NFL regular season by a team** In 2007, the New England Patriots (U.S.A.) scored 589 points, topping the 556 points by the Minnesota Vikings (U.S.A.) in 1998.

In that same season, the Patriots scored the **most touchdowns by a team in an NFL season** with 75, surpassing the previous high of 70 by the Miami Dolphins (U.S.A.) in 1984.

First NFL regular season game played in Europe On October 28, 2007, the New York Giants beat the Miami Dolphins (both U.S.A.) 13–10 at Wembley Stadium in London, UK, in the first NFL regular season game to be played in Europe.

AUTOSPORTS

CARS

Dakar rally The ★ **most consecutive Dakar rallies completed** is 20, by Yoshimasa Sugawara (Japan), from 1983 to 2009.

He also holds a record for the ★ **most consecutive Dakar rallies raced**, having entered 26 competitions during the same time period.

☆ **Most F1 fastest laps in a career** The greatest number of fastest laps achieved by one driver in a Formula One career is 76 by Michael Schumacher (Germany) between August 25, 1991, and October 22, 2006.

The ☆ **most fastest laps by one driver in a Formula One season** is 10, by Michael Schumacher in 2004 and Kimi Raikkonen (Finland) in 2005 and 2008.

Most F1 pole positions The prolific Michael Schumacher also holds the record for the ☆ **most Formula One pole positions**: 68, achieved while he was driving for the Benetton and Ferrari teams between 1991 and 2006.

The ☆ **most consecutive Formula One pole positions** is eight, by Ayrton Senna (Brazil) for McLaren between the 1988 Spanish Grand Prix and the 1989 U.S.A. Grand Prix.

☆ **MOST FORMULA ONE GRANDS PRIX** The greatest number of Formula One (F1) Grand Prix wins by a driver is 91, by Michael Schumacher (Germany) between August 30, 1992, and October 1, 2006. Schumacher also holds the record for the ☆ **most points scored in a Formula One career**: he amassed 1,377 points from races between August 25, 1991, and March 14, 2010.

BRO'!: Michael Schumacher (pictured above) and his younger brother, Ralph, are the only brothers in Formula One history to have both won F1 races.

★ **MOST NASCAR TRUCK SERIES CHAMPIONSHIPS** Ron Hornaday Jr. (U.S.A.) has been National Association for Stock Car Auto Racing (NASCAR) Truck Series champion four times, from 1996–2009.

☆ **Most F1 wins by a manufacturer** Ferrari (Italy) won 211 Formula One Grands Prix between 1961 and 2010, the greatest number of Grand Prix wins by a manufacturer.

Ferrari has also achieved the ☆ **most Formula One Constructors' World Championship titles**, with 16, in 1961, 1964, 1975–77, 1979, 1982–83, 1999–2004, and 2007–08.

☆ **Most F1 Grand Prix starts** Rubens Barrichello (Brazil) had 284 Formula One Grand Prix starts from 1993 to 2009.

★ **Youngest driver to finish an F1 race** Jaime Alguersuari (Spain, b. March 23, 1990) was just 19 years 125 days old when he completed the Hungarian Grand Prix in Budapest, Hungary, on July 26, 2009.

World rally championships The ☆ **most FIA World Rallying Championship title wins** is six and was achieved by Sebastien Loeb (France) in 2004–09. This achievement also gives Loeb the record for the ☆ **most consecutive FIA World Rally Championship titles**, with six titles between 2004 and 2009. He won his sixth title on October 25, 2009, by just one point (93 points to 92) over his Finnish rival, Mikko Hirvonen.

QUIZ!: Michael Schumacher is an F1 legend, but he is not the youngest driver to finish an F1 race. Who is? See p. 544 for the answer.

☆ **MOST MOTO GRAND PRIX CHAMPIONSHIPS** Valentino Rossi (Italy) has won six Moto Grand Prix championships, in 2002–05 and 2008–09. Racing for the FIAT Yamaha Team, he acquired 306 points, winning six of the 17 races he took part in. The Moto GP was instituted in 2002, replacing the World Motorcycling Championship 500 cc Grand Prix.

The ☆ most **World Rally Championship race wins** is 53 and was achieved—yes, you've guessed it—by Sebastien Loeb, in 2002–09.

☆ **Most wins at the Le Mans 24-hour race** The greatest number of wins by a driver at the Le Mans 24-hour race is eight, by Tom Kristensen (Denmark), in 1997, 2000–05, and 2008.

BIKES

Superbike championships The ☆ most **American Motorcyclist Association (AMA) Superbike titles won by an individual rider** is seven, by Matt Mladin (Australia), in 1999–2001, 2003–05, and 2009.

Between 1979 and 2009, Suzuki and Kawasaki (both Japan) won the championship 13 times, the ☆ most **AMA Superbike titles won by a manufacturer**.

The ☆ most **Superbike world championship manufacturer's titles won** is 16, by Ducati, in 1991–96, 1998–2004, 2006, and 2008–09.

....

MONTREAL, QC, CANADA (45°30'N 73°33'W): The world's **largest jazz festival** is the Festival International de Jazz de Montreal in Québec, Canada, which attracted 1,913,868 people for its 25th anniversary year in July 2004.

....

F1!: The term "Formula One" refers to rules (the "formula") to which all drivers and manufacturers taking part in the race must agree.

★ **MOST CONSECUTIVE SPRINT CUP SERIES CHAMPIONSHIPS** Jimmie Johnson (U.S.A.) won four consecutive National Association for Stock Car Racing (NASCAR) Sprint Cup Series championships, from 2006 to 2009.

★ **MOST E1 CLASS ENDURO WORLD CHAMPIONSHIPS** Two riders have won the E1 class Enduro World Championships on two occasions: Ivan Cervantes (Spain), in 2005–06, and Mika Ahola (Finland, pictured at left), in 2008–09.

PROVIDENCE, RI, U.S.A. (41°49'N 71°25'W): Ashrita Furman (U.S.A.) simultaneously balanced 700 eggs vertically on one end at the Rhode Island School of Design in Providence, Rhode Island, on October 29, 2006—the **most eggs balanced by an individual**.

★ **MOST WORLD TOURING CAR CHAMPIONSHIPS BY A DRIVER** Guernsey-born racer Andy Priaulx has won three World Touring Car Championships driving for BMW Team UK, from 2005 to 2007.

Isle of Man TT races The ☆ **fastest average speed by a rider at the Isle of Man TT** is 131.578 mph (211.754 km/h) by John McGuinness (UK) on a Honda CBR1000RR in 2009.

The ★ **fastest lap recorded by a rider at the Isle of Man TT in the Superbike TT class** is 17 min. 21.29 sec., also by John McGuinness, on a Honda CBR1000RR, in 2009.

John McGuinness also recorded the ★ **fastest time by a rider in an Isle of Man TT Superbike race (six laps)**. Riding a 1000 HM Plant Honda, he registered a time of 1 hr. 46 min. 7.16 sec. in 2009.

The ☆ **fastest lap by a woman** on the 37.73-mile (60.75-km) Isle of Man TT course is 19 min. 22.6 sec. at an average speed of 116.83 mph (188.02 km/h) and was achieved by Jenny Tinmouth (UK) on June 12, 2009.

☆ **Most Motocross des Nations wins** The Motorcross des Nations, also known as the "Olympics of Motocross," has been contested annually since 1947. The national team with the greatest number of wins is the U.S.A., with 20 between 1981 and 2009.

BALL SPORTS

AUSSIE RULES

★ **Most Leigh Matthews Trophies** Gary Ablett Jr. (Australia) has been awarded a record three Leigh Matthews Trophies, the highly coveted award presented to the most valuable player in the Australian Football League over a season. Ablett earned the awards playing for Geelong in 2007–09.

☆ **MOST ALL-IRELAND FINAL WINS** Kerry (Ireland) have won Gaelic football's All-Ireland Senior Football Championships, the sport's premier knockout competition, 36 times between 1903 and 2009.

★**Most players used in an AFL season** In 1911, St. Kilda used 62 players over the course of the season, a record for the Australian Football League (then Victorian Football League).

CANADIAN FOOTBALL

★**Largest Grey Cup TV audience** The Canadian Football League's (CFL) Grey Cup is the biggest TV sports event in Canada. A total of 6.1 million viewers watched the Grey Cup match between the Montreal Alouettes and Saskatchewan Roughriders at Calgary, Canada, on November 29, 2009. The Alouettes won the game 28–27.

★**Most touchdown passes in a CFL season (by a quarterback)** Doug Flutie (U.S.A.) threw 48 touchdown passes playing for the Calgary Stampeders in the Canadian Football League in 1995.

DID YOU KNOW?

The **most consecutive volleyball passes** is 92 and was set by SV Bayer Wuppertal (Germany) in the Bayerhall, Wuppertal, Germany, on November 25, 2006.

TRIVIA

The Brazil men's pair has won the beach volleyball World Championships title four times, in 1997, 1999, 2003, and 2005.

QUEBEC CITY, QC, CANADA (46°48'N 71°13'W): The **most goals scored by an individual in an NHL game** is seven by Joe Malone for the Quebec Bulldogs in their game against the Toronto St. Patricks in Quebec City, Canada, on January 31, 1920.

> *"I'm five nine . . . For indoor volleyball I'd be short, but for beach I'm average. People say I play tall."*
> **Beach volleyball star Misty May-Treanor**

★ **MOST POINTS IN A PRO BEACH VOLLEYBALL MATCH** When Larissa Franca and Juliana Felisberta Silva (Brazil, pictured) defeated Misty May-Treanor and Kerri Walsh (U.S.A.) 28–26, 40–42, 15–13 in Acapulco, Mexico, on October 30, 2005, the two teams clocked up a record 164 points in the match.

EXTRA! Prefer bats to balls? Check out Tennis & Racket Sports on p. 483.

☆ **MOST VOLLEYBALL GRAND PRIX WINS** Brazil's female volleyball team has won the Grand Prix event eight times: in 1994, 1996, 1998, 2004–06, and 2008–09.

CASH!: Misty May-Treanor (U.S.A.) has won a record $1,833,658 in beach volleyball earnings through to the end of the 2009 season.

HANDBALL

★**Highest combined score in a World Championship final** The 2005 Men's Handball World Championship final between Spain and Croatia saw an aggregate of 74 points scored. Spain won 40–34.

★The **highest combined score recorded in a Women's Handball World Championship final** is 61 points, in the match between France and Hungary in 2003. France won the match 32–29.

HURLING

☆**Most wins of All-Ireland finals** Between 1904 and 2009, Kilkenny won a total of 32 All-Ireland Hurling Championships, the most wins by one team.

Part of Kilkenny's success included the **greatest number of successive wins in the All-Ireland Hurling Final**, with four in a row from 2006 to 2009, equaling Cork's run from 1941 to 1944.

★ **MOST NETBALL GOALS SCORED IN ONE HOUR (TEAM)** A record 257 netball goals were scored in one hour at an event organized by The Co-operative World Netball Series, at Piccadilly Gardens, Manchester, UK, on September 16, 2009.

BOSTON, MA, U.S.A. (42°21'N 71°03'W): The **first telephone call** was made in March 1876 in Boston, Massachusetts, U.S.A., when Alexander Graham Bell (UK) phoned his assistant in a nearby room and said, "Come here Watson, I want you."

KORFBALL

★**Most Indoor European Cups** Dutch korfball club Papendrechtse have won the indoor Korfball European Cup five times, in 1985, 1990, 1999–2000, and 2002.

☆**Most World Games wins** The Netherlands holds the record for the most wins of the korfball tournament at the World Games with seven victories, in 1985, 1989, 1993, 1997, 2001, 2005, and 2009.

VOLLEYBALL

☆**Most women's beach volleyball world championships** The world championships were first staged for both men and women in 1997. The U.S.A. women's pair has won the title four times, in 2003, 2005, 2007, and 2009.

☆**Most men's World League titles** Two national sides have each won eight gold medals in the World League: Italy were victorious in 1990–92, 1994–95, 1997, and 1999–2000, while Brazil won in 1993, 2001, 2003–07, and 2009.

··

SANTIAGO, CHILE (33°27'S 70°40'W): The official Fédération Equestre Internationale record for the **highest jump by a horse** is 8 ft. 1.25 in. (2.47 m) by Huaso ex-Faithful, ridden by Captain Alberto Larraguibel Morales (Chile) at Viña del Mar, Santiago, Chile, on February 5, 1949.

··

BASEBALL

WORLD SERIES

★**Most games pitched in the World Series in a career** Mariano Rivera (Panama) of the New York Yankees (U.S.A.) pitched a record 24 games in World Series play in 1996, 1998, 1999, 2000, 2001, 2003, and 2009. The right-handed relief pitcher has won five World Series with the Yankees (1996, 1998, 1999, 2000, and 2009).

Most home runs in a World Series game Two batters have hit three home runs in a World Series game: Reggie Jackson (U.S.A.) of the New York Yankees (U.S.A.) in Game 6 of the 1977 World Series against the Los Angeles Dodgers (U.S.A.) on October 18, 1977; and Babe Ruth (U.S.A.) of the New York Yankees in Game 4 of the 1926 World Series against the St. Louis Cardinals (U.S.A.) on October 6, 1926, and in Game 4 of the 1928 World Series, also against the St. Louis Cardinals, on October 9, 1928.

☆**MOST HOME RUNS IN A SINGLE WORLD SERIES** Chase Utley of the Philadelphia Phillies (both U.S.A.) hit five home runs in the 2009 World Series against the New York Yankees (U.S.A.), equaling the record set by Reggie Jackson (U.S.A.) of the New York Yankees in the 1977 World Series against the Los Angeles Dodgers (U.S.A.).

WOW!: Lawrence Peter "Yogi" Berra (U.S.A.) played in a record 14 World Series for the New York Yankees (U.S.A.) between 1947 and 1963.

★ **MOST STRIKEOUTS
BY A BATTER IN A
SINGLE WORLD SERIES**
Ryan Howard of the
Philadelphia Phillies
(both U.S.A.) holds the
unfortunate record for
the most strikeouts by a
batter in a World Series,
with 13 in the 2009
World Series against the
New York Yankees
(U.S.A.).

☆**Most runs batted in a World Series game** Hideki Matsui (Japan)
equaled the record for most runs batted in a World Series game when he hit
six, playing for the New York Yankees against the Philadelphia Phillies (both
U.S.A.) in Game 6 of the 2009 World Series on November 4, 2009. Matsui
equaled the record of Robert C Richardson (U.S.A.) of the New York Yankees against the Pittsburgh Pirates (U.S.A.) in Game 3 of the 1960 World
Series on October 8, 1960.

★**Largest television audience for a World Series** The highest average viewing figures per game for a baseball World Series is 44,278,950
viewers for the 1978 World Series between the New York Yankees and the
L.A. Dodgers (both U.S.A.), on October 10–17, 1978. The games were
broadcast on NBC and averaged a 56% share, meaning that they reached
around 24.5 million homes.

☆**Most wins of the World Series** The New York Yankees (U.S.A.)
have won the World Series on 27 occasions: 1923, 1927–28, 1932, 1936–39,
1941, 1943, 1947, 1949–53, 1956, 1958, 1961–62, 1977–78, 1996,
1998–2000, and 2009.

MLB CAREER RECORDS

☆**Most ejections from a game** Robert J. Cox (U.S.A.) has been ejected
from an MLB game 150 times while managing the Toronto Blue Jays
(Canada) and Atlanta Braves (U.S.A.) from 1978 to 2009.

☆ **MOST CONSECUTIVE 200-HIT SEASONS** Playing for the Seattle Mariners (U.S.A.) from 2001 to 2009, Ichiro Suzuki (Japan) became the first player in Major League Baseball history to record 200 or more hits in nine straight seasons.

☆ **Most games played at shortstop** Omar Vizquel (Venezuela) set a Major League Baseball record by playing 2,681 games in the shortstop position. Since 1989, he has played for the Seattle Mariners, Cleveland Indians, San Francisco Giants, Texas Rangers, and Chicago White Sox (all U.S.A.).

The venerable Vizquel also tops the list for ★ **most double-plays by a shortstop**, having participated in a record 1,720 double-plays during a 20-year career in which he has received 11 Gold Glove awards in recognition of his fielding expertise.

★ **Most postseason wins by a manager** Joe Torre (U.S.A.) has achieved a record 84 postseason wins as a manager while at the helm of the Atlanta Braves, New York Yankees, and Los Angeles Dodgers (all U.S.A.) from 1982 to 2009.

☆ **Most home runs in postseason** The Dominican Republic's Manny Ramirez has hit a record 29 postseason home runs playing for the Cleveland Indians, Boston Red Sox, and Los Angeles Dodgers (all U.S.A.) from 1995 to 2009.

EXTRA! For more displays of strength and balance, pitch into p. 141.

★ **MOST GAMES PLAYED AT CATCHER** In 2009, Ivan Rodriguez (Puerto Rico) celebrated his 2,288th career game as catcher with the Texas Rangers, Florida Marlins, Detroit Tigers, New York Yankees, and Houston Astros (all U.S.A.) since he made his Major League debut on June 20, 1991.

☆ **Most home runs scored under one manager** Chipper Jones (U.S.A.) has hit 426 home runs playing for the Atlanta Braves under manager Robert J. Cox (both U.S.A.) from 1993 to 2009.

☆ **Most strikeouts by a left-handed pitcher** Left-handed pitcher Randy Johnson (U.S.A.) has recorded 4,875 strikeouts playing for the Montreal Expos (Canada), Seattle Mariners, Houston Astros, Arizona Diamondbacks, and New York Yankees (all U.S.A.) from 1988 to 2009.

★ **Most combined wins and saves** Andy Pettitte (U.S.A.) and Mariano Rivera (Panama) have combined for a win and a save on 59 occasions pitching for the New York Yankees (U.S.A.) from 1996 to 2009. Pettitte and Rivera surpassed the previous mark of 57 by Bob Welch and Dennis Eckersley (both U.S.A.) playing for the Oakland Athletics (U.S.A.) in the 1980s and 1990s.

★ **MOST ASSISTS BY A FIRST BASEMAN IN A SEASON** Albert Pujols (Dominican Republic) achieved 185 assists as first baseman for the St. Louis Cardinals (U.S.A.) during the 2009 season.

LA PAZ, BOLIVIA (16°30'S 68°09'W): La Paz, administrative and de facto capital of Bolivia, stands at an altitude of 11,913 ft. (3,631 m) above sea level, the **highest altitude for a capital city**. Its airport, El Alto, is at 13,385 ft. (4,080 m). Sucre, the legal capital of Bolivia, stands at 9,301 ft. (2,834 m) above sea level.

MLB MILESTONES

First professional franchise to lose 10,000 matches The Philadelphia Phillies (U.S.A.) became the first professional sports franchise ever to lose 10,000 games, dropping a 10–2 decision to the St. Louis Cardinals (U.S.A.) on July 15, 2007. The franchise has a long history of losing, having played—and lost—its first game in May 1883.

★**First person with 2,000 wins as a manager and 2,000 hits as a player** Joe Torre (U.S.A.) is the only person in baseball history to record at least 2,000 games as a manager and 2,000 hits as a player.

First person to record 500 saves in a career as a relief pitcher The first relief pitcher in Major League Baseball (MLB) history to record 500 saves in a career is Trevor Hoffman (U.S.A.), playing for the Florida Marlins and San Diego Padres (both U.S.A.) from 1993 to 2007.

★**Fewest games to reach 200 home runs** Ryan Howard of the Philadelphia Phillies (both U.S.A.) needed just 658 games to reach 200 career home runs, achieving the feat on July 17, 2009.

☆ **MOST STRIKEOUTS IN AN MLB SEASON BY A BATTER** Playing for the Arizona Diamondbacks (U.S.A.) in 2009, Mark Reynolds (U.S.A.) scored a Major League Baseball record 223 strikeouts in the season.

PHEW!: The **fastest recorded baseball pitch** is 100.9 mph (162.3 km/h) and was achieved by Lynn Nolan Ryan (U.S.A.) on August 20, 1974.

CARACAS, VENEZUELA (10°30'N 66°55'W): The **longest regularly scheduled bus route**, known as the "Liberator's Route," is 6,003 miles (9,660 km) long and is operated by Expreso Internacional Ormeño S.A. of Lima, Peru. It links Caracas, Venezuela, and Buenos Aires, Argentina, passing through the capitals of six South American countries.

EXTRA! For bats of a winged nature, go look at Mammals on p. 88.

★ **MOST CAREER HOME RUNS BY A DESIGNATED HITTER** David Ortiz (Dominican Republic) hit a grand total of 274 home runs during a career in which he played for the Minnesota Twins and Boston Red Sox (both U.S.A.). Ortiz achieved his record playing between 1997 and 2009.

★ **First team with 500 consecutive sellouts** The Boston Red Sox (U.S.A.) recorded 500 consecutive regular-season sellout crowds at Fenway Park from May 15, 2003, to June 16, 2009.

Most seasons with 40 or more saves Trevor Hoffman (U.S.A.) has recorded at least 40 saves in nine seasons for the San Diego Padres (U.S.A.) in 1996, 1998–2001, and 2004–07.

Youngest person to hit 50 home runs in a season At 23 years 139 days, Prince Fielder (U.S.A., b. May 9, 1984) became the youngest Major League player ever to hit 50 home runs in a season, when he homered while playing for the Milwaukee Brewers against the St. Louis Cardinals (both U.S.A.) at Miller Park in Milwaukee, Wisconsin, U.S.A., on September 25, 2007.

INSTANT EXPERT

• The first officially recorded baseball game in U.S. history took place on June 19, 1846, in Hoboken, New Jersey, U.S.A. the "New York Nine" defeated the New York Knickerbockers 23–1 in four innings.

• The National Association of BaseBall Players (NABBP) was the first governing organization in U.S. baseball. It was founded in 1857.

• In 1903, Boston played the Pittsburgh Pirates in the first World Series, which Boston won.

Youngest person to hit 500 home runs At the age of just 32 years 8 days, Alex Rodriguez (U.S.A., b. July 27, 1975) became the youngest player in baseball history to reach 500 career home runs when he homered off Kyle Davies (U.S.A.)—who was pitching for the Kansas City Royals (U.S.A.) against Rodriguez's New York Yankees (U.S.A.) team—at Yankee Stadium in the Bronx, New York City, U.S.A., on August 3, 2007.

MOST IN A ROW

★**Postseason games driving in a run** Three players have recorded eight consecutive postseason games with at least one run batted in. Alex Rodriguez of the New York Yankees (both U.S.A.) achieved the feat between October 8, 2007, and October 20, 2009, just one day after Ryan Howard of the Philadelphia Phillies (both U.S.A.) had completed his own eight-game sequence on October 7–19, 2009. The first player to set the mark was Lou Gehrig (U.S.A.) while playing for the New York Yankees between October 4, 1928, and October 2, 1932.

★**Losing seasons by a team** The Pittsburgh Pirates (U.S.A.) recorded 17 consecutive losing seasons from 1993 to 2009, surpassing the 16 straight losing seasons by the Philadelphia Phillies (U.S.A.) from 1933 to 1948.

☆**LONGEST BASEBALL MARATHON** The Jonny G. Foundation Cardinals and the Edward Jones Browns (both U.S.A.) played baseball for 48 hr. 9 min. 27 sec. at the T. R. Hughes Ballpark in St. Louis, Missouri, U.S.A., on October 9–11, 2009. Money raised by the event was donated to the SSM Cardinal Glennon Children's Medical Center.

☆ **MOST BATTERS CONSECUTIVELY RETIRED BY A PITCHER** Mark Buehrle (U.S.A.) set a Major League Baseball record when he retired 45 batters in a row pitching for the Chicago White Sox (U.S.A.) on July 18–28, 2009.

Hits in MLB On June 19–21, 1938, right-handed third baseman Michael Franklin "Pinky" Higgins (U.S.A.) recorded 12 consecutive hits playing for the Boston Red Sox (U.S.A.). Walter "Moose" Dropo (U.S.A.) equaled this on July 14–15, 1952, playing for the Detroit Tigers (U.S.A.).

Games batted safely Joseph Paul DiMaggio (U.S.A.), playing for the New York Yankees (U.S.A.), safely batted in 56 consecutive games between May 15 and July 16, 1941.

DiMaggio played for nine World Series champions, but this was deemed his greatest feat and elevated him to the ranks of celebrity.

★ **Games without an error** The New York Yankees (U.S.A.) recorded 18 consecutive games without error from May 14, 2009, to June 1, 2009.

THROUGH THE GATE

Largest attendance at a World Series A record 420,784 people attended the six-match series between the Los Angeles Dodgers and the Chicago White Sox (both U.S.A.) on October 1–8, 1959. The **largest attendance for a single World Series game** is 92,706 for the fifth game of the series, at the Memorial Coliseum in Los Angeles, U.S.A., on October 6, 1959.

Largest attendance at a baseball club in one year The record for annual attendance at an individual team is 4,483,350, for the home games of the Colorado Rockies (U.S.A.) at Mile High Stadium, Denver, Colorado, U.S.A., in 1993.

Formed in 1993, the Colorado Rockies originally played at the Mile High Stadium, which had a capacity of 76,100. In 1995, they relocated to the Coors Field, with a smaller capacity of 50,381.

SAN JUAN, PUERTO RICO (18°27'N 66°04'W): Wilfred Benitez (b. New York, September 12, 1958) of Puerto Rico was 17 years 176 days old when he won the WBA light welterweight title in San Juan, Puerto Rico, on March 6, 1976—making him the **youngest boxing world champion**.

☆**Largest attendance at a baseball game** A 115,300-strong crowd attended an exhibition game played between the Los Angeles Dodgers and the Boston Red Sox (both U.S.A.) at the Los Angeles Memorial Coliseum, California, U.S.A., on March 29, 2008.

BASKETBALL

NBA

★**Highest margin of victory in a playoff game** On April 27, 2009, the Denver Nuggets (U.S.A.) beat the New Orleans Hornets (U.S.A.) by 58 points in a playoff game that they won 121–63, matching the Minneapolis Lakers' (U.S.A.) 133–75 win over the St. Louis Hawks (U.S.A.) in 1956.

★**Highest 3-point field goal percentage (career)** Steve Kerr (U.S.A.) recorded a 3-point field goal percentage of .454 playing for six different teams from 1988–89 to 2002–03.

★**Youngest individual to score 12,000 points in a career** At 24 years 35 days, Lebron James (U.S.A., b. December 30, 1984) is the youngest player in NBA history to score 12,000 career points. James reached the mark playing for the Cleveland Cavaliers (U.S.A.) on February 3, 2009.

★**YOUNGEST INDIVIDUAL TO SCORE 25,000 POINTS IN AN NBA CAREER** Kobe Bryant (U.S.A., b. August 23, 1978) was 31 years 151 days old when he reached the landmark of 25,000 National Basketball Association (NBA) career points. He achieved this feat playing for the Los Angeles Lakers (U.S.A.) on January 21, 2010.

ST JOHN'S, ANTIGUA AND BARBUDA (17°07'N 61°51'W):
The **fastest Test match century** was made from 56 balls by Viv Richards (Antigua), playing for the West Indies against England at St. John's, Antigua and Barbuda, on April 11–16, 1986.

★ **MOST BLOCKED SHOTS IN AN NBA FINALS GAME** Dwight Howard (U.S.A.) holds the record for the most blocked shots in an NBA Finals game with nine, playing for the Orlando Magic (U.S.A.) in Game 4 of the NBA Finals against the Los Angeles Lakers (U.S.A.) on June 11, 2009.

☆ **Most playoff games won by a coach** As coach of the Chicago Bulls (U.S.A.) between 1989 and 1997 and the Los Angeles Lakers (U.S.A.) during two stints in charge, 1999–2003 and 2005–10, Phil Jackson (U.S.A.) won an unprecedented 219 playoff games.

★ **Most assists in one quarter** Steve Blake (U.S.A.) of the Portland Trail Blazers (U.S.A.) recorded 14 assists in the first quarter of a game against the Los Angeles Clippers (U.S.A.) on February 22, 2009. Blake matched the mark set by John Lucas (U.S.A.) of the San Antonio Spurs (U.S.A.) during the second quarter of a game against the Denver Nuggets (U.S.A.) on April 15, 1984.

★ **Most consecutive losses to start a season** The New Jersey Nets (U.S.A.) started the 2009–10 season with a record 18 defeats in a row from October 28 to December 3, 2009.

☆ **MOST NBA CHAMPIONSHIP TITLES WON BY A COACH** In 2009, Phil Jackson (U.S.A.) won his 10th NBA title as head coach, surpassing Red Auerbach's (U.S.A.) nine titles. Jackson won six NBA titles with the Chicago Bulls (U.S.A.) in 1991–93 and 1996–98, and four with the Los Angeles Lakers (U.S.A.) in 2000–02 and 2009.

★ **MOST CONSECUTIVE LOSSES BY AN NBA TEAM** The National Basketball Association (NBA) record for most consecutive losses by a team is 24 by the Cleveland Cavaliers (U.S.A.). The Cavaliers' record stretched over two seasons, 1981–82 and 1982–83.

QUIZ!: How many countries have the Harlem Globetrotters played in to date? See p. 544 for the answer.

EXTRA! Want to find out about the NBA All-Star Jam Session? take a trip to p. 471.

★ **HIGHEST 3-POINT FIELD GOAL PERCENTAGE (WNBA)** The highest 3-point field goal percentage (minimum 100 attempts) in Women's National Basketball Association (WNBA) games is .458 by Jennifer Azzi (U.S.A.) for the Detroit Shock (1999), the Utah Starzz (2000–02), and the San Antonio Silver Stars (all U.S.A.) in the 2003 season.

WNBA

★ **Highest free throw percentage** Eva Nemcova (Czech Republic) made a free throw percentage of .897 playing for the Cleveland Rockers (U.S.A.) from 1997 to 2001.

☆ **Most field goals in a career** Lisa Leslie (U.S.A.) scored 2,332 field goals in a 12-year career playing for the Los Angeles Sparks (U.S.A.) between 1997 and 2009.

★ **Highest rebounds per game average** Cheryl Ford (U.S.A.) averaged 9.7 rebounds per game playing for the Detroit Shock (U.S.A.) since 2003.

☆ **Highest point-scoring average in a career** Seimone Augustus (U.S.A.) has scored 2,230 points in 105 games for the Minnesota Lynx (U.S.A.) since 2006, giving her a record point-scoring average of 21.2.

PORT OF SPAIN, TRINIDAD AND TOBAGO (10°40'N 61°31'W): India scored 413–5 to beat Bermuda (156 all out) by 257 runs at Queen's Park Oval, Port of Spain, Trinidad and Tobago, on March 19, 2007, the **highest margin of victory in a cricket World Cup match**.

SKILLS

☆ **Most basketball bounces in one minute** Kiran Harpal (the Netherlands) made 384 bounces of a basketball in one minute at the Hiernasst Youth Center in Wijchen, the Netherlands, on Guinness World Records Day, November 12, 2009.

☆ **Farthest slam dunk using a trampoline** Jordan Ramos (UK) set the record for the farthest slam dunk from a trampoline with a 23-ft.-5-in. (7.15-m) effort on the set of *Blue Peter*, at BBC Television Studios, UK, on March 30, 2010.

☆ **Most free throws in one hour** Perry Dissmore (U.S.A.) made an incredible 1,926 basketball free throws in one hour at Chipola College's Milton Johnson Health Center in Marianna, Florida, U.S.A., on October 9, 2009.

COMBAT SPORTS

★ **Most full-contact kicks in an hour by a team** A team of 36 members of the Cobh Martial Arts Academy performed a total of 12,428 contact kicks in one hour in Cobh, Cork, Ireland, on April 22, 2009.

★ **Most wrestling chokeslams in one minute** A chokeslam is a move in which a wrestler grasps an opponent's neck and slams him or her down. Italian wrestlers Nury Ayachi (aka Kaio), Carlo Lenzoni (aka Charlie Kid), and Mariel Shehi performed 34 chokeslams in a minute on the set of *Lo Show dei Record* in Rome, Italy, on February 25, 2010.

★ **OLDEST FEMALE PRO BOXER** Kazumi Izaki (Japan, b. March 2, 1963) was 46 years 304 days old when she fought Naoko Fujioka (Japan) in a flyweight bout in Tokyo, Japan, on November 30, 2009, although she was defeated by her younger opponent with a technical knockout (TKO) in round two.

QUIZ!: Who wrote the Marquess of Queensbury rules? See p. 544 for the answer.

☆**Most competitive full-contact rounds** Between February 1993 and November 12, 2009, Paddy Doyle (UK) achieved 6,324 competitive full-contact rounds in boxing and other martial arts.

★**Most martial arts kicks in one minute (one leg, female)** Chloe Bruce (UK) performed 212 martial arts kicks in a minute using just her right leg on the set of *Zheng Da Zong Yi—Guinness World Records Special* in Beijing, China, on June 19, 2009. Chloe's kicks were so swift that slow-motion footage was required to verify her feat.

★**Most martial arts throws in one minute** Veteran television comedian Joe Pasquale (UK) performed 29 martial arts throws in one minute on the set of *Guinness World Records—Smashed* at Pinewood Studios, UK, on April 15, 2009.

☆ **MOST UFC MIDDLEWEIGHT CHAMPIONSHIP WINS Lean, keen fighting machine Anderson Silva (Brazil) won a total of seven Ultimate Fighting Championship (UFC) Middleweight Championship bouts between 2006 and 2009.**

BRIDGETOWN, BARBADOS (13°05'N 59°37'W): The **youngest captain in the history of Test (international) cricket** was the Nawab of Pataudi (later Mansur Ali Khan), who captained India v. West Indies at Bridgetown, Barbados, on March 23, 1962, aged 21 years 77 days.

★ **MOST CONSECUTIVE SOLO OLYMPIC GOLDS IN FOIL FENCING (FEMALE)** Foil fencer Valentina Vezzali (Italy) cut out a niche for herself in the world of fencing with three consecutive individual Olympic gold medals in foil fencing to her name, achieved in 2000, 2004, and 2008.

★ **Most punches landed in a championship boxing match** Troy Dorsey (U.S.A.) landed a bone-shaking 620 punches during the course of a 12-round IBF featherweight title match against Jorge Paez (Mexico) in Las Vegas, Nevada, U.S.A., on February 4, 1990. Perhaps surprisingly, this feat of fast-flying fists didn't result in Dorsey's victory. He eventually lost the fight in a split decision, despite the fact that Paez landed only 340 punches in reply.

BUENOS AIRES, ARGENTINA (34°36'S 58°22'W): The **largest cattle market** is Liniers Market in Buenos Aires, Argentina, where between 12,000 and 18,000 heads of cattle reach the market every day to be bought or sold. The market covers an area of 84 acres (34 ha), has 450 pens for the cattle and 2,000 corrals for selling, and employs about 4,000 people.

EXTRA! For sports of a more x-treme nature, head for X Games, starting on p. 502.

★ **MOST JUDO WORLD CHAMPIONSHIP WINS** Ryoko Tani (Japan) won a record seven women's World Judo Championship titles in the 48 kg (105 lb.) category between 1993 and 2007—her first win came when she was just 18 years and 27 days old.

★ **Most punches thrown in a championship boxing match** Antonio Margarito (Mexico) threw 1,675 punches in a 12-round WBO Welterweight title match victory against Joshua Clottey (Ghana) in Atlantic City, New Jersey, U.S.A., on December 2, 2006.

★ **Most martial arts throws of the same person in one minute** Martial artist Vito Zaccaria (Italy) performed a total of 30 martial arts throws on his fellow countryman Michele Vallierion in one minute on the set of *Lo Show dei Record* in Milan, Italy, on April 25, 2009.

★ **Most Sumo top division wins** The most Makunouchi wins in Sumo wrestling by an individual *rikishi* is 815 by Kaio (Japan, born Hiroyuki Koga) from 1993 to 2010.

INSTANT EXPERT

• There are four official sanctioning bodies for the sport of boxing—the World Boxing Association (WBA), the World Boxing Council (WBC), the International Boxing Federation (IBF), and the World Boxing Organization (WBO).

• Despite being named after the ninth marquess of Queensbury, the famous rules that bear his name were actually written by Welshman John Graham Chambers.

• Boxing first became an Olympic sport at the 1904 Olympic Games held in St. Louis, Missouri, U.S.A.

☆**MOST BOXING WORLD TITLES IN DIFFERENT WEIGHT DIVISIONS** Two men have held boxing titles at five different weight divisions. Thomas Hearns (U.S.A.) established his record between 1980 and 1988 while Manny Pacquiao (Philippines) recently equaled the feat with titles in the WBO Welterweight, WBC Lightweight, WBC Super Featherweight, IBF Super Bantamweight, and WBC Flyweight divisions.

☆**Tallest UFC Fighter** In the world of UFC fighting there is no one taller than Stefan Struve (the Netherlands), who measures 6 ft. 11 in. (2.11 m). The ★**shortest UFC fighters** are the 5-ft.-6-in. (1.65-m) Manny Gamburyan, Tyson Griffin, Matt Serra, and Sean Sherk (all U.S.A.).

CYCLING

MOST WINS . . .

★**UCI Time Trial World Championships (female)** France's Jeannie Longo-Ciprelli has won four Time Trial World Championships, in 1995–97 and 2001.

She also holds the record for the ★ **most UCI Road Race World Championships won by a female**, with five wins in 1985–87, 1989, and 1995.

☆**UCI Time Trial World Championships (male)** Two men have won the Time Trial World Championships on three occasions: Michael Rogers (Australia) triumphed in 2003–05, and Fabian Cancellara (Switzerland) in 2006–07 and 2009.

★**Trials Cycling World Championships (team)** Spain is the only team to have won the Trials Cycling World Championships twice, in 2008 and 2009.

> *"It's about winning gold medals, and I'd rather have one gold than three silvers."*
> **Sir Chris Hoy displays the mentality of a winner**

☆ **MOST MOUNTAIN BIKE CROSS-COUNTRY WORLD CUPS (MALE)** Julien Absalon (France) has won more mountain bike cross-country World Cup titles than any other man. His record five victories came in 2003 and from 2006 to 2009. Absalon has also won two Olympic gold medals in the discipline, in 2004 and 2008.

★**UCI ProTour** Spain's Alejandro Valverde is the only rider to have won the UCI ProTour on two occasions, in 2006 and 2008.

★**UCI women's Road World Cups** Four women have won the UCI Road World Cup on two occasions: Diana Ziliute (Lithuania) in 1998 and 2000; Nicole Cooke (UK) in 2003 and 2006; Oenone Wood (Australia) in 2004 and 2005; and Marianne Vos (Netherlands) in 2007 and 2009.

☆**Trials Cycling World Championships—elite class (male)** Benito Ros Charral (Spain) has won the Elite Men's Trials World Championships a record six times, in 2003–05 and 2007–09.

GEORGETOWN, GUYANA (6°48'N 58°10'W): Sir Lionel Luckhoo (Guyana), senior partner of Luckhoo and Luckhoo of Georgetown, Guyana, succeeded in securing 245 successive murder-charge acquittals between 1940 and 1985, making him the **most successful lawyer** on record.

★FASTEST 3 KM TEAM PURSUIT (WOMEN'S TEAM) The Great Britain trio of Elizabeth Armitstead, Wendy Houvenagel, and Joanna Rowsell set a new record for the women's 3 km team pursuit of 3 min. 21.875 sec. in Manchester, UK, on November 1, 2009.

☆**UCI Trials Cycling World Championships (female)** Switzerland's Karin Moor has won the Trials Cycling World Championships title on eight occasions, in consecutive years from 2001 to 2007 and again in 2009.

☆**Mountain Bike World Championships (Marathon, male)** Only two male riders have secured the UCI Mountain Bike Marathon World Championships on two occasions: Thomas Frischknecht (Switzerland), in 2003 and 2005, and Roel Paulissen (Belgium), in 2008–09.

The most wins of the **Mountain Bike World Championships marathon by a female rider** is four by Gunn-Rita Dahle Flesjå (Norway), in 2004–06 and 2008.

☆**Mountain Bike World Cups (Four-Cross, female)** Anneke Beerten (Netherlands) has won the women's Four-Cross Mountain Bike World Cup on three occasions, in 2007–09.

Brian Lopes (U.S.A.) has won three Four-Cross World Cups, in 2002, 2005 and 2007, the greatest number by a male rider.

★MOST UCI MEN'S ROAD WORLD CUPS Paolo Bettini (Italy) has won the UCI Road World Cup three times, which is a record for a male rider. The wins came in 2002–04. This competition was replaced by the UCI ProTour in 2005.

★ **UNPACED 200 M FLYING START (MALE)** Kevin Sireau (France) set a new record of 9.572 seconds for the unpaced 200 m flying start sprint in Moscow, Russia, on May 30, 2009.

FASTEST . . .

★ **Unpaced 500 m, standing start (women's team)** The Australia team of Kaarle McCulloch and Anna Meares set the team record for the women's unpaced 500 m cycle from a standing start with a time of 33.149 seconds at Pruszkow, Poland, on March 26, 2009.

The day before, Simona Krupeckaite (Lithuania) had set the individual female fastest time for the discipline, with 33.296 seconds at the same event in Poland.

MONTEVIDEO, URUGUAY (34°53'S 56°10'W): The **first player to score a hat-trick** (three goals in a match) at a FIFA World Cup is Bert Patenaude (U.S.A.) playing for the U.S.A. against Paraguay at the 1930 World Cup, in Estadio Gran Parque Central, Montevideo, Uruguay, on July 17, 1930.

★ MOST GIRO D'ITALIA FEMMINILE WINS
Fabiana Luperini (Italy) has won the Tour of Italy women's race (Giro d'Italia Femminile) on five occasions, consecutively from 1995 to 1998 and again in 2008.

★ Unpaced 750 m, standing start (men's team) The Great Britain team of Chris Hoy, Jason Kenny, and Jamie Staff recorded a time of 42.950 seconds for the unpaced 750 m cycle from a standing start at Beijing, China, on August 15, 2008. The time came en route to the trio winning the team sprint gold medal at the Beijing Olympic Games, in which they beat France in the final in a time of 43.128 seconds.

LAND'S END TO JOHN O'GROATS

A classic cycling challenge, the 874-mile (1,407-km) route from Land's End in Cornwall, England, UK, to John O'Groats in Caithness, Scotland, UK, requires riders to travel the length of Great Britain between its two most distant points.

The ☆**fastest time by a male rider to cycle from Land's End to John O'Groats** is 44 hr. 4 min. 19 sec., by Gethin Butler (UK) in September 2001.

The ☆**fastest time by a female rider to cycle from Land's End to John O'Groats** is 52 hr. 45 min. 11 sec., set by Lynne Taylor (UK) on October 3, 2002.

Lynne is also the co-holder of the ★**fastest time to cycle from Land's End to John O'Groats on a tandem bicycle (mixed team)**, having achieved a time of 51 hr. 19 min. 23 sec. with Andy Wilkinson (UK) in 2000.

GOLF

☆**Highest prize money for a golf tournament** The Professional Golfer's Association (PGA) tour Players Championships contested at Sawgrass, Florida, U.S.A., in 2008 and 2009 had a total prize pool of $9,500,000 each year—with a spectacular $1,710,000 going to the winner.

★**Highest combined prize money for the WGC Match Play Championship** The World Golf Championships (WGC) Match Play Championship played at the Ritz-Carlton Golf Club, Marana, Arizona, U.S.A., in 2009 had a total prize pool of $8,500,000.

★ MOST BIRDIES RECORDED IN A U.S. MASTERS ROUND Anthony Kim (U.S.A.) scored 11 birdies in his second round at The Masters tournament at Augusta National, Augusta, Georgia, U.S.A., on April 10, 2009. The previous record of 10 birdies had been set by Nick Price (Zimbabwe) in 1986.

★ Lowest score below par in 72 holes in a PGA Tour event Ernie Els (South Africa) had a score of -31 (31 under par) after 72 holes of the 2003 Mercedes Championships, Maui, Hawaii, U.S.A., on January 9–12, 2003.

★ Lowest score in 72 holes in a PGA Tour event Tommy Armour III (U.S.A.) posted a four-round score of 254 (26 strokes under par) at the 2003 Valero Texas Open, San Antonio, Texas, U.S.A., on September 25–28, 2003.

★ Most birdies in a 72-hole golf PGA Tour event Mark Calcavecchia (U.S.A.) hit 32 birdies in 72 holes at the 2001 Phoenix Open in Phoenix, U.S.A., on January 25–28, 2001. The feat was equaled by Paul Gow (Australia) at the 2001 B.C. Open, in New York, U.S.A., on July 19–22, 2001.

EXTRA! For a different kind of birdie, spread your wings and fly over to p. 84.

For a different kind of birdie, spread your wings and fly over to p. 84.

PARAMARIBO, SURINAME (5°52'N 55°10'W): Suriname, with a population of 436,494, has only one cinema, which can be found in the capital Paramaribo—the **fewest cinemas per head of population**. In 1997, this cinema saw a total of 103,626 admissions.

★ **LONGEST SEATED GOLF SHOT** Dale Sheppard (Australia) hit a golf ball 372 ft. 6 in. (113.55 m), while seated, on the Moonah Links Golf Club's Open Course 11th hole in Mornington Peninsula, Victoria, Australia, on November 27, 2009.

★ **Most consecutive birdies in a PGA Tour event** Playing "preferred lies" on a rain-sodden course, U.S. PGA tour veteran Mark Calcavecchia (U.S.A.) scored nine consecutive birdies in the third round of the Canadian Open at Oakville, Ontario, Canada, on July 25, 2009.

★ **Most consecutive U.S. Amateur golf titles** Before embarking on a stellar professional career, Tiger Woods (U.S.A.) recorded three consecutive U.S. Amateur Championship wins between 1994 and 1996.

Most Curtis Cup appearances Carole Semple-Thompson (U.S.A.) played in 12 ties and won a record 18 matches from 1974 to 2002.

★ **Most Solheim Cup appearances** Laura Davies (UK) has played for Europe in every Solheim Cup from 1990 to 2009, making 11 appearances.

★ **LONGEST 19TH HOLE** The "Extreme 19th" at the Legend Golf and Safari Resort, South Africa, measures 1,312 ft. 4 in. (400 m) in horizontal distance, with the tee and hole separated by a 1,410-ft.-9-in. (430-m) drop. The tee is located on Hanglip Mountain.

★ **Most Solheim Cup points scored** Sweden's Annika Sorenstam scored 24 Solheim Cup points playing for the Europe team in the biennial event from 1994 to 2007.

Sorenstam also holds the record for the **highest career earnings on the U.S. LPGA Tour**, with $22,573,192 between 1993 and 2009.

★ **Most holes played by a pair in 12 hours (cart)** Using a golf cart to speed their progress, Jason Casserly and Chris Woods (both Australia) played 189 holes of golf in 12 hours at Grafton District Golf Club, Grafton, Australia, on April 26, 2009. The golfers used foursome rules (taking alternate shots), starting at 5:30 a.m., just before sunrise, and finishing just before sunset at 5:30 p.m. They were raising money for the Grafton Oncology Ward. The final score after 10-and-a-half rounds was 952 (206 over par).

★ **Most holes played by fourball teams in 24 hours** In an event organized by PGA Design Consulting Ltd, MBC ESPN, and AHA Golf Inc. at Gunsan Country Club, South Korea, 93 fourball teams played 6,974 holes of golf in 24 hours on June 28, 2009.

DID YOU KNOW?

Aided by a golf cart, Thomas Bucci (U.S.A.) played 1,801 golf holes in seven days at the Albany Country Club, Voorheesville, New York, U.S.A., on June 14–20, 2009.

TRIVIA

The longest golf course in British Open history was Carnoustie, Scotland, which measured 7,421 yd. (6,785 m) in 2007.

ST. JOHN'S, NL, CANADA (47°34'N 52°42'W): Ann Keane (Canada) ran across Canada from St. John's, Newfoundland and Labrador, to Tofino, British Columbia, in 143 days (April 17 to September 8, 2002)— the **fastest time to cross Canada on foot by a woman**.

★ **HIGHEST WINNING U.S. MASTERS SCORE** The highest score recorded by a golfer to win The Masters golf tournament is 289, by three golfers: Sam Snead (U.S.A.) in 1954, Jack Burke Jr. (U.S.A.) in 1956, and Zach Johnson (U.S.A., far left) in 2007.

★ **Oldest golfer to win a club championship** Tom S. Bennett (U.S.A., b. January 26, 1934) won the Valencia Golf and Country Club championship aged 75 years 56 days in Naples, Florida, U.S.A., on March 23, 2009.

★ **Fewest strokes to complete a marathon distance** Jake Sand (U.S.A.) took 494 strokes to complete the marathon distance of 26 miles 385 yd. (42.195 km) playing golf at Desert Mountain Golf Resort, Arizona, U.S.A., on May 28, 2009. Sand averaged a very creditable 93.4 yd. (85.4 m) per shot and completed the marathon distance in a time of 9 hr. 57 min. 25.14 sec.

☆ **Largest one-day golf tournament** A one-day golf tournament featuring 1,019 participants was held by Golfers512 Fund Raising Campaign (China) at Mission Hills Golf Club in Shenzhen, China, on June 12, 2009.

☆ **Most 18-hole golf courses played in one year** Cathie and Jonathan Weaver (both Canada) played a total of 449 different 18-hole golf courses in one year. Their golfing bonanza was staged at a variety of locations across Canada and the U.S.A., from April 1, 2008, to March 31, 2009.

YOUNGEST WINNER ON THE PGA EUROPEAN TOUR Danny Lee (New Zealand, b. July 24, 1990) was just 18 years 213 days old when he won the Johnnie Walker Classic at The Vines Resort and Country Club, Perth, Australia, on February 22, 2009.

ICE HOCKEY

GOALIES

★**Most matches won by an NHL goaltender** Martin Brodeur is no
stranger to these pages, but as the Canadian netminder's career goes on and
on, the records just keep tumbling. Brodeur has now recorded 598 regular-
season wins in his career playing for the New Jersey Devils (U.S.A.) since
the 1993–94 season to January 2010.

• Brodeur also holds the NHL record for ★**most regular-season games
played by a goaltender**, having played 1,069 times for the Devils in his
career.

• Such career longevity has seen Brodeur take the records for ★**most
regular-season minutes played**, with 63,091, and also the ★**most regular-
season shutouts by a goaltender**, with 108 career clean sheets.

★**Most stanley Cup playoff games played by a goaltender** Retired goaltending great Patrick Roy (Canada) still holds the NHL record for
most games played by a goaltender in the Stanley Cup playoffs, having featured in 247 matches playing for the Montreal Canadiens (Canada) and Colorado Rockies (U.S.A.) from 1985–86 to 2002–03.

• Having played in so many playoff games for two exceptional teams, it's perhaps no surprise that Roy, dubbed "St. Patrick" by fans, holds the NHL record

for **most wins by a goaltender in the Stanley
Cup playoffs** with 151 career victories.

• Roy is the **only player to have won the
Conn Smythe Trophy on three occasions**, in
1986, 1993, and 2001. The prestigious trophy
is awarded each year to the Most Valuable
Player in the Stanley Cup playoffs.

★**YOUNGEST CAPTAIN OF A STANLEY
CUP–WINNING TEAM At 21 years
10 months 5 days, Sidney Crosby (Canada,
b. August 7, 1987) became the youngest
captain of a Stanley Cup–winning team
when the Pittsburgh Penguins defeated the
Detroit Red Wings (both U.S.A.) in the
2009 finals.**

NUUK, GREENLAND (64°10'N 51°45'W): The Ameralik Span is
the **longest span of an electrical overhead powerline** in the world. It is
situated near Nuuk on Greenland and crosses Ameralik Fjord with a span
width of 3.34 miles (5.37 km).

★ **MOST REGULAR-SEASON GOALS CONCEDED BY A GOALTENDER** Gilles Meloche (Canada) has allowed more regular-season goals in his career than any other NHL goaltender, having conceded 2,756 goals playing for the Chicago Black Hawks, California Golden Seals, Cleveland Barons, Minnesota North Stars, and Pittsburgh Penguins (all U.S.A.) from the 1970–71 season to 1987–88.

★**Most regular-season losses by a goaltender** In a career that stretched from 1989 to 2009, Curtis Joseph (Canada) tied the unfortunate record for most regular-season career losses by an NHL goaltender, which had been set by Lorne "Gump" Worsley (Canada) between 1952 and 1974. Both long-playing netminders have experienced 352 defeats.

SCORING

Fastest goals scored in an NHL match The quickest goals in an NHL match came five seconds after the opening whistle. This record is held jointly by three players. Doug Smail (Canada), for the Winnipeg Jets (Canada) against the St. Louis Blues (U.S.A.) at Winnipeg, Manitoba, Canada, on December 20, 1981; Bryan John Trottier (Canada), for the New York Islanders against the Boston Bruins (both U.S.A.) at Boston, U.S.A., on March 22, 1984; and Alexander Mogilny (Russia), for the Buffalo Sabres (U.S.A.) against the Toronto Maple Leafs (Canada) at Toronto, Ontario, Canada, on December 21, 1991.

EXTRA! For warmer, more relaxing pastimes, try out some Toys & Games on p. 259.

★**MOST-TRADED PLAYERS** Mike Sillinger (near left) and Brent Ashton (far left) (both Canada) have each been traded (sold to another team) a record nine times during their careers playing in the NHL.

★**MOST SHOOTOUT GOALS** As of March 2010, Vyacheslav Kozlov (Russia) has scored 27 NHL ice hockey shootout goals in his career, playing for the Detroit Red Wings, Buffalo Sabres, and Atlanta Thrashers, from 1991 to 2010.

★**FIRST TEAM TO WIN 3,000 REGULAR-SEASON GAMES** The Montreal Canadiens (Canada) beat the Florida Panthers (U.S.A.) 5–2 on December 29, 2008, in Sunrise, Florida, U.S.A.—their 3,000th regular-season victory. The Canadiens are the first team in NHL history to achieve the feat.

"Try to just carry a positive attitude and try to be a good teammate every day."

Mike Sillinger on playing for a number of teams (see p. 465)

Only players to score in their first six games Joe Malone, Newsy Lalonde, and Cy Denneny (all Canada) each scored in their first six games during the NHL's inaugural season way back in 1917–18.

On November 1, 2006, Evgeni Malkin (Russia) became the first NHL player in 89 years to score in his first six games while playing for the Pittsburgh Penguins (U.S.A.). His scoring streak had begun on October 18, 2006.

★Most consecutive seasons scoring more than 100 points The Detroit Red Wings (U.S.A.) became the first team in the history of the NHL to top 100 points in 10 straight seasons, from 1999–2000 to 2009–10.

★Most consecutive games in which an NHL defenseman has scored Mike Green (Canada) set a record for defensemen by scoring a goal in eight consecutive games for the Washington Capitals (U.S.A.) during the 2008–09 season, his last goal coming in a 5–1 win over the Tampa Bay Lightning (U.S.A.) on February 14, 2009.

MARATHONS

★Fastest marathon on crutches (one leg) Simon Baker (UK) completed the fastest marathon on crutches using one leg when he crossed the finish line at the 2008 Dublin City Marathon in Dublin, Ireland, in 6 hr. 42 min. 47 sec. on October 27, 2008.

FASTEST TIME TO RUN THE LONDON MARATHON (MALE) Kenya's Samuel Wanjiru recorded the fastest time to complete the London Marathon by a male athlete when he completed the 26-mile-385-yard (42.195-km) course, which winds through the streets of London, UK, in 2 hr. 5 min. 10 sec. on April 26, 2009.

CURITIBA, BRAZIL (25°25'S 49°15'W): The **shortest married couple**—Douglas Maistre Breger da Silva and Claudia Pereira Rocha (both Brazil)—measured 35 in. (90 cm) and 36 in. (93 cm) respectively when married on October 27, 1998, in Curitiba, Brazil.

AMAZING AUSSIE The ★most wins of the wheelchair event at the New York Marathon by a male athlete is four by Kurt Fearnley (Australia) in 2006–09. Kurt also holds the record for the ★**fastest time to complete the London Marathon by a male wheelchair athlete** with 1 hr. 28 min. 57 sec. on April 26, 2009.

★**Fastest marathon by a relay team** The fastest time in which a relay team has completed a marathon is 2 hr. 10 min. 50 sec., by the Team Jack & Adam's Bicycles/Zapata Roadrunners (U.S.A.), formed by Rueben Ondari, Stephen Ariga, Kibet Cherop, Scott Kimbell, and Derek Yorek (Kenya/U.S.A.), in the Silicon Laboratories Austin Marathon Relay, at Auditorium Shores in Austin, Texas, U.S.A., on September 27, 2009.

★**Fastest marathon wearing armor** On September 21, 2008, Peter Pedersen (Denmark) completed the HC Andersen Marathon in Odense, Denmark, in 6 hr. 46 min. 59 sec. wearing a full suit of armor for the entire run.

FAST: The **fastest time to complete the London Marathon by a female wheelchair athlete** is 1 hr. 48 min. 4 sec. by Sandra Graf (Switzerland) in 2008.

BRASÍLIA, BRAZIL (15°48'S 47°54'W): The **widest city street in the world** is the Monumental Axis, a 1.8-mile-long (2.4-km) six-lane boulevard in Brasília, the capital of Brazil. Opened in April 1960, the street is 820 ft. 2 in. (250 m) wide.

LONDON MARATHON RECORDS

RECORD TITLE	RECORD RESULT & RUNNER
A ★ *Fastest marathon carrying a 60-lb. pack*	5 hr. 28 min. 53 sec. by Benjamin Harrop (UK)
B ☆ *Fastest marathon in a firefighter's uniform*	5 hr. 32 min. 55 sec. by Nigel Addison-Evans (UK)
C ★ *Fastest marathon in school uniform (female)*	4 hr. 14 min. 46 sec. by Louise Winstanley (UK)
D ☆ *Fastest marathon in an animal costume (male)*	3 hr. 30 min. 10 sec. by Kevin Robins (UK) dressed as a tiger
E ★ *Fastest marathon dressed as a golfer (male)*	3 hr. 43 min. 20 sec. by Bertrand Bodson (Belgium)
F ☆ *Fastest marathon in a superhero costume (female)*	3 hr. 8 min. 55 sec. by Jill Christie (UK)
G ★ *Fastest marathon dressed as a baby*	3 hr. 13 min. 30 sec. by Tony Audenshaw (UK)
H ★ *Fastest marathon dressed as a jester*	3 hr. 33 min. 55 sec. by David Smith (UK)
I ★ *Fastest marathon dressed as a television character (male)*	4 hr. 1 min. 40 sec. by Paul Franks (UK) dressed as a Dalek
J ★ *Fastest marathon dressed as a bottle (female)*	4 hr. 54 min. 36 sec. by Gill Begnor (UK)
K ☆ *Fastest marathon dressed as a leprechaun*	3 hr. 9 min. 40 sec. by Ben Afforselles (UK)
L ☆ *Tallest costume worn running in a marathon*	23 ft. 1 in. (7.04 m) by Jean Paul Delacy (UK)
M ★ *Longest crochet chain while running a marathon*	253 ft. (77.4 m) by Susie Hewer (UK)
N ★ *Fastest marathon in a martial arts suit*	3 hr. 39 min. 20 sec. by Peter Kelly (UK)
O ☆ *Fastest marathon dressed as a cartoon character*	3 hr. 7 min. 34 sec. by David Ross (UK) dressed as Fred Flintstone
P ★ *Fastest marathon dressed as a doctor (male)*	4 hr. 21 min. 9 sec. by Tom Solomon (UK)
Q ★ *Fastest marathon in a nurse's uniform (male)*	3 hr. 46 min. 27 sec. by Andrew White (UK)
R ★ *Fastest marathon dressed as a book character*	4 hr. 1 min. 47 sec. by Ian Young (UK) dressed as Sherlock Holmes

VIRGIN LONDON MARATHON 2010 On April 25, 2010, an incredible 36,549 runners completed the Virgin London Marathon (UK), a record for this great city marathon, which was celebrating its 30th anniversary. Once again Guinness World Records was proud to be involved, with 75 runners competing in 27 record categories and an astounding 19 new Guinness World Records awarded on the day. Well done, everyone!

☆ **MOST SIBLINGS TO COMPLETE A MARATHON** An incredible 16 siblings from the Kapral family—Chris, Vince, Steve, Tony, Joe, Doug, Angela, Allison, Theresa, Phil, Michelle, Mary, Nick, Mike, David, and Sarah (all U.S.A.)—ran the Community First Fox City Marathon, Appleton, Wisconsin, U.S.A., on September 20, 2009.

TEAM CATERPILLAR The ☆ **most runners linked to complete a marathon is 34**, by Team Caterpillar at the Virgin London Marathon, London, UK, on April 25, 2010. The team, organized by Phil Nevin (UK), included Princess Beatrice (UK), the first royal to run the London Marathon, and Virgin boss Richard Branson (UK), and finished in a time of 5 hr. 13 m. 3 sec.

SÃO PAULO, BRAZIL (23°33'S 46°38'W): The **fastest guitar player** is Tiago Della Vega (Brazil), who successfully played "Flight of the Bumblebee" by Nikolai Rimsky-Korsakov (Russia) at 320 BPM without error at EM&T, São Paulo, Brazil, on May 7, 2008.

NBA JAM

★**Largest sports trading card** At the NBA All-Star Jam Session in Dallas, Texas, U.S.A., on February 13, 2010, a sports trading card measuring 59.75 x 84 in. (151 x 213 cm) was unveiled by Panini (U.S.A.). The colossal card featured LA Lakers star Kobe Bryant (U.S.A.).

★**Most points scored as Kobe Bryant on the NBA 2K10 video game** At the NBA All-Star Jam Session, fans and players get the chance to show off their skills on the latest NBA video game. On February 13, 2010, Chico Kora (U.S.A.) scored 29 points playing as Kobe Bryant on 2K Sports *NBA 2K10* (playing a four-minute game, with one minute per quarter).

Several other video-game records were set at the NBA All-Star Jam Session. The ★**most steals on 2K Sports *NBA 2K10* (playing a four-minute game, with one minute per quarter)** is seven by Wesley Parker (U.S.A.), on February 10, 2010.

The ★ **most assists**, within the same parameters, is 16 by Andrew Frost and J. R. Wildly (both U.S.A.), on February 11, 2010.

The ★**most points scored in the first half of a 2K Sports *NBA 2K10* video game**, within the same parameters, is 17 by Cody Redrick and Brandon McJunlain (both U.S.A.), on February 12, 2010.

Highest slam dunk with a backflip
Jerry Burrell (U.S.A.) made a slam dunk, having performed a backflip from a 15-ft.-4-in.-tall (4.67-m) platform. Burrell achieved the feat during the NBA All-Star Jam Session in Phoenix, Arizona, U.S.A., on February 16, 2009.

★**FARTHEST HOOK SHOT Special K Daley (U.S.A.) of the Harlem Globetrotters recorded a hook shot measured at 46 ft. 6 in. (14.15 m) at the NBA All-Star Jam Session, Dallas, Texas, U.S.A., on February 13, 2010.**

SANTOS, BRAZIL (23°58'S 46°20'W): The **tallest cemetery** is the Memorial Necrópole Ecumônica, in Santos, near São Paulo, Brazil. The cemetery is 10 stories high and occupies an area of 4.4 acres (1.8 ha). Its first burial was on July 28, 1984.

★FARTHEST SHOT MADE WHILE SITTING ON COURT Orlando Magic (U.S.A.) center Dwight Howard (U.S.A.) made a shot measured at 52 ft. 6 in. (15.99 m) while sitting on the court at the NBA All-Star Jam Session in Dallas, Texas, U.S.A., on February 13, 2010

★LONGEST TIME SPINNING A BASKETBALL ON THE NOSE Harlem Globetrotter Scooter Christensen (U.S.A.) kept a ball spinning on his nose for 5.1 seconds during the NBA All-Star Jam Session in Dallas, Texas, U.S.A., on February 13, 2010.

Longest time spinning two basketballs using one hand During the NBA All-Star Jam Session held in Phoenix, Arizona, U.S.A., on February 14, 2009, professional basketball freestyler Tommy Baker (UK) spun two basketballs using one hand for 32.88 seconds. Baker achieved the record by spinning one ball on top of the other. At the same event, Baker also performed the **most headers while spinning two basketballs**, with 40 bounces of the ball on his forehead.

Longest time spinning a basketball on one toe Jack Ryan (U.S.A.) spun a basketball on his toe for 9.53 seconds at the NBA All-Star Jam Session in New Orleans, Louisiana, U.S.A., on February 13, 2008.

EXTRA! For more all-court action, track back to Basketball on pp. 446–450.

☆ **LARGEST ATTENDANCE FOR A BASKETBALL GAME** The NBA All-Star Game played at Cowboys Stadium in Arlington, Texas, U.S.A., on February 14, 2010, watched by 108,713 fans, the largest ever basketball crowd. The game saw the East beat the West 141–139.

DID YOU KNOW?

The ★ **farthest six-person tandem before a dunk using a trampoline** is 20 ft. (6 m) and was achieved by Team Acrodunk (U.S.A.).

TRIVIA

The **most consecutive three-pointers scored on *NBA 2K9*** is eight by Marcus Platt (U.S.A.).

★ **MOST FREE THROWS MADE IN TWO MINUTES WHILE ALTERNATING HANDS** Jeff Harris (U.S.A.) made 44 basketball free throws in two minutes using alternate hands at the NBA All-Star Jam Session in Dallas, Texas, U.S.A., on February 10, 2010.

....

RIO DE JANEIRO, BRAZIL (22°54'S 43°14'W): Rio de Janeiro's annual carnival, normally held during the first week of March, is the **largest carnival** in the world, attracting approximately 2 million people each day.

....

MOST UNDERHANDED HALF-COURT SHOTS IN ONE MINUTE Only two people have achieved two underhanded half-court shots in one minute: Jason Kidd (U.S.A.) of the Dallas Mavericks (U.S.A.) and Bucket Blades (U.S.A., left) of the Harlem Globetrotters. Kidd set the record during the NBA All-Star Jam Session in New Orleans, Louisiana, U.S.A., on February 16, 2008, and Blades equaled it during the NBA All-Star Jam Session in Dallas, Texas, U.S.A., on February 13, 2010.

Longest time spinning a basketball on one finger Joseph Odhiambo (U.S.A.) spun a basketball continuously for 4 hr. 15 min. on February 19, 2006 in Houston, Texas, U.S.A.

Most free throws At the NBA All-Star Jam Session in New Orleans, Louisiana, U.S.A., on February 16, 2008, Becky Hammon of the San Antonio Silver Stars (both U.S.A.) made the **most free throws in one minute by a female player**: 38.

At the same event three days earlier, NBA Hall of Famer Rick Barry (U.S.A.) had recorded the **most underhanded free throws in one minute**: 24.

National Wheelchair Basketball Association (NWBA) player Jeff Griffin (U.S.A.) scored the **most consecutive free throws from a wheelchair**, with three successful throws in a row, on February 12, 2009, at the NBA All-Star Jam Session in Phoenix, Arizona, U.S.A.

Most three-pointers in two minutes On February 17, 2008, Jason Kapono (U.S.A.) of the Toronto Raptors (Canada) scored 43 three-pointers in two minutes at the NBA All-Star Jam Session in New Orleans, Louisiana, U.S.A.

SOCCER

★**Lowest goal average in FIFA World Cup finals** The goal average at the 1990 FIFA World Cup Finals in Italy was just 2.21 per game, the lowest since the competition began in 1930. The overall average for the 18 World Cup Finals to Germany 2006 is 2.91 goals per match.

SOCCER

It is widely believed that the word "soccer" is a contraction of "Association" from "Association Football."

★ MOST GOALS SCORED IN A WORLD CUP FINALS A record 171 goals were scored by the 32 teams in the FIFA World Cup Finals held in France in 1998.

MOST WINS OF THE CONFEDERATIONS CUP When Brazil came back from a 0–2 halftime deficit to beat the U.S.A. 3–2 in the final of the 2009 Confederations Cup in South Africa on June 28, 2009, it saw the South American country register its third victory in the competition. Previous wins had occurred in 1997 and 2005.

....

REYKJAVÍK, ICELAND (64°08'N 21°56'W): The **most northerly city**, and the northernmost national capital, is Reykjavík, Iceland. As of 2010, its population was nearly 200,000, approximately two-thirds of the overall population of Iceland.

....

EXTRA! Turn to p. 244 to find out who's the most expensive soccer player of all time.

★**Most FIFA Fair Play Trophy wins** Brazil have won the FIFA Fair Play Trophy four times, in 1982, 1986, 1994, and 2006. The trophy is awarded to the team with the best record of fair play during a World Cup Final.

★**Longest unbeaten run in international soccer** Two international soccer teams have achieved unbeaten runs stretching to the 35-game mark: Brazil was the first team to set the record, between December 16, 1993, and January 18, 1996, and Spain from October 11, 2006, until June 20, 2009.

In this period, Brazil won the 1994 World Cup, reached the 1995 Copa America final, and reached the final of the 1996 Gold Cup. Their run was

AFRICA CUP OF NATIONS The ★**most consecutive matches played in Africa Cup of Nations tournaments** is 34, by Rigobert Song (Cameroon) between 1996 and 2010. During his run, Song was part of the victorious Cameroon teams of 2000 and 2002.

MOST AFRICA CUP OF NATIONS WON BY A PLAYER Ahmed Hassan has played in eight Africa Cup of Nations tournaments for Egypt between 1996 and 2010. During that period he has been on the winning side a record four times, in 1998, 2006, 2008, and 2010.

DAKAR, SENEGAL (14°41'N 17°26'W): Ari Vatanen (Finland) has won the Dakar Rally four times, first in 1987 and then on three more occasions from 1989 to 1991 inclusively—the **most Dakar Rally wins**.

ended with a 2–0 defeat in the Gold Cup final to Mexico. During the 35-game run Brazil did lose one game by penalty shoot-out (the 1995 Copa America final to hosts Uruguay), but were still unbeaten after extra-time.

Spain's undefeated sequence, meanwhile, saw them win the 2008 European Championships and reach the semifinals of the 2009 Confederations Cup before losing to the U.S.A.

☆ **Most goals scored in a FIFA Beach Soccer World Cup career**
Madjer (Portugal) is the most prolific goal scorer in FIFA Beach Soccer World Cups, with 67 goals between 2005 and 2009. Madjer also has the **most FIFA Beach Soccer World Cup Golden Shoe awards**, having won three times.

☆ **Most goals scored in Africa Cup of Nations** Cameroon's Samuel Eto'o has scored a total of 18 goals in Africa Cup of Nations tournaments from 1996 to 2010. He has also won the African Footballer of the Year award three times, a record he shares with Abedi Pelé (Ghana) and George Weah (Liberia).

★ **MOST CONSECUTIVE WINS IN INTERNATIONALS** Between June 26, 2008, and June 20, 2009, Spain won 15 consecutive international soccer matches. The sequence began when they beat Russia 3–0 in the semifinals of the 2008 European Championships. Their 15th consecutive win came with a 2–0 victory over South Africa in their final group game in the 2009 Confederations Cup.

MOST WINS OF THE BEACH SOCCER WORLD CUP Brazil has won the FIFA Beach Soccer World Cup on four of the five occasions it has been held (2006–09). Before it became officially recognized by FIFA in 2005, a version of the Beach Soccer World Cup had been running since 1995, and Brazil had won nine out of the 10 events.

Most goals scored in FIFA Women's World Cup matches Brigit Prinz (Germany) has scored a total of 14 goals in FIFA Women's World Cup matches. Her latest goal was scored in the FIFA World Cup Final at the Hongkou Stadium in Shanghai, China, on September 30, 2007.

Fastest hat trick in international soccer Japanese international Masashi "Gon" Nakayama scored a hat trick in 3 min. 15 sec. against Brunei during an Asian Cup qualifying match played on February 16, 2000. Nakayama netted on 1 min., 2 min., and 3 min. 15 sec., beating the 62-year-old mark set by George William Hall (England), who scored three goals in 3 min. 30 sec. against Ireland at Old Trafford, Manchester, UK, on November 16, 1938.

Most goals scored in a Copa America tournament Three soccer players have scored nine goals in a single Copa America tournament: Jair Rosa Pinto (Brazil) in 1949, and Humberto Maschio (Argentina) and Javier Ambrois (Uruguay), both in 1957.

Most appearances as captain in FIFA World Cup finals Argentina's Diego Maradona captained his country in 16 World Cup Finals matches between 1982 and 1994. Maradona's tenure as captain included leading his country to World Cup victory in the 1986 final against West Germany.

EXTRA! Prefer to play soccer with a controller in your hand? Go to video games on p. 291.

★ **FIRST ALL-FOREIGN PREMIER LEAGUE MATCH SQUAD** The squad selected by Arsenal (UK) for the match against Crystal Palace (UK) on February 14, 2005, was the first all-foreign lineup to play in an English Premier League match. The squad consisted of: Jens Lehmann (Germany); Lauren (Cameroon); Kolo Touré (Ivory Coast); Pascal Cygan, Gaël Clichy, Robert Pirès, Patrick Vieira, and Thierry Henry (all France); Edu (Brazil); Jose-Antonio Reyes (Spain); and Dennis Bergkamp (Netherlands). Subs: Manuel Almunia and Cesc Fàbregas (both Spain); Philippe Senderos (Switzerland); Mathieu Flamini (France); and Robin van Persie (Netherlands). Arsenal won 5–1.

PREMIER LEAGUE BAD BOYS The ☆ **most yellow cards received by a player in the English Premier League** is 93 by Lee Bowyer (UK, above right) between 1996 and 2010. The most red cards received by a player in the English Premier League is eight, by three players: Richard Dunne (Ireland, above left), between 1996 and 2008; Duncan Ferguson (UK), between 1994 and 2006; and Patrick Vieira (France), between 1996 and 2005.

LONGEST HOME UNBEATEN STREAKS IN THE TOP DIVISION OF THE LEADING DOMESTIC LEAGUES

NO.	CLUB	START DATE	END DATE	WON	DRAWN	LEAGUE
121	Real Madrid	February 17, 1957	February 21, 1965	112	9	La Liga (SPA)
93	PSV	February 17, 1983	March 4, 1989	77	16	Eredivisie (NED)
92	FC Nantes	June 4, 1976	March 14, 1981	80	12	Ligue 1 (FRA)
88	Torino	January 31, 1943	October 23, 1949	78	10	Série A (ITA)
86	Chelsea	March 20, 2004	October 5, 2008	62	24	Premier League (ENG)
73	Bayern Munich	April 11, 1970	September 14, 1974	62	11	Bundesliga (GER)
68	Palmeiras*	February 23, 1986	September 2, 1990	45	23	Série A (ITA)
49	Banfield**	May 7, 1950	May 24, 1953	35	14	Primera División (ARG)
25	Urawa Red Diamonds	September 24, 2005	April 7, 2007	22	3	J-League (JPN)
25	Gamba Osaka	March 29, 2006	August 11, 2007	20	5	J-League (JPN)
24	Columbus Crew	June 28, 2008	September 26, 2009	18	6	MLS (U.S.A.)

Notes:
*Palmeiras' streak also includes São Paulo Championship (Paulista); **Banfield's streak does not include 1951 championship decider against Racing, which was played on a neutral pitch.

Source: Infostrada Sports

LISBON, PORTUGAL (38°42'N 9°11'W): The **shortest reign ever** was that of Crown Prince Luis Filipe of Portugal, who was King of Portugal for about 20 minutes on February 1, 1908. His father, the King, was shot dead in Lisbon, and he was mortally wounded at the same time.

FASTEST SPOT KICK Francisco Javier Galan Màrin (Spain, left) spot-kicked a ball at 80.1 mph (129 km/h) for *El Show de los Récords* in Madrid, Spain, on October 29, 2001. The fastest known shot on goal was by David Hirst (UK) for Sheffield Wednesday vs. Arsenal on September 16, 1996. It clocked in at 114 mph (183 km/h)—but hit the bar!

☆**Most goals scored in international soccer (male or female)** The record for most career international goals scored, by a man or woman, is 158 by Mia Hamm (U.S.A.) from 1987 to 2004. Hamm's stellar career included 275 appearances for the U.S.A. national team and two Women's World Cup titles, in 1991 and 1999.

★**Youngest soccer player in a top division** Mauricio Baldivieso (Bolivia) was aged 12 years 362 days when he represented Aurora FC against La Paz in the Clausura competition of the Liga de Fútbol Profesional Boliviano at Estadio Hernando Siles, La Paz, Bolivia, on July 19, 2009.

★**Youngest goal scorer in La Liga** The youngest goal scorer in the top division of Spanish soccer is Iker Muniain (Spain), who was 16 years 289 days old when he scored for Athletico Bilbao in a 2–2 draw with Real Valladolid, in Valladolid, Spain, on October 4, 2009.

★**Most Bundesliga titles won by a coach** Udo Lattek (Poland) secured eight Bundesliga titles in his career as a soccer coach. Six titles came in his two spells as coach of Bayern Munich, winning in 1972–74 and 1985–87, and two with the Borussia Mönchengladbach team in 1976–77.

PORTO, PORTUGAL (41°09'N 8°38'W): The **largest patchwork quilt** measured 270,174 ft.^{2} (25,100 m^2). The project was carried out by Realizar—Eventos Especiais, Lda of Parque da Cidade, Porto, Portugal, and completed on June 18, 2000.

★ **MOST WINS OF BUNDESLIGA BY A PLAYER** Two players have won Germany's Bundesliga title on eight occasions: Mehmet Scholl (Germany, left) in 1994, 1997, 1999–2001, 2003, and 2005–06; and Oliver Kahn (Germany) in 1997, 1999–2001, 2003, 2005–06, and 2008. Both players were part of the Bayern Munich team.

★ **Most Coppa Italia wins** Two teams have won the Coppa Italia, the premier cup competition in Italian soccer, on a record nine occasions: Juventus in 1938, 1942, 1959–60, 1965, 1979, 1983, 1990, 1995; and Roma in 1964, 1969, 1980–81, 1984, 1986, 1991, 2007–08.

☆ **Most wins of the Tippeligaen** The Tippeligaen is the top division of league soccer competition in Norway. The most successful team in the league, in terms of titles won, is Rosenborg, who have been league champions a record 21 times between 1967, when they won their first title, and 2009, when they won their latest.

★ **Most goals scored in a Premier League match by an individual player** Three players have scored five goals in a single English Premier League match: Andy Cole (UK) for Manchester United versus Ipswich at Old Trafford, Manchester, UK, on March 4, 1995; Alan Shearer (UK) for Newcastle United versus Sheffield Wednesday at St James' Park, Newcastle, UK, on September 19, 1999; and most recently Jermain Defoe (UK) for Tottenham Hotspur versus Wigan Athletic at White Hart Lane, London, UK, on November 22, 2009.

☆ **Most durable soccer referee** Hungary's Csernyi Géza (b. March 25, 1932) has been an active soccer referee for 57 years. Géza gained his refereeing qualification on June 7, 1950, and officiated his last match in Hungary in February 2007.

☆Most soccer management rejection letters Between 2000 and 2010, Patrick Rielly (UK) has received 46 rejection letters from soccer clubs to whom he has applied to be manager. His first rejection came from Millwall FC; others include Celtic, Manchester City, and West Ham United (all UK).

TENNIS & RACKET SPORTS

TENNIS

★Most aces served in a Davis Cup match Ivo Karlovic (Croatia) served 78 aces against Radek Stepanek (Czech Republic) in the semifinal of the Davis Cup, held at Porec, Croatia, on September 18, 2009. Sadly, Karlovic's serving power was not enough to grant him victory—he lost the match 7–6, 6–7, 6–7, 7–6, 14–16.

☆Largest single-day attendance at Wimbledon A total of 45,955 people watched the second day of the Wimbledon tournament, at London, UK, on June 23, 2009.

☆Most tennis club championships (male) Stuart Foster (UK) secured 55 championships at Leverstock Green Lawn Tennis Club in Hemel Hempstead, Hertfordshire, UK, from 1985 to 2009.

Stuart also holds the record for the ☆**most tennis club men's doubles championships with multiple partners**, with 24 titles won from 1985 to 2009 at the same club.

★MOST CONSECUTIVE GRAND SLAM TOURNAMENTS PLAYED From her first appearance at Wimbledon on June 20, 1994, to her first match at the 2009 U.S. Open on August 31, 2009, Ai Sugiyama (Japan) played 62 consecutive Grand Slam tournaments.

CORK, IRELAND (51°53'N 8°28'W): The **largest attendance at a hurling match** was 84,865 for the All-Ireland final between Cork and Wexford at Croke Park, Dublin, Ireland, in 1954.

EXTRA! For more of Roger Federer's tennis records, turn to p. 415.

★ **MOST GAMES IN A WIMBLEDON FINAL** The Wimbledon final held on July 5, 2009, was a particularly punishing affair, with Andy Roddick (U.S.A.) forcing Roger Federer (Switzerland) to play 77 games before the Swiss tennis legend finally claimed a 5–7, 7–6, 7–6, 3–6, 16–14 victory.

THE BODY-SLAMMING BRYANS Twins Bob and Mike Bryan (both U.S.A., aka "the Bryans") scored the ★ **most wins of the International Tennis Federation Men's Doubles World Championship by the same pair** with six, in 2003–07 and 2009.

POWER PLAYER Squash maestro Jonathon Power (Canada) claimed the record for the ★most wins of the Professional Squash Association Masters singles tournament with a total of three victories, in 2001–02 and 2005. Shortly after his last win, Jonathon announced his retirement from the sport.

★Highest earnings in a season (female) Serena Williams (U.S.A.) earned a whopping $6,545,586 in 2009. This is just a small chunk of the $30,491,460 she earned in her career between 1997 and 2009. While this gives her the record for the ☆ **highest earnings in a professional career (female)**, her wealth is a fraction of the $55,350,788 Roger Federer (Switzerland) won between 1998 and 2010—the ☆ **highest earnings in a tennis career (male)**.

★Tallest Grand Slam winner Juan Martín del Potro (Argentina) measured 6 ft. 6 in. (198 cm) when he won the 2009 U.S. Open in Flushing Meadows, New York City, U.S.A., on September 14, 2009.

BADMINTON WORLD CHAMPIONSHIPS In the struggle for the ☆ **most Badminton World Championships men's singles titles, Lin Dan** (China) takes the honors, with wins in 2006, 2007, and 2009. His latest victory saw Lin finally take the record from his fellow countryman, Yang Yang.

BADMINTON

★ **Most World Team Badminton Championship appearances** The men's team from Denmark has put in 25 appearances at the final stage of the World Team Badminton Championships, otherwise known as the Thomas Cup, between 1949 and 2008.

★ **Longest badminton doubles marathon** Dedicated sportsmen Joost Berkelmans, Rick Blok, Thijs Maassen, and Steven van Puffelen (all the Netherlands) played an extended doubles badminton marathon lasting 27 hours at De Toekomstgroep badminton sports center, Almere, the Netherlands, on February 27–28, 2009.

RACQUETBALL

★ **Most Men's team wins at the World Racquetball championships** Instituted in 1984 and based on the U.S. game of racquetball, the World Racquetball Championships has been won a total of eight times by the U.S. men's team, between 1984 and 2008.

The achievements of the men's team pale in comparison to those of the U.S. women's team, however, which has won the competition on 13 occasions. This represents the record for the ☆ **most women's team wins at the World Racquetball Championships**.

CASABLANCA, MOROCCO (33°32'N 7°35'W): Measuring 656 ft. (200 m), the **tallest minaret** in the world is that of the Great Hassan II Mosque, Casablanca, Morocco. The mosque cost 5 billion dirhams ($513.5 million) to build.

TABLE TENNIS

★ **Most Men's team European Table Tennis Championships** Sweden's table tennis team won a total of 14 European Table Tennis Championship team titles between 1964 and 2002.

TRACK & FIELD

Highest pole vault (female) Despite missing out in the 2009 World Championships, Yelena Isinbayeva (Russia) has continued to break records in women's pole-vaulting over the past year, both indoors and outdoors.

The ☆ **highest pole vault (female) (indoors)** now stands at 5.00 m (16 ft. 4 in.) and was set in Donetsk, Ukraine, on February 15, 2009, while on August 29, 2009, in Zurich, Switzerland, Isinbayeva extended the record for the ☆ **highest pole vault (female)** to 5.06 m (16 ft. 7 in.) on her first attempt at the height at the Zurich Weltklasse event.

FAST: The **fastest 400 m** ever run is 43.18 seconds by Michael Johnson (U.S.A.) in Seville, Spain, on August 26, 1999. Usain Bolt's fastest 400 m is 45.28 seconds, so far . . .

FASTEST MAN Usain Bolt's (Jamaica) incredible career continues, quite literally, apace. In 2009, his amazing form saw him break the following sprint records: ☆ **Fastest run 100 m (male)** in 9.58 seconds in Berlin, Germany, on August 16, 2009; ★ **Fastest run 150 m (male)** in 14.35 seconds in Manchester, UK, on May 17, 2009; ☆ **Fastest run 200 m (male)** in 19.19 seconds in Berlin, Germany, on August 20, 2009.

VAST: Arvind Pandya (India) ran backward across the U.S.A. from Los Angeles to New York City in 107 days in 1984.

☆FARTHEST HAMMER THROW (FEMALE) Poland's Anita Wlodarczyk threw the hammer an unprecedented distance of 77.96 m (255 ft. 9 in.) to win the gold medal at the 12th IAAF World Championships in Berlin, Germany, on August 22, 2009.

MOST IAAF WORLD ATHLETE OF THE YEAR AWARDS The IAAF World Athlete of the Year Award is organized by the International Association of Athletics Federations, and given annually to the most outstanding global track and field athlete. The ★most Men's IAAF World Athlete of the Year trophies won is three by Hicham El Guerrouj (Morocco), each year from 2001 to 2003. The ★most Women's IAAF World Athlete of the Year trophies won is also three, by Yelena Isinbayeva (Russia) in 2004–05 and 2008.

☆LONGEST TRIPLE JUMP (MALE) (INDOORS) Teddy Tamgho (France) jumped 17.9 m (58 ft. 9 in.) in Doha, Qatar, on March 14, 2010. Tamgho set the mark on his last jump of the competition to surpass the record of 17.83 m (58 ft. 5.96 in.) held jointly by Aliecer Urrutia (Cuba) and Christian Olsson (Sweden).

DUBLIN, IRELAND (53°20'N 6°16'W): The **tallest windmill** in the world is the St. Patrick's Distillery Mill in Dublin, Republic of Ireland, now without sails. It is 150 ft. (45.7 m) tall.

☆**FASTEST RUN 4 X 1,500 M RELAY** On September 4, 2009, in Brussels, Belgium, William Biwott Tanui, Gideon Gathimba, Geoffrey Kipkoech Rono, and Augustine Kiprono Choge, representing Kenya, ran the 4 x 1,500 m relay in 14 min. 36.23 sec. The time was almost two seconds better than the previous best set by West Germany in 1977.

☆**Fastest run 5,000 m (female) (indoors)**   Meseret Defar (Ethiopia) ran 5,000 m in 14 min. 24.37 sec. at the GE Galan Meeting in Stockholm, Sweden, on February 18, 2009.

☆**Fastest relay running 100 miles by a team of 10**   The fastest time to complete 100 miles (160.9 km) by a team of 10 runners in relay is 8 hr. 19 min. 53 sec. by members of the ECU Cross-Country Alumni (U.S.A.). The record-breaking relay took place at Ada High School Track, Ada, Oklahoma, U.S.A., on December 31, 2009.

★**Fastest relay 100 x 10 kilometers**   The record for the fastest 100 x 10-km (6.2-mile) relay is 77 hr. 17 min. 25 sec. and was set by the Florida Striders Track Club (U.S.A.) at Bishop John J. Snyder High School, Jacksonville, Florida, U.S.A., on December 3–6, 2009.

☆**Fastest 100 km ultra distance track (women)**   Norimi Sakurai (Japan) ran 100 km (62.1 km) in 7 hr. 14 min. 6 sec. in Verona, Italy, on September 27, 2003.

SEVILLE, SPAIN (37°22'N 5°59'W): The Cathedral Church of Santa María de la Sede in Seville, Spain, covers the **greatest area of any Roman Catholic cathedral**. Built between 1402 and 1519, it is 414 ft. (126.2 m) long, 271 ft. (82.6 m) wide, and 100 ft. (30.5 m) high to the vault of the nave.

> **EXTRA!** For more exceptional track and field records, go to our sports reference section, starting on p. 512.

Most mountain running titles The ★ **most wins of the Mountain Running World Championship (male)** is six by Jonathan Wyatt (New Zealand), who was victorious in 1998, 2000, 2002, 2004–05, and 2008.

The ★ **most wins of the Mountain Running World Championship (female)** is four, which has been achieved by two runners: Isabelle Guillot (France) in 1989, 1991, 1993, and 1997; and Gudrun Pfluger (Austria) in 1992, 1994, 1995, and 1996.

Most European Athlete of the Year awards The ★ **most Men's European Athlete of the Year Trophies** won by an individual athlete is two, by three different athletes: Jonathan Edwards (UK) in 1995 and 1998; Jan Železný (Czech Republic) in 1996 and 2000; and Christian Olsson (Sweden) in 2003–04.

Similarly, the ★ **most Women's European Athlete of the Year Trophies** won by an individual athlete is also two, by Carolina Klüft (Sweden) in 2003 and 2006; and Yelena Isinbayeva (Russia) in 2005 and 2008. This annual award is decided by votes from members of the European Athletic Association, media, and fans.

WACKY WORLD CHAMPIONSHIPS

Largest audience at a camel wrestling festival At the 1994 Camel Wrestling Festival in Selçuk, Turkey, 20,000 people watched 120 dromedaries wrestle in a 2,000-year-old stadium in the city of Ephesus.

☆ **Most worms charmed** Sophie Smith (UK) charmed a record 567 worms in 30 minutes from a 9.84-ft.^{2} (3-m^2) plot at the 2009 World Worm Charming Championships, held in Willaston, Cheshire, UK, on June 17, 2009.

....

BELFAST, UK (54°36'N 5°55'W): Annalisa Wray (UK) achieved a shout of 121.7 dBA—the **loudest shout**—at the Citybus Challenge, Belfast, Co. Antrim, Northern Ireland, UK, on April 16, 1994. Ironically, the word she shouted out was "quiet."

....

FASTEST SNAIL The annual World Snail Racing Championships is held in July outside St. Andrew's Church in Congham, Norfolk, UK. Races are conducted on a 13-in. (33-cm) circular course, on which the snails race from the center to the perimeter. The all-time record holder is a snail named Archie, trained by Carl Bramham (UK), who "sprinted" to the winning post in 2 min. 20 sec. in 1995.

★ **FIRST REDNECK GAMES** In 1996, radio DJ Mac Davis (U.S.A.) of station Y-96 of East Dublin, Georgia, U.S.A., conceived the Redneck Games as an antidote to that year's Olympic Games in nearby Atlanta. "The media kept saying that the Olympics were going to be run by a bunch of rednecks," said Davis, "so we figured if that's what the world expects, we'll give it to them." The Games feature events such as the cigarette flip, bobbing for pig's trotters, and the mud-pit belly flop.

OLDEST SHIN-KICKING CHAMPIONSHIPS Competitive shin-kicking is known to have been taking place since 1636 as part of Robert Dover's Cotswold Olimpicks, held in England since 1612. These Olimpicks were hosted continually until 1644, then again from 1660 to 1852, revived in 1951, and then held annually from 1965. Competitors must wear soft shoes and can protect their shins with straw.

Most elephant polo World Championships
The Tiger Top Tuskers team (Nepal) have won the World Elephant Polo Association Championships in Nepal on eight occasions, in 1983–85, 1987, 1992, 1998, 2000, and 2003.

☆**Most Horseshoe Pitching World Championships (MALE)** Alan Francis (U.S.A.) has won a record 15 Horseshoe Pitching World Championships in the men's category, in 1989, 1993, 1995–99, 2001, and 2003–09. Historically the championships have been played at irregular intervals, but have been held every year since their inception in 1909.

Most consecutive World Pea Shooting Championships Three people have won the World Pea Shooting Championships, held annually in Witcham, Cambridgeshire, UK, on three consecutive occasions: Dennis Minett (UK) in 1971–73, Mike Fordham (UK) in 1983–85, and David Hollis (UK) in 1999–2001. Hollis was also the **youngest World Pea Shooting champion** when he scooped the title in 1999, age just 13 years old.

MOST TIDDLY-WINKS TITLES
Larry Khan (U.S.A.) won 19 singles titles at the Tiddlywinks World Championships between 1983 and 2003. He also won 10 pairs titles between 1978 and 1998.

QUIZ!: What number do you get if you add together the **most worms charmed** and the **most horseshoe pitching titles won**? See p. 544 for the answer.

FASTEST WIFE CARRYING Margo Uusarj and Sandra Kullas (both Estonia) completed the 831-ft.-8-in. (253.5-m) obstacle course at the World Wife-Carrying Championships, held annually in Sonkajärvi, Finland, in 56.9 seconds on July 1, 2006. This is the fastest time achieved since the rule for a minimum wife weight of 108 lb. (49 kg) was introduced in 2002.

DID YOU KNOW?

David Jones (UK) carried a record 110-lb. (50-kg) bag of coal over a 3,321-ft.-9-in. (1,012.5-m) course in 4 min. 6 sec. at the Coal Carrying Championship race at Gawthorpe, UK, on April 1, 1991.

TRIVIA

In tiddlywinks, the large disk, which is used to flip the smaller disks into the air, is called a "squidger."

☆ **Most wins of the Sauna World Championships** The Sauna World Championships are held in Heinola, Finland, each year. The title is awarded to the person who stays in the sauna for the longest time. Timo Kaukonen (Finland) has won the event five times, in 2003, 2005–07, and 2009.

Most World Conker Championships won (male) Two men have won the World Conker Championship in Ashton, Northamptonshire, UK, on three occasions: P. Midlane (UK) in 1969, 1973, and 1985, and J. Marsh (UK) in 1974, 1975, and 1994.

....

GIBRALTAR (36°08'N 5°21'W): The **most densely populated territory** is the British Crown Colony of Gibraltar, which has an estimated population of 27,714 (2002) in an area of 2.2 miles² (5.8 km²), giving a density of 12,597.2 people/mile² (4,778.2 people/km²).

....

SPORT STACKING Sport stacking involves stacking plastic cups in specific sequences in the fastest time possible. The current master of sport stacking is Steven Purugganan (U.S.A.), who holds many world records, including:
• The ★fastest sport stacking individual cycle stack, in 5.93 seconds on January 3, 2009.
• On April 19, 2009, at the WSSA World Sport Stacking Championships in Denver, Colorado, U.S.A., Team U.S.A. (comprising Purugganan along with Joel Brown, Luke Myers, and Alex Schumann, all U.S.A.) completed the ★fastest sport stacking 3-6-3 timed relay in 12.72 seconds.
• At the same event, Steven Purugganan and his brother Andrew Purugganan (U.S.A.) completed the ★fastest sport stacking doubles cycle stack in 7.58 seconds.

WATERSPORTS

DIVING

★**Most gold medals won at a single European championship** Tania Cagnotto (Italy) won an impressive three golds at the 2009 European Diving Championships in Turin, Italy, on April 5, 2009.

☆**Most World championships** Jingjing Guo (China) won a grand total of 10 FINA diving world titles, in the women's 3 m springboard, individual, and synchronized categories in 2001, 2003, 2005, 2007, and 2009.

CANOEING

★**Oldest Olympic medalist (female)** Josefa Idem (Italy, b. September 23, 1964) was age 43 years 335 days when she won silver in the K1 class 500 m flatwater event at the 2008 Olympic Games in Beijing, China, on August 23, 2008.

FES, MOROCCO (54°36'N 5°55'W): The **oldest existing and continually operating educational institution** in the world is the University of Karueein, founded in 859 A.D. in Fez, Morocco. The University of Bologna, Italy, was founded in 1088 and is the oldest university in Europe.

Greatest distance on flowing water in 24 hours Ian Adamson (U.S.A.) paddled 261.6 miles (421 km) down the Yukon River, Canada, on June 20–21, 2004.

SCUBA DIVING

★ **Longest dive in an enclosed environment** Cem Karabay (Turkey) spent 135 hr. 2 min. 19 sec. inside a water tank, breathing via scuba equipment, at the Beylikduzu Migros Shopping Mall in Istanbul, Turkey, from August 30 to September 5, 2009.

DOUGLAS, ISLE OF MAN (54°08'N 4°29'W): The **oldest trams in revenue service** are cars 1 and 2 of the Manx Electric Railway, dating from 1893. These run regularly on the 28.5-km (17.7-mile) railway between Douglas and Ramsey, Isle of Man, UK.

☆**FASTEST LONG COURSE 100 M BACKSTROKE (FEMALE)** Gemma Spofforth (UK) claimed her first World Championship title, and a world record into the bargain, with her 58.12-second swim in Rome, Italy, on July 28, 2009.

SWIMMING

The Marathon Swimming World Cup was an endurance swimming event organized by FINA and held between 1993 and 2006. Petar Stoychev (Bulgaria) holds the record for the ★ **most men's Marathon Swimming World Cups**, with six wins from 2001 to 2006.

The ★ **most women's Marathon Swimming World Cups** is the three wins racked up by Edith van Dijk (the Netherlands) in 2000–01 and 2005.

In 2007, the event was superseded by the FINA 10 km Marathon Swimming World Cup. Three swimmers share the record for the ★ **most FINA 10 km Marathon Swimming World Cups (male)**—Vladmir Dyatchin (Russia), Valerio Cleri (Italy), and Thomas Lurz (Germany) for their respective victories in 2007, 2008, and 2009.

Angela Maurer (Germany) has earned the distinction of winning the **most FINA 10 km Marathon Swimming World Cups (female)**, with a total of two victories, in 2007 and 2008.

☆**Largest race (open water)** A total of 13,755 participants swam the 2009 Midmar Mile at Midmar Dam, Howick, near Pietermaritzburg, South Africa, on February 7–8, 2009.

EXTRA! For more swimming records, dive into our sports reference section, starting on p. 512.

WIND: Björn Dunkerbeck also holds the records for ★ **most wave windsurfing titles** (seven wins) and ★ **most race windsurfing titles** (12 wins).

BRILLIANT BJÖRN World-beating windsurfer Björn Dunkerbeck (Switzerland) has the ★ **most Professional Windsurfers Association (PWA) World Championship titles**, with 33 wins between 1988 and 2001, including a PWA Freestyle World Championship victory in 1998 and a PWA Speed World Championship title in 1994.

☆ **FASTEST 2,000 M ROWING SINGLE SCULLS (MEN)** New Zealand rower Mahe Drysdale completed the 2,000 m course in the men's sculls in 6 min. 33.35 sec. at Poznań, Poland, on August 29, 2009.

BAGGED: In the course of his windsurfing career, Björn Dunkerbeck has picked up an impressive total of six Guinness World Records achievements.

UNIVERSITY BOAT RACE

The annual Boat Race held each spring between teams from the UK universities of Oxford and Cambridge was inaugurated on June 10, 1829, with a race from Hambledon Lock to Henley Bridge on the River Thames; Oxford won. Outrigged eights boats were first used in 1846 and have since been adopted as the standard vessel for the event.

In the 156 races to 2010, Cambridge has won a total of 80 times, Oxford 75 times, and there was a dead heat on March 24, 1877, handing Cambridge the record for the ☆ **most wins**.

Cambridge also holds the record for the ☆ **most consecutive wins**, with a series of 13 victories from 1924 to 1936.

The ☆ **oldest rower** was Mike Wherley (U.S.A., Oxford) at 36 years 14 days, in the 2008 race, although cox Andrew Probert (UK, Cambridge) was aged 38 years 3 months for the 1992 race.

Finally, the ☆ **lightest individual oarsman** was Alfred Higgins (UK), who weighed 132 lb. 6 oz. (60.1 kg) for the April 1, 1882, race.

WHEEL SKILLS

BICYCLE

• Xavi Casas (Andorra) recorded the ★ **most people stepped over by bicycle in two minutes** when he cleared 97 people on the set of *Guinness World Records*, Madrid, Spain, on January 14, 2009.

• Benito Ros Charral (Spain) recorded the ☆ **highest bunny hop on a bicycle**, achieving a hop of 4 ft. 8 in. (1.42 m) at the 2009 Bike the Rock festival in Heubach, Germany, on May 17, 2009.

• Charral has also accomplished the ★ **fastest time to bunny-hop 15 hurdles on a trials bicycle**, with a time of 26.08 seconds on the set of *Zheng Da Zong Yi—Guinness World Records Special* in Beijing, China, on November 20, 2009.

• Also on the set of *Zheng Da Zong Yi—Guinness World Records Special*, the UK's Ben Wallace recorded the ★ **highest bicycle backflip** with a flip of 8 ft. 6 in. (2.60 m).

• Austria's Thomas Öhler completed the ★ **highest bicycle wall climb** with a 9-ft.-5.9-in. (2.89-m) climb at the MTB Freestyle night, Kaprun, Austria, on August 7, 2009.

MÁLAGA, SPAIN (36°43'N 4°25'W): Robert Lantsoght of Málaga, Spain, has a collection of 4,393 individual golf clubs that he has been collecting since 1992—the **largest golf club collection**.

• Lance Trappe (U.S.A.) executed the ★ **most continuous front wheel hops on a bicycle**, with 108 hops at Lake Buena Vista, Florida, U.S.A., on June 16, 2009.

☆ **MOST 180° JUMPS (SWITCHES) ON A BICYCLE IN ONE MINUTE** Kenny Belaey (Belgium) performed 35 jumps of 180° at the Safety Jogger Classic bike festival held in Belgium, on September 20, 2009.

★ **MOST WORLD UNICYCLE HOCKEY TITLES** UNICON, the world championships of unicycling, has been held biennially since 1984. Unicycle hockey was added to the program of events in 1994, since when nine tournaments have been contested. The Swiss Power Team (Switzerland) has won the title a record three times, in 2004, 2006 and 2010 (pictured, dark jersey at left).

MISTY FLIP

Front flip with a 180° twist. The skater (or rider) either goes off the jump backward or lands backward.

WOW!: Stefan Akesson (Sweden) skateboard wheelied for a record 224 ft. 10 in. (68.54 m) in Stockholm, Sweden, on November 2, 2007.

★ **LONGEST JUMP IN A RALLY CAR** On December 31, 2009, in Long Beach, California, U.S.A., Travis Pastrana (U.S.A.) made a record leap of 269 ft. (81.9 m) in his Subaru rally car. The ramp-to-ramp jump was made off the Pine Street Pier onto a floating barge anchored in Long Beach's Rainbow Harbor as part of the "RedBull: New Year. No Limits" event.

> *"Our goal is to make this as authentic as possible . . . Just a full-on, old-school stunt."*
>
> **Travis Pastrana keeps rally-car jumping real**

☆ **MOST DOWNHILL SKATEBOARD CHAMPIONSHIPS (FEMALE)** Three women have won the International Gravity Sports Association Women's Downhill Championships on two occasions: Angelina Nobre (Switzerland) in 2004–05, Jolanda Vogler (Switzerland) in 2006–07, and Brianne Davies (Canada, pictured at left) in 2008–09.

LOW!: The **lowest motorcycle backflip** ever was 3 ft. (91 cm) off the ground, achieved by Travis Pastrana (U.S.A.) on November 17, 2008.

QUIZ!: Just how high was the highest wall climb on a bicycle? See p. 544 for the answer.

★**FASTEST INLINE SPEED SKATER OVER 300 M** On September 19, 2009, Joey Mantia (U.S.A.) set the fastest track 300 m by an individual male inline speed skater, as ratified by the sport's governing body, the Fédération Internationale de Roller Sports, when he recorded a time of 24.25 seconds in Haining, China.

INLINE SKATES

• Steve Swain (UK) completed the ★**highest misty flip on inline skates** with a 6-ft.-10-in. (2.08-m) attempt in London, UK, on April 23, 2009.

• The ☆**highest ramp jump on inline skates** is 15 ft. 5 in. (4.7 m) and was achieved by Zhang Baoxiang (China) in Beijing, China, on November 5, 2009.

• Paul Randles (UK) completed the ★**fastest 20-cone backward slalom on inline skates** in 5.62 seconds on the set of *Guinness World Records*, in Madrid, Spain, on January 23, 2009.

EXTRA! For more fun on wheels, take a long run and jump over to Autosports on p. 429.

GLASGOW, UK (55°51'N 4°15'W): The **tallest cinema complex** in the world is the Glasgow Cineworld, UK, with an overall height of 203 ft. 4 in. (62 m). Opening its doors on September 21, 2001, it is 12 stories high, holds 18 screens, and has a seating capacity of 4,277.

MOTORCYCLE

• The **longest motorcycle ramp jump** is 351 ft. (106.98 m), achieved by Robbie Maddison (Australia) at the Crusty Demons Night of World Records at Calder Park Raceway in Melbourne, Victoria, Australia, on March 29, 2008.
• Minibike master Ricardo Piedras (Spain) set the ★ **longest jump with a backflip performed on a minimoto** with his 41-ft.-9-in. (12.72-m) attempt on the set of *Lo Show dei Record* in Milan, Italy, on April 11, 2009.
• Michele Pradelli (Italy) performed the **longest standing jump on a motorcycle** with an attempt measuring 13 ft. 11 in. (4.26 m) on the set of *Lo Show dei Record* in Milan, Italy, on April 25, 2009.

SKATEBOARD

• The UK's Alex DeCunha recorded the ★ **most skateboarding no-comply flips in one minute** by achieving 56 flips in 60 seconds on the set of *Guinness World Records Smashed* at Pinewood Studios, UK, on April 15, 2009.
• Rob Dyrdek (U.S.A.) recorded the ★ **most skateboard 720 kick flips in one minute**—a total of seven—on MTV's *The Rob & Big Show* in Los Angeles, California, U.S.A., on September 17, 2007.
• On the same show, Dyrdek recorded the ★ **most heel-flip shove-its in one minute** with 10.
• With an effort of 4 ft. 11 in. (1.5 m), Terence Bougdour (France) set the record for the **highest skateboard 540 McTwist off a halfpipe** on the set of *L'Été De Tous Les Records* in La Tranche-sur-Mer, France, on July 27, 2005.

X GAMES

SUMMER

Longest skateboard ramp jump Pro skateboarder Danny Way (U.S.A.) performed a skateboard ramp jump with a 79-ft. (24-m) 360 air on his Mega Ramp at X Games 10 in Los Angeles, California, U.S.A., on August 8, 2004.

Youngest X games gold medalist On August 17, 2003, Ryan Sheckler (U.S.A., b. December 30, 1989) won the Skateboard Park gold medal at ESPN X Games 9 in Los Angeles, California, U.S.A. He was 13 years 230 days old.

ABIDJAN, IVORY COAST (5°20'N 4°01'W): The **highest altitude recorded for a bird** is 37,000 ft. (11,300 m) for a Rüppell's vulture (*Gyps rueppellii*), which collided with a commercial aircraft over Abidjan, Ivory Coast, on November 29, 1973.

EXTRA! For world championship games of a truly wacky nature, flip back to p. 490.

Lyn-z Adams Hawkins (U.S.A., b. September 1, 1989) became the **youngest female to win a gold medal at the X Games** in any discipline when she won the Skateboard Vert competition at age 14 years 321 days at X Games 10, Los Angeles, California, U.S.A., on August 7, 2004.

☆**Most medals** Dave Mirra (U.S.A.), who competes in BMX Freestyle, has won a total of 24 ESPN X Games medals.

Mirra also holds the record for the ☆**most BMX Freestyle medals**, with 23. Fourteen of those are gold, giving Mirra another record for the **most ESPN Summer X Games gold medals won**.

Most Moto X Medals at Summer X Games As of ESPN Summer X Games 12, held in 2006, Travis Pastrana (U.S.A.) had won 11 Moto X medals, including seven gold.

☆**MOST SUMMER X GAMES SKATE MEDALS** The greatest number of ESPN Summer X Games Skateboard medals is 19 and was achieved by Andy Macdonald (U.S.A.) between 1999 and 2009.

YOUNGEST X GAMES ATHLETE Nyjah Huston (U.S.A., b. November 30, 1994) was 11 years 246 days old when he made his debut at X Games 12 (August 3–6, 2006). He competed in the Men's Skateboard Street event.

★ MOST SNOWSKATE KICK FLIPS IN 30 SECONDS Max Hilty (U.S.A.) completed a total of 14 kick flips on his snowskate board in 30 seconds at Winter X Games 14 in Aspen, Colorado, U.S.A., on January 29, 2010.

Greatest attendance for a summer action sports event ESPN Summer X Games Five, held in San Francisco, California, U.S.A., were attended by 268,390 visitors over its 10-day duration

WINTER

☆**Most gold medals** Shaun White (U.S.A.) has won 10 ESPN Winter X Games gold medals. White's tally of gold medals all come from the snowboard SuperPipe and Slopestyle disciplines. He won his 10th gold medal at Winter X Games 14 in 2010.

☆**Most medals** Prolific X Games star Shaun White also holds the record for the most ESPN Winter X Games medals won, with 15. His 15th medal came at Winter X Games 14 in 2010.

★**FIRST AMPUTEE TO WIN A SUMMER X GAMES GOLD MEDAL** Riding a 2009 Suzuki RMZ450F, Chris Ridgway (U.S.A.) won gold in the X Games adaptive Moto X class at X Games 15 in Los Angeles, California, U.S.A., on July 31, 2009.

LONGEST MOTO X DIRT-TO-DIRT BACKFLIP Jeremy Stenberg (left), and Nate Adams (both U.S.A.) completed a Moto X dirt-to-dirt backflip of 100 ft. (30.48 m) during the Moto X Freestyle Finals at X Games 11 in. Los Angeles, California, U.S.A., on August 6, 2005.

DID YOU KNOW?

X Games knows no age limit. **Oldest medalist** Angelika Casteneda (U.S.A.) was 53 years old when she won gold in 1996 for the X Venture Race.

★ **MOST BMX WHEELIE HOPS** Manuel Torres (U.S.A.) performed 62 wheelie hops in 30 seconds at X Games 15 in Los Angeles, California, U.S.A., on July 30, 2009. A wheelie hop consists of lifting only the front wheel of a bike off the ground.

WINTER OLLIE DAYS Phil Smage (U.S.A.) is ollie royalty! He holds records for the **highest ollie** (27.75 in.; 70.5 cm), **longest ollie** (11 ft. 4 in.; 3.45 m), and **most ollies** (14) on a snowskate board.

Most skier X medals The largest medal haul for Skier X Men's is six by Enak Gavaggio (France). He took gold in 1999, four bronze in 2001–04, and a fifth at ESPN Winter X Games 11 in. Aspen/Snowmass, Colorado, U.S.A., on January 28, 2007.

Aleisha Cline (Canada), Magdalena Jonsson (Sweden), and Ophélie David (France) have all won five medals for Skier X, the ☆ **most Skier X Women's medals**. Out of that total, both Cline and David have won four golds.

STIRLING, UK (56°07'N 3°56'W): During an excavation project at Stirling Castle, Scotland, UK, in the mid-1970s, a gray leather ball was discovered behind oak paneling in a bedroom once used by Mary, Queen of Scots, during her reign in the 16th century. It is the world's **oldest soccer ball**.

★ **MOST SKATEBOARD SHOVE-ITS IN 30 SECONDS** The greatest number of skateboard shove-its achieved in 30 seconds is 14 by Eddie Davis (U.S.A.), at X Games 15 in Los Angeles, California, U.S.A., on July 30, 2009.

EXTRA! Are you mad for Mega Motors? Then put your foot down and head for p. 397.

☆ **Most skiing medals** Tanner Hall (U.S.A.) has won 11 ESPN Winter X Games medals in skiing disciplines, as of the ESPN Winter X Games 11 in. Aspen/Snowmass, Colorado, U.S.A., on January 28–31, 2007. Hall has won a gold for Big Air, three golds and one silver for Slopestyle, and three golds and three silvers for SuperPipe Men's.

Jon Olsson (Sweden) holds the record for the ☆ **most skiing Slopestyle medals**, with five: bronze in 2002–05 and 2008.

☆ **Most snocross medals** Tucker Hibbert (U.S.A.) has won nine SnoCross medals since 1999, comprising five golds, three silvers and one bronze.

Hibbert also holds the record for the ★ **most consecutive gold medals won in Winter X Games snowmobile SnoCross**, with four. He won his last gold at Winter X Games 14 in 2010. It was the first "four-peat" (four gold medals) in snowmobile history.

Greatest attendance for a winter action sports event A total of 85,100 spectators attended Winter X Games 5 in 2001 at Mount Snow, Vermont, U.S.A.

MADRID, SPAIN (40°24'N 3°41'W): Kinepolis Madrid, which opened in Spain on September 17, 1998, is the **world's largest movie theater complex**. It has a seating capacity of 9,200 from its 25 screens, which can, individually, seat between 211 and 996 people.

★**Highest ollie on a snowskate board** Phil Smage (U.S.A.) achieved a 28.5-in. (72.4-cm) ollie on a snowskate board at Winter X Games 14 in Aspen, Colorado, U.S.A., on January 29, 2010.

★**Most gold medals in women's Skier X** Ophélie David (France) has won a record four individual Winter X Games women's Skier X medals, a feat that represents the first "four-peat" in Winter X Games skiing history.

★**Highest air on skis on a SuperPipe** At Winter X Games 14 in Aspen, Colorado, U.S.A., on January 31, 2010, Peter Olenick (U.S.A.) managed a 24-ft.-11-in. (7.58-m) air on skis on a SuperPipe.

SKATEBOARD

★**Most backside grinds in 30 seconds** On July 31, 2009, Terrance Covington (U.S.A.) achieved 17 backside grinds in 30 seconds at X Games 15 in Los Angeles, California, U.S.A.

★**MOST OLLIES IN 30 SECONDS** Sten Carr (U.S.A.) performed a total of 34 ollies in 30 seconds at X Games 15 in Los Angeles, California, U.S.A., on August 2, 2009.

OLLIE
A no-hands aerial skateboard trick, named after skateboard legend Alan "Ollie" Gelfand.

★ **HIGHEST HIPPY JUMP ON A SNOWSKATE** Kyle Williams (U.S.A.) achieved an 18.5-in. (47-cm) hippy jump on a snowskate at Winter X Games 14 in Aspen, Colorado, U.S.A., on January 31, 2010.

★ **MOST HEELFLIPS AND NOLLIES IN 30 SECONDS** Ivan Sebastian Cordova (U.S.A.) performed a record nine skateboard heelflips in 30 seconds at X Games 15 in Los Angeles, California, U.S.A., on August 1, 2009.

At the same event, Ivan performed the ★ **most nollies in 30 seconds**: 15.

★ **Most rock and rolls in 30 seconds** Terrance Covington and Dalton Price (both U.S.A.) achieved a total of 16 rock and rolls in 30 seconds at X Games 15 in Los Angeles, California, U.S.A., on July 31, 2009.

★ **Most 360 frontside spins in 30 seconds** Lunati Hamilton (U.S.A.) performed six 360 frontside spins in 30 seconds at X Games 15 in Los Angeles, California, U.S.A., on July 30, 2009.

SNOWBOARD

★ **Highest air on a snowboard on a SuperPipe** On January 30, 2010, at Winter X Games 14 in Aspen, Colorado, U.S.A., Shaun White (U.S.A.) performed a 23-ft. (7-m) air on a snowboard on a SuperPipe.

HIGH!: Danny Way (U.S.A.) performed the **highest skateboard air off a quarterpipe**—23 ft. 6 in. (7.1 m)— off a 27-ft. (8.2-m) ramp on June 19, 2003.

WINTER WINNERS GWR truly established a presence at Winter X Games 14 in January 2010, carrying out a host of record attempts with skating, biking, snowboarding kids. Pictured above are some of those who set new records.

HIGHER!: The **highest air on a BMX bike** is 26 ft. 6 in. (8.07 m) by Mat Hoffman (U.S.A.), on March 20, 2001. He was towed by a motorcycle in the run-up.

★**Most consecutive Snowboarder X gold medals** Nate Holland (U.S.A.) had won five consecutive gold medals at the Winter X Games Snowboarder X competition as of January 2010. Holland won his fifth gold medal (an achievement known as the "five-peat")—the first in the history of the tournament—at Winter X Games 14 in 2010.

CARDIFF, UK (51°29'N 3°11'W): On November 29, 2005, scientists at Cardiff University in Wales, UK, announced the development of machinery that can drill holes just 22 microns (0.00087 inches) across, making them the **smallest holes ever drilled**.

☆**Most snowboarder x medals** Seth Wescott (U.S.A.) has won an unprecedented seven medals for Snowboarder X Men's: he picked up four silvers in 2002, 2004, 2005, and 2010 and three bronzes in 1998, 2001, and 2007.

The ☆**most medals for Snowboarder X Women's** won at Winter X Games competitions is seven by Lindsey Jacobellis (U.S.A.), who won six golds in 2003–05 and 2008–10 and silver at Winter X Games 11 in. Aspen/Snowmass, Colorado, U.S.A., in January 2007.

☆**Most slopestyle medals** Shaun White (U.S.A.) has picked up an unprecedented eight snowboard Slopestyle Winter X Games medals. He won five golds in 2003–06 and 2009, a silver in 2002, and two bronze medals in 2007–08.

The ☆**most women's snowboard Slopestyle medals** won at the Winter X Games is six by Janna Meyen-Weatherby (U.S.A.). She collected four gold medals in 2003–06, a silver medal in 2002, and a bronze medal in 2010.

☆**Most SuperPipe medals** Shaun White has seven medals in the men's snowboard SuperPipe at the Winter X Games: five gold medals (2003, 2006, and 2008–10) and two silvers (2002 and 2007).

He has also won the most ☆**medals overall** (14) and the ☆**most gold medals** (10) in Winter X Games history.

Kelly Clark (U.S.A.) has won the ☆**most women's snowboard SuperPipe medals**, with seven: gold in 2002 and 2006, silver in 2003–04 and 2009–10, and bronze in 2008.

SPORTS REFERENCE

★ TRACK & FIELD—OUTDOOR TRACK EVENTS ★

MEN	TIME/DISTANCE	NAME & NATIONALITY
☆ 100 m	9.58	Usain Bolt (Jamaica)
☆ 200 m	19.19	Usain Bolt (Jamaica)
400 m	43.18	Michael Johnson (U.S.A.)
800 m	1:41.11	Wilson Kipketer (Denmark)
1,000 m	2:11.96	Noah Ngeny (Kenya)
1,500 m	3:26.00	Hicham El Guerrouj (Morocco)
1 mile	3:43.13	Hicham El Guerrouj (Morocco)
2,000 m	4:44.79	Hicham El Guerrouj (Morocco)
3,000 m	7:20.67	Daniel Komen (Kenya)
5,000 m	12:37.35	Kenenisa Bekele (Ethiopia)
10,000 m	26:17.53	Kenenisa Bekele (Ethiopia)
20,000 m	56:26.00	Haile Gebrselassie (Ethiopia)
1 hour	21,285 m	Haile Gebrselassie (Ethiopia)
25,000 m	1:13:55.80	Toshihiko Seko (Japan)
30,000 m	1:29:18.80	Toshihiko Seko (Japan)
3,000 m steeplechase	7:53.63	Saif Saaeed Shaheen (Qatar)
110 m hurdles	12.87	Dayron Robles (Cuba)
400 m hurdles	46.78	Kevin Young (U.S.A.)
4 x 100 m relay	37.10	Jamaica (Asafa Powell, Nesta Carter, Michael Frater, Usain Bolt)
4 x 200 m relay	1:18.68	Santa Monica Track Club, U.S.A. (Michael Marsh, Leroy Burrell, Floyd Heard, Carl Lewis)
4 x 400 m relay	2:54.29	U.S.A. (Andrew Valmon, Quincy Watts, Harry Reynolds, Michael Johnson)
4 x 800 m relay	7:02.43	Kenya (Joseph Mutua, William Yiampoy, Ismael Kombich, Wilfred Bungei)
☆ 4 x 1,500 m relay	14:36.23	Kenya (Geoffrey Kipkoech Rono, Augustine Kiprono Choge, William Biwott Tanui, Gideon Gathimba)

WOMEN	TIME/DISTANCE	NAME & NATIONALITY
100 m	10.49	Florence Griffith-Joyner (U.S.A.)
200 m	21.34	Florence Griffith-Joyner (U.S.A.)
400 m	47.60	Marita Koch (GDR)
800 m	1:53.28	Jarmila Kratochvílová (Czechoslovakia)
1,000 m	2:28.98	Svetlana Masterkova (Russia)
1,500 m	3:50.46	Qu Yunxia (China)
1 mile	4:12.56	Svetlana Masterkova (Russia)
2,000 m	5:25.36	Sonia O'Sullivan (Ireland)
3,000 m	8:06.11	Wang Junxia (China)
5,000 m	14:11:.15	Tirunesh Dibaba (Ethiopia)

LOCATION	DATE
Berlin, Germany	Aug. 16, 2009
Berlin, Germany	Aug. 20, 2009
Seville, Spain	Aug. 26, 1999
Cologne, Germany	Aug. 24, 1997
Rieti, Italy	Sep. 5, 1999
Rome, Italy	Jul. 14, 1998
Rome, Italy	Jul. 7, 1999
Berlin, Germany	Sep. 7, 1999
Rieti, Italy	Sep. 1, 1996
Hengelo, the Netherlands	May 31, 2004
Brussels, Belgium	Aug. 26, 2005
Ostrava, Czech Republic	Jun. 26, 2007
Ostrava, Czech Republic	Jun. 27, 2007
Christchurch, New Zealand	Mar. 22, 1981
Christchurch, New Zealand	Mar. 22 1981
Brussels, Belgium	Sep. 3, 2004
Ostrava, Czech Republic	Jun. 12, 2008
Barcelona, Spain	Aug. 6, 1992
Beijing, China	Aug. 22, 2008
Walnut, U.S.A.	Apr. 17, 1994
Stuttgart, Germany	Aug. 22, 1993
Brussels, Belgium	Aug. 25, 2006
Brussels, Belgium	Sep. 4, 2009

MEN'S OUTDOOR 1,500 M In a record that has stood for more than 12 years, Hicham El Guerrouj (Morocco) won the 1,500 m event at the IAAF Golden League Golden Gala in Rome, Italy, in a time of 3 min. 26 sec. on July 14, 1998. He also holds the world records for the mile and the 2,000 m.

LOCATION	DATE
Indianapolis, U.S.A.	Jul. 16, 1988
Seoul, South Korea	Sep. 29, 1988
Canberra, Australia	Oct. 6, 1985
Munich, Germany	Jul. 26, 1983
Brussels, Belgium	Aug. 23, 1996
Beijing, China	Sep. 11, 1993
Zurich, Switzerland	Aug. 14, 1996
Edinburgh, UK	Jul. 8, 1994
Beijing, China	Sep. 13, 1993
Oslo, Norway	Jun. 6, 2008

OFF THE TRACK?: Aside from Usain Bolt's remarkable 100 m and 200 m runs (see above), very few track & field records were broken in 2009.

WOMEN	TIME/DISTANCE	NAME & NATIONALITY
10,000 m	29:31.78	Wang Junxia (China)
20,000 m	1:05:26.60	Tegla Loroupe (Kenya)
1 hour	18,517 m	Dire Tune (Ethiopia)
25,000 m	1:27:05.90	Tegla Loroupe (Kenya)
30,000 m	1:45:50.00	Tegla Loroupe (Kenya)
3,000 m steeplechase	8:58.81	Gulnara Samitova-Galkina (Russia)
100 m hurdles	12.21	Yordanka Donkova (Bulgaria)
400 m hurdles	52.34	Yuliya Pechonkina (Russia)
4 x 100 m relay	41.37	GDR (Silke Gladisch, Sabine Rieger, Ingrid Auerswald, Marlies Göhr)
4 x 200 m relay	1:27.46	United States "Blue" (LaTasha Jenkins, LaTasha Colander-Richardson, Nanceen Perry, Marion Jones)
4 x 400 m relay	3:15.17	USSR (Tatyana Ledovskaya, Olga Nazarova, Maria Pinigina, Olga Bryzgina)
4 x 800 m relay	7:50.17	USSR (Nadezhda Olizarenko, Lyubov Gurina, Lyudmila Borisova, Irina Podyalovskaya)

★ TRACK & FIELD—INDOOR TRACK EVENTS ★

MEN	TIME	NAME & NATIONALITY
50 m	5.56	Donovan Bailey (Canada)
60 m	6.39	Maurice Green (U.S.A.)
	6.39	Maurice Green (U.S.A.)
200 m	19.92	Frankie Fredericks (Namibia)
400 m	44.57	Kerron Clement (U.S.A.)
800 m	1:42.67	Wilson Kipketer (Denmark)
1,000 m	2:14.96	Wilson Kipketer (Denmark)
1,500 m	3:31.18	Hicham El Guerrouj (Morocco)
1 mile	3:48.45	Hicham El Guerrouj (Morocco)
3,000 m	7:24.90	Daniel Komen (Kenya)
5,000 m	12:49.60	Kenenisa Bekele (Ethiopia)
50 m hurdles	6.25	Mark McKoy (Canada)
60 m hurdles	7.30	Colin Jackson (GB)
4 x 200 m relay	1:22.11	Great Britain & N. Ireland (Linford Christie, Darren Braithwaite, Ade Mafe, John Regis)
4 x 400 m relay	3:02.83	U.S.A. (Andre Morris, Dameon Johnson, Deon Minor, Milton Campbell)
4 x 800 m relay	7:13.94	Global Athletics & Marketing, U.S.A. (Joey Woody, Karl Paranya, Rich Kenah, David Krummenacker)
5,000 m walk	18:07.08	Mikhail Shchennikov (Russia)

EDINBURGH, UK (55°57'N 3°09'W): The world's **largest performing arts festival** is the annual Edinburgh Festival Fringe, instituted in 1947. Between August 7 and 31, 2009, its record year, there were 18,901 artists and 34,265 performances of 2,265 shows, and the box office sold no less than 1,859,235 tickets.

LOCATION	DATE
Beijing, China	Sep. 8, 1993
Borgholzhausen, Germany	Sep. 3, 2000
Ostrava, Czech Republic	Jun. 12, 2008
Mengerskirchen, Germany	Sep. 21, 2002
Warstein, Germany	Jun. 6, 2003
Beijing, China	Aug. 17, 2008
Stara Zagora, Bulgaria	Aug. 20, 1988
Tula, Russia	Aug. 8, 2003
Canberra, Australia	Oct. 6, 1985
Philadelphia, U.S.A.	Apr. 29, 2000
Seoul, South Korea	Oct. 1, 1988
Moscow, Russia	Aug. 5, 1984

LOCATION	DATE
Reno, U.S.A.	Feb. 9, 1996
Madrid, Spain	Feb. 3, 1998
Atlanta, U.S.A.	Mar. 3, 2001
Liévin, France	Feb. 18, 1996
Fayetteville, U.S.A.	Mar. 12, 2005
Paris, France	Mar. 9, 1997
Birmingham, UK	Feb. 20, 2000
Stuttgart, Germany	Feb. 2, 1997
Ghent, Belgium	Feb. 12, 1997
Budapest, Hungary	Feb. 6, 1998
Birmingham, UK	Feb. 20, 2004
Kobe, Japan	Mar. 5, 1986
Sindelfingen, Germany	Mar. 6, 1994
Glasgow, UK	Mar. 3, 1991
Maebashi, Japan	Mar. 7, 1999
Boston, U.S.A.	Feb. 6, 2000
Moscow, Russia	Feb. 14, 1995

DUNDEE, UK (56°28'N 2°59'W): Jenny Wood-Allen (b. 1911) from Dundee, UK, is the **oldest female to complete a marathon**. She ran the 2002 London Marathon in 11 hr. 34 min., age 90 years 145 days.

★ TRACK & FIELD—INDOOR TRACK EVENTS ★

WOMEN	TIME	NAME & NATIONALITY
50 m	5.96	Irina Privalova (Russia)
60 m	6.92	Irina Privalova (Russia)
	6.92	Irina Privalova (Russia)
200 m	21.87	Merlene Ottey (Jamaica)
400 m	49.59	Jarmila Kratochvílová (Czechoslovakia)
800 m	1:55.82	Jolanda Ceplak (Slovenia)
1,000 m	2:30.94	Maria de Lurdes Mutola (Mozambique)
1,500 m	3:58.28	Yelena Soboleva (Russia)
1 mile	4:17.14	Doina Melinte (Romania)
3,000 m	8:23.72	Meseret Defar (Ethiopia)
5,000 m	14:24.37	Meseret Defar (Ethiopia)
50 m hurdles	6.58	Cornelia Oschkenat (GDR)
60 m hurdles	7.68	Susanna Kallur (Sweden)
4 x 200 m relay	1:32.41	Russia (Yekaterina Kondratyeva, Irina Khabarova, Yuliya Pechonkina, Yulia Gushchina)
4 x 400 m relay	3:23.37	Russia (Yulia Gushchina, Olga Kotlyarova, Olga Zaytseva, Olesya Krasnomovets)
4 x 800 m relay	•8:12.41	Moskow 1 (Tatyana Andrianova, Oksana Sukhachova-Spasovkhodskaya, Elena Kofanova Yevgeniya Zinurova)
3,000 m walk	11:40.33	Claudia Stef (Romania)

•Still awaiting ratification at the time of going to press

★ TRACK & FIELD—ULTRA-LONG DISTANCE [TRACK] ★

MEN	TIME/DISTANCE	NAME & NATIONALITY
50 km	2:48:06	Jeff Norman (GB)
100 km	6:10:20	Donald Ritchie (GB)
100 miles	11:28:03	Oleg Kharitonov (Russia)
1,000 km	5 days 16:17:00	Yiannis Kouros (Greece)
1,000 miles	11 days 13:54:58	Peter Silkinas (Lithuania)
6 hours	97.2 km (60.4 miles)	Donald Ritchie (GB)
12 hours	162.4 km (100.91 miles)	Yiannis Kouros (Greece)
24 hours	303.506 km (188.59 miles)	Yiannis Kouros (Greece)
48 hours	473.495 km (294.21 miles)	Yiannis Kouros (Greece)
6 days	1,038.851 km (645.51 miles)	Yiannis Kouros (Greece)

WOMEN	TIME/DISTANCE	NAME & NATIONALITY
50 km	3:18:52	Carolyn Hunter-Rowe (GB)
100 km	7:14:06	Norimi Sakurai (Japan)
100 miles	14:25:45	Edit Berces (Hungary)
1,000 km	7 days 01:28:29	Eleanor Robinson (GB)
1,000 miles	13 days 1:54:02	Eleanor Robinson (GB)
6 hours	83.2 km (57.7 miles)	Norimi Sakurai (Japan)
12 hours	147.6 km (91.71 miles)	Ann Trason (U.S.A.)
24 hours	250.106 km (155.40 miles)	Edit Berces (Hungary)
☆48 hours	385.130 km (239.31 miles)	Mami Kudo (Japan)
6 days	883.631 km (549.06 miles)	Sandra Barwick (New Zealand)

LOCATION	DATE
Madrid, Spain	Feb. 9, 1995
Madrid, Spain	Feb. 11, 1993
Madrid, Spain	Feb. 9, 1995
Liévin, France	Feb. 13, 1993
Milan, Italy	Mar. 7, 1982
Vienna, Austria	Mar. 3, 2002
Stockholm, Sweden	Feb. 25, 1999
Moscow, Russia	Feb. 18, 2006
East Rutherford, U.S.A.	Feb. 9, 1990
Stuttgart, Germany	Feb. 3, 2007
Stockholm, Sweden	Feb. 18, 2009
Berlin, Germany	Feb. 20, 1988
Karlsruhe, Germany	Feb. 10, 2008
Glasgow, UK	Jan. 29, 2005
Glasgow, UK	Jan. 28, 2006
Moscow, Russia	Feb. 28, 2010
Bucharest, Romania	Jan. 30, 1999

INDOOR 5,000 M
Meseret Defar (Ethiopia) is elated after winning the women's 5,000 m in a time of 14 min. 24.37 sec. at the Stockholm Globe Arena, Sweden, on February 18, 2009.

LOCATION	DATE
Timperley, UK	Jun. 7, 1980
London, UK	Oct. 28, 1978
London, UK	Oct. 20, 2002
Colac, Australia	Nov. 26–Dec. 1, 1984
Nanango, Australia	Mar. 11–23, 1998
London, UK	Oct. 28, 1978
Montauban, France	Mar. 15–16, 1985
Adelaide, Australia	Oct. 4–5, 1997
Surgères, France	May 3–5, 1996
Colac, Australia	Nov. 20–25, 2005

LOCATION	DATE
Barry, UK	Mar. 3, 1996
Verona, Italy	Sep. 27, 2003
Verona, Italy	Sep. 21–22, 2002
Nanango, Australia	Mar. 11–18, 1998
Nanango, Australia	Mar. 11–23, 1998
Verona, Italy	Sep. 27, 2003
Hayward, U.S.A.	Aug. 3–4, 1991
Verona, Italy	Sep. 21–22, 2002
Surgères, France	May 22–24, 2009
Campbelltown, Australia	Nov. 18–24, 1990

OFFICIAL WEBSITES

TRACK & FIELD:
www.iaaf.org

ULTRARUNNING:
www.iau.org.tw

★ TRACK & FIELD—ROAD RACE ★

MEN	TIME	NAME & NATIONALITY
☆ 10 km	27:01	Micah Kipkemboi Kogo (Kenya)
15 km	41:29	Felix Limo (Kenya)
	41:29	Deriba Merga (Ethiopia)
☆ 20 km	55:21	Zersenay Tadese (Eritrea)
☆ Half marathon	58:23	Zersenay Tadese (Eritrea)
☆ 25 km	•1:11:50	Samuel Kiplimo Kosgei (Kenya)
☆ 30 km	1:27:49	Haile Gebrselassie (Ethiopia)
Marathon	2:03:59	Haile Gebrselassie (Ethiopia)
100 km	6:13:33	Takahiro Sunada (Japan)
Road relay	1:57:06	Kenya (Josephat Ndambiri, Martin Mathathi, Daniel Mwangi, Mekubo Mogusu, Onesmus Nyerere, John Kariuki)

WOMEN	TIME	NAME & NATIONALITY
10 km	30:21	Paula Radcliffe (GB)
☆ 15 km	46:28	Tirunesh Dibaba (Ethiopia)
20 km	1:02:57	Lornah Kiplagat (the Netherlands)
Half marathon	1:06:25	Lornah Kiplagat (the Netherlands)
25 km	1:22:13	Mizuki Noguchi (Japan)
30 km	1:38:49	Mizuki Noguchi (Japan)
Marathon	2:15:25	Paula Radcliffe (GB)
100 km	6:33:11	Tomoe Abe (Japan)
Road relay	2:11:41	China (Jiang Bo, Dong Yanmei, Zhao Fentgting, Ma Zaijie, Lan Lixin, Li Na)

•Still awaiting ratification at the time of going to press

★ TRACK & FIELD—RACE WALKING ★

MEN	TIME	NAME & NATIONALITY
20,000 m	1:17:25.6	Bernardo Segura (Mexico)
20 km (road)	1:17:16	Vladimir Kanaykin (Russia)
30,000 m	2:01:44.1	Maurizio Damilano (Italy)
50,000 m	3:40:57.9	Thierry Toutain (France)
50 km (road)	3:34:14	Denis Nizhegorodov (Russia)

WOMEN	TIME	NAME & NATIONALITY
10,000 m	41:56.23	Nadezhda Ryashkina (USSR)
20,000 m	1:26:52.3	Olimpiada Ivanova (Russia)
20 km (road)	1:25:41	Olimpiada Ivanova (Russia)

LOCATION	DATE
Brunssum, the Netherlands	Mar. 29, 2009
Nijmegen, the Netherlands	Nov. 11, 2001
Ras Al Khaimah, UAE	Feb. 20, 2009
Lisbon, Portugal	Mar. 21, 2010
Lisbon, Portugal	Mar. 21, 2010
Berlin, Germany	May 9, 2010
Berlin, Germany	Sep. 20, 2009
Berlin, Germany	Sep. 28, 2008
Tokoro, Japan	Jun. 21, 1998
Chiba, Japan	Nov. 23, 2005

☆ **MEN'S HALF MARATHON** On March 21, 2010, Zersenay Tadese (Eritrea) won the 20th Lisbon Half Marathon in Portugal. He did so in a time of 58 min. 23 sec., and during the same race ran 20 km in a record 55 min. 21 sec.

LOCATION	DATE
San Juan, Puerto Rico	Feb. 23, 2003
Nijmegen, the Netherlands	Nov. 15, 2009
Udine, Italy	Oct. 14, 2007
Udine, Italy	Oct. 14, 2007
Berlin, Germany	Sep. 25, 2005
Berlin, Germany	Sep. 25, 2005
London, UK	Apr. 13, 2003
Tokoro, Japan	Jun. 25, 2000
Beijing, China	Feb. 28, 1998

LOCATION	DATE
Bergen, Norway	May 7, 1994
Saransk, Russia	Sep. 29, 2007
Cuneo, Italy	Oct. 3, 1992
Héricourt, France	Sep. 29, 1996
Cheboksary, Russia	May 11, 2008

LOCATION	DATE
Seattle, U.S.A.	Jul. 24, 1990
Brisbane, Australia	Sep. 6, 2001
Helsinki, Finland	Aug. 7, 2005

★ TRACK & FIELD—INDOOR FIELD EVENTS ★

MEN	RECORD	NAME & NATIONALITY
High jump	2.43 m (7 ft. 11.66 in.)	Javier Sotomayor (Cuba)
Pole vault	6.15 m (20 ft. 2.12 in.)	Sergei Bubka (Ukraine)
Long jump	8.79 m (28 ft. 10.06 in.)	Carl Lewis (U.S.A.)
☆ Triple jump	17.90 m (58 ft. 9 in.)	Teddy Tamgho (France)
Shot	22.66 m (74 ft. 4.12 in.)	Randy Barnes (U.S.A.)
☆ Heptathlon*	•6,499 points	Ashton Eaton (U.S.A.)

*60 m 6.71 seconds; long jump 7.73 m; shot 13.12 m; high jump 2.11 m; 60 m hurdles 7.77 seconds; pole vault 5.10 m; 1,000 m 2 min. 32.67 sec.

WOMEN	RECORD	NAME & NATIONALITY
High jump	2.08 m (6 ft. 9.8 in.)	Kajsa Bergqvist (Sweden)
Pole vault	5.00 m (16 ft. 4 in.)	Yelena Isinbayeva (Russia)
Long jump	7.37 m (24 ft. 2.15 in.)	Heike Drechsler (GDR)
Triple jump	15.36 m (50 ft. 4.72 in.)	Tatyana Lebedeva (Russia)
Shot	22.50 m (73 ft. 9.82 in.)	Helena Fibingerová (Czechoslovakia)
Pentathlon†	4,991 points	Irina Belova (Russia)

†60 m hurdles 8.22 seconds; high jump 1.93 m; shot 13.25 m; long jump 6.67 m; 800 m 2 min. 10.26 sec.

•Still awaiting ratification at time of going to press

★ TRACK & FIELD—OUTDOOR FIELD EVENTS ★

MEN	RECORD	NAME & NATIONALITY
High jump	2.45 m (8 ft. 0.45 in.)	Javier Sotomayor (Cuba)
Pole vault	6.14 m (20 ft. 1.73 in.)	Sergei Bubka (Ukraine)
Long jump	8.95 m (29 ft. 4.36 in.)	Mike Powell (U.S.A.)
Triple jump	18.29 m (60 ft. 0.78 in.)	Jonathan Edwards (GB)
Shot	23.12 m (75 ft. 10.23 in.)	Randy Barnes (U.S.A.)
Discus	74.08 m (243 ft. 0.53 in.)	Jürgen Schult (USSR)
Hammer	86.74 m (284 ft. 7 in.)	Yuriy Sedykh (USSR)
Javelin	98.48 m (323 ft. 1.16 in.)	Jan Železný (Czech Republic)
Decathlon*	9,026 points	Roman Šebrle (Czech Republic)

*100 m 10.64 seconds; long jump 8.11 m; shot 15.33 m; high jump 2.12 m; 400 m 47.79 seconds; 110 m hurdles 13.92 seconds; discus 47.92 m; pole vault 4.80 m; javelin 70.16 m; 1,500 m 4 min. 21.98 sec.

....

LIVERPOOL, UK (53°24'N 2°59'W): The **most European Cups won by a soccer manager** is three by Bob Paisley (UK) for Liverpool FC in 1977–78 and 1981.

....

LOCATION	DATE
Budapest, Hungary	Mar. 4, 1989
Donetsk, Ukraine	Feb. 21, 1993
New York City, U.S.A.	Jan. 27, 1984
Doha, Qatar	Mar. 14, 2010
Los Angeles, U.S.A.	Jan. 20, 1989
Fayetteville, U.S.A.	Mar. 13, 2010

LOCATION	DATE
Arnstadt, Germany	Feb. 4, 2006
Donetsk, Ukraine	Feb. 15, 2009
Vienna, Austria	Feb. 13, 1988
Budapest, Hungary	Mar. 6, 2004
Jablonec, Czechoslovakia	Feb. 19, 1977
Berlin, Germany	Feb. 15, 1992

☆HEPTATHLON Ashton Eaton (U.S.A.) is shown above during the pole vault competition of the heptathlon in Fayetteville, U.S.A., on March 13, 2010. He set a new mark of 6,499 points, thereby breaking Dan O'Brien's 17-year-old record.

LOCATION	DATE
Salamanca, Spain	Jul. 27, 1993
Sestriere, Italy	Jul. 31, 1994
Tokyo, Japan	Aug. 30, 1991
Gothenburg, Sweden	Aug. 7, 1995
Los Angeles, U.S.A.	May 20, 1990
Neubrandenburg, Germany	Jun. 6, 1986
Stuttgart, Germany	Aug. 30, 1986
Jena, Germany	May 25, 1996
Götzis, Austria	May 27, 2001

OFFICIAL WEBSITES

TRACK & FIELD & RACE WALKING:
www.iaaf.org

CYCLING:
www.uci.ch

DID YOU KNOW?

Track racing dates back to the end of the 19th century. The first track World Championships were held in 1895. Cycling was also included as an event in the first modern Olympic Games of 1896.

★ TRACK & FIELD—OUTDOOR FIELD EVENTS ★

WOMEN	RECORD	NAME & NATIONALITY
High jump	2.09 m (6 ft. 10.28 in.)	Stefka Kostadinova (Bulgaria)
☆ Pole vault	5.06 m (16 ft. 7.21 in.)	Yelena Isinbayeva (Russia)
Long jump	7.52 m (24 ft. 8.06 in.)	Galina Chistyakova (USSR)
Triple jump	15.50 m (50 ft. 10.23 in.)	Inessa Kravets (Ukraine)
Shot	22.63 m (74 ft. 2.94 in.)	Natalya Lisovskaya (USSR)
Discus	76.80 m (252 ft.)	Gabriele Reinsch (GDR)
☆ Hammer	77.96 m (255 ft. 9 in.)	Anita Wlodarczyk (Poland)
Javelin	72.28 m (253 ft. 6 in.)	Barbora Spotáková (Czech Republic)
Heptathlon†	7,291 points	Jacqueline Joyner-Kersee (U.S.A.)
Decathlon**	8,358 points	Austra Skujyte (Lithuania)

†100 m hurdles 12.69 seconds; high jump 1.86 m; shot 15.80 m; 200 m 22.56 seconds; long jump 7.27 m; javelin 45.66 m; 800 m 2 min. 8.51 sec.

**100 m 12.49 seconds; long jump 6.12 m; shot 16.42 m; high jump 1.78 m; 400 m 57.19 seconds; 100 m hurdles 14.22 seconds; discus 46.19 m; pole vault 3.10 m; javelin 48.78 m; 1,500 m 5 min. 15.86 sec.

★ CYCLING—ABSOLUTE TRACK ★

MEN	TIME/DISTANCE	NAME & NATIONALITY
☆ 200 m (flying start)	9.572	Kevin Sireau (France)
500 m (flying start)	24.758	Chris Hoy (GB)
1 km (standing start)	58.875	Arnaud Tournant (France)
4 km (standing start)	4:11.114	Christopher Boardman (GB)
Team 4 km (standing start)	3:53.314	Great Britain (Ed Clancy, Paul Manning, Geraint Thomas, Bradley Wiggins)
1 hour	*49.7 km	Ondrej Sosenka (Czech Republic)

WOMEN	TIME/DISTANCE	NAME & NATIONALITY
200 m (flying start)	10.831	Olga Slioussareva (Russia)
500 m (flying start)	29.655	Erika Salumäe (Estonia)
☆ 500 m (standing start)	33.296	Simona Krupeckaite (Lithuania)
3 km (standing start)	3:24.537	Sarah Ulmer (New Zealand)
1 hour	*46.065 km	Leontien Zijlaard–Van Moorsel (the Netherlands)

*Some athletes achieved better distances within an hour with bicycles that are no longer allowed by the Union Cycliste Internationale (UCI). The 1-hour records given here are in accordance with the new UCI rules.

BILBAO, SPAIN (43°15'N 2°55'W): The Guggenheim Museum in Bilbao, Spain, which opened on October 18, 1997, has a length of 450 ft. (137.16 m), making it the **largest single gallery space**.

LOCATION	DATE
Rome, Italy	Aug. 30, 1987
Zurich, Switzerland	Aug. 28, 2009
St. Petersburg, Russia	Jun. 11, 1988
Gothenburg, Sweden	Aug. 10, 1995
Moscow, Russia	Jun. 7, 1987
Neubrandenburg, Germany	Jul. 9, 1988
Berlin, Germany	Aug. 22, 2009
Stuttgart, Germany	Sep. 13, 2008
Seoul, South Korea	Sep. 24, 1988
Columbia, U.S.A.	Apr. 15, 2005

☆ **WOMEN'S POLE VAULT**
Russia's Yelena Isinbayeva is regarded by many as the greatest female pole vaulter of all time. She holds 27 world records (15 outdoor and 12 indoor). Here she celebrates after breaking her own outdoor record by clearing 16 ft. 7.21 in. (5.06 m) at the IAAF Golden League Athletics meeting in Zurich, Switzerland, on August 28, 2009.

LOCATION	DATE
Moscow Russia	May 30, 2009
La Paz, Bolivia	May 13, 2007
La Paz, Bolivia	Oct. 10, 2001
Manchester, UK	Aug. 29, 1996
Beijing, China	Aug. 18, 2008
Moscow, Russia	Jul. 19, 2005

LOCATION	DATE
Moscow, Russia	Apr. 25, 1993
Moscow, Russia	Aug. 6, 1987
Pruszków, Poland	Mar. 25, 2009
Athens, Greece	Aug. 22, 2004
Mexico City, Mexico	Oct. 1, 2003

MEN'S CYCLING 500 M FLYING START Chris Hoy (UK) celebrates breaking the world 500 m altitude record at the Alto Irpavi Velodrome on May 13, 2007, in La Paz, Bolivia. He achieved a time of 24.758 seconds.

MEN'S DEPTH DISCIPLINES

MEN'S DEPTH DISCIPLINES	DEPTH/TIME	NAME & NATIONALITY
☆ Constant weight with fins	•124 m (406 ft. 9 in.)	Herbert Nitsch (Austria)
☆ Constant weight without fins	•95 m (311 ft. 8 in.)	William Trubridge (New Zealand)
☆ Variable weight	142 m (465 ft. 10 in.)	Herbert Nitsch (Austria)
No limit	214 m (702 ft.)	Herbert Nitsch (Austria)
☆ Free immersion	•120 m (393 ft. 8 in.)	Herbert Nitsch (Austria)

•Please note that these records were still awaiting ratification at the time of going to press.

MEN'S DYNAMIC APNEA

With fins	250 m (800 ft. 2 in.)	Alexey Molchanov (Russia)
Without fins	213 m (698 ft. 9 in.)	Tom Sietas (Germany)
	213 m (698 ft. 9 in.)	Dave Mullins (New Zealand)

MEN'S STATIC
☆ APNEA

Duration	11 min. 35 sec.	Stephanie Mifsud (France)

WOMEN'S DEPTH DISCIPLINES

Constant weight with fins	96 m (314 ft. 11 in.)	Sara Campbell (UK)
☆ Constant weight without fins	62 m (203 ft. 5 in.)	Natalia Molchanova (Russia)
Variable weight	122 m (400 ft. 3 in.)	Tanya Streeter (U.S.A.)
No limit	160 m (524 ft. 11 in.)	Tanya Streeter (U.S.A.)
Free immersion	85 m (278 ft. 10 in.)	Natalia Molchanova (Russia)

WOMEN'S DYNAMIC APNEA

☆ With fins	225 m (738 ft. 2 in.)	Natalia Molchanova (Russia)
☆ Without fins	160 m (524 ft. 11 in.)	Natalia Molchanova (Russia)

WOMEN'S STATIC APNEA

Duration	8 min. 23 sec.	Natalia Molchanova (Russia)

LOCATION	DATE
The Bahamas	Apr. 22, 2010
The Bahamas	Apr. 26, 2009
The Bahamas	Dec. 7, 2009
Spetses, Greece	Jun. 14, 2007
The Bahamas	Apr. 25, 2010
Lignano, Italy	Oct. 5, 2008
Hamburg, Germany	Jul. 2, 2008
Wellington, New Zealand	Aug. 12, 2008
Hyères, France	Jun. 8, 2009
The Bahamas	Apr. 2, 2009
The Bahamas	Dec. 3, 2009
Turks and Caicos Islands	Jul. 19, 2003
Turks and Caicos Islands	Aug. 17, 2002
Crete, Greece	Jul. 27, 2008
Moscow, Russia	Apr. 25, 2010
Aarhus, Denmark	Aug. 20, 2009
Aarhus, Denmark	Aug. 21, 2009

☆ **WOMEN'S CYCLING 500 M STANDING START** Simona Krupeckaite (Lithuania) rode the women's 500 m in a time of 33.296 seconds at the UCI Track Cycling World Championships held at the BGZ Arena in Pruszków, Poland, on March 25, 2009.

☆ **MEN'S STATIC APNEA** On June 8, 2009, in Hyères, France, freediver Stephane Mifsud (France) held his breath underwater in the men's static apnea event, clocking a time of 11 min. 35 sec.

MEN

	TIME	NAME & NATIONALITY
☆ Single sculls	6:33.35	Mahe Drysdale (New Zealand)
Double sculls	6:03.25	Jean-Baptiste Macquet, Adrien Hardy (France)
Quadruple sculls	5:36.20	Christopher Morgan, James McRae, Brendan Long, Daniel Noonan (Australia)
Coxless pairs	6:14.27	Matthew Pinsent, James Cracknell (GB)
Coxless fours	5:41.35	Sebastian Thormann, Paul Dienstbach, Philipp Stüer, Bernd Heidicker (Germany)
Coxed pairs*	6:42.16	Igor Boraska, Tihomir Frankovic, Milan Razov (Croatia)
Coxed fours*	5:58.96	Matthias Ungemach, Armin Eichholz, Armin Weyrauch, Bahne Rabe, Jörg Dederding (Germany)
Eights	5:19.85	Deakin, Beery, Hoopman, Volpenhein, Cipollone, Read, Allen, Ahrens, Hansen (U.S.A.)

LIGHTWEIGHT

	TIME	NAME & NATIONALITY
Single sculls*	6:47.82	Zac Purchase (GB)
Double sculls	6:10.02	Mads Rasmussen, Rasmus Quist (Denmark)
Quadruple sculls*	5:45.18	Francesco Esposito, Massimo Lana, Michelangelo Crispi, Massimo Guglielmi (Italy)
Coxless pairs*	6:26.61	Tony O'Connor, Neville Maxwell (Ireland)
Coxless fours	5:45.60	Thomas Poulsen, Thomas Ebert, Eskild Ebbesen, Victo Feddersen (Denmark)
Eights*	5:30.24	Altena, Dahlke, Kobor, Stomporowski, Melges, März, Buchheit, Von Warburg, Kaska (Germany)

WOMEN

	TIME	NAME & NATIONALITY
Single sculls	7:07.71	Rumyana Neykova (Bulgaria)
Double sculls	6:38.78	Georgina and Caroline Evers-Swindell (New Zealand)
Quadruple sculls	6:10.80	Kathrin Boron, Katrin Rutschow-Stomporowski, Jana Sorgers, Kerstin Köppen (Germany)
Coxless pairs	6:53.80	Georgeta Andrunache, Viorica Susanu (Romania)
Coxless fours*	6:25.35	Robyn Selby Smith, Jo Lutz, Amber Bradley, Kate Hornsey (Australia)
Eights	5:55.50	Mickelson, Whipple, Lind, Goodale, Sickler, Cooke, Shoop, Francia, Davies (U.S.A.)

LIGHTWEIGHT

	TIME	NAME & NATIONALITY
Single sculls*	7:28.15	Constanta Pipota (Romania)
Double sculls	6:49.77	Dongxiang Xu, Shimin Yan (China)
Quadruple sculls*	6:23.95	Hua Yu, Haixia Chen, Xuefei Fan, Jing Liu
Coxless pairs*	7:18.32	(China) Eliza Blair, Justine Joyce (Australia)

*Denotes non-Olympic boat classes

MANCHESTER, UK (53°28'N 2°14'W): Liverpool Road Station in Manchester, UK, is the **oldest railroad station**. It was first used on September 15, 1830, and was finally closed on September 30, 1975.

LOCATION	DATE
Poznan, Poland	Aug. 29, 2009
Poznan, Poland	Jun. 17, 2006
Beijing, China	Aug. 10, 2008
Seville, Spain	Sep. 21, 2002
Seville, Spain	Sep. 21, 2002
Indianapolis, U.S.A.	Sep. 18, 1994
Vienna, Austria	Aug. 24, 1991
Athens, Greece	Aug. 15, 2004

Eton, UK	Aug. 26, 2006
Amsterdam, the Netherlands	Jun. 23, 2007
Montreal, Canada	Aug. 1992
Paris, France	1994
Lucerne, Switzerland	Jul. 9, 1999
Montreal, Canada	Aug. 1992

Seville, Spain	Sep. 21, 2002
Seville, Spain	Sep. 21, 2002
Duisburg, Germany	May 19, 1996
Seville, Spain	Sep. 21, 2002
Eton, UK	Aug. 26, 2006
Eton, UK	Aug. 27, 2006

Paris, France	Jun. 19, 1994
Poznan, Poland	Jun. 17, 2006
Eton, UK	Aug. 27, 2006
Aiguebelette-le-Lac, France	Sep. 7, 1997

OFFICIAL WEBSITES

FREEDIVING:
www.alda-international.org

ROWING:
www.worldrowing.com

SPEED SKATING:
www.isu.org

★ SPEED SKATING—LONG TRACK ★

MEN	TIME/POINTS	NAME & NATIONALITY
500 m	34.03	Jeremy Wotherspoon (Canada)
2 x 500 m	68.31	Jeremy Wotherspoon (Canada)
1,000 m	1:06.42	Shani Davis (U.S.A.)
☆ 1,500 m	•1:41.04	Shani Davis (U.S.A.)
3,000 m	3:37.28	Eskil Ervik (Norway)
5,000 m	6:03.32	Sven Kramer (the Netherlands)
10,000 m	12:41.69	Sven Kramer (the Netherlands)
500/1,000/500/1,000 m	137.230 points	Jeremy Wotherspoon (Canada)
500/3,000/1,500/5,000 m	146.365 points	Erben Wennemars (the Netherlands)
500/5,000/1,500/10,000 m	145.742 points	Shani Davis (U.S.A.)
Team pursuit (8 laps)	3:37.80	The Netherlands (Sven Kramer, Carl Verheijen, Erben Wennemars)

WOMEN	TIME/POINTS	NAME & NATIONALITY
☆ 500 m	•37.00	Jenny Wolf (Germany)
2 x 500 m	74.42	Jenny Wolf (Germany)
1,000 m	1:13.11	Cindy Klassen (Canada)
1,500 m	1:51.79	Cindy Klassen (Canada)
3,000 m	3:53.34	Cindy Klassen (Canada)
5,000 m	6:45.61	Martina Sáblíková (Czech Republic)
500/1,000/500/1,000 m	149.305 points	Monique Garbrecht-Enfeldt (Germany)
	149.305 points	Cindy Klassen (Canada)
500/1,500/1,000/3,000 m	155.576 points	Cindy Klassen (Canada)
500/3,000/1,500/5,000 m	154.580 points	Cindy Klassen (Canada)
☆ Team pursuit (6 laps)	2:55.79	Canada (Kristina Groves, Christine Nesbitt, Brittany Schussler)

•Still awaiting ratification at time of going to press

★ SPEED SKATING—SHORT TRACK ★

MEN	TIME	NAME & NATIONALITY
☆ 500 m	•40.651	Sung Si-Bak (South Korea)
1,000 m	1:23.454	Charles Hamelin (Canada)
1,500 m	2:10.639	Ahn Hyun-Soo (South Korea)
3,000 m	4:32.646	Ahn Hyun-Soo (South Korea)
5,000 m relay	6:38.486	South Korea (Kwak Yoon-Gy, Lee Ho-Suk, Lee Jung-Su, Sung Si-Bak)

WOMEN	TIME	NAME & NATIONALITY
500 m	•42.609	Wang Meng (China)
☆ 1,000 m	•1:29.049	Zhou Yang (China)
1,500 m	2:16.729	Zhou Yang (China)
3,000 m	4:46.983	Jung Eun-Ju (South Korea)
☆ 3,000 m relay	•4:06.610	China (Sun Linlin, Wang Meng, Zhang Hui, Zhou Yang)

•Still awaiting ratification at time of going to press

LOCATION	DATE
Salt Lake City, U.S.A.	Nov. 9, 2007
Calgary, Canada	Mar. 15, 2008
Salt Lake City, U.S.A.	Mar. 7, 2009
Salt Lake City, U.S.A.	Dec. 11, 2009
Calgary, Canada	Nov. 5, 2005
Calgary, Canada	Nov. 17, 2007
Salt Lake City, U.S.A.	Mar. 10, 2007
Calgary, Canada	Jan. 18–19, 2003
Calgary, Canada	Aug. 12–13, 2005
Calgary, Canada	Mar. 18–19, 2006
Salt Lake City, U.S.A.	Mar. 11, 2007

MEN'S 1,500 M LONG TRACK Shani Davis (U.S.A.) skates during the ISU World Cup Speed Skating Championships at the Utah Olympic Oval in Kearns, Salt Lake City, U.S.A. Here he finished the 1,500 m in a time of 1 min. 41.04 sec. He holds two more records: the "big combination" (with 145.742 points), which he has held since March 2006, and the 1,000 m (in 1 min. 6.42 sec).

LOCATION	DATE
Salt Lake City, U.S.A.	Dec. 11, 2009
Salt Lake City, U.S.A.	Mar. 10, 2007
Calgary, Canada	Mar. 25, 2006
Salt Lake City, U.S.A.	Nov. 20, 2005
Calgary, Canada	Mar. 18, 2006
Salt Lake City, U.S.A.	Mar. 11, 2007
Salt Lake City, U.S.A.	Jan. 11–12, 2003
Calgary, Canada	Mar. 24–25, 2006
Calgary, Canada	Mar. 15–17, 2001
Calgary, Canada	Mar. 18–19, 2006
Calgary, Canada	Dec. 6, 2009

LOCATION	DATE
Marquette, U.S.A.	Nov. 14, 2009
Montreal, Canada	Jan. 18, 2009
Marquette, U.S.A.	Oct. 24, 2003
Beijing, China	Dec. 7, 2003
Salt Lake City, U.S.A.	Oct. 19, 2008

☆ **WOMEN'S 3,000 M SHORT TRACK RELAY** China's gold medalists Sun Linlin, Wang Meng, Zhang Hui, and Zhou Yang (from left to right) attend the medal ceremony at the Vancouver Winter Olympics in Canada. They skated the women's 3,000 m relay in a time of 4 min, 6.61 sec, on February 24, 2010.

LOCATION	DATE
Beijing, China	Nov. 29, 2008
Vancouver, Canada	Feb. 26, 2010
Salt Lake City, U.S.A.	Feb. 9, 2008
Harbin, China	Mar. 15, 2008
Vancouver, Canada	Feb. 24, 2010

★ SWIMMING—LONG COURSE [50 M POOL] ★

MEN	TIME	NAME & NATIONALITY
☆ 50 m freestyle	20.91	Cesar Cielo Filho (Brazil)
☆ 100 m freestyle	46.91	Cesar Cielo Filho (Brazil)
☆ 200 m freestyle	1:42.00	Paul Biedermann (Germany)
☆ 400 m freestyle	3:40.07	Paul Biedermann (Germany)
☆ 800 m freestyle	7:32.12	Zhang Lin (china)
1,500 m freestyle	14:34.56	Grant Hackett (Australia)
4 x 100 m freestyle relay	3:08.24	U.S.A. (Michael Phelps, Garrett Weber-Gale, Cullen Jones, Jason Lezak)
☆ 4 x 200 m freestyle relay	6:58.55	U.S.A. (Michael Phelps, Ricky Berens, David Walters, Ryan Lochte)
50 m butterfly	22.43	Rafael Muñoz (Spain)
☆ 100 m butterfly	49.82	Michael Phelps (U.S.A.)
☆ 200 m butterfly	1:51.51	Michael Phelps (U.S.A.)
☆ 50 m backstroke	24.04	Liam Tancock (UK)
☆ 100 m backstroke	51.94	Aaron Peirsol (U.S.A.)
☆ 200 m backstroke	1:51.92	Aaron Peirsol (U.S.A.)
☆ 50 m breaststroke	26.67	Cameron van der Burgh (South Africa)
☆ 100 m breaststroke	58.58	Brenton Rickard (Australia)
☆ 200 m breaststroke	2:07.31	Christian Sprenger (Australia)
☆ 200 m medley	1:54.10	Ryan Lochte (U.S.A.)
400 m medley	4:03.84	Michael Phelps (U.S.A.)
☆ 4 x 100 m medley relay	3:27.28	U.S.A. (Aaron Peirsol, Eric Shanteau, Michael Phelps, David Walters)

WOMEN	TIME	NAME & NATIONALITY
☆ 50 m freestyle	23.73	Britta Steffen (Germany)
☆ 100 m freestyle	52.07	Britta Steffen (Germany)
☆ 200 m freestyle	1:52.98	Federica Pellegrini (Italy)
☆ 400 m freestyle	3:59.15	Federica Pellegrini (Italy)
800 m freestyle	8:14.10	Rebecca Adlington (UK)
1,500 m freestyle	15:42.54	Kate Ziegler (U.S.A.)
☆ 4 x 100 m freestyle relay	3:31.72	The Netherlands (Inge Dekker, Ranomi Kromowidjojo, Femke Heemskerk, Marleen Veldhuis)
☆ 4 x 200 m freestyle relay	7:42.08	China (Yang Yu, Zhu Qian Wei, Liu Jing, Pang Jiaying)
☆ 50 m butterfly	25.07	Therese Alshammar (Sweden)
☆ 100 m butterfly	56.06	Sarah Sjostrom (Sweden)
☆ 200 m butterfly	• 2:01.81	Liu Zige (China)
☆ 50 m backstroke	27.06	Zhao Jing (China)
☆ 100 m backstroke	58.12	Gemma Spofforth (UK)
☆ 200 m backstroke	2:04.81	Kirsty Coventry (Zimbabwe)

•Still awaiting ratification at time of going to press

....

BIRMINGHAM, UK (52°29'N 1°53'W): Crufts, held every year at the National Exhibition Centre (NEC) in Birmingham, UK, is the world's **largest dog show**. It attracted 22,993 canine entries from January 9 to 12, 1991.

....

LOCATION	DATE
Sao Paulo, Brazil	Dec. 18, 2009
Rome, Italy	Jul. 30, 2009
Rome, Italy	Jul. 28, 2009
Rome, Italy	Jul. 26, 2009
Rome, Italy	Jul. 29, 2009
Fukuoka, Japan	Jul. 29, 2001
Beijing, China	Aug. 11, 2008
Rome, Italy	Jul. 31, 2009
Málaga, Spain	Apr. 5, 2009
Rome, Italy	Aug. 1, 2009
Rome, Italy	Jul. 29, 2009
Rome, Italy	Aug. 2, 2009
Indianapolis, U.S.A.	Jul. 8, 2009
Rome, Italy	Jul 31, 2009
Rome, Italy	Jul. 29, 2009
Rome, Italy	Jul. 27, 2009
Rome, Italy	Jul. 30, 2009
Rome, Italy	Jul. 30, 2009
Beijing, China	Aug. 10, 2008
Rome, Italy	Aug. 2, 2009

☆ **MEN'S 200 M BREASTSTROKE**
Christian Sprenger (Australia)
competes in the 200 m
breaststroke final during the
13th Fédération Internationale
de Natation (FINA) World
Championships on July 30, 2009
in Rome, Italy. He finished in
2 min. 7.31 sec.

LOCATION	DATE
Rome, Italy	Aug. 2, 2009
Rome, Italy	Jul. 31, 2009
Rome, Italy	Jul. 29, 2009
Rome, Italy	Jul. 26, 2009
Beijing, China	Aug. 16, 2008
Mission Viejo, U.S.A.	Jun. 17, 2007
Rome, Italy	Jul. 26, 2009
Rome, Italy	Jul. 30, 2009
Rome, Italy	Jul. 31, 2009
Rome, Italy	Jul. 27, 2009
Jinan, China	Oct. 21, 2009
Rome, Italy	Jul. 30, 2009
Rome, Italy	Jul. 28, 2009
Rome, Italy	Aug. 1, 2009

☆ **MEN'S 50 M BACKSTROKE**
Great Britain's Liam Tancock
stands on the podium after
winning the 50 m backstroke at
the FINA World Championships
in Rome, Italy, on August 2,
2009. Tancock won gold and set
a new world record of 24.04
seconds.

OFFICIAL WEBSITE

SWIMMING:
www.fina.org

★ SWIMMING—LONG COURSE [50 M POOL] ★

WOMEN	TIME	NAME & NATIONALITY
☆ 50 m breaststroke	29.80	Jessica Hardy (U.S.A.)
☆ 100 m breaststroke	1:04.45	Jessica Hardy (U.S.A.)
☆ 200 m breaststroke	2:20.12	Annamay Pierse (Canada)
☆ 200 m medley	2:06.15	Ariana Kukors (U.S.A.)
400 m medley	4:29.45	Stephanie Rice (Australia)
☆ 4 x 100 m medley relay	3:52.19	China (Zhao Jing, Chen Huijia, Jiao Liuyang, Li Zhesi)

★ SWIMMING—SHORT COURSE [25 M POOL] ★

MEN	TIME	NAME & NATIONALITY
☆ 50 m freestyle	20.30	Roland Schoeman (South Africa)
100 m freestyle	44.94	Amaury Leveaux (France)
☆ 200 m freestyle	1:39.37	Paul Biederman (Germany)
☆ 400 m freestyle	3:32.77	Paul Biederman (Germany)
800 m freestyle	7:23.42	Grant Hackett (Australia)
1,500 m freestyle	14:10.10	Grant Hackett (Australia)
☆ 4 x 100 m freestyle relay	3:03.30	U.S.A. (Nathan Adrian, Matt Greves, Garrett Weber-Gale, Michael Phelps)
☆ 4 x 200 m freestyle relay	6:51.05	Canada (Colin Russel, Stefan Hirniak, Brent Hayden, Joel Greenshields)
☆ 50 m butterfly	22.80	Steffen Deibler (Germany)
☆ 100 m butterfly	48.48	Evgeny Korotyshkin (Russia)
☆ 200 m butterfly	1:49.11	Kaio Almeida (Brazil)
☆ 50 m backstroke	22.61	Peter Marshall (U.S.A.)
☆ 100 m backstroke	48.94	Nick Thoman (U.S.A.)
☆ 200 m backstroke	1:46.11	Arkady Vyatchanin (Russia)
☆ 50 m breaststroke	25.25	Cameron van der Burgh (South Africa)
☆ 100 m breaststroke	55.61	Cameron van der Burgh (South Africa)
☆ 200 m breaststroke	2:00.67	Daniel Gyurta (Hungary)
☆ 100 m medley	50.76	Peter Mankoc (Slovenia)
☆ 200 m medley	1:51.55	Darian Townsend (South Africa)
☆ 400 m medley	3:57.27	Laszlo Cseh (Hungary)
☆ 4 x 100 m medley relay	3:19.16	Russia (Stanislav Donets, Sergey Geybel, Evgeny Korotyshkin, Danila Izotov)

WOMEN	TIME	NAME & NATIONALITY
50 m freestyle	23.25	Marleen Veldhuis (the Netherlands)
☆ 100 m freestyle	51.01	Lisbeth Trickett (Australia)
☆ 200 m freestyle	•1:51.17	Federica Pellegrini (Italy)
400 m freestyle	3:54.92	Joanne Jackson (UK)
☆ 800 m freestyle	8:04.53	Alessia Filippi (Italy)

•Still awaiting ratification at time of going to press

....

LEEDS, UK (53°48'N 1°33'W): The **earliest surviving film** is a sensitized 2.1-in.-wide (53.9-mm) paper roll that runs at 10 to 12 frames per second. It was shot by Louis Aimé Augustin Le Prince (UK), who filmed the garden of his father-in-law, Joseph Whitley, in Roundhay, Leeds, West Yorkshire, UK, in October 1888.

....

LOCATION	DATE
Federal Way, U.S.A.	Aug. 7, 2009
Federal Way, U.S.A.	Aug. 7, 2009
Rome, Italy	Jul. 30, 2009
Rome, Italy	Jul. 27, 2009
Beijing, China	Aug. 10, 2008
Rome, Italy	Aug. 1, 2009

LOCATION	DATE
Pietermaritzburg, South Africa	Aug. 8, 2009
Rijeka, Croatia	Dec. 13, 2008
Berlin, Germany	Nov. 15, 2009
Berlin, Germany	Nov. 14, 2009
Melbourne, Australia	Jul. 20, 2008
Perth, Australia	Aug. 7, 2001
Manchester, UK	Dec. 19, 2009
Leeds, UK	Aug. 7, 2009
Berlin, Germany	Nov. 14, 2009
Berlin, Germany	Nov. 15, 2009
Stockholm, Sweden	Nov. 10, 2009
Singapore, Singapore	Nov. 22, 2009
Manchester, UK	Dec. 18, 2009
Berlin, Germany	Nov. 15, 2009
Berlin, Germany	Nov. 14, 2009
Berlin, Germany	Nov. 15, 2009
Istanbul, Turkey	Dec. 13, 2009
Istanbul, Turkey	Dec. 12, 2009
Berlin, Germany	Nov. 15, 2009
Istanbul, Turkey	Dec. 11, 2009
St. Petersburg, Russia	Dec. 20, 2009

LOCATION	DATE
Manchester, UK	Apr. 13, 2008
Hobart, Australia	Aug. 10, 2009
Istanbul, Turkey	Dec. 13, 2009
Leeds, UK	Aug. 8, 2009
Rijeka, Croatia	Dec. 12, 2008

☆ **MEN'S 50 M BUTTERFLY**
Steffen Deibler (Germany)
swimming in a men's 50 m
butterfly heat at the FINA short
course World Cup in Berlin,
Germany, on November 14,
2009. He set a record 21.80
seconds in the event.

☆ **WOMEN'S 1,500 M**
FREESTYLE Lotte Friis
(Denmark) swam the women's
1,500 m short course freestyle
in a time of 15 min. 28.65 sec. in
Birkerod, Denmark, on
November 28, 2009.

★ SWIMMING—SHORT COURSE (25 M POOL) ★

WOMEN	TIME	NAME & NATIONALITY
☆ 1,500 m freestyle	15:28.65	Lotte Friis (Denmark)
4 x 100 m freestyle relay	3:28.22	The Netherlands (Hinkelien Schreuder, Inge Dekker, Ranomi Kromowidjojo, Marleen Veldhuis)
4 x 200 m freestyle relay	7:38.90	The Netherlands (Inge Dekker, Femke Heemskerk, Marleen Veldhuis, Ranomi Kromowidjojo)
☆ 50 m butterfly	24.38	Therese Alshammar (Sweden)
☆ 100 m butterfly	•55.05	Diane Bui-Duyet (France)
☆ 200 m butterfly	2:00.78	Liu Zige (China)
☆ 50 m backstroke	•25.70	Sanja Jovanovic (Croatia)
☆ 100 m backstroke	55.23	Sakai Shiho (Japan)
☆ 200 m backstroke	2:00.18	Sakai Shiho (Japan)
☆ 50 m breaststroke	28.80	Jessica Hardy (U.S.A.)
☆ 100 m breaststroke	1:02.70	Rebecca Soni (U.S.A.)
☆ 200 m breaststroke	2:14.57	Rebecca Soni (U.S.A.)
☆ 100 m medley	57.74	Hinkelien Schreuder (the Netherlands)
☆ 200 m medley	2:04.60	Julia Smit (U.S.A.)
☆ 400 m medley	4:21.04	Julia Smit (U.S.A.)
☆ 4 x 100 m medley relay	3:47.97	U.S.A. (Margaret Hoelzer, Jessica Hardy, Dana Vollmer, Amanda Weir)

•Still awaiting ratification at time of going to press

★ WEIGHTLIFTING ★

MEN	CATEGORY	WEIGHT LIFTED	NAME & NATIONALITY
56 kg	Snatch	138 kg	Halil Mutlu (Turkey)
	Clean & jerk	168 kg	Halil Mutlu (Turkey)
	Total	305 kg	Halil Mutlu (Turkey)
62 kg	Snatch	153 kg	Shi Zhiyong (China)
	Clean & jerk	182 kg	Le Maosheng (China)
	Total	326 kg	Zhang Jie (China)
69 kg	Snatch	165 kg	Georgi Markov (Bulgaria)
	Clean & jerk	197 kg	Zhang Guozheng (China)
	Total	357 kg	Galabin Boevski (Bulgaria)
77 kg	☆ Snatch	174 kg	Lu Xiaojun (China)
	Clean & jerk	210 kg	Oleg Perepetchenov (Russia)
	☆ Total	378 kg	Lu Xiaojun (China)
85 kg	Snatch	187 kg	Andrei Rybakou (Belarus)
	Clean & jerk	218 kg	Zhang Yong (China)
	Total	394 kg	Andrei Rybakou (Belarus)
94 kg	Snatch	188 kg	Akakios Kakhiasvilis (Greece)
	Clean & jerk	232 kg	Szymon Kolecki (Poland)
	Total	412 kg	Akakios Kakhiasvilis (Greece)
105 kg	Snatch	200 kg	Andrei Aramnau (Belarus)
	Clean & jerk	237 kg	Alan Tsagaev (Bulgaria)
	Total	436 kg	Andrei Aramnau (Belarus)

LOCATION	DATE
Birkerod, Denmark	Nov. 28, 2009
Amsterdam, the Netherlands	Dec. 19, 2008
Manchester, UK	Apr. 9, 2008
Singapore, Singapore	Nov. 22, 2009
Istanbul, Turkey	Dec. 12, 2009
Berlin, Germany	Nov. 15, 2009
Istanbul, Turkey	Dec. 12, 2009
Berlin, Germany	Nov. 15, 2009
Berlin, Germany	Nov. 14, 2009
Berlin, Germany	Nov. 15, 2009
Manchester, UK	Dec. 19, 2009
Manchester, UK	Dec. 18, 2009
Berlin, Germany	Nov. 15, 2009
Manchester, UK	Dec. 19, 2009
Manchester, UK	Dec. 18, 2009
Manchester, UK	Dec. 18, 2009

LOCATION	DATE
Antalya, Turkey	Nov. 4, 2001
Trencín, Slovakia	Apr. 24, 2001
Sydney, Australia	Sep. 16, 2000
Izmir, Turkey	Jun. 28, 2002
Busan, South Korea	Oct. 2, 2002
Kanazawa, Japan	Apr. 28, 2008
Sydney, Australia	Sep. 20, 2000
Qinhuangdao, China	Sep. 11, 2003
Athens, Greece	Nov. 24, 1999
Goyang, South Korea	Nov. 24, 2009
Trencín, Slovakia	April 27, 2001
Goyang, South Korea	Nov. 24, 2009
Chiang Mai, Thailand	Sep. 22, 2007
Ramat Gan, Israel	Apr. 25, 1998
Beijing, China	Aug. 15, 2008
Athens, Greece	Nov. 27, 1999
Sofia, Bulgaria	Apr. 29, 2000
Athens, Greece	Nov. 27, 1999
Beijing, China	Aug. 18, 2008
Kiev, Ukraine	Apr. 25, 2004
Beijing, China	Aug. 18, 2008

☆ MEN'S 77 KG SNATCH
Lu Xiaojun (China) lifts
174 kg in the snatch in the
men's 77 kg category at
the World Weightlifting
Championships in
Goyang, South Korea, on
November 24, 2009.
Xiaojun also holds the
record for the total,
having successfully lifted
378 kg at the same event.

MEN	CATEGORY	WEIGHT LIFTED	NAME & NATIONALITY
105+ kg	Snatch	213 kg	Hossein Rezazadeh (Iran)
	Clean & jerk	263 kg	Hossein Rezazadeh (Iran)
	Total	476 kg	Hossein Rezazadeh (Iran)

WOMEN	CATEGORY	WEIGHT LIFTED	NAME & NATIONALITY
48 kg	Snatch	98 kg	Yang Lian (China)
	Clean & jerk	120 kg	Chen Xiexia (China)
	Total	217 kg	Yang Lian (China)
53 kg	Snatch	102 kg	Ri Song-Hui (North Korea)
	Clean & jerk	129 kg	Li Ping (China)
	Total	226 kg	Qiu Hongxia (China)
58 kg	Snatch	111 kg	Chen Yanqing (China)
	Clean & jerk	141 kg	Qiu Hongmei (China)
	Total	251 kg	Chen Yanqing (China)
63 kg	Snatch	116 kg	Pawina Thongsuk (Thailand)
	Clean & jerk	142 kg	Pawina Thongsuk (Thailand)
	Total	257 kg	Liu Haixia (China)
69 kg	Snatch	128 kg	Liu Chunhong (China)
	Clean & jerk	158 kg	Liu Chunhong (China)
	Total	286 kg	Liu Chunhong (China)
75 kg	☆ Snatch	132 kg	Svetlana Podobedova (Kazakhstan)
	☆ Clean & jerk	160 kg	Svetlana Podobedova (Kazakhstan)
	☆ Total	292 kg	Svetlana Podobedova (Kazakhstan)
75+ kg	Snatch	140 kg	Jang Mi-Ran (South Korea)
	☆ Clean & jerk	187 kg	Jang Mi-Ran (South Korea)
	Total	326 kg	Jang Mi-Ran (South Korea)

EXTRA! For tales of record-breaking achievements on the world's oceans, turn to p. 330.

ZARAGOZA, SPAIN (41°39'N 0°53'W): On May 18, 2003, a total of 157 mixed couples performed the folk dance "The Jota of Aragon" for eight minutes in Zaragoza, Spain, making this the **largest castanet dance** ever performed.

LOCATION	DATE
Qinhuangdao, China	Sep. 14, 2003
Athens, Greece	Aug. 25, 2004
Sydney, Australia	Sep. 26, 2000

LOCATION	DATE
Santo Domingo, Dominican Republic	Oct. 1, 2006
Taian City, China	Apr. 21, 2007
Santo Domingo, Dominican Republic	Oct. 1, 2006
Busan, South Korea	Oct. 1, 2002
Taian City, China	Apr. 22, 2007
Santo Domingo, Dominican Republic	Oct. 2, 2006
Doha, Qatar	Dec. 3, 2006
Taian City, China	Apr. 23, 2007
Doha, Qatar	Dec. 3, 2006
Doha, Qatar	Nov. 12, 2005
Doha, Qatar	Dec. 4, 2006
Chiang Mai, Thailand	Sep. 23, 2007
Beijing, China	Aug. 13, 2008
Beijing, China	Aug. 13, 2008
Beijing, China	Aug. 13, 2008
Goyang, South Korea	Nov. 28, 2009
Goyang, South Korea	Nov. 28, 2009
Goyang, South Korea	Nov. 28, 2009
Beijing, China	Aug. 16, 2008
Goyang, South Korea	Nov. 28, 2009
Beijing, China	Aug. 16, 2008

☆ **WOMEN'S 75+ KG CLEAN & JERK** Jang Mi-Ran (South Korea) celebrates after lifting 187 kg in the clean and jerk in the women's 75+ kg category at the World Weightlifting Championships in Goyang, South Korea, on November 28, 2009. She also holds the records for the snatch and the total in this category.

OFFICIAL WEBSITES

WEIGHTLIFTING:
www.iwf.net

WATERSKIING:
www.iwsf.com

VALENCIA, SPAIN (39°29'N 0°22'W): On the last Wednesday in August the town of Buñol, near Valencia, Spain, holds its annual tomato festival. At the 2004 Tomatina, 38,000 people spent one hour at the world's **largest food fight** throwing about 275,500 lb. (125 tonnes) of tomatoes at one another.

MEN	RECORD	NAME & NATIONALITY
Slalom	1.5 buoy/9.75-m line/ 58 km/h	Chris Parrish (U.S.A.)
Barefoot slalom	20.6 crossings of wake in 30 sec.	Keith St. Onge (U.S.A.)
Tricks	12,400 points	Nicolas Le Forestier (France)
☆ Barefoot tricks	11,250 points	Keith St. Onge (U.S.A.)
☆ Jump	75.2 m (246 ft. 8 in.)	Freddy Krueger (U.S.A.)
Barefoot jump	27.4 m (89 ft. 11 in.)	David Small (GB)
Ski fly	91.1 m (298 ft. 10 in.)	Jaret Llewellyn (Canada)
Overall	2,818.01 points*	Jaret Llewellyn (Canada)

*5@11.25 m, 10,730 tricks, 71.7 m jump

WOMEN	RECORD	NAME & NATIONALITY
Slalom	1 buoy/10.25-m line/ 55 km/h	Kristi Overton Johnson (U.S.A.)
		Karina Nowlan (Australia)
☆		Regina Jaquess (U.S.A.)
Barefoot slalom	17.0 crossings of wake in 30 sec.	Nadine de Villiers (South Africa)
☆ Tricks	9,080 points	Natallia Berdnikava (Belarus)
☆ Barefoot tricks	4,400 points	Nadine de Villiers (South Africa)
☆ Jump	56.6 m (186 ft.)	Elena Milakova (Russia)
Barefoot jump	20.6 m (67 ft. 7 in.)	Nadine de Villiers (South Africa)
Ski fly	69.4 m (227 ft. 8.2 in.)	Elena Milakova (Russia)
☆ Overall	2,934.36 points**	Regina Jaquess (U.S.A.)

**4@10.75 m, 8,180 tricks, 52.2 m jump; calculated with the 2006 scoring method

★ LONGEST SPORTS MARATHONS ★

SPORT	TIME	NAME & NATIONALITY
☆ Aerobics	26 hours	Dinaz Vervatwala (India)
☆ Baseball	48 hr. 9 min. 27 sec.	Jonny G Foundation Cardinals and Edward Jones Browns (U.S.A.)
☆ Basketball	82 hours	Treverton College (South Africa)
Basketball (wheelchair)	26 hr. 3 min.	University of Omaha students and staff (U.S.A.)
☆ Bowling (tenpin)	120 hours	Andy Milne (Canada)
☆ Bowls (indoor)	36 hours	Arnos Bowling Club (UK)
☆ Bowls (outdoor)	170 hr. 3 min.	Goulburn Railway Bowling Club (Australia)
☆ Cricket	67 hr. 9 min.	New South Wales Police Force officers (Australia)
☆ Curling	54 hr. 1 min.	The Burlington Golf and Country Club (Canada)

LOCATION	DATE
Trophy Lakes, U.S.A.	Aug. 28, 2005
Bronkhorstspruit, South Africa	Jan. 6, 2006
Lac de Joux, Switzerland	Sep. 4, 2005
Maize, U.S.A.	Aug. 15, 2009
Seffner, U.S.A.	Nov. 2, 2008
Mulwala, Australia	Feb. 8, 2004
Orlando, U.S.A.	May 14, 2000
Seffner, U.S.A.	Sep. 29, 2002

☆ **WOMEN'S OVERALL**
Waterskier Regina Jaquess
(U.S.A.) in action on July 17,
2009 at Santa Rosa, California,
U.S.A.. She achieved an overall
score of 2,934.36 points.

LOCATION	DATE
West Palm Beach, U.S.A.	Sep. 14, 1996
Sacramento, U.S.A.	Sep. 22, 2008
Santa Rosa, U.S.A.	Jul. 4, 2009
Witbank, South Africa	Jan. 5, 2001
Polk City, U.S.A.	Oct. 31, 2009
Witbank, South Africa	Jan. 5, 2001
Rio Linda, U.S.A.	Jul. 21, 2002
Pretoria, South Africa	Mar. 4, 2000
Pine Mountain, U.S.A.	May 26, 2002
Santa Rosa, U.S.A.	Jul. 17, 2009

LOCATION	DATE
Secunderabad, India	Jan. 9–10, 2010
St. Louis, Missouri, U.S.A.	Oct. 9–11, 2009
Mooi River, South Africa	Aug. 7–10 2009
Omaha, Nebraska, U.S.A.	Sep. 24–25, 2004
Mississauga, Ontario, Canada	Oct. 24–29, 2005
Southgate, London, UK	Apr. 20–21, 2002
Goulburn, NSW, Australia	Jan. 19–26, 2009
Bateau Bay, NSW, Australia	Feb. 8–11, 2009
Burlington, Ontario, Canada	Mar. 12–14, 2010

SPORT	TIME	NAME & NATIONALITY
☆ Darts (doubles)	30 hours	Richard Saunders, Lee Hannant, Andrew Brymer, Paul Taylor (UK)
Darts (singles)	26 hr. 42 min.	Stephen Wilson and Robert Henderson (UK)
Floorball	24 hr. 15 min.	TRM Floorball and Hornets Regio Moosseedorf Worblental (Switzerland)
☆ Soccer	37 hours	TSV Mutlangen & FC Raron II (Germany)
☆ Soccer (five-a-side)	27 hr. 15 min.	Collingwood College Challengers & Radio Basingstoke Bandits (UK)
Hockey (ice)	241 hr. 21 min.	Brent Saik and friends (Canada)
Hockey (indoor)	50 hours	Bert & Macs and Mid-Town Certigard teams (Canada)
Hockey (inline/roller)	24 hours	8K Roller Hockey League (U.S.A.)
Hockey (street)	105 hr. 17 min.	Molson Canadian and Canadian Tire teams (Canada)
Korfball	30 hr. 2 min.	Kingfisher Korfball Club (UK)
Netball	58 hours	Sleaford Netball Club (UK)
☆ Pétanque (boules)	52 hours	Gilles de B'Heinsch (Belgium)
Pool (singles)	53 hr. 25 min.	Brian Lilly and Daniel Maloney (U.S.A.)
Skiing	202 hr. 1 min.	Nicky Willey (Australia)
Snowboarding	180 hr. 34 min.	Bernhard Mair (Austria)
Table soccer	51 hr. 52 min.	Alexander Gruber, Roman Schelling, Enrico Lechtaler, Christian Nägele (Austria)
Table tennis (doubles)	101 hr. 1 min. 11 sec.	Lance, Phil, and Mark Warren, Bill Weir (U.S.A.)
Table tennis (singles)	132 hr. 31 min.	Danny Price and Randy Nunes (U.S.A.)
Tennis (doubles)	50 hr. 0 min. 8 sec.	Vince Johnson, Bill Geideman, Brad Ansley, Allen Finley (U.S.A.)
☆ Tennis (singles)	36 hr. 36 min. 36 sec.	Jeroen Wagenaar and Serge Fernando (the Netherlands)
Volleyball (beach)	24 hr. 10 min.	Krzysztof Garbulski, Michael Fuks, Adam Jankowski, Tomasz Konior (Poland)
Volleyball (indoor)	76 hr. 30 min.	Zespól Szkól Ekonomicznych students (Poland)

LONDON, UK (51°30'N 0°07'W): Davenports in London is the **oldest magic shop**. The family-run business was founded in 1898 by Lewis Davenport (UK) and opened at his home on Ryles Road, Plaistow, London, UK, in 1903.

LOCATION	DATE
Twyford, Berkshire, UK	Jan. 9–10, 2009
Palnackie, Scotland, UK	Jun. 20–21, 2008
Zollikofen, Switzerland	Apr. 27–28, 2007
Mutlangen, Germany	Jul. 16–17, 2009
Camberley, Surrey, UK	Oct. 17–18, 2009
Strathcona, Alberta, Canada	Feb. 8–18, 2008
Lethbridge, Alberta, Canada	Mar. 25–27, 2008
Eastpointe, Michigan, U.S.A.	Sep. 13–14, 2002
Lethbridge, Alberta, Canada	Aug. 20–24, 2008
Larkfield, Kent, UK	Jun. 14–15, 2008
Sleaford, Lincolnshire, UK	Jul. 25–27, 2008
Arlon, Belgium	Sep. 18–20, 2006
Spring Lake, North Carolina, U.S.A.	Oct. 10–12, 2008
Thredbo, NSW, Australia	Sep. 2–10, 2005
Bad Kleinkirchheim, Austria	Jan. 9–16, 2004
Bregenz, Austria	Jun. 27–29, 2008
Sacramento, California, U.S.A.	Apr. 9–13, 1979
Cherry Hill, New Jersey, U.S.A.	Aug. 20–26, 1978
Hickory, North Carolina, U.S.A.	Nov. 7–9, 2008
Hellevoetsluis, the Netherlands	
Ustka, Poland	Jun. 27–28, 2008
Sosnowiec, Poland	Dec. 4–7, 2009

CREDITS & ACKNOWLEDGMENTS

Quiz answers

Q1, p. 13. What was the name given to NASA's first Space Shuttle?
A: *Columbia*

Q2, p. 57. No tall tales—how long is the aye-aye's tale?
A: 20 in. (50.5 cm)

Q3, p. 69. To which group do the following creatures belong, mollusk or crustacean? A: Crab; B: Octopus; C: Slug
A: A) Crustacean; B) Mollusk; and C) Mollusk

Q4, p. 72. Of all the fish in the sea, which is the largest?
A: The whale shark

Q5, p. 78. Which classic arcade video game features an amphibian attempting to cross a busy road and a fast-flowing river?
A: *Frogger*

Q6, p. 123. Which of these measures the most: the longest beard, the longest mustache, or the highest hairstyle?
A: The longest mustache, at 14 ft. (4.29 m), held by Ram Singh Chauhan (India)

Q7, p. 148. Anssi Vanhala solved a Rubik's cube in 36.77 seconds using which bodypart?
A: The feet

Q8, p. 189. How long after the sound barrier was first broken did Andy Green set the current land speed record?
A: 50 years and 1 day

Q9, p. 198. In 1911, Norway's Roald Amundsen became the first man to reach the South Pole. What other polar record did he achieve 15 years later?
A: The first flight over the North Pole, in the airship *Norge*

Q10, p. 212. On average, how many graves did Johann Heinrich Karl Thime dig every year throughout his 50-year career?
A: Over 466 graves—that's more than one a day!

Q11, p. 225. How old was the oldest person to be accused of murder?
A: 98 years old

Q12, p. 231. Who did Carlos Slim Helú replace as the world's richest man?
A: Bill Gates

Q13, p. 247. On May 2, 2007, Lup Fun Yau (UK) set a new record for the most jam doughnuts eaten in three minutes. But how many did he eat?
A: Six

Q14, p. 334. Who is *Hurt Locker* director Katheryn Bigelow's famous ex?
A: James Cameron

Q15, p. 338. Which animated movie was the first to be produced in stereoscopic 3D?
A: *Monsters vs. Aliens*

Q16, p. 431. Michael Schumacher is an F1 legend, but he is not the youngest driver to finish an F1 race. Who is?
A: Jaime Alguersuari

Q17, p. 448. How many countries have the Harlem Globetrotters played in to date?
A: 120 countries450

Q18, p. 450. Who wrote the Marquess of Queensbury rules?
A: John Graham Chambers

Q19, p. 493. What number do you get if you add the most worms charmed to the most horseshoe pitching titles won?
A: 582 (567 worms + 15 horseshoe titles)

Q20, p. 501. Just how high was the highest wall climb on a bicycle?
A: 9 ft. 5.9 in. (2.89 m)

Guinness World Records would like to thank the following individuals, companies, groups, websites, societies, schools, colleges, and universities for their help in the creation of the 2011 edition:

Academy of Motion Picture Arts & Sciences, Oscar Rogelio Antillon Aceituno, Heather Anderson, Ulla Anlander, Roberta Armani, Arriva London, All at Ascent Media, Astoria Park (Queens, NYC), Ted Batchelor and family, Bender Media Services (Sally Treibel, Susan Bender), Beano Max, British Film Institute, Robert Bierfreund, Oliver Blair (Dyson), Bleedingcool.com (Rich Johnston), Luke and Joseph Boatfield, Brian Bolland, Boostamonte Mountainboarding (Brad Beren), Richard Booth, Olivia and Alexander Boulton, Ceri, Katie, Georgie, and Emily Boulton, Alfie Boulton-Fay, Victor Bourdariat, Pete Bouvier, Box Office Mojo, Jason Bradbury, Matthew R. I. Bradford, Bragster team (Dan Barrett, Andy Dust, Luke Forsythe, Adam Moore, Peter Vandenberk), British Waterways Scotland (Donald Macpherson), Sarah Brown, Vittorio 100% Brumotti, Rachel Buchholz (NGK Magazine), *BusinessWeek,* Kirk, Beth, and Gavin Butterfield, CCTV (Guo Tong, Wang Wei, and Tony), Kwang-Sung Chun, Simone Ciancotti, Cinefex, Adam Cloke, Mark Collins, Columbus Zoo, Ohio, U.S.A., Commission for the Geological Map of the World, Connexion Cars (Rob and Tracey), Julia Cottrell, Gerard Danford, Debby DeGroot, Deno's Wonder Wheel Amusement Park, Coney Island, U.S.A., Jose Torres Diaz, *Doctor Who* (BBC America, Russell T. Davies, Stephen Moffat, Matt Smith, and David Tennant), Doctor Who Magazine, Electric Sky (Jakki Hart and David Pounds), Louis Epstein, ESPN X Games (Marc Murphy, Dan Gordner, Valerie Benardinelli, Katie Moses Swope, Danny Chi, Crystal Yang, and Amy Lupo), Eurodata TV Worldwide, Europroducciones TV, Europroducciones, Europroduzzione and Veralia (Renato Vacatello, Stefano Torrisi, Carlo Boserman, Marco Fernandez De Araoz, Gabriela Ventura, Marco Boserman, Mar Izquierdo, Maria Ligues, Dario Viola, Amato Penasilico and Chiara Duranti), Amelia Ewen, Toby Ewen, Eyeworks Australia & New Zealand (Julie Christie, Joanne Law, Philippa Rennie, Erin Downton, Georgina Sinclair, Marc Ellis, and James Kerley), Eyeworks Europe (Wim, Kathe, Oliver, and Pian), Molly & Isobel Fay, Finnish Naval Academy (Sr lt Tero Hanski), *First News* (Serena Lacy, Kelane Henderson, and the team), FJT Logistics Limited, *Forbes,* Formulation Inc, *The Gadget Show,* Alfons Gidlöf, Vilgot Gidlöf, Karen Gillen, Go' Morgen Danmark/Go' Aften Danmark, Google, Alan Green (International Regulations Commission, International Sailing Federation), Jordan, Ryan, and Brandon Greenwood, Victoria Grimsell, Kris Growcott, GXT (Paula, Giuliano, and Francesco), Haaga-Helia University of Applied Sciences, Hachette Book Group (Craig Young, Vanessa Vasquez, and Todd McGarity), Kari Haering (Zone Living), Dan Hall, Hampshire Sports and Prestige Cars, Ray Harper, Roger Hawkins, Merja Hedman and the Finnish Sauna Society, Stuart Hendry, Gavin Hennessey, Tamsin Holman, Hollywood Press Association, Marsha K. Hoover, Alistair Humphreys, ICM (Michael Kagan and Greg Lipstone), I Gri.siani hair salon, Rome, Italy, Infomag (Emin Gorgun and Ipek Hazneci), Infostrada Sports (Philip Hennemann and Erik Kleinpenning), INP Media (Bryn

Downing), International Commission on Stratigraphy, Internet Movie Database, *The Irish Sun* (Helen Morrogh), ITV Productions (Jeremy Philips, Caz Stuart, and Bernard Kelly), Melanie Johnson, Richard Johnston, Andy Jones, Todd Klein, Dr. Erwin J. O. Kompanje and family, Sultan and Hasan Kösen, Kathrine Krone, Olaf Kuchenbecker, Josh Kushins (Lucasfilm), Orla and Thea Langton, Jony Levi, Paul Levitz, Carey Low, Jim Lyngvild, Sean Macaulay, Manda, Macmillan Distribution, Norman D. Mangawang, Médiamétrie, Melia White House Hotel, London, Clare Merryfield, Mark Messenger, Dan Meyer, Millennium Seed Bank (Sarah Moss), Steven Moffat, Sophie and Joshua Molloy, Monte-Carlo Television Festival, National Geographic Kids, NBA (Gail Hunter, Patrick Sullivan, Jason Lodato, and Karen Barberan), David Nelson, the New York City Police Department, The Nielsen Company, Jan Nielsen, Norddeich (York and Jurgen), Andrea Oddone, Outline Productions (Laura Mansfield, Diana Hunter, and Helen Veale), Andres Ostrofsky, Paley Center for Media, New York, U.S.A. (Ron Simon), Eddie Palmer, Dan Phillips, Stuart Phillips, POD Worldwide (Christy Chin, Alex Iskandar Liew, and Yip Cheong), Rob Pullar, Queen's Head and Artichoke, RCAF Trenton, Ontario, Canada, Ryan Reiter (Hollywood Almost Free Outdoor Cinema), R&G Productions (Stephane Gateau, Jerome Revon, Patrice Parmentier, Vanina Latcheva, and Deborah Amar), Martyn Richards Research (Martyn Richards), Ristorante Sant'Eustorgio (Paolo e Filippo Introini), Stephen Rodriguez (MLS), Jimmy Rollins, Roma Medical (John Pitt and John Dalton), Edward Russell, Eric Sakowski, Scottish Canoe Association (Margaret Winter), The Scottish Sun (Gill Smith and Graeme Donohue), Screecher's Pix (Hayma, Monique, and Ryan), Secondskin Makeup Artist, Alex Segura (DC Comics), Victor Hugo Camacho Sedano, Joshua Selinger, Tom Sergeant, SET Japan (Adrian Grey), Dean Shaw (Game Stores Group), Chris Sheedy, *The Simpsons* (Matt Groening, Antonia Coffman, and Art Villanueva), Richard Sisson, Sky 1 (James Townley), Glori Slater (K9 Storm Inc.), Carlton J. Smith, Matt Smith, Nick Smith, Phee Smith, Sean Sorensen (Motion Theory), Southern California Steampunks, Tom Spilsbury, Ian Starr, Start Licensing (Ian Downes), Daniel Stolar, St Pancras International (Kate Fisher), Nick Steel, Ri Streeter (Weta Workshop), Seyda Subasi-Gemici, The Sultan's Tent restaurant, Toronto, Canada, *The Sun* (Caroline Iggulden and Dave Masters), Atichart Tavornmard, Charlie Taylor, Holly Taylor, Stephen Taylor, Torfaen County Borough Council (Ben Payne, communications officer), TNR (Claire, Sophie, and Tessa), Virgin London Marathon (Natasha Grainger, Nicola Okey, and Tiffany Osborne), UCLH (Sharon Spiteri), Maria Vivas, Wandsworth Film Office, Louisa, Jessica, Isabel, and Sam Way, Westminster City Council (Francesca Pipe), Adam Wide, Dan Woods, World Health Organization, World Health Statistics, Oz Wright, David Wyatt, X Games, Zippy Productions.

IN MEMORIA

Henry Allingham (**oldest living man**), Gertrude Baines (**oldest living woman**), Melvin Boothe (**longest fingernails—male**), Terry Calcott (**fastest motocycle wheelie**), Chanel and Otto (**oldest dogs**), Gibson (**tallest dog**), Michael Jackson (**most successful pop artist**), Lurch (**largest horn circumference—steer**), He Pingping (**shortest living man [mobile]**), Tomoji Tanabe (**oldest living man**), Helen Wagner (**longest serving soap star**), Don Vesco (**fastest wheel-driven vehicle**)

PICTURE CREDITS

xii, xiii Ranald Mackechnie/GWR; Tristan Savatier; Takezo2000 **xiv, xv** Robert Vos/Photoshot

INTRO

xvii, xviii Nate Christenson; Rob Fraser/GWR; Paul Michael Hughes/GWR **xix** Joe Murphy/Getty Images; Paul Michael Hughes/GWR **xxiii** Adam Bouska

xxv, xxvi Paul Michael Hughes/GWR **xxvii, xxviii** *Adam Bouska*; Paul Michael Hughes/GWR **xxix-xxxii** Paul Michael Hughes/GWR; Getty Images **xxxiii, xxxv** Paul Michael Hughes/GWR; John Wright/GWR **xxxvi, xxxvii** Paul Michael; Hughes/GWR **xxxviii, xxxix** Paul Michael Hughes/GWR **xl, xlii** Paul Michael Hughes/GWR **xliii** Paul Michael Hughes/GWR **xliv, xlv** Tim Anderson/GWR; Yuri Ceschin/GWR; Press Eye **xlvi, xlviii** Tim Anderson/GWR; Hakan Eijkenboom; Yuri Ceschin/GWR **1** NASA **4, 5** NASA; Robert Gendler/Science Photo Library **3, 6** Steve A. Munsinger/Science Photo Library; NASA/Science Photo Library; David Ducros/Science Photo Library **8, 9** NASA **9, 10** NASA **11, 12** Getty Images; NASA **12, 14** Lori Losey/Getty Images; NASA **15, 16** NASA **17, 19** Dorling Kindersley; G Scharmer; L Rouppe van der Voort (KVA)/Reel EFX Inc. **23** Getty Images **23** M. Timothy O'Keefe/Alamy **24, 27** Daniel Riordan Tom Fox/Corbis **26, 28** Corbis; Grant Dixon/Getty Images **31, 38** Alamy Eitan; Simanor/Getty Images **30, 32** Kevin Schafer/Getty Images; Getty Images; John Beatty/Getty Images **34, 35, 37** Paul Nicklen/Getty Images; NASA; Stephen Belcher/FLPA **36** Steven Miller/NRL NOAA/National Science Foundation **38, 39** Reuters; Jeff Hunter/Getty Images **40-41** Alamy; Albert Moldvay/Getty Images **42, 43** NOAA; Merrick Davies **44, 45** Radek Dolecki; Simon Battensby/Getty Images **48, 49** Michael Appleton/Getty Images; Rex Features; Colin Braley/Reuters **46, 47, 49** John Russell/Getty Images; Rex Features; Ricardo Mazalan/AP/PA **53** Getty Images **53** H. Schmidbauer/Still Pictures **54, 58** BBC/Random House; Ron Blakey **55, 59** BBC/Random House **60, 61** BBC/Random House **62, 63** BBC/Random House; BBC **65** Sarefo; Satoshi Kuribayashi/Photolibrary; Anna Eksteen **66** Ondřej "Spídy" Řehák Darlyne A. Murawski/Getty Images **67, 68, 71** Dante Fenolio/Science Photo Library; Corbis; Gunter Marx/Alamy; Piotr Naskrecki/FLPA **69, 70** Norbert Wu/National Geographic; Daniel Gotshall/Getty Images; Alamy; David C Tomlinson/Getty Images **72, 73, 74** Karen Gowlett-Holmes/Photolibrary; SeaPics; Cole Brandon/Still Pictures; Rodger Klein/Photolibrary **74, 75** Chris Newbert/FLPA; Corbis **76, 78** Heidi & Hans-Juergen Koch/FLPA; Francesco Tomasinelli/Natural Visions **77, 79** LiveScience; Rex Features; Albert Feng **80, 81, 83** Chris Matti-

Science Photo Library; Sheng Li/Reuters; Jamie Rector/Getty Images **234, 235, 236** Paul Michael Hughes/GWR; Mark Bassett **236, 237, 238, 239** Getty Images; Thomas E. Franklin/Getty Images; Jeff Haynes/Getty Images Bruce Glikas/Getty Images; Harry Langdon/Getty Images; Carsten Koall/ Getty Images; Jorg Greuel/Getty Images **237, 239, 240, 241** Munawar Hosain/Getty Images; Alfred Eisenstaedt/Getty Images; Bob Thomas/Getty Images; Martin Mills/Getty Images; Alfred Eisenstaedt/Getty Images; Mike Clarke/Getty Images; Brad Barket/Getty Images; Getty Images **242, 243, 245** Stefan Wermuth/Reuters; Cate Gillon/Getty Images **242, 244** Finbarr O'Reilly/Reuters; Oli Scarff/Getty Images; Alejandro Gonzalez/Getty Images **246, 247** Hussein Malla/AP/PA; Richard Bradbury/GWR **251** Larry Marano/Getty Images **252, 253** Mark Campbell/Rex Features; Richard Bradbury/GWR **255** Ranald Mackechnie/GWR **257** Caters News Agency; Paul Michael Hughes/GWR **259, 260** Itsuo Inouye/AP/PA; Maria Ricci; Steve Parsons/PA; Steve Parsons/PA **261, 262** Ranald Mackechnie/GWR; Josette Lenars/Corbis; Corbis **263, 264** Oklahoma Historical Society; Erwin Bud Nielsen/Getty Images; Peter Pearson/Getty Images **265, 266** Paul Michael Hughes/GWR **270, 271** David Parry/Press Association; Richard Bradbury/GWR **272, 273** Paul Michael Hughes/GWR **274, 275** Paul Michael Hughes/GWR; Marc Henrie/Getty Images **276, 277, 278** Jacob Chinn/GWR; Jeffery R. Werner/Barcroft Media **279, 281** Richard Bradbury/GWR **280, 281** David Silverman/Getty Images; Richard Bradbury/GWR **283, 284** Ranald Mackechnie/GWR **291** Twentieth Century Fox **291** Twentieth Century Fox **293** Eidos Activision **292, 294, 295** Paul Michael Hughes/GWR; EA **296, 297, 298** Jenny Duval/Getty Images; Manpreet Romana/Getty Images **297, 298, 299** The British Library **304, 307** BBC; Frank Ockenfels/AMC **305, 306, 308** Gilles Toucas; Jamie McCarthy/Getty Images; Michael Tran/Getty Images; Ken McKay/Rex Features; Topfoto **309, 311, 313** Scope Features; NBC/Rex Features; ITV/Rex Features; Getty Images **312, 314, 315** Scope Features; NBC/Rex Features; ITV/Rex Features; Rex Features; ITV/Rex Features **310, 316, 317, 319** Corbis; Paramount Pictures; Rex Features; BBC; Rex Features **318, 319** Lucasfilm; BBC **320, 321, 322** BBC; Phil Rees/Rex Features; Tony Kyriacou/Rex Features; BBC **322, 323, 324, 325** BBC; Rex Features **326, 327** Disney/Rex Features; Hanna Barbera/Moviestore Collection **327, 328** Fox Broadcasting; DreamWorks Animation; Pixar Animation **329, 330** Warner Bros.; Summit Entertainment; 20th Century Fox/Rex Features **331** Warner Bros.; Lionsgate; **332, 333** Jeff Vespa/Getty Images; Miramax/Rex Features; Stephen Lovekin/Getty Images; Gareth Cattermole/Getty Images **324, 325, 326** Leon Neal/Getty Images; Frank Micelotta/Getty Images; Summit Entertainment; Summit Entertainment/Kobal **336, 337** Disney/Rex Features; Getty Images; Rex Features **338, 339, 340** Warner Bros./Kobal; 20th Century Fox; DreamWorks Animation **341, 342** Jean Baptiste Lacroix/Getty Images; Giuseppe Cacace/Getty Images; James Devaney/Getty Images **342, 343, 344** Jon Kopaloff/Getty Images; John Schults/Reuters; Frazer Harrison/Getty Images; Jake Holly/Rex Features; Christopher Polk/Getty Images **346, 347** Venturelli/Getty Images; 20th Century Fox/Rex Features **348, 349** Rex Features **349, 350** Jeff Kravitz/Getty Images; John Wright/GWR;

Columbia Pictures **352, 354** Rainer Wohlfahrt; Joe Kohen/Getty Images; Sara Krulwich/Eyevine **353, 354** Michael Kovac/Getty Images; Brad Barket/Getty Images; Ranald Mackechnie/GWR **355, 356, 357** Paul Michael Hughes/GWR; Jim Denevan/Barcroft Media; Jim Denevan **356, 358** Richard Bradbury/GWR **361** Paul Michael Hughes/GWR **361** Paul Michael Hughes/GWR **362, 363** Qilai Shen/Getty Images Mosab Omar/Reuters **364, 365** Feng Li/Getty Images **366, 367, 368** Benjamin D. Esham; Stefan Scheer **371, 372** Haakman; Nathan Benn/Corbis **373, 374** Peter Brenneken/Getty Images; Stephen Brashear/Getty Images **375, 378** Wu Hong/Corbis; Train web.org; Rex Features **376, 377** Justin Lane; Simon De Trey-White/Barcroft Media; Richard A. Cooke/Corbis **379, 380** John Wright/GWR **382, 383** Bobby Yip/Reuters **388, 389** AFP **390, 391** Michael Urban/Getty Images; Bob Strong/Reuters **393, 394** Barcroft Media; Lockheed Martin Corporation; Chris Ison/PA **395, 396** Dmitry Kostyukov/Getty Images; Crown Copyright **397, 398, 399** PA; Andy Willsheer/Rex Features; Volker Hartmann/AFP **398, 399, 400** Darin Schnabel/RM Auctions; WENN **403** Yoshikazu Tsuno/Getty Images **404, 405** Russell Kightley/Science Photo Library; G. Otto/Carola Pomplun/GSI; AP/PA **405, 407, 408** Donna Coveney/MIT **409, 410** Carla Cioffi/NASA; National Geographic; Jeff Kravitz/Getty Images **410, 411, 412** Justin Sullivan/Getty Images; Mike Epstein; Kevin Winter/Getty Images **415** Glyn Kirk/Getty Images **416, 417** Michał Sacharewicz; Mari Sterling **419, 420** Craig Parker/Getty Images **421, 422** Al Messerschmidt/Getty Images; Andy Lyons/Getty Images **423, 424** Andy Lyons/Getty Images; Dilip Vishwanat/Getty Images **425, 426** Gregory Shamus/Getty Images; Al Messerschmidt/Getty Images **426, 427, 428** Ronald Martinez/Getty Images; Getty Images; Christian Petersen/Getty Images **429, 430, 431** Rusty Jarrett/Getty Images; Javier Sorano/Getty Images; Malcolm Griffiths/Getty Images **432, 433** Dario Agrati; James Cheadle/Alamy; Robert Laberge/Getty Images **434, 435** David Maher/Sportsfile; Christian Petersen/Getty Images; Yuriko Nakao/Reuters **436, 437** Laurence Griffiths/Getty Images **438, 439** Nick Laham/Getty Images; Jed Jacobsohn/Getty Images **440, 441** Doug Pensinger/Getty Images; Otto Greule Jr/Getty Images; Dilip Vishwanat/Getty Images **442, 443** Jonathan Willey/Getty Images; Elsa/Getty Images **444, 445** Scott Rovak; Ron Vesely/Getty Images **446, 447** Jae C. Hong/AP/PA; John Raoux/AP/PA **448, 449** D. Clarke Evans/Getty Images; Juan Ocampo/Getty Images; Dick Raphael/Getty Images **450, 451** Issei Kato/Reuters; Jon Kopaloff/Getty Images **452, 453, 454** Rex Features; Clive Rose/Getty Images; Kim Kyung-Hoon/Reuters **455, 456** Mathieu Belanger/Reuters; Jon Super/AP/PA **456, 457, 458** Delmati; Damien Meyer/Getty Images; Peter Andrews/Reuters **459, 460** Desmond Boylan/Reuters; Karim Sahib/Getty Images **461, 462** Paulo Whitaker/Reuters; Gianluigi Guercia/Getty Images; Laurence Griffiths/Getty Images **463, 464** Thomas Niedermueller/Getty Images; Alex Livesey/Getty Images Darren Staples/Reuters; Roy Beardsworth/Offside **465** John Wright/GWR **466, 467, 470** Andrew Redington/Getty Images; Caters News Agency **468, 469, 470** David Cannon/Getty Images; Timothy A Clary/Getty Images; Andrew Redington/Getty Images **472, 473** Gregory Shamus/Getty Images; Bruce Bennett/Getty Images **471, 472, 473, 474**

This year's index is organized into two parts: by subject and by superlative. **Bold** entries in the subject index indicate a main entry on a topic, and entries in **BOLD CAPITALS** indicate an entire chapter. Neither index lists personal names.

SUBJECT INDEX

bite, 88
blackouts, 250
black smokers, 37
blizzards, 46
blockbusters, 329–331
Bloodhound SSC, 190
blood transfusions, 131
Bluebird, 191
The Blue Flame, 188
blue jets, 45
BMX, 138, 506, 510
board games, 258
boat lifts, 373
boats, *see "ships and boats"*
body-building, xxix
body parts, 107–111
body-piercings, 103, 115
body revolutions, 145
bomb disposal suits, 184
bombardier beetle, 66
bones, 90; broken, 129
bookmarks, 258
books, 42, 176, 297, 299, 324; graphic
    novels, 300–303
bottles, 236, 247, 255, 385
bowling (tenpin) 538
bowls, 538
boxing, 137, 253, 445, 452, 453
brains, 59, 215
bras, 149
bread, 67, 249
breakdancing, 152
breakfasts, 250, 253
breath, holding, 165, 184
bridges, 128, 371
British Open (golf) 461
brooches, 256
brushes, xliv, 213, 381
Brussels sprouts, 246
buildings, 124, 351, 363–365, 374;
    climbing, 150
bumper stickers, 258
bungee jumps, 140, 417
Burj Khalifa, Dubai, UAE, 363
Burning Man festival, xiii
burns, xii–xiv, 132; full-body, xii
burps, 146
bus tickets, 255
buses, xlv, 442

C

cable walking, 137
caecilians, 79

caimans, 83
cakes, 246, 252
calendars, 243, 255
Call of Duty: Modern Warfare 2, 293
camcorders, 403
camel wrestling, 490
cameras, 256, 401
Canada Basin, 37
canals, 373
candles, 258
canoeing, 201, 204, 494–495
cans, xxviii, 156, 235, 384
canyons, slot, 23
Cape Cod Canal, U.S.A. 373
capital cities, 254, 441, 475
caps & internationals: soccer, 477
car number plates, 165, 255
caravans, 400
carbon dioxide emissions, 233
cardboard boxes, 384
carnivals, 473
carol singers, 386
carp, 72
carpets, 385
cars, 397–400; amphibious, 183, 398;
    autosports, 429–433; bio, 392;
    circumnavigation, 183; crashes, 189;
    journeys, 31; limousines, 361; model,
    258; most people in, 163; parades,
    167; pushed, 142; rocket, 188; slot,
    263; speed records, 187–191; steam,
    398; stunts, 136, 137, 500; supersonic,
    187, 188; veteran, 399; washing, 168
cartoons, 325–329, 358
cartwheels, 146
casino chips/tokens, 256
castles, 87
catacombs, 211
catchers (baseball) 441
Cathedral Caverns, U.S.A. 29
cathedrals, 489
cats, 57, 274, 277, 278
cattle markets, 452
caves, 27, 28, 29
CDs, 149
celebrities, 305–307, 340–344
cemeteries, 471
Ceres, 7
chains, 155, 333, 387
Challenger space shuttle, 13
champagne corks, xlviii, 169
Champions League (soccer) xxix
chandeliers, 169
Chandra X-ray Observatory, 14

fuels, 388
funerals, 163, 214
furniture, 380, 384, 385

G

galaxies, 3
gambling, 294
Gamburtsev Mountains, Antarctica, 26
games, 259–262; board, 258; chess, 107, 259, 384; party, 259–260; *see also "video games"*
Gangkar Punsum, Bhutan, 25
gape, 107
garden gnomes, 386
gardens, xxvii, 66, 96
garlic, 246
garlic bread, 254
geckos, 80
genomes, 90
geomagnetic storms, 19
gerbils, 278
gharials, 81
ghosts, 214
giant pandas, 89, 91
Gigantocypris, 67
gingerbread men, xlvii
giraffes, 88, 281
glaciers, 254
glass, stained, 63
gliders, 14, 416–417
glow sticks, 384
goals & field goals: basketball, 392, 446, 449; football, 474, 475, 481; ice hockey, 434, 464, 465
goaltenders (ice hockey) 464
goats, 288
gold panning, 164
golden oldies, 124–128
Golden Raspberry Awards, 334
goldfish, 277
golf, 458–462
balls, 168; clubs, 380, 498; tees, 381
goliath beetle, 64
gorges, 28
gorillas, 280
Govind Devji's Temple, India, 362
Graf Zeppelin, 200
graffiti, 153
Grand Canyon, Arizona, 28
Grand Slams (tennis) 415, 483, 485
grand tours, 173–178
grapes, 149, 246
Great Barrier Reef, 38

Great Rift Valley, Africa, 31
greenhouse gases, 235
Greenland, 37
Grey Cup (Canadian football), 434
grouse, 88
guillotine, 15
guinea pigs, 274
Guitar Hero, 292
guitars, 470
guns, 393, 394
Gutenberg Bible, 42
GWR Day, xliv–xlviii
GWR live! xxxvi–xxxix
GWR TV, xxix–xxxv

H

haggis, 253
hair, 119–123
balls, 119; body hair, 120, 122; dreadlocks, 123; hairstyles, 121, 123; vehicles pulled by, 121, 141
haircuts, 121
Halloween, 170
Halo Wars 294
halva, 253
hammer throwing, 488
hamsters, 278
handball, 109, 436
handcuffs, 139, 156
hands, 106, 108, 109, 132
handshakes, 187
hang gliders, 198
hanging baskets, xliii
harps, 417
hats, 258, 383
hat-tricks, football, 234, 457, 478
head kicking, 148
headspins, 145, 152
hearses, 215
heart, 335; transplants, 105, 397
heart-shaped motifs, 256
heat waves, 49
heather, 94
hedgehogs, 256
helicopters, 182, 198, 199
Helios 2 spacecraft, 19
heptathlon, 520
high achievers, 192–195
Himalayas, 24, 195
hockey, 540
    see also "ice hockey"
home runs (baseball) 378, 438, 440, 441
hominids, 60

trolls, 256
trousers, stripper, xxxiv
trucks, 365, 430
Trump International Hotel & Tower,
   Chicago, 365
tsunamis, 46, 49
tuataras, 80, 82
tummy tucks, 128, 131
tunnels, xvi, 18, 376
Turkana, Lake, Kenya, 31
turkeys: carving, 248; plucking, 248, 285
tusks, 60
TV, 304–319; audiences, 214, 310, 439;
   cop & crime shows, 311–315;
   earnings, 305, 306, 311, 344; sci-fi &
   fantasy, 316–325; screens, 239, 382;
   sets, 401, 402
twins, 124, 209, 210, 406; conjoined,
   124
Twitter, 343, 408

U

UCI (Union Cycliste Internationale) 454,
   455, 456
UEFA Champions League, xxix
ultimate fighting, 451, 454
Ulysses spacecraft, 15
underground: lab, 404; railways, 148, 377,
   425
underwater: escapes, 139; geographical
   features, 27; holding breath, 165; road
   tunnel, 376; Rubik's cube solved, 263;
   swimming, 204
unicycles, 177, 348, 499
United Nations, 221, 222
universities, 231, 494
University Boat Race, 498
Unmanned Aerial Vehicles (UAVs) 394
urban arts, 150–154
US Air Force, 393
US Masters (golf) 459, 462

V

vacuum cleaners, 402
valleys, 28
vampire finches, 86
vehicles, 397–400; model, 261; drifts, 136;
   pulled, xlv, 116, 140, 141, 142;
   restrained, 141
veils, bridal, 211
Venice, Italy, 69
Venus of Hohle Fels, 356

Victoria Falls, 32
Victoria, Lake, 32
video games, xxxvii, 166, **292–296,** 471
vines, 88
viruses, 408; computer, 408
vision, 67, 80
volcanoes, xvi, 25, 28, 35, 48; submarine,
   35
volleyball, 434, 435, 436, 540

W

wacky world championships 490–494
waists, 110
wakeboarding, 418
walking, xxi, 175; Atlantic crossing, 203;
   backward, 175; on hot plates, 185;
   mass participants, 166, 191; race
   walking, 518–519
wall climbing, 417; ice, 141
wall of death, 137
war, 220–223, 395–397
warships, 395, 396
waterfalls, 32
water polo, 7, 495
waterskiing, 204, 539
waterslides, xlv
water sports, 494–498
waves, 33, 284, 389
wealth & commerce, 228–232
weapons, 392–397
weather & climate, 42–46
weaver birds, 85
wedding dresses, 387; veils, 211
wedding vow renewals, 209
weddings, 96, 208, 209;
   celebrity, 342, 344; dog, 272
weevils, 64, 67
weightlessness, 211
weightlifting, 142, 145, 156, 158; elephant,
   162, 534–537
West Mata volcano, Pacific Ocean, 36
whales, 90
what's on TV, 304–311
wheel skills, 498–502
wheelchairs, 175, 467
wheelies: BMX, 506; skateboard, 502
whip cracks, 156, 161
wife carrying, 493
wigs, 123
Wii Sports, 292
Wikipedia, 410
Willis Tower, Chicago, 364
willow trees, 93

X Y Z

SUPERLATIVES INDEX

object on Earth, 375
roller coaster, 366
telegram, 39
3D animation, 337
Top, 40 box set, 349
TV, 402; advertisement, 311; costume, 319
weapon system, 397
Most (number)
180° jumps on bicycle, 499
360° spins on tightrope, 161
albino siblings, 209
animated, 3D features, 336
Annie nominations, 327
audio books per author, 297
backflips: against wall, 150; pogo, 151;
    stilts, 139
backing dancers, 168
badminton players, 168
ballet dancers on pointe, 354
balloons blown up, 146; with nose, 147
balls caught no hands, xxxix
bananas snapped, 248
BASE jumps, 153
basketball: bounces, xlvi, 450; free throws,
    450, 473, 474
bicycle: back wheel bar jumps, 139; front
    wheel hops, 499
bird songs recorded, 88
BMX stunts, 138, 506
body-piercings, 103, 115–118
body revolutions, 145
books written, 221
boxing punches, 452
bras worn & removed, 149
breakdance moves, 152
broken bones, 129
buildings climbed, 154
bullwhip cracks, 161
cars driven on two wheels, 138
cars washed, 168
cartwheels, 146
CDs flipped & caught, 149
champagne bottles sabered, 169
characters in animation, 328
chess games, simultaneous, 259
child soldiers, 220
chromosomes: mammal, 90; plant, 93
coconuts smashed, 249
concrete blocks smashed, xlvii
countries in military tattoo, 197
couples married, 209
crime cases worked on by psychic, 422
custard pies in face, 248
cycle racers, 80

Dakar Rally wins, 476
dance spins, 145
dogs in fancy dress, 269
drink cans broken with whip, 156
eating feats, xxxi, 246
eggs: balanced, 432; held in hand, 248
Emmys won, 307
Everest conquests, 192
eye tests carried out, 128
fingers and toes, 130, 278
fire torches extinguished, xxxii
flamenco taps, 352
flaming torches juggled, xiii
flying discs caught, 271
flying hours by pilot, 367
free throws (basketball) 450
generations born on same day, 208
giraffe offspring, 281
golf balls hit, 168
golf courses played, 462
Grand Slam titles, 415
grapes caught in mouth, 149
Guinness World Records, 135
hair: cuts, 121; dyed, 121; styles, 121
hand amputations, 132
hat-tricks, soccer, 234
headspins, 145, 152
horizontal bar backward spins, 145
horns on a sheep, 159
hours on US TV, 311
hula hoops spun, 159
human rights activists killed, 219
ice-cream scoops stacked, 248
Internet users in country, 410
islands, 37–39
jokes told, 224, 380
journeys by scheduled flight, 199
juggling catches, 159
karaoke participants, 170
kicks to the head, 148
kites flown, 166
knee bends on Swiss ball, 143
knives thrown around human target, 155
knockdowns in boxing, 137
Maltesers caught in mouth, 148
marathon runners linked, 470
martial arts: kicks, 451; throws, 451, 453
mass participants, 163–170
Mentos-soda fountains, 118
models in fashion show, 168
motorcycle: donuts, 138; pirouettes, 29
multi-legged racers, 167
murders of any country, 224
music awards, 412

STOP PRESS

☆**Fastest violin player** Ben Lee (UK), of violin duo FUSE, played "Flight of the Bumblebee" in 1 min. 4.21 sec. in London, UK, on April 7, 2010. The quality of the performance was verified by Rodney Friend, the leader/concert master who has performed with the London Symphony Orchestra, New York Philharmonic Orchestra, and the BBC Symphony Orchestra in a career spanning 30 years.

★**Most pork scratchings eaten** Scott Dustan (UK) ate 0.95 oz. (27 g) of deep-fried cured pork rind in one minute at The Union, London, UK, on April 30, 2010. At the same event, Courtney Shapiro (U.S.A./UK) consumed 0.74 oz. (21 g) in 30 seconds.

☆**OLDEST LIVING PERSON** Just as we were going to press we received this image of Eugénie Blanchard (St. Barts, France, b. February 16, 1896), who became the oldest person on the planet upon the death of the previous record holder, Kama Chinen (Japan), on May 2, 2010. Eugénie shares her nationality with the oldest person ever; see p. 126 for details.

★**FASTEST TIME TO KAYAK/CANOE LOCH NESS** A team of 26 Asda employees and suppliers led by senior meat buyer Jim Viggars (all UK) kayaked the length of Loch Ness, Scotland, UK, from Fort Augustus to Dores (a distance of 17.9 nautical miles; 20.59 miles; 33.15 km) in 5 hr. 19 min. 17 sec. on May 18, 2010. The record attempt was organized to raise funds for the Tickled Pink breast cancer charity. All of the team members lined up to cross the finish line together and therefore achieved the same time.

VW: The ☆ **largest car mosaic** was created with 460 Volkswagen automobiles in an event organized by Volkswagen do Brasil in São Paulo, Brazil, on April 10, 2010.

☆ **Largest game of musical statues** A total of 1,079 participants took part in a game of musical statues at an event organized by Danone Finland in Helsinki, Finland, on April 25, 2010.

☆ **Greatest prize money for a horse race** The largest prize fund for a single horse race is $10 million for the Dubai World Cup, held at Meydan Racecourse in Dubai, United Arab Emirates (UAE), on March 27, 2010.

Shortest person to perform a wing walk The **shortest professional stuntman**, Kiran Shah (UK), stands at 4 ft. 1.7 in. (1 m 26.3 cm) and performed his first wing walk in Cirencester, Gloucestershire, UK, on April 30, 2010.

☆ **LARGEST PASTA BOWL** Buca di Beppo Italian Restaurant (U.S.A.) served up a 13,786-lb. (6,253-kg) bowl of pasta at the chain's Anaheim restaurant, Garden Grove, California, U.S.A., on March 12, 2010.

APNEA

The suspension of breathing, particularly that practiced by divers, from the Greek verb "to breathe."

☆ **LARGEST ICE MAZE** The Arctic Glacier Ice Maze (U.S.A.) at the Buffalo Powder Keg Festival in Buffalo, New York, U.S.A., featured an ice maze measuring 12,855.68 ft.² (1,194.33 m²) on February 26, 2010. The maze was constructed using 2,171 blocks of ice, each weighing 300 lb. (36.08 kg).

☆**Largest sculpture made from recycled material** Under the auspices of RESUR, the local government consortium for the recycling of solid waste materials, a team of students from the Granada School of Architecture in Granada, Spain, designed and built a castle measuring 95 ft. 1.7 in. (29 m) long, 46 ft. 1.9 in. (14.07 m) wide, and 22 ft. 11.5 in. (7 m) tall from approximately 50,000 tetra pak milk cartons on May 17, 2010. The cartons were collected by students at the primary schools in the Granada region in the weeks before the record attempt. The structure had no internal frame and was held together with staples and string.

☆**Freediving/dynamic apnea with fins (women)** Natalia Molchanova (Russia) dived to a depth of 738 ft. 2 in. (225 m) without an external oxygen supply in Moscow, Russia, on April 25, 2010, breaking her own record.

☆ **LONGEST BUBBLE CHAIN** Just as we were finishing off this year's book, bubble blower Sam Heath (aka Sam Sam the Bubbleman) popped into the GWR offices in London, UK, where he created a chain of 26 bubbles.

Sam used a standard drinking straw and bubble wand to make the chain.

★ **MOST CANS CRUSHED WITH A VEHICLE IN THREE MINUTES** Ian Batey crushed 61,106 cans in three minutes driving a 10-ton (9-tonne) monster truck for Burn Energy Drink (UAE) at the Jumeirah Beach Residence in Dubai, UAE, on March 6, 2010.